# MOCKINGBIRD SONG

# Mocking-bird Song

## Song

ECOLOGICAL
LANDSCAPES OF
THE SOUTH

JACK TEMPLE KIRBY

THE UNIVERSITY OF NORTH CAROLINA PRESS

CHAPEL HILL

Set in Arnhem types by Tseng Information Systems, Inc.

Manufactured in the United States of America

This book was published with the assistance of the
William R. Kenan Jr. Fund of the University of North Carolina Press.
The paper in this book meets the guidelines for permanence and
durability of the Committee on Production Guidelines for Book
Longevity of the Council on Library Resources.

Library of Congress Cataloging-in-Publication Data

Kirby, Jack Temple.

Mockingbird song : ecological landscapes of the South /
by Jack Temple Kirby.

　　p. cm.

Includes bibliographical references and index.

ISBN-13: 978-0-8078-3057-4 (cloth : alk. paper)

ISBN-10: 0-8078-3057-7 (cloth : alk. paper)

1. Human ecology—Southern States. 2. Geographical perception—
Southern States. 3. Landscape assessment—Southern States.
4. Southern States—Environmental conditions. I. Title.

GF504.S6K57 2006

304.20975—dc22　　　2006011353

The Epilogue was previously published, in somewhat different form,
as "Postmodern Landscapes of the American South," in *Revolution in
the Land: Southern Agriculture in the Twentieth Century*, ed. Connie L.
Lester (Mississippi State University: Department of History, 2003). It is
reprinted here with permission.

cloth　10 09 08 07 06　5 4 3 2 1

FOR CONSTANCE

# CONTENTS

Preface  *xi*

Prologue: An Orientation Mostly along St. Johns River  *1*

Chapter 1. Original Civilizations  *38*

Chapter 2. Plantation Traditions  *75*

Chapter 3. Commoners and the Commons  *113*

Chapter 4. Matanzas and Mastery  *156*

Chapter 5. Enchantment and Equilibrium  *201*

Chapter 6. Cities of Clay  *257*

Epilogue: Postmodern Landscapes  *312*

Notes  *331*

Index  *357*

# ILLUSTRATIONS AND MAPS

ILLUSTRATIONS

Marjorie Kinnan Rawlings and her first husband in Florida, 1928  *3*

William Bartram's drawing of alligators in St. Johns River, 1773  *21*

Chesapeake Corporation Paper Mill at West Point, Virginia, 1920s  *36*

Interracial Native Americans called "Brassankles," near Sommerville, South Carolina, 1938  *41*

Ruins of a plantation house near Marshall, Texas, 1939  *94*

Soil erosion, Stewart County, Georgia, 1937  *96*

Loading cotton, Natchez, Mississippi, 1935  *97*

Florida migrant workers bound for New Jersey, 1940  *107*

Migrant construction worker and his family, Portsmouth, Virginia, 1941  *108*

Marjorie Kinnan Rawlings at her garden fence, Cross Creek, ca. 1940s  *122*

Overboxed turpentine pine near Valdosta, Georgia, 1936  *127*

Massachusetts soldiers carrying away fence rails, North Carolina, 1862  *130*

View of a farm from Blue Ridge Parkway, Virginia, 1940  *151*

Audie Murphy displays his medals, ca. 1950s  *159*

Alvin York posing in uniform, Pall Mall, Tennessee, 1919  *161*

Alvin York at a community turkey shoot, early 1930s  *181*

Headquarters, People for the Ethical Treatment of Animals, Norfolk, Virginia, ca. 2000  *190*

Working in a school garden, Gees Bend, Alabama, 1939  *221*

Zora Neale Hurston, ca. 1930  *227*

Greensboro, Georgia, on a Saturday afternoon, 1941  *249*

Eugene P. Odum greets a bronze bust of himself, 1984  *254*

Terminal Hotel and Beach Park, West Point, Virginia, ca. 1900  *262*

Residential D Street, West Point, Virginia, ca. 1912  *266*

Street scene, St. Augustine, Florida, 1893  *272*

Hotel Ponce de Leon, St. Augustine, Florida, 1920  *275*

Petersburg, Virginia, featuring a railroad, ca. 1845  *282*

Edmund Ruffin, ca. 1850  *284*

Construction of a sewage disposal plant, Slagheap Village, Alabama, 1937  *288*

Cabin with mud chimney, Gees Bend, Alabama, 1937  *305*

MAPS

Subregions of the South *xxii*
Northeastern Florida and St. Johns River *26*
De Soto's route from Apalachee to Apafalaya, 1540 *44*
De Soto's route from Apafalaya to Guachoya, 1540–1542 *48*
Black Mountains of Western North Carolina *147*

# PREFACE

Back in the halcyon days of comparative history centered on the American South, C. Vann Woodward brilliantly addressed opportunities (and deep problems) presented by the works of the Brazilian scholar Gilberto Freyre, who had been educated at Baylor and Columbia and who cherished the plantation patriarchies of his own Old North and of our Old South. Woodward generously supported analytical studies of plantation societies around the globe but rightly suggested cautionary perspective. "The culture contrast," he wrote, "suggests setting a flock of gray and white mockingbirds down in a tropical jungle filled with gaudy parakeets." New Englanders, he averred, may have found "life along the James, the S[u]wannee, or the Lower Mississippi . . . lushly exotic and outlandishly bizarre. But set side-by-side with life along the Amazon, the colors of antebellum society in the Old South fade to temperate-zone grays and russets and muted saffrons that went well enough with magnolias or Spanish moss, but were not quite the thing for promenades under palm and breadfruit."[1]

Conceded. Yet confined to our own continent, we may still legitimately think about, say, New Orleans (pre-Katrina) versus, say, Bath, Maine. Both are lovely riverside cities, Bath much the cleaner but with few promenades (of which the French Quarter and Garden District have many) and scarce mockingbird sighting. Woodward's juxtaposition of tropical "gaudy parakeets" with mockingbirds as avian symbol of the South was simultaneously appropriate and wrong. Appropriate because of traditional, popular-cultural allusions that include the nineteenth-century song "Listen to the Mockingbird" (reportedly a favorite of Abraham Lincoln, who also liked "Dixie") and innumerable associations of the birds with (as Woodward wrote) magnolias and Spanish moss, in print and film. The mockingbird is also the official avian of five southern states: Texas, Arkansas, Mississippi, Tennessee, and Florida. Yet this creature, a resident, nonmigrating animal, is found over most of the contiguous United States except the Pacific Northwest, northern Idaho, and western Montana—although, it is true, mockingbird counts are always highest in the South and Southwest.[2]

Gray is indeed the mockingbird's predominant color, particularly on the head and upper parts. Under parts are whitish, and the bird has a long black tail with white on the outer feathers, black legs, white wing bars, and yellow eyes. Males and females are similar in appearance and prefer urban, suburban, and scrub habitats, where they eat insects and fruit. Mockingbirds are small, too, adults usually measuring hardly ten inches from beak to tail-tip, and they are slimmer than robins. Nonetheless they are aggressive; the males are particularly bellicose at challenging rivals for mates, and males and females alike ferociously defend feeding territory. In pairs and bands of four or more, mockingbirds have long been observed mobbing intruders, including other avians, snakes, cats, dogs, and humans. J. J. Audubon famously painted mockingbirds furiously defending a nest against rattlesnakes. That rattlesnakes do not climb troubled Audubon not at all, for he was a showman as well as a naturalist and painter. The non-viper rat snake, skillful climber and devourer of birds as well as rodents, would have been the truer subject, albeit less dramatic.

It is the mockingbird's voice—or better, voices—that makes it something much more than "gray," something far more colorful, and more interesting, than squawking parakeets. *Mimus polyglottos*, the bird's perfect taxonomic designation, mimics other birds—thus the common name given by the eighteenth-century naturalist Mark Catesby. Mockingbirds will mock parakeets' squawks but also warblers' warbles, kingfishers' rattles, and the sounds of at least three dozen other birds. Some ornithologists and bird-watchers declare that mockers *compose* songs as well as imitate others, and that they never cease learning new expressions. An old mockingbird always has the largest repertoire. Mockingbirds can sing low, whisperingly, and raucously loud. They also perform what should be called sound effects rather than song—for example, dogs barking, chickens cackling, frogs croaking, and wheelbarrows' wheels groaning. Males, particularly unattached ones during the spring, sing day and night. All will emote on perches, from nests, in flight, endlessly. To human auditors, this can be charming or annoying.

In Harper Lee's beloved *To Kill a Mockingbird* (1960), kindly elders advise sweet children that it would be sinful to rub out such a creature. Why? Because mockingbirds expend their remarkable, perhaps exhausting talents for *our* pleasure. I think not. First, mockingbirds—especially males in the spring, particularly at night—are not pleasurable at all, but rather the opposite. But even when they are a delight to hear—paired, in the fall, happily gathering food, or tuneful and/or in the whispering mode—our pleasure makes no difference to them. (Lee's elders were raising yet more homocentric naturalists.) While neither an ornithologist nor a consistent, learned birder, I do observe that of all the songbirds in this continent's temperate and subtropical regions, the mockingbird may be least responsive to, most indifferent to, us upright mammals.

For example: male cardinals, especially unmated yearlings, sing out their locations, challenges, and yearnings, the call ending with two or three monotonal whistles. They hardly ever fail to respond to a human mocker whose ending whistles exceed the cardinal's most recent call by one. The cardinal will go one more, and so on. I have played this game with those scarlet birds (who are no dumber than I) up to thirteen or so before conceding defeat. More charming, though, is the responsive white-throated sparrow, which summers in Canada, migrating back and forth from far south. It is a tiny creature, six inches long, and elusive, preferring thick brushy places and forests, and I have seldom seen one. But its call is sublimely sad, reedy and dulcet, by far exceeding my own attempts at admiring duplication. Yet the white-throats generously correct my pathetic imitation of their haunting message: "Sweet sweet, Canada Canada Canada," they sing; or, as a Canadian ornithologist once translated: "O-oh my! Can-a-da, can-a-da, can-a-da." The latter version is what I think I hear, and how enchanting it is to know the sparrow communicates with *me*—not another avian.

Never so with the mockingbird, whose hyperkinetic days are engrossed with itself and its own kind. Its imitations of others mock, I must think, rather than flatter (as imitation reputedly does, sincerely). The generalization was demonstrated to me yet again as I was considering a title and composing this preface. While sitting on my balcony one fine fall afternoon, I watched a mockingbird alight upon the railing hardly five feet from my Panama-hatted, newspaper-reading self. Stepping in place and stretching, looking about, it took no notice of my large presence so close by. So I tried to gain its attention with little whistles, my version of mockingbirds' whispering, then shriller calls. No response at all. Except that shortly the bird deposited one fecal pellet upon my railing, then flew away. Still—however annoying, sometimes maddening, and occasionally endearing—mockingbirds remind us that we of the large brains are not alone the dominators of earth's attention, nor the centers of all universes, either. This seems information most useful when thinking about ecological, or environmental, history. Mockingbirds live mostly among and near human-built landscapes, relishing the creator's and our own fruity bounty and surviving (somehow) our chemical dependencies. Yet if one thing about them is utterly understandable, it is that mockingbirds are not *our* creatures but singers of themselves. Their cacophony seems to me useful as metaphor, both for human conceptual limitations and nature's uncomprehended mysteries. For how can we know all, really? Meanwhile, we should not kill because we can, but instead demonstrate respectful restraint.

🏵 Neither a text nor a comprehensive survey nor a specialized monograph is this book. Principally, my narratives attempt to foster understanding by presenting the poetics, politics, and portions of the sciences of the human relationship with the rest of nature in what is called the American South, from earliest habitation to approximately the present. The South is American, to be sure, but different from other American regions and deserving of such attention. Most of the South is hot and humid most of every year, and well watered. Such a place has more flowers and weeds, more insect life, exuberant avian activity, and more and more varied vipers as well as nonpoisonous snakes, alligators, and a few crocodiles. There are and have been more infectious diseases among all animals, including ourselves. As in other American regions, the South's humanity has been ever in flux — Americans are rootless, migrating, commuting folks — so landscapes have changed drastically from generation to generation, from overgrown derelict settlements to rough new farming frontiers, from mature rural cultures to abandonment (again) and reforestation, urbanization, suburbanization, and so on. But because a great war was waged by millions of soldiers over much of the South, its landscapes arguably suffered more extreme change and different patterns of redevelopment than less cursed regions. During the twentieth century, I shall suggest, too, southerners helped invent and embraced a particular reformist version of scientific ecology whose thesis and goals centered upon nature's own system of self-correction, equilibrium, and human emulation of nature's harmony. Finally, the South is distinct in the extreme brevity of southerners' experience with densely built landscapes and the urban life.

Humans (many of them named) are my principal actors, but I am interested in humans upon *landscapes* — from the low and tropical to the montane and chilly. Landscapes have powers to invite, constrain, and occasionally prohibit human occupance, even while ultimately most have been susceptible to civilization. Nature's own violent agency in the history of the earth is demonstrated not only in the periodic wrecking by hurricane and earthquake of Charleston, South Carolina, but steadier phenomena, such as humidity, temperature, altitude, morphology and cover, the function (or malfunction) of wetlands, and the meanderings of rivers. Humans nonetheless have ever shaped landscapes as best (or worst) they could, given their cultures and technologies, to provide elemental necessities—food, water, and shelter—and, whenever possible, delights. The getting of all these, the last, especially, may involve methods we must call destructive and wasteful, although I must concede that human life without delight seems grim, indeed. So the ethical question about human behavior upon landscapes, from the origins of civilization through tomorrow, may well turn upon what really constitutes necessity, and especially the consequences of accumulating delights. The query is suggested in the prologue, lurks (at least) in all the chapters, and becomes the principal subject halfway through the epilogue.

Parts of the text following may seem to some readers not "environmental" history at all. I hope that they will be patient. There are, for instance, a few linear diversions—for example, attention to the arc and details of Hernando de Soto's barely credible expedition around "La Florida," which for a long time defined the South's boundaries and variety, at least to the Spanish. The objective in employing such a trope, yet again, is to frame the Mississippian natives the Spanish encountered, not only culturally and politically, but ecologically. There is much more nonlinear composition here, however, that offers odd (perhaps) but substantial as well as poetic juxtapositions. The famous friendship of Marjorie Kinnan Rawlings and Zora Neale Hurston, for instance, was a remarkable social-ecological phenomenon, given its chronology and location. But I hope readers will perceive that Hurston's and Rawlings's personal harmony (however imperfect) parallels and complements both women's declared commitment to the notion of equilibrium in nature, which must include human behavior appropriate to nature's harmony. Likewise my twining narratives of hunting and soldiering, with intertwined biographies of Alvin York and Audie Murphy, suggest much—so I must think—about the romantic ideal of subsistence gathering and the industrial-scale horrors of killing during two world wars, the latter making precedence for the industrial horrors of post–World War II meat production.

Some readers, the academic in particular, will be interested in an author's provenance, as it were—his intellectual inspirations and obligations. These are (mostly) represented in the endnotes and occasionally named in the text, but I am glad to acknowledge here powerful shoulders upon which I gladly squat. First are historians of the South and of agriculture and rural life who dominated my student and early professional days. Among these C. Vann Woodward was and remains paramount, for his forthright presentism and principled commitment to the region, his profound grasp of irony, and his elegant literary craftsmanship. Woodward was (to my knowledge) never termed an environmental historian, yet it was his *Origins of the New South* (1951) that first informed me that after the Civil War, distant bankers exploited landlords, who exploited sharecroppers, who had only the soil to exploit. Also Avery Craven, who while in error, I believe, about antebellum southern farming, was never wronghearted, and whose first book, published nearly eighty years ago, anticipated by half a lifetime what we now call environmental or ecological history. I remain an admirer, too, of Walter Prescott Webb, whose *The Great Plains* (1935) may have made excessive claims about landscape's and climate's dictation of human improvisation but remains so vivid and suggestive to me.

Among southernists *vivant* are several whose works have helped shape and fill more than a few of these pages: Eugene Genovese and Elizabeth Fox-Genovese made writing about the South in isolation impossible. Bertram Wyatt-Brown and Michael O'Brien have exfoliated generations of distracting discourse to reveal white (especially) Souths of mind, culture, and deliberation. Ed Ayers, a lovely writer and lately wizard of digitized history, is master of all southern cultures from the late antebellum into the twentieth century. Don Doyle has illuminated the declines and arrivals of nineteenth-century southern seaport and railroad cities (respectively), as well as the demographic chaos of Lafayette County, Mississippi. Pete Daniel, Nan Elizabeth Woodruff, and Lu Ann Jones—themselves natives of the southern countryside—persist in imaginative research and passionate revelation of a region that was overwhelmingly rural until the day before yesterday. Ted Ownby's first book (*Subduing Satan* [1990]) offers profound insight into the entanglement of modernization with a feminized, sectarian reformism that, as I read it, achieved a peace and order (of sorts) in a new southern world of lost commons. I still think Grady McWhiney's Celtic centrism (in *Cracker Culture* [1988]) misguided, yet his treatment of herdsmen, and their business and pleasures, remains not only accurate but essential to understanding antebellum southern landscapes. Steven Stoll, a Californian with the West Coast first on his mind, has lately come to the antebellum East, including the South, with refreshing perspective on upper-class would-be improvers of agricultural landscapes.

Development of flat-out environmental history of and in the South was much retarded for some time after the appearance of Albert Cowdrey's pioneering *This Land, This South* in 1983. Finally came marvelous first books by Timothy Silver (on southeastern forests, in 1990) and Mart Stewart (on Georgia islands and Low Country, in 1996). Then suddenly and (to me) unexpectedly, a raft of richly imaginative articles and books about southern subregions, beginning at the end of the 1990s and ongoing today, began to appear. Among these I am influenced by Conevery Bolton Valencius's *Health of the Country* (2002), which examines antebellum migrants to the trans-Mississippi South and their perceptions of landscape forms and their implications for human well-being. Many of the best new books concern the mountain South, not least Silver's 2003 work on Mount Mitchell and the Black Mountains in North Carolina, which ingeniously melds interdisciplinary archival research with Silver's own local experience as climber, hiker, fly fisherman, and naturalist. Margaret Lynn Brown's 2000 "biography" of the Great Smokies, too, is rich in scope and perspective on the hopeless inconsistencies of national park development and management. The southern lowlands have also received wise and diligent attention of late, notably in David McCally's book on the Everglades (1999) and Rob Outland's outstanding work on the naval stores industry among the longleaf forests (2004). And among younger historians of American regionalism and environmental ideas, Robert Dorman has actually had new things to say.

Geographers—both living and gone, and of rural and urban places—are irreplaceable to the student of landscapes. The late Merle C. Prunty Jr., for example, and his former students Sam Bowers Hilliard and Charles Aiken largely created the lexicons of rural occupance, economic organization, and food supply. And the contemporary urban geographers John A. Jakle and David Wilson confirm and elaborate the dereliction of cities predicted more than four decades ago by Jane Jacobs, whose classic *Death and Life of Great American Cities* (1961) is my own template for built landscapes. I am likewise obliged to geographers—but also to ethnographers, anthropologists, archaeologists, and historians—of Native America in the South. They have accomplished near-miracles of exposition and explanation during the past generation: Charles Hudson (the great patriarch), Shepard Kretch III, Theda Perdue, Michael Green, Robbie Ethridge, Helen Rountree, Daniel Usner, Patricia Galloway, William Doolittle, and others. Kretch, however, most directly engages native cultures and ecology, and Doolittle has (at long last) dispatched the myth of swidden (or "slash-and-burn") agriculture among natives.

Third (but hardly least), I am enormously influenced by the founders of contemporary environmental history. Samuel P. Hays's early book on forest industries (1959), now part of the canon of conservation history, led me, as a graduate student, to write Progressive Era political history with a more expansive and critical view. Only later did I and others connect Hays's portraits of corporate and government efficiency-mindedness with something else, something greener. Donald Worster, brother materialist, is my favorite agro-ecological historian; but he is also a historian of ideas, especially Anglo-American ecological science, and he is a literary stylist to admire. Alfred Crosby's extraordinary, global writings are essential, as are those of Stephen Pyne, global historian of fire. I have ever been a reader of Carolyn Merchant and Vera Norwood, genderers of environmental history and more, and of William Cronon, Richard White, Alan Taylor, and (on subjects European) Simon Shama. Robert Pogue Harrison's spellbinding meditation on forests, mostly European ones, as "shadow of civilization" continues to inform my own sensibilities about nature, too. John Reiger, indefatigable outdoorsman and historian, memorably tied upper-class hunters to the origins of conservation in nineteenth-century America.

Parallel to the development of environmental history, meanwhile, has been a school of landscape studies identified with the late John Brinkerhoff Jackson and Harvard's Graduate School of Design. Jacksonesque landscape studies never suffered early environmental historiography's plaguing preoccupation with "wilderness"—that is, nature without humanity, nature as monument.[3] To Jackson, most landscapes were "vernacular," or ever changing for whatever reason, especially the passing occupancy of people who reshape, rebuild, redecorate, and so on. Jackson's former student and successor at Harvard, John Stilgoe, carries on, teaching more graduate students in his own imaginatively interdisciplinary fashion. My own sensibilities about ourselves-in-nature comfortably comport with this tradition, to which the word "landscapes" in my subtitle alludes.

Finally, I have been a reader of fiction, memoirs, letters, biography, and a bit of poetry, as well as a green reader of certain movies. That I have been deeply in love with two dead literary women from Florida becomes obvious early in the text to come. Marjorie Kinnan Rawlings and Zora Neale Hurston themselves were forces of nature, and I regret beyond words that I did not know either of them in person. William Faulkner, yet another southern nature writer of note, makes appearances, too. The 2001 "southern" film, *O Brother, Where Art Thou?* (creation of the witty auteurs Joel and Ethan Coen) appears twice here, both times with landscape-ish interpretations. A few other films, plus some still photography, come into play, too. Of popular (or at least, admired) nature writing, I confess that I cannot read Annie Dillard's *Pilgrim at Tinker Creek* (1974), which is set in the upper South; likewise the neo-agrarian essays and poetry of Wendell Berry. But I have been an avid fan of Peter Matthiessen and of John McPhee's works, one of which, on oranges, is cited. Among nonacademic writers on matters natural, however, I have been the keenest student of Michael Pollan. Beginning with his 1991 book, *Second Nature*, Pollan wrote perhaps the most unusual gardening book ever, because he arose from perennial borders to re-delineate the great divide between First Nature—that is, wilderness—and his title subject, which includes *all* arranged and managed landscapes. The language of "first" and "second" natures was originally Marx's and Engels's, and it is good that Michael Pollan and the historian William Cronon have revived it.[4] Lately Pollan has turned to industrialized agriculture and food processing, which I think is one of the most important subjects an ecological scholar might address today.

There have been institutional as well as personal and private benefactors. I began this book while still W. E. Smith Professor at Miami University in Ohio. The professorship funded travel, research materials, and subscriptions, but my Miami colleagues Osaak Olumwullah, Bradley Schrager, and Peggy Shaffer knew their landscapes of (respectively) East Africa, Native America, and modern America. They talked great talk and often sent me packing to the library. Another former Miami colleague, Edwin Yamauchi, learned historian and philologist of ancient West Asia and Northeast Africa, kindly provided me a bundle of source materials when I inquired about brick manufacture during Old Testament times. A former Miami landscape ecologist, Gary Barrett—now of the University of Georgia—sent a huge packet of his and colleagues' offprint research reports on urban sewer sludge, its use on crop fields, and heavy metal uptake. Barrett, a co-founder of Miami's Ecology Research Center, was once a graduate student of Eugene Odum at the University of Georgia's world-famous Institute of Ecology. I readily express still-widening admiration for the late Gene Odum, too—I was slightly acquainted with him during his later years—since he and his brother, H. T. Odum, while internationally traveled and honored, represented a reformist and self-consciously southern mission to place science in service to their beloved native region. Even if their ecosystem paradigm for ecology is flawed (certainly now out of fashion), the determination of both Odums not only to reveal systemic harmony in nature but to *create* equilibrium where it was disrupted seems brave, good-hearted, and poignant to me.

Chuck Grench, assistant director and senior editor at the University of North Carolina Press, planted seed, or at least some latent fertilizer, for this project in my head during the course of an excellent dinner in Louisville, back toward the end of 2000. A chance viewing of the movie version of Rawlings's *The Yearling* and a rereading of the novel a little later, then a road trip down to the Okefenokee and on to Cross Creek, fully loosed the obsession. Later, two fortuitously timed conferences, at Mississippi State University and the University of Mississippi, gave me opportunity to present early, compressed versions of the epilogue and Chapter 4 in this book. The first has been published, the second is forthcoming, and I thank Connie Lester and Charles Reagan Wilson, generous hosts at Starkville and Oxford, for permission to include now-expanded forms here. Two other generous friends, Tim Silver and Constance Pierce, read and marked up an early version of the manuscript to my considerable benefit. Then Pierce read the whole again. Herself a writer of criticism, fiction, and poetry, she has also been my boonest companion in agro- and ecotourism through much of the United States and substantial parts of several other countries, not to mention principal landscapist and sister gardener on our successive plots in Indiana, Ohio, and Florida. She has ever been my best reader.

# MOCKINGBIRD SONG

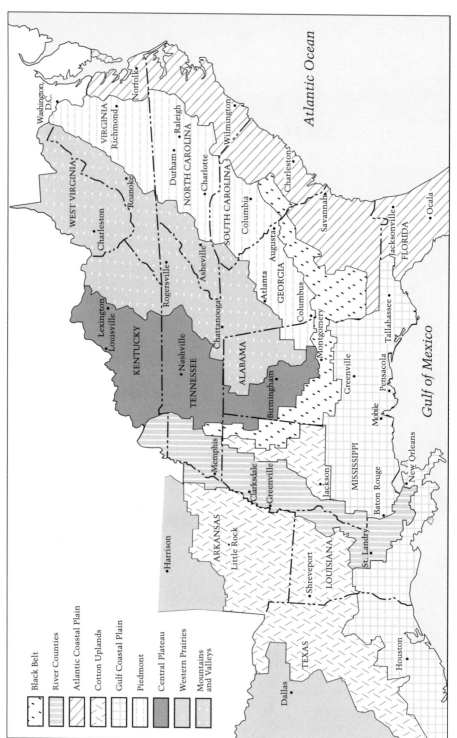

*Subregions of the South (courtesy Edward Ayers)*

**Legend:**
- Black Belt
- River Counties
- Atlantic Coastal Plain
- Cotton Uplands
- Gulf Coastal Plain
- Piedmont
- Central Plateau
- Western Prairies
- Mountains and Valleys

**States and places labeled:**

Atlantic Ocean

Washington, D.C.
VIRGINIA — Richmond, Norfolk
WEST VIRGINIA — Charleston, Roanoke
NORTH CAROLINA — Durham, Raleigh, Charlotte, Wilmington
SOUTH CAROLINA — Asheville, Columbia, Charleston
GEORGIA — Augusta, Savannah, Atlanta, Columbus
KENTUCKY — Lexington, Louisville, Rogersville
TENNESSEE — Nashville, Chattanooga
ALABAMA — Birmingham, Montgomery
FLORIDA — Jacksonville, Ocala, Tallahassee, Pensacola
MISSISSIPPI — Greenville, Jackson, Mobile
ARKANSAS — Memphis, Clarksdale, Greenville, Little Rock, Harrison
LOUISIANA — Baton Rouge, New Orleans, St. Landry, Shreveport
TEXAS — Dallas, Houston

Gulf of Mexico

*How happily situated is this retired spot of earth! What an
Elysium it is! Where the wandering Siminole, the naked red warrior,
roams at large, and after the vigorous chase retires from the
scorching heat of the meridian sun. Here he reclines, and reposes
under the odoriferous shades Zanthoxylon, her verdant couch
guarded by the Deity; Liberty, and the Muses, inspiring him with
wisdom and valour, whilst the balmy zephyrs fan him to sleep.*
—William Bartram on the St. Johns, 1774

*This wild, beautiful country, tucked off the tourists' highways . . .
is in itself a challenge to the imagination. I had met only two or
three of the neighboring crackers when I realized that isolation had
done something to these people. Rather, perhaps, civilization had
remained too remote, physically and spiritually, to take something
from them, something vital. They have a primal quality against
their background of jungle hammock. . . . The only ingredients of
their lives are the elemental things.*
—Marjorie Kinnan Rawlings at Cross Creek, Florida, 1930

*"Ole starvation, he's . . . meaner than ole Slewfoot!"*
—Ezra Baxter to his son, Jodie, in the film version of *The Yearling*,
1946

## PROLOGUE

# AN ORIENTATION MOSTLY
# ALONG ST. JOHNS RIVER

In March northern Florida is blessed with azure skies, shirt-sleeve-warm days, and best of all, the transporting perfume of orange blossoms wafted upon gentle breezes. Natives greet their early spring happy in a seasonal rhythm denied Floridians in the tropical South. Visitors from still-frigid northern places are simply overwhelmed with enchantment. Marjorie Kinnan Rawlings, a thirty-one-year-old journalist traveling from Rochester, New York, arrived in the lakeside citrus groves twenty-odd miles below Gainesville in March 1928, and her enchantment became permanent. She and her husband had come for a late-winter vacation, to visit her brothers-in-law, Yankee settlers who had established orchards. Rawlings, smitten, used a small inheritance to buy her own grove, which came with a primitive cottage and run-down outbuildings a few miles farther south at a hamlet called Cross Creek. Soon, however, a freeze ruined the orange harvest of her brothers-in-law, and they departed. Her husband, a disaffecting fellow disinclined to prune trees and mend fences, decamped a while later. Not Marjorie, whose fiction writing (more so than oranges) came to sustain her. She lived the rest of her life a Floridian, a countrywoman by preference, and she was buried in 1953 at Island Grove, just down the road from Cross Creek. Her old cottage, barn, tenant house, duck pen, and yard (now with new orange trees) have become a county-state park. Visitors come by the busload now, so many years later, to peer into the screened veranda where Marjorie typed letters to Ellen Glasgow, James Branch Cabell, Scott Fitzgerald, Ernest Hemingway, and Maxwell Perkins, the legendary editor at Scribner's. And here, too, she composed or rewrote so many stories published in *Scribner's* and other big-circulation magazines of the 1930s and 1940s, plus *South Moon Under* (1933), her first "Florida Cracker" long fiction; her best-selling memoir, *Cross Creek* (1942); and especially her most beloved novel, *The Yearling* (1938), which was made into an excellent Metro-Goldwyn-Mayer movie in 1946.[1]

The attraction of Cross Creek and especially the vast hammock swamps nearby was its anachronistic frontierish aspect. The countryside functioned in the world; it was hard by Henry Flagler's coastal railroad, after all, and modern cities, tourist resorts and attractions, and an industrialized agricultural landscape. Yet large sections of northeastern Florida's interior wetlands remained separate and almost independent of modernity, a sort of living museum of early Anglo-Floridian experience. Alachua County, for instance, had not yet closed its stock range as late as 1940. Cattle and especially hogs roamed at large and fed themselves in a still mostly wild countryside. Marjorie discovered (just as the first European newcomers had, centuries before) that, as a farmer, she must have good fences around her home garden and orange grove. Even then, cows broke in or out; worse, the occasional rogue boar wrought havoc with plantings, chickens (which would fly into trees), and pets. Once Marjorie dispatched one such mean hog with her trusty gun. The boar belonged to a distant neighbor, a rather menacing character actually, but Marjorie's and the neighbor's artfully indirect (and quite protracted) negotiations were ultimately successful. Neighborhood peace was restored—as was Marjorie's fence.

Beyond her hamlet other people, mostly whites, lived without scores of cattle and swine, much less oranges, on sandy pine ridges surrounded by al-

*Marjorie Kinnan Rawlings and her first husband in Florida, 1928.*
*Courtesy Florida State Archives.*

most impenetrable jungles swarming with snakes, including three species of vipers (rattlers, moccasins, and coral snakes), bears, and a few surviving panthers and alligators. (These last two species had been hunted almost to extinction by the 1930s, and wolves had been exterminated long before.) Marjorie went forth on horseback, as companion-assistant to the 1930 census taker, to meet and ultimately to know the swamp folk. She became friends with a "cracker" family, stayed in their cabin for extended periods, and learned to catch and cook turtles, hunt bear, and fish among the snakes and 'gators. The crackers lived from their gardens, the hunt, and fishing. They also grew some corn, which the men converted to whiskey and sold for cash money. This was illegal everywhere in the South for most of the twentieth century, so cracker men were often in hiding from sheriffs or in prison. Marjorie thought them nearly all admirably self-reliant, noble of sentiment and purpose, and irresistibly romantic; from them she made much of her fiction and more. She studied, then re-created in prose, the past in natural context, a dynamic rustic ecology that had been common through the seventeenth, eighteenth, and most of the nineteenth centuries, but one that hardly existed in the twentieth, except in comparably swampy, railroadless locales northward and westward, near the Atlantic and Gulf coasts, and in famously "primitive" spots of Appalachia and the Ozarks. Rawlings became an important nature writer (although she has seldom been recognized as such), not unlike her contemporary William Faulkner, in that her wild natural places have humans and human narratives in them, people and stories naturally, as it were, in *place*.

Nature without humans has manifest intrinsic value, to be sure, to human visitors who return to civilization: There are beauty gentle and awesome and a capacity for self-renewal in aftermaths of even colossal natural disasters. Humans have made their way for at least 3 million years, however, as members of the natural community everywhere on earth save Antarctica, and recently even there. Their objective has ever been the management of landscapes of every sort. For nature is sublime in the true meaning of the word—magnetically alluring yet dangerously wild, indifferent, and unpredictable. Humans must have shelter and food, and they achieve these through violence. Fire has ever been essential, destroying patches or great swaths of trees so people might establish sustaining gardens and also, for a very long time, big crop fields. The latter fed work animals, made huge bounties of corn so that whiskey might be distilled, or produced fiber to cover and protect human bodies. Not least, violence, especially fire, permitted extraction of surpluses of many commodities for trade for others' surpluses. Humans also have always used the best weapons they could contrive to kill wild and domesticated animals for meat, and they have used traps and poisons (arsenic, most commonly) as well as their weapons to control animals that civilization turned into pests and predators upon crops. Making shelter, tool and gun handles, plow frames, wagons, boats, and bridges in wooded landscapes necessitated more violence to forests, reduction of habitat, and alterations of drainage. Humans will manage landscapes as best (or worst) they can. Sometimes—and this hubris helps define what is called modernity—humans aspire to orchestrate utter security and predictability. This is but a dream, of course.[2]

Marjorie Rawlings's crackers understood this well. In *The Yearling* her wise spokesman-practitioner of human-"natural" environmental relationships is Ezra Baxter, who is called "Penny." (He is so named because in the novel Ezra is runty, yet in the film version, starring tall, broad-shouldered Gregory Peck, he is also called Penny as well as Ezra.) The story is set mainly in 1871, and Penny, his dour wife, and their only son, twelve-year-old Jodie, were inspired by hammock swamp families Marjorie knew during the 1930s. The Baxters live on Baxter's Island, a sandy pine ridge among watery marshes. They keep a horse for plowing, a cow for milk, a few hogs for meat (if they can), chickens for eggs, and dogs for hunting, home security (especially from snakes), and companionship. Penny shoots the occasional alligator—these were still plentiful then—so he may keep tail meat in his smokehouse for the dogs, since the Baxters seldom have leftovers from their own larder. Penny's crops, too, are seldom adequate for surpluses to trade for other things his family needs or craves—cloth, for example, or powder and shot, or candy. So he hunts deer, bear, and other wild animals for their meat and hides. Penny is an expert reader of forest signs, a relentless tracker, and a crack shot with an old, sometimes unreliable gun, probably the same one he carried for four years as a Confederate soldier. The gun problem is solved in a marvelous scene wherein Penny cleverly trades a dog of little utility for a fine shotgun—this with one of the brothers Forrester, rowdy neighbors who do not farm but range horses, drive them to distant trading places, and return with barrels of whiskey to swill while they saw fiddles, strum guitars, and sing uproariously in unselfconscious nakedness. They are one well-named and charming clan, except for the mean brother tricked in the dog-gun bargain, of course.

Unlike the Forresters, Penny is essentially a one-horse farmer without a labor force beyond himself and the small contributions of his growing son. In addition to the kitchen garden, worked mostly by Ma, Penny must grow corn and hay for his family, horse, and cow. He would like to have surpluses of both, plus maybe a little crop of cotton, for sale or trade. They must carry water uphill from a spring and would like to buy bricks for a well beside the house. Penny works steadily and hard, but experience has taught him that human effort is often foiled by nature. Seasons may become arhythmical, rain too sparse or ruinously abundant; unexpected pests and diseases may appear from nowhere. Penny's knowledge of nature's dynamics, its unpredictability, its local eccentricities, and its *lack* of balance subtly and brilliantly represents, I think, the revolutionary new science of the late twentieth century that overturned the notion of nature as *oikos* (a sentimental, equilibrious home) with chaos theory and what is called "patch dynamics," basically a roil of unpredictability in which human agency and the comfort of certainty are diminished if not actually dashed.[3] Penny's experience-based realism does not mean, however, that he himself was not devoted to *oikos* or oblivious to the ideal as well as the practicality of working within nature's nature.

Penny's crops for 1871 went in early and flourished in a spectacular northern Florida spring. Then came a storm. "Nor'easters" are common and expected in this country; they bring heavy winds and rain, usually for two or three days. Except this one continues for *eight* days and nights. Crops are washed away, farm animals lost, roofs compromised, stored feed spoiled. Beyond Baxter's Island, surviving wild animals starve in persisting deep floods. Millions of snakes are drowned, rattlers suffering worst, probably, in the gopher holes where many made their nests. Survivors crawl to pine ridges for safety, threatening people and their dogs. When the floods at last recede, a great deathly stench arises with the long-absent sun. A pack of about a dozen starving wolves—certainly the last of a once-large population—terrorizes the Baxters. Soon they will perish from Penny's marksmanship and in the Forresters' traps.

Rawlings's fictional eight-day nor'easter may represent elderly Florida swampers' memory of a historical storm recounted to her during the 1930s. There have always been such storms and worse. Until the twentieth century, however, if nor'easters and hurricanes were recorded at all, they became "historical" and "public" only to sparse populations affected and random readers of weather records thereafter. In 1871 in the hammocks of northern Florida, there was neither newspaper nor television nor a single meteorologist, much less a Simpson-Saffir scale (with categories 1 to 5) for measuring hurricane forces. Any notion that humans might know a storm was approaching, be able to prepare for it, and expect aid in relief during the aftermath, much less file insurance claims and request government subsidies, was faint or more likely nonexistent. Weather, especially the stormy, became public and subject to the ambition of management gradually, beginning notably during the 1890s. In September 1896, for instance, the fledgling U.S. Weather Service (a branch of the military) failed utterly to predict a Gulf hurricane that flattened the community of Cedar Key, Florida, killing 114. Two years later, President William McKinley, on the verge of war with Spain in the Caribbean, declared he feared hurricanes more than the Spanish fleet and prompted Congress to create a hurricane warning system. In 1900 came the giant tidal surge that destroyed Galveston and, during reconstruction, invited the city's introduction of the commission form of government—that is, an urban administration composed of expert-managers.[4]

There would be more great storms—most of them "southern"—as record keeping, scientific measurement, and relief organization improved and grew. The Great Florida Boom of the 1920s was practically silenced by awesome hurricanes in 1926 and 1928. The first inflicted property damage in Miami and environs exceeding that of the Galveston disaster, and the second killed probably more than 2,000 people in the Lake Okeechobee basin and inspired Zora Neale Hurston's bitter novel, *Their Eyes Were Watching God*, of 1937. In between came the Mississippi River's "flood of the century" in 1927. The Labor Day hurricane of 1935—when the national weather service failed again to warn sufficiently early—swept over the Florida Keys and drowned a thousand-odd government workers who were building a road alongside Henry Flagler's old railroad tracks.

During the 1940s, however, radar and aircraft reconnaissance propelled weather science and forecasting. The star of this essential public service was Grady Norton, whose calm Alabama drawl dominated radio airwaves during hurricane season. More than a voice, Norton revolutionized forecasting with his (correct) theory that the directions of hurricanes are determined not by surface high pressure areas but by wind flow in the upper troposphere. Technological confidence finally persuaded others in government employ to attempt actual management—not mere prediction—of great storms. Beginning during the late 1940s and most intensely during the 1960s, the National Hurricane Center, now a substantial bureaucracy, sent hurricane-hunter aircraft to seed hurricanes with silver iodide crystals in hopes of reducing their strength and dispersing them. Multiple seedings produced no measurable effects. The U.S. army, in the meantime, had turned down (in 1947) a serious offer from certain citizens in Lee County, Florida, to drop an atomic bomb on the next hurricane to approach Lee. Despite certain disappointments, then, great storms and floods had become public responsibilities, with forecasting, evacuation protocols, relief, government flood insurance, and appropriate bureaucracies fully in place, by the mid-1970s.

Famous storms roiled, still, now with names, all feminine until recently, the matches for the personable Grady Norton himself and all his successors as public faces of impending disaster—hurricanes Dora, Betsy, Camille, and many more, including another "storm of the century," Andrew, in 1992. The season of 2004 was a horror in Florida and coastal Alabama, when four hurricanes within a few weeks of August and September sent millions into retreat and hundreds to their graves. Then came Katrina in late August 2005, which must outrank all other "storms of the century": Coastal Alabama, Mississippi, and Louisiana were deluged, shrimp boats and floating palaces of gambling were blown well inland, public buildings and businesses were wrecked, and housing new, antebellum, brick, stone, and wood was demolished. In New Orleans, levees holding Lake Ponchartrain water in canals throughout the city failed, and much of the South's oldest great urban center and largest port were flooded. The National Hurricane Center had done its forecasting, but other public agencies—now long assumed as guarantors of safety—failed utterly, from the Corps of Engineers responsible for levees to the Federal Emergency Relief Administration. For all the recrimination against disaster management following Katrina—which was followed by yet another hurricane, Rita, onto the western Louisiana and eastern Texas coasts—the awful fate of the Gulf littoral in 2005 may have instructed us once more that technology, expertise, and managerial hubris cannot control nature's furies. Penny Baxter likely never entertained such a fantasy.

🌸 Yet Penny faced his own natural nemesis with a name. This is Ole Slewfoot. He is a huge, aged bear, a justified rogue named for a disfiguring encounter with a trap years before. Penny, a principled sporting man despite his lifelong struggles for existence, despises traps. But hungry Ole Slewfoot appears at the Baxters' place one night after the storm and mauls to death and partially devours the family's invaluable sow before the dogs chase the bear back into the swamp. Penny identifies the marauder from his unmistakable tracks: the deep impressions in rain-softened earth, the skewed hind paw. Slewfoot is nature primeval, furious over human incursions and depredations. He is known to raid settlements not only to eat but to commit mayhem. Slewfoot is not quite the metaphorical representative of wild nature that William Faulkner made of his Mississippian, "The Bear," in the novella of that name set about the same time as Rawlings's fiction. There is no forest-eating railroad penetrating her 1871 Florida swamp and no Christlike human moral agony over ownership, displacement, and power. Slewfoot's pursuers—all men want the honor of killing him—are uncomplicated fellows preoccupied with survival rather than the progress of civilization. Penny, especially—he the reflective, respectful man—understands and sympathizes with his bear adversary's history and necessities. Yet it is Penny who, after superhuman chase, finally brings Slewfoot to his end. Penny never hesitated; rather, the opposite. It was Slewfoot or starvation, after all, as simple and profound as that.

It was an earlier, unsuccessful tracking of Ole Slewfoot that situated the title theme of *The Yearling*, that is, the "boy's story." Penny is treading carefully through thick underbrush, crouching to see the bear's trail, young Jodie and the dogs behind him. Reaching down to move ground cover, Penny is struck on the arm by a "big'un," an enormous rattlesnake. Far from home and farther from the only doctor in the territory, Penny figures himself a goner. But he spots a doe deer, fells her with shot, and orders Jodie to remove her offal. Penny presses the liver against his snakebite wound and staggers off toward the Island. Penny will survive because the doe died. Jodie, at first terrified at the prospect of his father's death, soon calculates that the doe lingered close to humans because she had a fawn. With his father's permission, he returns to the doe's body and soon finds the speckled offspring. Jodie wants a pet, something of "his own"— the dogs are all Penny's creatures. Ma, ever fretful about the family's food supply, says no, but Penny, who always prevails through patience, tells Jodie he may fetch home the fawn. Jodie shares his own table rations with his pet and, over his mother's new objections, brings the fawn to sleep with him in his bed. Now he wants a fitting name for the animal, and for that he must visit the Forresters, the youngest of whom is a crippled boy about his age called Fodderwing, who keeps birds and, among other mammals, a raccoon named Racket. (Marjorie Rawlings herself had a young 'coon named thus for a while.) Fodderwing has observed that running deer hold their tails aloft, like flags, so Jodie's fawn assumes the affectionate identity Flag. Jodie's life becomes nature idyll: He and the growing Flag race through the woods, splash in the spring, and disappear for hours while Penny recovers and farmwork is neglected.

Inevitably, tragically, Flag grows, becoming (like Jodie) a yearling on the brink of adulthood. Now Penny is abed again, unable to work owing to an old, recurring malady. (A result of the war? Rawlings, curiously, considering hers was a work in the age of *Gone with the Wind*, barely mentions Penny's previous history.) Jodie must be a farmer now, meaning he must guarantee also the security of the family's crops from Flag. Jodie builds a fence; Flag easily jumps it and devours corn seedlings. Jodie builds the fence higher, six feet now, a heroic effort for a boy. But as any twenty-first-century suburbanite might predict, six feet is pathetically inadequate. Flag has, in effect, reincarnated Ole Slewfoot and so must die. Penny, from his sickbed, grimly gives the order. Ma tries to execute but merely wounds the yearling. Jodie must finish off Flag. Heartbreak hardly describes his despair, and doubtlessly many thousands of young (and old) readers of *The Yearling* have wept with Jodie. The boy flees to the great St. Johns River, determined to quit forever the cruel elements of Baxter's Island. He will get to faraway Jacksonville, then to civilized Boston, where a Floridian sailor friend might shelter him. But three hard days and nights later he returns, overcome by love of his parents as much as the impenetrably dark heart of the St. Johns. Penny commiserates. Even Ma's reserve melts. Jodie becomes a man, sadder and wiser, like his father. Any reader, however young or old, will know absolutely that as Jodie grows yet older, and no matter how old, he will ever be, like Penny, a respectful negotiator with nature rather than a would-be conqueror.

Jodie's brief but memorable attempt at flight from his destiny evokes much. Before creation of railroads, hard-surface highways, and automobiles, rivers were the best roads. The English sometimes named great watery junctions "roads," as in Hampton Roads, Virginia, where the mighty James, the Nansemond, and the Elizabeth empty into the bottom of Chesapeake Bay. Jamestown is nearby, up the James a distance sufficient for safety yet close enough readily to ship Virginia's gold, which was tobacco, to Europeans. Dutchmen brought Africans up this road in 1619. Much later the world's first battle between ironclad ships took place here, the event appropriate to the highway's strategic importance. Jodie Baxter tried to escape eastern Florida via that region's great thoroughfare, which the Spanish had named Rio San Juan, then the English translated directly as St. Johns. This was the road to Florida's interior, more-or-less parallel to the Atlantic coast, from present-day Jacksonville southward, past Palatka, through broad, often-stormy Lake George, through more lakes to Sanford, then narrowing and winding to the river's still-mysterious origins among swampy springs in the neighborhood of Melbourne—more than 300 miles of first dark, vegetation-stained, and then blue waters, moving slowly (for the gradient is almost flat), a rare northward-flowing highway. The southern reaches of the St. Johns—the "upper" river, owing to its flow direction— are the blackest, illustrating metaphorically, one could say, Jodie's frustration as well as south-sailing Europeans' apprehensions, centuries earlier, as they encountered lean prospects and considerable danger, not only from native peoples on the banks, but from huge populations of alligators and deadly snakes.[5]

About midway, chronologically, between the Spaniards and the fictional Jodie, the first great American-born naturalist, William Bartram, sailed, paddled, botanized, and camped along the St. Johns. William (1739–1823) was a son of John (1699–1777), the first famous Bartram naturalist, who established on his farm near Philadelphia North America's largest and best-known plant nursery and pleasure garden and who corresponded with and sent specimens to every important European taxonomist, including Sweden's Carl von Linné (Linnaeus). John sailed and paddled much of the St. Johns in 1759 and took William there in 1765. William was smitten (not unlike Marjorie Rawlings) and decided to remain in Florida as a planter of rice and indigo. John's half-brother, also named William, a planter near Wilmington, North Carolina, was probably model and inspiration. John, ever the indulgent father, bought slaves in Charleston and sent them down to young William early the next year, but William promptly failed. He was no good at business and returned to Philadelphia as a farm laborer, for a while. Finally, capitalizing on his father's contacts with English collectors, William gained commissions to draw pictures and gather specimens of North American fauna and flora and ship them to London. Botanical and other natural life collections had been a passion of Europeans and European settlers in the Americas since 1492. Possession of natural exotica enhanced collectors' social status and entertained collectors' fascinated friends, but collecting was also about the business of commodifying nature. Europeans sought plant medicines and perfumes. Europe was becoming deforested, and kings sought replacements and/or new sources of wood for ships, especially. William himself had sought to extract wealth from Florida in 1766. Like other fortune seekers, he would tear out natural vegetation, drain and dike extensive rich lands, and introduce semitropical cultivars from Asia and West Africa. Now he would collect and draw sea, river, and land shells, then mollusks and turtles, for Londoners' study and amusement. This was an agreeable profession for William. It would be conducted alone, without supervision, and it permitted William to wander, especially in wild places, by foot, horse, and boat. In 1773 he won a commission from a wealthy London physician to gather Floridian plants for the doctor's elaborate city garden. So William was happily off to the South Atlantic coast again.

In April 1774—just a year before the Revolution began—he approached the mouth of St. Johns River again (as he recorded in his *Travels*) aboard "a handsome pleasure-boat, manned with four stout negro slaves, to row in case of necessity."[6] There was no need for rowing as the party sailed past Amelia Narrows, then bore shoreward through Fort George Sound into the river's broad mouth. William and a companion, a Mr. Egan, took pleasure in watching diving pelicans—brown pelicans, presumably, since the larger white variety are not divers. Egan promptly "shot one of them, and brought it into the boat," delighting Bartram, who described the dead bird at length: "The pouch or sack, which hangs under the bill: it is capable of being expanded to a prodigious size. One of the people on board, said, that he had seen more than half a bushel of bran crammed into one of their pouches. The body is larger than that of a tame goose, the legs extremely short, the feet webbed." This was observation both scientific and artistic, for that day and many years to come, before photography presented a less sanguinary means to study birds closely.

William Bartram was hardly a slouch, but bird study is better associated with his younger contemporary, John James Audubon (1785–1851). The most vivacious painter of North American birds, immortal in his books and the bird-protection society founded in his name during the 1880s, Audubon "captured" his subjects first with his gun before posing their carcasses with the aid of sticks and wires. Audubon also wrote unselfconsciously of his participation in slaughters of birds for mere sport on the east coast of Florida early in the nineteenth century. As his vessel cleared a coral reef and made safe harbor, Audubon's "heart swelled with uncontrollable delight," he wrote, for "the birds which we saw were almost all new to us; their lovely forms appeared to be arrayed in more brilliant apparel than I had ever before seen." Nonetheless the men fired "shot after shot . . . and down came whirling through the air the objects of our desire." Still unsatisfied, a companion invited Audubon onward, to another site: "'Come along, I'll shew you something better worth your while,'" "'rare sport.'" This was soon revealed in a mangrove swamp: "a multitude of pelicans. A discharge of artillery seldom produced more effect;—the dead, the dying, and the wounded, fell from the trees upon the water, while those unscathed flew screaming through the air in terror and dismay." Still this was not enough for the men. The boat pilot insisted on a trip of another half-mile over water, this time to "four hundred cormorants' nests over our heads." Audubon and the others blasted away at sitting birds, "and when we fired, the number that dropped as if dead, and plunged into the water was such, that I thought by some unaccountable means or other we had killed the whole colony." *Unaccountable?*

There is a famous fictional slaughter of birds, almost contemporaneous with Audubon's Florida mischief, in the first of James Fenimore Cooper's Leatherstocking novels, *The Pioneers* (1823). The scene here is a frontier town in upstate New York where one day townsmen and local farmers are blasting passenger pigeons, a species later to become extinct. Cooper's hero, Natty Bumppo, appears and condemns the shooters' "wasty ways," recommending the common sense of killing only what one needed for food. But all to no avail. So-called binge killing—of birds, alligators, deer, and other animals—was in fact a phenomenon common across the continent well into the twentieth century. Frontiersmen (as one historian suggests) quite logically hate wild nature. They dwell on an edge of civilization not yet won for human security and convenience. Trees are the enemy, also wolves and other predators, naturally, and birds believed to endanger various crops. By the late nineteenth century, evidence had accumulated that crows, more commonly associated with consuming grain than were passenger pigeons, actually fed principally on grubs and insects, the greater danger to crops. Yet farmers persisted in shooting them and setting out arsenic-laced bait in their fields, especially in the South. Binge-slaughters of deer, meanwhile, were common in the same region through the nineteenth century until about World War I. Rural men and older boys, always drinking liquor, would hunt on Saturday nights, killing and leaving animals to rot in the woods, sometimes concluding their rampages by disrupting church services the next morning. The same males, apparently, also enjoyed circuses and fairs where bears and exotic animals were poked and tortured. Here was a premodern masculine culture so wasteful and violent as to prompt women and their preacher allies to organize reforms and see to enactment of liquor laws and hunting regulations.[7]

The casual killing of one pelican by Bartram's shipmate, Egan, and the instrumental killing of pairs (sometimes six individuals) of a species by J. J. Audubon for his portraits of birds might be explained another way: Bartram and Audubon admired, perhaps even loved, birds, but nature in their age was so abundant that the taking of one or two or half a dozen for study would matter not to anyone, save perhaps God. Bartram addressed this subject himself after his St. Johns River journey, as he accompanied white traders in Alachua Indian country, west of St. Augustine. The hunters had killed and cooked for William an enormous soft-shelled turtle. William thought it delicious but could eat hardly half the meat and regretted waste. His "companions," he wrote, "seemed regardless, being in the midst of plenty and variety, at any time within our reach, and to be obtained with little or no trouble or fatigue on our part; when herds of deer were feeding in the green meadows before us; flocks of turkeys walking in the groves around us, and myriads of fish, of the greatest variety and delicacy, sporting in the crystalline floods before our eyes." Besides, "vultures and ravens, crouched on the crooked limbs of the lofty pines, at a little distance from us, sharpening their beaks, in low debate, waiting to regale themselves on the offals, after our departure from camp." Still, there is much more on the killing of wild nature.

Once Bartram had landed by the St. Johns and procured from a planter a little sailboat, then set out southward, on his own, one of his first observations was of "parroquets . . . hovering and fluttering" about treetops. He meant Carolina Parakeets, foot-long multicolored birds that became extinct about 1900. Their range extended northward past Virginia and westward past the Appalachian Mountains. During the seventeenth and eighteenth centuries, Europeans and Africans exclaimed that parakeet migrations blackened the skies—like those of passenger pigeons—the birds being so numerous. Already, though, by William Bartram's time, these colorful creatures had become brethren to Ole Slewfoot, and settlers were laboring toward the parakeet's extinction with gun, net trap, and poison.

What parakeets threatened was apples. Europeans brought apple seed and tree seedlings to America, the last great migratory destination of the Asian species. Mature trees bloom magnificently and grace any homestead. The fruit may be beautiful, too, and delicious. Apples dried and stored might also supplement winter's diminishing food stores, for people and hogs. But apples had more important economic utility: They became brandy, for home and local consumption, to be sure, but especially as a form of cash money. Apples reduced in bulk to demijohns and casks might be transported relatively easily from backwater farms to trading points great and small. The overwhelming majority of Euro-Americans, from Florida through Virginia and Maryland, were not great riverside planters with large labor forces and enormous commodity production for ready trade with the world. They were instead common folk subsisting, mostly, and dependent first on their cattle and hogs to feed themselves sufficiently in the woods and marshes to multiply into surplus meat-on-the-hoof for trade. How else to pay taxes, support remote churches and schools, and buy cloth, shot, and powder? But if drought wilted grasses and reduced forest mast (nuts, root shoots, and berries), there would be no meat surpluses, and hard times would follow. Apple and other fruit brandies were the standby. The war on parakeets, then, like the ongoing war to exterminate wolves that attacked livestock, was a democratic one in the simple sense that nearly everyone had elemental reason to kill. So for the better part of two centuries, southerners blasted away (and poisoned or netted and clubbed) the parakeet population. This was hardly binge killing but, to them, grim necessity. One must think, nonetheless, that diminished parakeets corresponded to more abundant brandy production, which doubtlessly fueled southern men's sanguinary rampages in the woods.[8]

Another celebrated avian, common in Florida and throughout the lower Gulf territories and states in the Bartrams' era, was the ivory-billed woodpecker. Closely resembling the pileated woodpecker, a large, aggressive black creature with a red head and dramatic plume—which thrives still within a range much larger than the semitropics—the ivory-billed woodpecker apparently succumbed, early in the twentieth century, to habitat reduction. Relentless amateur birders and ornithologists never gave up on the ivory-billed, however, and sixty-odd years after the putative last bird was sighted, trackers sighted another in an eastern Arkansas swamp in 2004.[9] Critics of the evidence soon publicized plausible doubt, yet whether or not the ivory-billed's resurrection ultimately proves real, something marvelous began to transpire in the Arkansas wetlands: Federal, state, and private interests moved to protect and extend the wetlands, which had once been much larger, modestly reversing a sorry old story of compromised wild places.

In northeastern Florida, for example, William Bartram casually described riverscapes already long managed and revised by humans. Many of the aboriginals—some Timucua chiefdoms to the north (before their eighteenth-century extinction) and later many Seminoles and other peoples to the south—had been farmers, clearing land with fire. Early during his trip south on the St. Johns, William passed a substantial native settlement with large crop fields and a well-tended orange grove. The natives also fished from permanent villages and built large shell mounds that were landform features of considerable interest to both Bartrams, to Marjorie Kinnan Rawlings, and to tourists even now, although many mounds have been plundered, reduced, or removed for modern agricultural operations and road paving. The Indians made trails, too, permanent roads for trade and commuting to hunting grounds as well as for transport to once-permanent native towns. Towns, the highest expression of what is called civilization, were common throughout most of Florida and the greater Southeast as well. (More on these later.) By the time William Bartram navigated the St. Johns, most Indian settlements were gone, and surviving natives had become lively traders with the Spanish, then the English and Americans. They persisted in year-round settlements by the river, incorporating European introductions of plants and animals with their own.

The orange, for example, seemed utterly ubiquitous by 1774. The cultivar of the fruit the Spanish brought to Florida (so that seamen might consume it and avoid scurvy) came originally from eastern Asia. Arabs adopted oranges via the Indian Ocean trade more than a thousand years ago and then, as Muslim conquerors, introduced them to Spain, probably by the tenth or eleventh century. Valencia, especially, is associated with oranges, and English speakers used the name of the Spanish city to label several varieties of orange in Florida. Here, whites and natives alike tended them in groves, but birds spread the plant indiscriminately. William Bartram often camped in unsettled places with mixed assemblages of trees—huge live oaks (under which William preferred to camp), palms, bay, longleaf pine (in northern Florida), magnolia grandiflora, and many other species—virtually always including the stray orange. These were handy even if the juice was sometimes bitter, typical of the variety called Seville after yet another Spanish city. William packed oil for cooking but lacked vinegar or other seasonings. So when he caught and cleaned fat fish for roasting on his fire, he usually pulled an orange or two and squeezed juice on his catch, rhapsodizing about the effect.[10]

Of introduced animals—horses, asses, mules, cattle, and hogs—Bartram saw few in the deep swamps. Elsewhere, by the coast and in the open pine forests and plains of Alachua, for instance, natives and whites alike adopted and used all these creatures, plus dogs, the one (relatively) tame animal natives possessed before the Europeans came. The riverine landscape was too boggy, for the most part, to support beasts of burden, and riverside ridges that might easily be cultivated with draft animals were few. In 1774, too, the swamps still harbored too many large predators for the safe ranging of domesticated dairy and meat creatures. Bears singly and in pairs, wolves in packs, and panthers in numbers prowled everywhere. So the range for cattle and swine was really not yet open here. Native vipers were a considerable inconvenience if not deadly danger to beasts and humans, as well.

Much, much later, after Marjorie Kinnan Rawlings had moved to Florida, she was frequently preoccupied with snakes in her fiction, her famous memoir, and her private letters. Rawlings was terrified of snakes, and to her great credit she sought out a University of Florida herpetologist, who taught her respect and tolerance and took her rattlesnake hunting in the Everglades—not to kill them, but to collect. Still, Rawlings had many unpleasant surprise encounters. Once she picked up a coral snake in her garden before recognizing it. She almost trod on a moccasin lying next to her front step, and much later, after she had acquired fame, moderate wealth, and plumbing in her Cross Creek cottage, a four-foot-long moccasin appeared in her toilet.[11] (The snake had entered through a broken drainage tile outside.) Bartram, by contrast, wrote little of serpents, although he must have seen them every time he went ashore. Still, within his *Travels* there is a brief catalog of Florida and southeastern snakes. Here William lingered more passionately on the appearance and habits of the rattlesnake, which he rather liked—"a wonderful creature," potentially deadly to be sure, but retiring, slow of motion, and ultimately "magnanimous." Once he awoke in camp to discover that a rattler had slept at his feet. When both were awake, each simply withdrew. He recalled an earlier encounter with a huge rattler on Sapelo Island, Georgia, that had permitted him and his companions to pass close by, in the dark, time and again on their way to a spring. William, discovering the snake, demanded that his friends not harm it. In Florida, he only reluctantly killed a large rattlesnake in an Indian town, at the natives' command.

William was quite fearless, except in the presence of another native, the alligator, which he also called the crocodile. On this animal his prose became darkly ominous, sometimes almost hysterical and straining credulity (as he himself admitted), nullifying in considerable measure the enchantment he usually perceived in semitropical nature. Late one day he put ashore below Lake George, where a narrow inlet opened into a pond, or lagoon. Discovering his supply of food low, he set out again to fish for "trout"—just as the sun began to set and slumbering alligators awoke and, as he observed with mounting apprehension, "gathered around my harbour from all quarters." Fearful the animals might swamp or tip his little bark, with its low gunwales, he unloaded his gun, papers, and specimens and selected a stout club for self-defense. He pressed through the alligators that blocked his "harbour" but found that "several very large ones" pursued him. He "paddled with all my might" but "was attacked on all sides, several endeavouring to overset the canoe. My situation now became precarious to the last degree: two very large ones attacked me closely, at the same instant, rushing up with their heads and part of their bodies above the water, roaring terribly and belching floods of water over me. They struck their jaws together so close to my ears, as almost to stun me, and I expected every moment to be dragged out of the boat and instantly devoured." But William saved himself by bashing the attackers on their snouts with his club, driving them off long enough to make his retreat. William still needed his fish, so he worked to make his way to the entrance to the lagoon. It was here, though, that alligators "formed a line" that he boldly penetrated; then he luckily caught his sufficiency without delay. An "old daring" alligator, "about twelve feet in length," shadowed him back to his camp landing. When William pulled his boat out of the water and began to unpack his gear, "he rushed up near my feet, and lay there for some time, looking me in the face, his head and shoulders out of the water." William "resolved he should pay for his temerity," and remembering that his gun was already prepared with "a heavy load," he raced the few yards to his camp and, returning, found his antagonist "with his foot on the gunwale of the boat, in search of fish." William "soon dispatched him by lodging the contents of my gun in his head." Now William began on the same spot to clean his hard-won fish. But another alligator—again "a very large" one—appeared next to him, and "with a sweep of his tail, he brushed off several of my fish." Bartram recalled that had he not "looked up" the instant the creature appeared, he might have been killed. "This incredible boldness of the animal disturbed me greatly," he wrote, and William knew he would have to remain on alert the entire night.

Later he discerned the reason for the alligators' ferocity. The St. Johns had become alive with hundreds of thousands of "trout" — more likely largemouth bass[12]—pressing to enter the lagoon. This was doubtlessly a seasonal event and presumably well known to the amphibian predator population. Alligators had thickly lined the entrance, awaiting a frenzy of feeding. This was "a scene," William wrote, so "new and surprising, which at first threw my senses into such a tumult, that it was some time before I could comprehend what was the matter." Had not the waiting host been so dangerous, William figured, he might have walked across the waters on their heads and backs. The great feeding was a nightmare. "The horrid noise of their closing jaws, their plunging amidst the broken banks of fish, the rising with their prey some feet upright above the water, the floods of water and blood rushing out of their mouths, and the clouds of vapour issuing from their wide nostrils, very truly frightful. This scene continued at intervals during the night, as the fish came to the pass." William concluded he was now safe, the alligators being preoccupied. But then danger appeared from behind. Two bears, smelling his supper, approached to within thirty yards. William's gun misfired but made sufficient noise to send the would-be marauders into retreat, "leaping and plunging a long time" through the underbrush and swamps. There were no further close encounters that night, but poor William knew scant repose owing to screeching owls and bellowing alligators. Finally he slept a bit toward morning, arising to "perfect peace." The alligators themselves now were asleep with bellies full.

William paddled southward, then, and considering his terrifying experiences the previous evening and night, readers of his *Travels* may justly be alarmed to learn that, observing by a shady riverbank what had been described to him earlier as alligator nests, he steered without hesitation to the closest landing so he might inspect them! Curiosity always overcame fright with William. (During my own brief excursion on the St. Johns in 2002, a young mother alligator swam vigorously toward our boat, which had paused near her nest.) That evening, however, as he sought another bankside camp, he was startled when "a huge crocodile rising up from the bottom close to me . . . plunged down again under my vessel." Knowing again he was obliged "to be on my guard," he spent another restless, watchful night, during which he discovered the "crocodile . . . dashing my canoe against the roots of a tree [to which it was tied], endeavouring to get into her for the fish." "Another time in the night I believe I narrowly escaped being dragged into the river by him; for when again through excessive fatigue I had fallen asleep, but was again awakened by the screaming owl, I found the monster on the top of the bank, his head towards me not above two yards distant." William jumped up with his gun, and the alligator "plunged back into the water." He got no more sleep but maintained a high campfire, and he stole away as soon as light permitted.

William Bartram's summary report on alligators mixes awe and fear with the naturalist's compulsion to inform:

The alligator when full grown is a very large and terrible creature, and of prodigious strength, activity, and swiftness in water. I have seen them twenty feet in length, and some are supposed to be twenty-two and twenty-three feet. Their body is as large as a horse; their shape exactly resembles that of a lizard, except their tail, which is flat or cuneiform . . . the whole body is covered with horny plates or squammae, impenetrable when on the body of a live animal, even to a rifle ball, except about their head and just behind their fore-legs or arms. . . . Only the upper jaw moves, which they raise almost perpendicular, so as to form a right angle with the lower one. . . . But what is yet more surprising to a stranger, is the incredible loud and terrifying roar, which they are capable of making, especially in the spring season, their breeding time. It most resembles very heavy distant thunder, not only shaking the air and waters, but causing the earth to tremble; and when hundreds and thousands are roaring at the same time, you can scarcely be persuaded, but that the whole globe is violently and dangerously agitated.

William's summary was possibly even better expressed in his extraordinary drawings of the beasts. Normally a skilled draftsman of plants and other animals, Bartram botched his alligators. They are less representational than any other subject he drew, to my mind more like movie monsters than recognizable amphibians. One must concede, though, that his monsters are an honest match for his experience.

William Bartram was hardly responsible for the near-extermination of the American alligator during the late nineteenth and twentieth centuries. He bashed a few of them on their snouts but shot and killed only one that we know of. About a century later, Marjorie Kinnan Rawlings's fictional Penny Baxter shot one only occasionally, when he needed dog food. Alligators do not figure large in Rawlings's oeuvre. They are nocturnal creatures, after all, who laze about, sleeping mostly, while humans are awake and afoot. Shooting one during daylight is nearly the equivalent of taking a barnyard chicken. But not long after the gentle Penny's time, the great slaughter began. Excursion boat operators as far away as Charleston and Savannah invited tourists to cruise down the St. Johns with their rifles and take target practice at birds and alligators. In 1875 the Georgia-born poet Sidney Lanier, in hire to a railroad, advised infirm Yankees to winter in St. Augustine and plunder the adjacent riverine environment for sustenance: "You may," he wrote, "kill alligators and sell their teeth . . . or shoot herons, and collect their plumes for market—an occupation by which at least one invalid . . . has managed to support himself." Prospective visitors with means sufficient to live without work might simply shoot "for pleasure." (One must think of the beloved conservationist ex-president

*Photo of William Bartram's drawing of alligators in St. Johns River, 1773.*
*Courtesy Florida State Archives.*

Theodore Roosevelt, blasting away at Amazonian fauna from a big, comfortable river cruiser.) As early as the 1880s, alligators had become rare on the St. Johns north of Lake George. Trophy hunters traveled a bit farther, then. In 1932 George Herman "Babe" Ruth descended to Florida and "bagged a gator" for himself. A *New York Times* photographer recorded the triumphal coda: It is daytime, and Ruth, his shoes and lower trouser legs muddy from the hunt, cradles his rifle in his right arm and stands beside his trophy, an eight-and-a-half-footer, perhaps, which is hooked and roped from its snout and suspended from a tree limb. Another man, probably Ruth's guide, stands on the other side, and he and Ruth hold the dead 'gator's hind feet outward, spread-eagle style.[13] Sad business.

It was market hunting, however, more than potshotting and the getting of trophies that drove alligator populations nearly out of sight throughout the South Atlantic and Gulf states by about 1960. Tail meat is edible by humans as well as dogs, when properly prepared, but alligator hides were the prize commodity, for shoes and boots, belts, luggage, and handbags. One December in the 1940s, Marjorie Kinnan Rawlings's second husband, a St. Augustine hotelier, begged Marjorie for suggestions of a Christmas present. She offered only one, a bag, and related later to a friend that her husband went to "the Alligator Farm" (presumably the same Anastasia Island attraction that persists today) and purchased an enormous alligator case for her gift. Rawlings, who early in her writing career in effect paid tribute to alligators in a *Saturday Evening Post* story titled "Alligators," was complicit, then, in a world market, as were millions of others. Florida at last protected alligators by law in 1972, and their population recovered to an estimated 1 million by 1999. Some of these are bred in captivity and displayed as tourist attractions in such institutions as the venerable "Farm" in St. Augustine, yet others are bred for meat and hides in a market that has revived with the amphibian population.

Most of Florida's alligators live not in captivity yet not quite in the wild, either. The 2000 federal census recorded more than 15 million people in the state, and demographers predicted at least another 5 million by 2010. Nearly everyone alive, it seems, Florida natives and newcomers alike, covets a home by the water. The ocean and gulf strands are more-or-less taken, so the shores and banks of rivers, creeks, lakes, and canals—alligator habitat—grow crowded. Alligators have become the problem with paradise, and the Florida Fish and Wildlife Conservation Commission, which takes complaint calls, is the stalwart mediator. Between 1948 and 1998, the commission recorded 236 alligator attacks upon humans. These included bites from foot-long babies imprudently picked up, but also fifteen fatalities (six of whom may have been dead before opportunistic alligators arrived). The 1990s average of about eighteen reported attacks annually seems smaller than one might expect, actually. But after all, alligators (like snakes) are reclusive animals. They become trouble for humans usually when humans effectively invite contact by feeding them.

Then there is the large, unmeasurable matter of domestic serenity associated especially with suburbs, and dogs and cats. New settlements of people that are neither rural nor urban occupy a middle landscape dear to Americans since the nineteenth century. Here one lives quietly in nature but certainly not wild nature. Slewfoot is gone, forgotten in the household and neighborhood idyll. Alligators, at least potentially, are a threat worse than Slewfoot, though, since Slewfoot was a menace with reasoned (as it were) cause for his antipathy to humans. Alligators better resemble Faulkner's Bear, representing the fiercely primeval, that which must be destroyed if human supremacy and security are to be maintained. If loathing for alligators is mitigated, however, by education in the creatures' remote threat to humans, loathing seems justified, maybe heightened, by the creatures' presumed threat to pets. Suburbanites' domestic companions, cursed with curiosity about the contents of swamps and waterways, are the vulnerable ones, a potential feast, it is thought, no less tantalizing that William Bartram's "trout."

Alligators may indeed kill pets, although imaginative talk doubtlessly overwhelms statistics that seem dubious anyway. At the Okefenokee State Park in southeastern Georgia, a short distance from the mouth of the mighty St. Johns, unfenced alligators small and very large lounge about in broad daylight near the entrance to the reception center, in the gardens, in the water near the reconstructed pioneer farmhouse, and among the verdant tangles of adjacent swamps. A strange landscape, indeed, for ranger-conducted tours for crowds of visitors, a few of whom have brought their dogs. The dogs may not tour, and rangers advised me several times (in March 2001) to mind Nando, my collie-sheltie. He must absolutely remain on leash because (I heard variously), since the park's opening, twenty, twenty-three, forty, or sixty dogs had been gruesomely minced. Nando, meanwhile, who was programmed to encircle, trap, and control other moving creatures, never pulled his lead, expressing no interest in a close inspection, much less a dashing charge upon the lazing monsters. Smart dog.

Live and let live: the most ancient, armored, and fearsome beside (but not too close to) the most preciously bred.

🐾 Enough of animals for a while. Both Bartrams were much more enthralled by the botanical marvels of the Southeast. In the Georgia uplands they discovered and named a "new" tree, *Franklinia altamaha*, which John then cultivated in his Philadelphia nursery. William found another specimen (or the very same one) during his 1774–76 travels, but the tree exists now only as a cultivar, all apparently descending from John's plantings. Along the St. Johns, meanwhile, William filled his journal pages with sightings of bird species within their lush botanical habitats, trees soaring, squat, florid, or dark, and hardly a nonwoody plant escaped his notice either. Some of the last he represented as illustrations to accompany the *Travels*. Later settlers and travelers were no less enchanted. These included, of course, Marjorie Kinnan Rawlings, who made identification of native and introduced trees and other plants, and mastery of their names, her mission. She also gardened, relishing especially the glory of rose culture in northern Florida. Marjorie replanted her rose garden every other year, she said, because they "literally bloomed themselves to death."

William Bartram was fascinated also by aquatic plants. Early in his voyage south on the river, on "a fine cool morning, and fair wind," he marveled at "vast quantities of the *Pistia stratiotes*, a very singular aquatic plant. It associates in large communities, or floating islands, some of them a quarter mile in extent, which are impelled to and fro, as the wind and current may direct." William thought the mature plant resembled lettuce, although the leaves were greener, and he knew that *Pistia* sent down fibrous roots toward muddy river and lake bottoms. All the descriptive detail paled with the effects of the plant islands on his imagination, though. They were

> a very entertaining prospect; for although we behold an assemblage of the primary production of nature only, yet the imagination seems to remain in suspense and doubt; as in order to enliven the delusion, and form a most picturesque appearance, we see not only flowery plants, clumps of shrubs, old weather-beaten trees, hoary and barbed, with the long moss waving from their snags, but we also see them completely inhabited, and alive, with crocodiles, serpents, frogs, otters, crows, herons, curlews, jackdaws, etc. There seems, in short, nothing wanted but the appearance of a wigwam and a canoe to complete the scene.

William complained little that the floating islands sometimes confounded navigation, especially in the lakes, where channels were mazes of choice. This was not the case with later river travelers, who discovered islands not yet imagined when William paddled and sailed.

In March 1933, Marjorie Rawlings undertook with a young woman friend what Rawlings told Maxwell Perkins was "a very foolish trip" on the St. Johns. Local men warned her against the dangers of the wild, yet concluded (to her delight), "No fool, no fun." So the women would navigate most of the St. Johns, beginning not on the easy, broad northern or (relatively) straight middle sections of the river but at its presumed source, just west of Melbourne, in a lake named Hell 'n' Blazes. (Marjorie rendered it "Hellenblazes.") This upper region of the river was notorious for its narrow, mazelike channels—if channels could be found at all—and lakes so covered with drifting vegetation that they were avoided by all but a few local fishing people. The worst of the lakes was properly named Puzzle. Marjorie and her friend, Dessie Vinson, would take an eighteen-foot rowboat with a small outboard motor (plus another motor for safety), gasoline, a tent, food, and Marjorie's dutch oven. Dessie brought a rod and reel and packed a pistol. If they made it to Sanford, beginning of the "middle" part of the river, where banks and channels were obvious, they would proceed northward through Lake George and then, at Welaka, steer westward into Marjorie's "home river," the Ocklawaha, a tributary of the St. Johns originating far inland toward the south.[14]

Even as late as 1933, women generally did not attempt such adventures. Marjorie, however, was deeply depressed. Her long-faltering marriage had just ended, and now she identified herself to Max Perkins as "an old woman of 36." Dessie, twenty-six and athletic, was the adventurer who insisted on the trip to distract the troubled Marjorie, and simply because she relished the notion. Married to a Tampa physician, Dessie "lives a sophisticate's life among worldly people," Marjorie wrote, but "at the slightest excuse she steps out of civilization, naked and relieved, as I should step out of a soiled chemise. . . . Guns and campfires and fishing-rods and creeks are corpuscular in her blood." So off they drove in Marjorie's Oldsmobile, trailing her rowboat piled with gear. Lake Hellenblazes turned out to be a dry, yellowing marsh. A drought that had begun in 1929 forced the adventurers northward, where they finally discovered the navigable head of the St. Johns at Fort Christmas. They pushed off (a boy drove the car back) and started the motor in the narrowest of streams, surrounded by endless marsh.

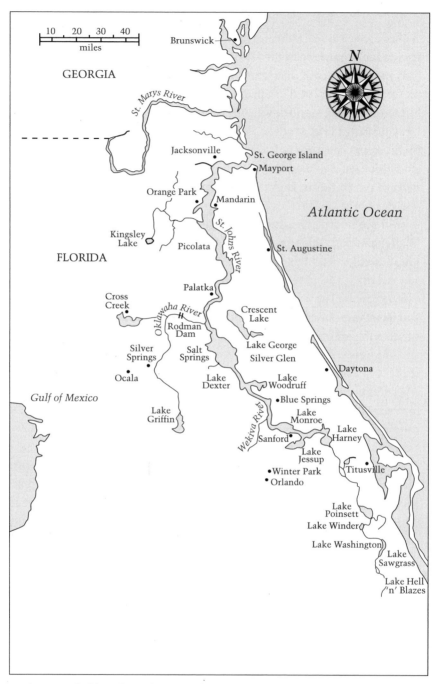

*Northeastern Florida and St. Johns River (from Bill Belleville,* River of Lakes:
A Journey on Florida's St. Johns River *[2000], courtesy University of Georgia Press)*

Dessie womaned the outboard, whistling and requesting directions. Marjorie sat toward the bow with her compass and Coast and Geodetic Survey chart of the river. Her first bad news, from the chart, was that there would be no "lights, beacons nor buoys for at least a hundred miles." A kindly fisherman and his wife, from their shack leaning over the riverbank, pointed downriver and named a certain tree that would guide them to the proper channel. (The fisherman also asked them to send him a postcard when they arrived safely at home, so he might stop worrying about two women in the wilderness.) But they could not find the tree and were soon lost in a maze of water hyacinths. Trying one opening after another, they found nothing but false channels. Finally they turned off the motor, drifted, and felt and watched the river for definite motion. This tactic, and Marjorie's dogged persistence with her compass, led to the true channel, at last. Marjorie had navigated Puzzle Lake—all the while thinking they were on Lake Harney.

The puzzle-maker was the hyacinths. The women were not charmed by drifting, dividing, recombining islands of hyacinths, as William Bartram had been by islands of *Pistia*, or "watterlettuce." Water lettuce itself was probably an introduction, brought to the St. Johns by European ships long before 1774. It was regarded as a hazard to navigation and a threat to the river's quality, too, since rotting *Pistia* fouled sandy shores and the river's bottom. Water hyacinth was a more recent introduction, made foolishly for aesthetic effect. In 1884 Mrs. W. F. Fuller, Brooklyn-born but a resident of Edgewater, Florida, attended the Cotton Exposition in New Orleans and came home with souvenirs: a few filched clippings of water hyacinth. By the St. Johns once more, she set the hyacinths in her fish pond. Soon spikes of stunning lavender flowers appeared. Mrs. Fuller so loved the effect in her pond that she set more hyacinth into the river in front of her house. The rest, as it is said, is the history of yet another disaster of unintended consequences. By 1897 water hyacinth was universally condemned as a pest, and a century later the editor of Jacksonville's principal newspaper demanded the plant's extermination. During the 1970s, hydrilla, yet another aquatic floater, got into the St. Johns.

Back in 1933, meanwhile, Marjorie and Dessie plowed through and around hyacinth islands not only in the puzzling upper reaches of the river but past Sanford and through Lake George and beyond, where yachts, tugboats, and large ships negotiated the great plant drifts. Neither woman complained. To Marjorie, the passage through "Hyacinth Drift" (the name of a story in *Scribner's Magazine* later in 1933, then a chapter in *Cross Creek*) was psychological therapy that returned happiness. To Dessie, the sports-woman, it was another splendid lark. The best was surviving Puzzle Lake to find an idyllic campsite by Lake Harney. They found "a deserted cabin, gray and smooth as only cypress weathers. There was no door for its doorway, or panes or shutters for its windows, but the roof was whole, with lichens thick across the shingles." Dessie made a fire and Marjorie "broiled shad and shad roe over fragrant coals, and French-fried potatoes, and found I had the ingredients for Tartar sauce." At night they bathed in water from a bucket, then put on pajamas. "The moon shone through the doorway and windows and the light was patterned with the shadows of Spanish moss waving from the live oaks. There was a deserted grove somewhere behind the cabin, and the incredible sweetness of orange bloom drifted across us." Next morning, a "mocking-bird sang from a palm tree at sunrise." Marjorie hated to leave the spot.

Soon they arrived at Sanford, where the river widens and the channel is broad and deep. It was Sunday morning, and they tied up next to a yacht from Long Island. The city marina's gas station was closed for church, but the yacht's owner gave Marjorie, Dessie, and their gas cans a ride in his limousine into town to an open station. They returned shortly with cans filled and that day's New York City newspapers. Off once more, crossing Lake Monroe (and ignoring their Sunday papers), they spotted "a white sand bar and had a swim in water clear as amber." A little earlier Marjorie had spotted a six-foot-long water moccasin, one with "a magnificent mot-tled hide" swimming between "a spider lily and a swamp laurel." There is no mention or apparent fear of alligators. Later the travelers approached the giant Lake George toward dark, an awkward time. Looking for a camp, they spied a shack on poles occupied by unfriendly squatters. Marjorie sort of wished to stay, anyway, rather than backtrack several miles to an open but maybe dangerous bank. At the pole-shack, meanwhile, Dessie noticed that hyacinths gathered thickly around their boat's stern, and she declared to her friend, "I'd rather sleep with a moccasin over each shoulder than get caught in a hyacinth block." So back they went, and as darkness fell, they encountered some fishermen who had camped across from their own dark resort. The men shouted an inquiry: Were they the women who had set out from Fort Christmas about a week earlier? Watermen had sent word north-ward, down the river, to look out for the two. Marjorie liked this and wrote that the men's "campfire flickered sociably all night."

Next morning they avoided Lake George's middle (and shortest) channel, because squalls threatened and that route would have put them out of sight of land for at least an hour, not to mention in the path of large vessels. The safer western channel crossing was rough enough. Stiff winds and choppy waters pitched the rowboat, its stern and propeller rhythmically out of the water in a trip of two and a half hours. Finally, "at Welaka one afternoon we left the hyacinths swirling leisurely and turned up our home river, the Ocklawaha," Marjorie wrote. "I thought in a panic, I shall never be happy on land again." Yet then, "when the dry ground was under us, the world no longer fluid, I found a forgotten loveliness in all the things that have nothing to do with men. Beauty is pervasive, and fills, like perfume, more than the object that contains it. Because I had known intimately a river, the earth pulsed under me. The Creek was home, Oleanders were sweet past bearing, and my own shabby fields, weed-tangled, were newly dear. I knew, for a moment, that the only nightmare is the masochistic human mind."

❧ So Marjorie returned to Cross Creek slightly battered, a bit older and wiser, and altogether enchanted once more. That was three-quarters of a century ago. There is enchantment to be found, still. Beholders are, after all, various, with idiosyncratic criteria for beauty. Commonly held notions seem ever to include quiet, purity—a quality of natural cleanliness—and the possibility of solitude, or something close to that. Well before the end of the twentieth century, though, hardly a place in the South remained clean and/or quiet, especially Florida. The world had become noisy with motors and dirty with smoke from trucks and cars and factories and power plants. Chemical and sewage spills compromised or ruined water. Public works to reduce mosquito populations (and create salable plots of land) drained more than half of the vast wetlands that supplied the source of the St. Johns. Human populations surged, demanding more forest and wetlands clearance and pavement. Mounting consciousness of earthly degradation, culminating perhaps with Bill McKibben's announcement of nature's actual "death" in 1989, cast a grim if not defeatist pall over the latest version of conservation, called environmentalism. Enchantment became memory, then, usually borrowed from a past ever more remote. The present is for disaffected dreamers.

An excellent representative of these is the Florida writer and environmental activist Gail Fishman. Miami-born and lately based in Tallahassee, where she has worked for the Nature Conservancy, Fishman is the daughter of a father who loved to drive on weekends. During the late 1950s and 1960s, then, as a child she knew not only a relatively simple Miami and an uncluttered Dade County but Keys uncrowded and with coral reefs intact and, throughout the peninsula's southern interior, seas of relatively undisturbed wetlands. Fishman is just old enough, in other words, to have experienced enchantment and then lost its sources and sensation. Her recourses have been conservation action and study—of old landscape photographs, drawings, paintings, and writings. During the late 1990s she developed an idea for a book that perfectly suits our nostalgic and disaffected situation. The result, published in 2000, is tellingly called *Journeys through Paradise: Pioneering Naturalists in the Southeast*.

Fishman reread the journals, memoirs, books, and sometimes the private letters of "classic" naturalists who visited or lived in and portrayed the American South. These included the famous Bartrams, John and William, of course, and Mark Catesby (1683–1749), the Englishman who spent time in Williamsburg as a young fellow, then returned and stayed longer in Charleston and the lower South, plus Bermuda. She also read André Michaux (1746–1802?), the adventurous French botanical collector; J. J. Audubon; and John Muir (1838–1914), the eccentric who walked from Indiana to Florida in 1867 and wrote an engrossing book about it after he walked to California. Fishman's traveling scheme, once her reading was done, was to revisit her naturalists' best or most interesting sites. Bartram's *Travels* in hand, for instance, she found a friend with a boat and sailed the middle leg of St. Johns River. Mostly she seems to have spent much of 1997 and 1999 dashing about Florida, Georgia, and South Carolina in her car, as one might expect.

To her credit, Fishman chose also to feature less well-known men, significant scientists anyway, a few of whom acted as strangely as William Bartram and John Muir. John Abbot (1751–1840) was a London attorney who abandoned his profession in order to collect insects in Virginia and Georgia. Like many naturalists, he was gifted at drawing and painting, producing luminously lifelike beetles. Hardy Bryan Croom (1797–1837) was a university-educated planter at New Bern, North Carolina, who with a brother migrated to northwestern Florida and established new plantations near the Apalachicola River. Botany was Croom's passion, and wealth freed him to become a fine taxonomist and brilliant gardener. Alvan Wentworth Chapman (1809–99) was a tall Yankee physician who began to collect plants early in life, before he moved to the Gulf port town of Apalachicola. Chapman's *Flora of the Southern United States* (1860) was the standard on the subject until the appearance of John Kunkel Small's *Flora of the Southeastern United States* in 1903. Small (1869–1938) is another of Fishman's subjects. Pennsylvania-born, he was a professional botanist (not merely a botanizer), a modern man who collected with the aid of an automobile packed with a "weed wagon." Finally, the brothers Roland (1878–1966) and Francis (1886–1972) Harper, New England–born botanists and workaholics, were devoted to the study and preservation of Okefenokee Swamp, which Roland first visited in 1902. Here was a place Fishman could visit, too.

Fishman's tightly scheduled 1997 and 1999 travels are of interest and revealing. There was hardly a trace of Mark Catesby to be found in Charleston or up the Ashley River, little surprise. But she documented Hardy Croom's connection with Alvan Chapman—Chapman was the young pupil to Croom—and she hiked the Apalachicola Bluffs, where the two had botanized together so long ago. The bluffs are a delight because they are protected by the Nature Conservancy. Fishman also found the Croom family monument in a Tallahassee churchyard. Earlier, Fishman canoed through parts of the Okefenokee with an informed companion, comparing landforms with seventy- and eighty-year-old works by the Harpers. The great swamp has been canalized, timbered, and mined for phosphates; comparisons did not encourage.

To the south, St. Johns River had been a thoroughfare for so many of her naturalists that Fishman persuaded an entomologist friend, a mosquito specialist with a twenty-two-foot motorized sailboat called *Gator*, to undertake a voyage from Sanford to the northern end of Lake George. They packed three coolers, "way too much food," guidebooks, Bartramiana, "binoculars, an assortment of cameras and lenses, clothes, sunscreens, hats, rain suits, a portable toilet," and more, for a week-long trip in May 1997—mildly embarrassed by the comparison with William Bartram's equipment. There was immediately much to see onshore: marinas, "yachts that reduced *Gator* to the size of a dinghy," housing developments, and power plants. Elsewhere wetland forests had returned from ruins of plantations; Bartram had viewed eastern bank landscapes more open, here and there. Fishman and the mosquito specialist, also a "Bartram aficionado," looked for places William had camped, had observed, or had battled alligators, and they saw a few. They spotted ruins of Timucuan shell mounds—opened and spoiled by artifact hunters, but especially carried off by highway departments, since shells made fine roadbeds. Fishman ventilated about Mrs. Fuller's folly, the hazards to navigation posed by water hyacinth, and especially the plant's despoliation of the river's bottom. A woman they met who lived on an island spoke effectively for Fishman and her companion: "The bottom was clear and sandy when I was a kid. We used to swim here, but not anymore. That stuff [dead hyacinth sludge] is a foot or more deep and it isn't going away.

We can't get the state to do anything about it either." What the state of Florida did accomplish was (in Fishman's words) to "run a spray program to control the plant. The plant dies, rots, and sinks to the bottom, leaving the surface water clear and the bottom deep in ooze."

Ooze is, indeed, broadly evocative of Fishman's Florida. For all the moments of pleasure she gathered in her visitations with historical places, the present mostly disgusted. In her Audubon chapter she complained defensively: "I could not bring myself to follow John James to the Keys. It has been about thirty-five years since the last visit and I do not want to disturb or replace the memories of quiet beaches, beautiful water, and real Key lime pie made by someone who knew how." Much later, following John Kunkel Small farther and farther southward, Fishman grew despondent: "I cannot honestly think of another region that has been so transformed and obliterated as South Florida," she wrote. "The places John Small loved were long gone before I arrived and even the Miami I loved as a child will never be seen again." Then, chillingly, she added, "These days, traveling much farther south than Gainesville in my home state leaves me drained, disappointed, frustrated, saddened, distraught—any emotion but happy." She might resist Audubon in the Keys, but following Small was essential to her self-assigned mission. Grimly, then, Fishman "face[d] that tropical journey one more time."

🌺 Comparable lamentation is chanted in other voices, too, with attachment to other subregions of the American South. Not just Fishman's Florida but virtually every inch of the rest of the coastal South is for sale or already developed. Tidal marshes and swamps, estuaries, coastal forests, and enormous drainage systems are compromised or obliterated. Building becomes as dense in some southern places as on the French and Italian rivieras, and auto traffic is arguably worse. My own version of Fishman's despair attaches to the Outer Banks of North Carolina, especially Nags Head and adjacent communities of Kitty Hawk and Kill Devil Hills, which was the nearly barren retreat of my youth from nearby metropolitan Hampton Roads, Virginia. Worse than the traffic and clutter of buildings, perhaps, is the callous dismissal of a delicious indigenous cuisine in what must be a monumentally stupid and unconfident appeal to perceived touristic appetites: New England clam chowder, New York steaks, and much pizza. Transformations of landscape from un- or barely built to densely built must be accepted (lest one go insane)—Fishman may disagree—but the compromising of local food cultures, whether real Key lime pie or the splendid simplicity of fried fish with slaw and hushpuppies, is an unmitigated disaster.

In parts of Appalachia, monster coal-mining machines have actually rendered a rugged vertical landscape flatter by cutting off ridges and filling valleys. Moving about is easier than before, and there are larger cattle pastures now, in a countryside rendered almost piedmontish. Such change amounts to irreparable loss to some folks, however, and they will point out as well that ancient streams are now fouled and/or buried, and toxic heavy metals are brought to the surface. Heavy, dirty smoke hovers over the Great Smokies, too, from upwind industries and especially power plants. Trees die here now from acid rain poisoning, as in New York's Adirondacks. And surely one of the most harrowing driving routes in eastern America today is Interstate 81 through the Valley of Virginia, between the Blue Ridge and Appalachian mountains. The valley's green and yellow checkerboard farmscape is as lovely as ever, but no participant in the torrent of north-south interstate traffic dare enjoy the view while driving. Some of us remember the enchantment of driving west from Charlottesville, over Afton Mountain —the same as in Earl Hamner's elegiac "The Waltons"—to Waynesboro, then leisurely down to, say, Christiansburg, on old U.S. Route 11, parallel to the present I-81. Graybeards have ever wept for *les temps perdu*.

More broadly, today's South is less associated with scenic delight than with the pathology of "environmental discrimination" (especially "racism") and campaigns for "environmental civil rights" that engage issues of pollution and social class and color. Arguably the problem is much older than environmental awareness. Poor and working-class people have always picked the crops amid pesticides; mined the coal, iron ore, and phosphates; and lived downwind of industrial smoke and sewage. The simple geography of pulp and paper mills illustrates this. The mills are always situated next to rivers, which carry in the raw materials and carry off the wastes. Mills' smokestacks arise there, too. Workers live near the mills and rivers, usually to the east. Owners, managers, and other professionals live upwind, to the west, on higher ground and often with separate (and clean) supplies of water. (A bit more on the paper industry appears below.) Making paper has been relatively safe, however, compared with a variety of chemical factories densely established since the 1940s, especially since the 1960s, always next to rivers. The Kanahwa, flowing past Charleston, West Virginia, is a notorious "chemical alley." So are sections of the James in Virginia. Recall the enormous and lethal pesticide (Kepone) spill at Hopewell in 1975 and, just as notoriously, the grimy Mississippi in southern Louisiana ("the American Ruhr") and Buffalo Bayou and other industry-impacted streams in Texas. Virtually none of these plants is unionized, and southern state governments have been loath to examine the effects of the operations' toxic effusions on either workers or surrounding environments.

The industrial-scale production and slaughter of chickens and hogs is arguably both a worse instance of environmental discrimination and a more insidious environmental poison than chemical refining and manufacturing. Chicken slaughtering plants employ women, especially black and, lately, Hispanic women. Hog disassembly operations workers are women and men, some white, most black and Hispanic. Chicken farms ("broiler factories" would be more descriptive) usually produce more wastes than farmers might reasonably return to crop fields as fertilizer. Such high-nitrogen wastes will wash into streams anyway, but dumping of excesses is not unknown in Arkansas, Alabama, and Maryland, among other big broiler-making states. In 1999, Maryland chicken wastes were apparently responsible for a fish-killing "red tide" in upper Chesapeake estuaries. This particular tide was the same as one earlier identified in eastern North Carolina—*Pfiesteria piscicida*—a "new" and particularly toxic dinoflagellate that caused lesions and death in fish and, more shocking, made humans sick and disoriented simply from breathing air or touching water affected by the tide. The source of *Pfiesteria* was eastern Carolina's newest industry: hog farms with many thousands of enclosed animals each. Since swine are astoundingly productive of wastes, each farm maintained a "lagoon" to hold urine and feces—enormous surpluses beyond any farmer's requirements for fertilizer. The subregion's soil is porous, its water tables are high, and rainfall is heavy. Field fertilizer and lagoons leached into drainage creeks and into rivers and sounds. Lagoons burst into the Cape Fear, New, Neuse, and Pamlico rivers. Watermen and swimmers became ill. The young North Carolina State University biologist who discovered and named *Pfiesteria* herself became ill. Yet as years pass since the "crisis" of the 1990s, meatpacking companies continue to merge, encouraging yet greater meat production in this dangerous industrial-scale mode. The Chesapeake, Carolina sounds, and many other southern waterways, meanwhile, seem bound for septic lifelessness. Southerners (and many others) have infested a lush country and imperiled, if not ruined, it.[15]

❧ Yet both despair and nostalgia are problematic. First, there is not a place on earth with a human history that is not soaked in blood and the scene of successive landscape transformations, most of them traumatic. Southeastern North America, later "The South" of the United States, has been home to heartbreak hardly less so than, say, the Italian peninsula. Consider hundreds of native civilizations gone; the degradations of Africans and landscapes during two and a half centuries of enslavement; more centuries of the wasteful slaughter of animals; awful wars waged as much against forests and farms as people; generations of conscious use of toxic chemicals, not only in agriculture but in the tanning of animal hides (perhaps the first serious pollution of streams); mining; and so on. Every time and human cohort have their tragedies and their nostalgias for places lost. Some of these are transparent of meaning, but many versions of nostalgia must be peculiar, arguably, to those with the peculiar experience. Consider again the making of paper.

The rural coastal South, from West Point, Virginia (about forty miles east of Richmond), to St. Marys, Georgia, across northern Florida into Louisiana and eastern Texas, is the great piney woods. It is a flat and monotonous landscape beloved to some of us. Beginning at West Point during the 1920s, the pulp and paper industry was established and gradually grew to dominate—and pollute—the countryside. Because the reduction of pine chips into pulp required heavy doses of sulfur, the huge mill region was known throughout most of the twentieth century by its pungent odor. When many mills switched from making heavy brown ("kraft") paper for boxes and packaging to white paper, which commands higher prices, enormous quantities of bleach entered the process—then exited, along with other "liquors" from paper chemistry, into waterways. Since the 1970s much of the industry has cleaned itself. Filters and "scrubbers" on stacks reduce if not quite eliminate mills' sulfurous odors. Progressive managers also oxygenated their impounded pools of liquor wastes with fountains, neutralizing or eliminating bleach and other contaminants before releasing them into adjacent rivers. By the 1990s many mills had also substituted ozone for bleach, and the federal government favored companies that used at least 30 percent recycled paper, instead of trees, as raw material.

I suspect that my father, who was born in West Point in 1908, would have been a little saddened by the cleanup, especially of the air. Before he was born, his hometown had been a prosperous rail center and summer tourist destination. (Two serpentine streams merge at West Point to form the broad York River and a superb expanse of tidal water for swimming, fishing, and boating.) But reorganization of cotton and other overseas-bound freight, then a great fire in 1903, reduced the town to near-penury. West

*Chesapeake Corporation Paper Mill at West Point, Virginia, 1920s.*
*Courtesy Virginia Historical Society, Richmond.*

Point's rescue began while my father was a schoolboy. A brilliant Swedish paper chemist and entrepreneur appeared and, with the help of some Richmond bankers, erected a pulp mill, the South's first. For a few years the mill chipped and pulped local pines and sent their product to an Ohio mill for finishing as paper. Then the Swede expanded his Chesapeake Corporation with a "Big Machine" to roll paper in West Point, and the town's future was secure.[16] My father worked at the mill a short time but spent most of his life elsewhere. Yet when I was a child and we drove up to visit, no matter the weather, my father would roll down his car window as we approached the bridge and the mill and inhale huge gulps of the sulfurous air, loudly proclaiming his pleasure in returning home. Sometimes heavy smoke from Chesapeake's stacks drifted low over Kirby Street, where daddy and his siblings and their daddy had been born and raised. My sisters and I gagged and protested, but to our father, this was the taste and smell of security and prosperity. Ole starvation was meaner than ole air pollution, sulfur his enchanted madeleine.

# 1

## ORIGINAL CIVILIZATIONS

A long century after the Chickasaws, Choctaws, Cherokees, Creeks, and Seminoles walked, rode, or sailed westward to the Territory, about seventy brutal years after the
white Mississippi kingdom of slavery fell in fire, and at the
very moment its successor, a reorganized cotton empire of
mules and sharecroppers, was disintegrating, Vernon Presley built a modest house in East Tupelo, a slightly raffish
town later incorporated into Tupelo proper. Presley's vivacious wife, Gladys, was heavily pregnant—there would be
twin sons—and Vernon made them adequate shelter reflecting their Depression-plagued class: a shotgun house
of two in-line rooms. (The name derives from the morbid
possibility of firing a shotgun through either the front or
rear doors, covering both rooms with one blast. Shotguns
were efficient architecture for narrow urban lots in workers'
neighborhoods. The design resembles "railroad" houses in
the Northeast, but shotguns were common in the southern countryside, too.) In January 1935 the twin boys came
forth, one of them dead. Later, Vernon, his wife, and their
surviving son, Elvis, moved to Memphis, living in rooming
houses and then a public housing project. Elvis already had

a guitar. Now he had also Beale Street emporiums (notably the talismanic Lansky's) that catered to black folks, and here he began to style an edgy, flamboyant persona. Before he was twenty, Elvis had discovered Sam Phillips and Sun Records, and vice versa, and the era of rock 'n' roll, already well under way, took off. Mississippians black and white—most illustriously Elvis Presley—were the astronauts.

Or were rock 'n' roll's pilots representative of all *three* of the country's so-called races? One of Gladys Presley's great-great-grandmothers was "a full-blooded Cherokee" named Morning Dove White (ca. 1800–35), whose remains lie about thirty-five miles east of Tupelo, over in Hamilton, Alabama. (Morning Dove had married one of Andrew Jackson's Tennessee soldiers, another Scots-Irish scourge of Redstick Creeks in the savage Alabama War of 1813–14.) Elvis was probably well aware of the connection (as well as a Jewish one, also on his mother's side). The native identity lives on, however blurred, in fans' memories, via films in which Elvis portrayed "half-breeds," especially an awkward movie he made with the uncomfortable director Don Siegel in 1960—*Flaming Star*—about a Euro-Kiowa named Pacer who, shunned by society, heads for the desert to die alone. It was Elvis and his rowdy entourage, all amphetamine-charged, who made Siegel uncharacteristically dysfunctional during filming. Chemistry may have enlarged the star's own genealogical consciousness, too. Yet Elvis's Indian heritage, confirmed by an Alabama genealogist, has larger, contextural credibility. Many southerners (Euro- and Afro-) have native ancestors; some are certified, but most are documented only by oral tradition. And if Elvis consciously situated himself, genealogically, as simultaneously "both colonizer and colonized," the notion is effectively enhanced by his and his family's repudiation of the anti-Negro ideology that prevailed during the age of Jim Crow. The Presleys often roomed on the borders of black neighborhoods; Elvis sometimes attended black church services in Tupelo, and in Memphis his transracial tastes in dress and hairstyle set him apart in high school. For all his shortcomings, Elvis was tolerant and receptive. He was a mama's boy, too, compounding the Indian aspect of his heritage in an odd yet illustrative sense: Cherokees, Chickasaws, and most other native peoples were matrilineal cultures; that is, social and political status derived from female connections and descent. So a poor white man might ascend through marriage to a native woman of noble rank. The son of such a union might be a "half-breed" and "trash" to whites, but among natives he would be a legitimate aristocrat, beloved and favored not only by his parents but by his mother's powerful brothers. It is interesting, then, to consider The King as conceivably the descendant of kings of another sort.[1]

Elvis's rise, meanwhile, occurred in the era of surging postwar prosperity, population takeoff, irrepressible bulldozing, and the early stages of suburban sprawl. The last, especially, brought Mississippians (and many other Americans) into contact with long-gone native civilizations, or their archaeological flotsam, unearthed incidentally. It is conceivable that Vernon Presley built his Tupelo shotgun house upon a Chickasaw site. Seventeenth- and eighteenth-century Chickasaw towns were centered just to the west, but the nation (as it would be known in the nineteenth century) ranged over much of the eastern Mississippi Black Prairie, northward to the Tennessee River, southward (especially in the fifteenth and sixteenth centuries) beyond the west bank of the Tombigbee, encompassing, that is, present-day West Point to Columbus and more. During the 1950s and 1960s, meanwhile, as builders of not shotguns but popular "ranch" style houses, new shopping areas, gas stations, and much else, extended Tupelo southward, workmen and watchful owners-to-be discovered troves of Chickasaw artifacts as foundations were excavated. The federal Park Service collected and preserved Indian remains turned up for a new furniture factory, but untold and unrecorded bones and materials exposed by construction of Lee Acres subdivision were retained by the new homeowners, who became private collectors. As late as 1981, an archaeologist attempted simply to catalog these collections, but most of the suburbanites were uncooperative. Still, protected materials from the factory site, the archaeologist's limited success in Lee Acres, and professional excavations of nearby protected sites yield much on the lives of the aboriginals. Archaeology, anthropology, and ethnohistory, supported by documents written by Europeans and Americans after contact, collectively present a sweeping, sometimes detailed, usually frustratingly incomplete, often tumultuous, and ultimately tragic narrative.[2]

The Chickasaws' ancestors were once a small part of the collection of Woodland cultures that spread all along the Gulf coast and uplands in the present-day Deep South. The Mesoamerican version of a "Neolithic revolution"—the domestication of maize, beans, and squashes (the invention, that is, of agriculture)—had diffused northward and eastward, revolutionizing the lifeways of these peoples, then of the Eastern Woodland peoples who lived to the north. Chickasaws were among the many groups to adopt farming and become a new "Mississippian" culture. Agriculture turned hunters-fishers-gatherers into more sedentary and probably healthier peo-

*Interracial Native Americans called "Brassankles," near Sommerville, South Carolina, 1938. Photo by Marion Post Wolcott. Courtesy Library of Congress (LC-USF34-050605-D DLC).*

ple, permitted creation of towns, doubtlessly accelerated trading between peoples, and promoted social hierarchy and ambitious architecture. Analysis of Eastern Woodland human bones near Chesapeake Bay revealed that, about a thousand years ago, maize suddenly increased from about 5 percent to half or more of local diets. The small early percentile may have been derived from trading with Mississippians to the south. The larger amount represents the diffusion of Mesoamerica's invention, finally, halfway up the Atlantic coast.[3]

Before 1450, the people later called Chickasaws were riverine, or wetlands, folk who clustered in villages along the Tombigbee River. There they built ceremonial "platform" earthen mounds, and among the many animals they hunted was the bison. For some unknown reason—conceivably the hostility of more-numerous people, proto-Creeks perhaps, east of the river in Alabama—they withdrew a distance to the west and resettled the greater Black Prairie. Here—again for reasons unknown—they ceased making platform mounds but continued to plant crops and hunt bison. And it was here that the Chickasaw encountered their first Europeans, late in 1540.

These were Spaniards, remainders of an army of 600 that had begun an expedition of conquest, enslavement, and looting in Florida the previous year. Their leader was Hernando de Soto, a wealthy and famous veteran of Francisco Pizarro's invasions of Panama, Nicaragua, and Peru. The foreigners had arrived at Tampa Bay with servants (some of them black slaves), horses and mules for soldiers to ride, a swarm of hogs for meat, a number of large dogs (some for herding swine, others for intimidating and maiming enemies), and a huge store of iron collars and chains for natives who would carry burdens. The Spaniards first headed northward through western and central Florida, robbing graves, appropriating natives' food stores, raping women, and (inadvertently) spreading diseases for which natives had no immunities. They stopped to rest their first winter in the panhandle, in or near present-day Tallahassee, but were obliged to fight fierce Apalachee warriors virtually every day. Undaunted, de Soto determined to press forward his exploration of the continent's interior, and at the beginning of 1540, his expedition forded dangerous rivers in present-day southwestern Georgia and meandered through the great piedmont in a north-northeasterly track, into and through South Carolina, and finally into western North Carolina and the mountains. De Soto and his men had passed east of Georgia's Etowah mounds, once the epicenter of the largest Mississippian society in the lower South. In South Carolina they sought in vain a town and people reportedly devoted to mining precious metals.

Much of the piedmont, indeed, was vacant in 1540—perhaps a result of a very long drought that had devastated agriculture and destabilized chiefdoms—and the Europeans went hungry.

The exception was their encounter by the Wateree River in South Carolina with a Mississippian culture called Cofitachequi. De Soto and his translators presented themselves as peaceable sojourners to subchiefs, then to a "brown but well-formed" woman they called the Lady of Cofitachequi. She arrived upon a fine fabric-covered litter carried by her servants. De Soto's Muskogean translator, Perico, thought the Lady a niece of the paramount chief, but the Spaniards accepted the Lady herself as chief. She brought gifts of food, fine cloth, and dressed skins and presented de Soto with strands of freshwater pearls from her own neck. Later, however, the Spanish broke into a burial temple to rob noble corpses of pearls and various metal and glass ornaments. In the principal tomb they found scarily lifelike wooden statues of warriors on guard. While the robbery continued, Spaniards and their horses consumed much of Cofitachequi's corn supplies. The Lady, now disaffected, disappeared, but de Soto had her hunted down and forced her to walk, as a hostage, as the expedition made its way into western North Carolina. One day the Spaniards, starving again and distracted, permitted the Lady and her native servant to enter the woods to urinate. They escaped and later connected with several other runaways from the expedition. One of these was an African slave whom the Lady of Cofitachequi took as mate as they made their way back to her kingdom and safety—a marvelous outcome to an otherwise dreadful intercultural collision. Assuming (plausibly, I think) that the romantic couple were striking physical specimens, I cannot resist the conjecture that among their remote descendants might be the most beautiful of the inventors of rock 'n' roll, the Georgia-born Little Richard.

🌿 In the mountains of North Carolina and the valleys of eastern Tennessee, meanwhile, the invaders found people and corn to extort, especially among the Coosa. At one point natives brought the white men barbequed turkeys, and here and several times later in the expedition there were gifts of small "dogs," barkless and edible, which the Spanish concluded Indians actually raised for food. The explorers were frustrated again in searches for valuable minerals; yet the northern trek did yield more stores of freshwater pearls, most of these in tombs of the native nobility, and the Spanish helped themselves. In the eastern Tennessee Valley, then along the Coosawattee in present-day northwestern Georgia, they encountered larger and larger

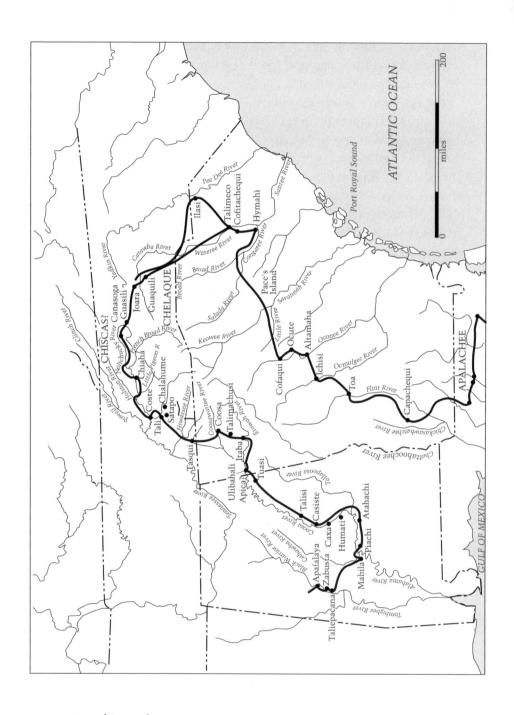

De Soto's route from Apalachee to Apafalaya, 1540 (from Charles Hudson, Knights of Spain, Warriors of the Sun: Hernando de Soto and the South's Ancient Chiefdoms [1997], courtesy University of Georgia Press)

native towns. Nearly all were palisaded; a few apparently were moated as well—these were powerful and warring peoples—with platforms and big chiefs' houses and ceremonial spaces that sometimes included tall poles. One such town was a new one, built upon the original and grander Etowah site. De Soto then followed the Coosa River south-southwestward, searching for an emerging giant—literally and politically—Tascaluza, the Black Warrior.[4]

Tascaluza was paramount chief of a growing confederation apparently of mixed ethnic peoples, rivals of the Coosas to the north. The chief's name is Choctaw or western Muskogean, but the name of his new town, Atahachi—in the neighborhood of the future Alabama capital, Montgomery—seems Creek. Native politics and identity evolved and sometimes changed radically, even before Europeans arrived. Tascaluza may have been a principal creator of a future nation called Upper Creek. Doubtlessly the chief already possessed an imperial persona when he invited the Spaniards to Atahachi in October 1540. They found Tascaluza seated on cushions beneath a portico atop his platform mound, above Atahachi's plaza. The chief, according to the visitors, was about seven feet tall, powerfully constructed, and regally attired in a cloak of feathers and a headcloth that reminded Iberians of the Moors. De Soto took Tascaluza's hand and led him to the shade of a tree for diplomatic talk. De Soto wanted supplies, women, guides, and porters. Later he presented the chief with a horse. Tascaluza mounted, and the Spanish observed that his toes nearly touched the ground, even though the horse was among the largest they had brought. The chief fed the visitors and entertained them with dancers. The Spanish performed cavalry games in the plaza, intended to intimidate the natives. Yet Tascaluza refused de Soto's demands, so the commander, following a tactic already successfully demonstrated in Mesoamerica and Peru, took the chief hostage. Finally Tascaluza agreed to supply food and some porters to assist the Spaniards' progress down the Alabama River to another town, Mabila (near present-day Selma), where the chief promised to provide more porters and the women. This was a trap.

At Mabila many of the Spanish rode and walked into town and permitted the captive chief to enter a house secretly secured by his own men. The great battle of Mabila broke out—the first outright combat the Spanish had faced since the Apalachees—when Tascaluza refused to leave. Suddenly a large force of warriors attacked. They forced most of the Europeans outside Mabila's strong palisade, wounded de Soto himself and many others, and killed a few men and horses. Horsemen outside saved their commander and lanced to death Indians brave enough to pursue the invaders onto open ground. Spanish reinforcements arrived; Mabila's walls were breached, and the town was set afire. Now fighting resumed inside the town. Tascaluza's fate is unknown, but his son and perhaps as many as 3,000 other Indians were killed in battle, burned, or committed suicide to escape capture. De Soto's victory cost his side 22 dead and 148 wounded men; seven horses died, and twenty-nine were wounded. Much of the Spaniards' baggage and equipment was burned or carried away early in the fury, including most of the looted pearls and the priests' and friars' sacramental wine. Soldiers now wished to head south to the Gulf, establish a coastal colony, and renew contact with Cuba, but de Soto, having yet to discover portable riches, was resolved to persist inland. The expedition would indeed progress many hundreds of leagues farther, extending an epic that, after Tascaluza and Mabila, would become ever more bizarre, appalling, and illuminating.

So with the approach of winter, wounded and ragged Spaniards slogged westward through cold swamps and over countless creeks, finally fording the river Apafalaya (now called Black Warrior). De Soto had been informed of a lush chiefdom and town called Chicaza a bit farther west, in present-day east-central Mississippi. When they arrived at Chicaza, the Spaniards found a town smaller than imagined, and empty. (News from Mabila had probably traveled ahead of de Soto.) The Spanish moved in for the winter, expanding shelter for a much-needed rest. Most nights throughout the frigid season of 1540–41, however, were disturbed by harassing local warriors. Finally soldiers captured two Chicazas, and de Soto used them to gain contact with the elusive chief. Frequent visits and flattering gifts ended nocturnal disturbances, and Spanish vigilance relaxed. De Soto feared that the chief schemed to entrap him, but rather than display suspicion or hostility, the commander invited the chief and his principals to a feast. It was the Spaniards' delectable entrée, pork, presumably barbequed in native fashion, that ultimately led to outright fighting. The Chicazas so loved the pig meat that they broke into Spanish sties at night and slaughtered and carried off a number of hogs. Here then, among linear ancestors of Chicka-saws, may have begun the most welcoming of native responses to European imperialism. Surely Indians craved possession of horses, guns, and iron pots and tools nearly everywhere, but it was the pig that found its place, ultimately, in native cosmology. More than a century and a half later, for instance, and more than a thousand miles to the northeast, near the Great Dismal Swamp, a Quaker smith explained to a missionary local native (probably Nansemond) eschatology: When a "good Indian" died, he would "go to a warm Country, where they had fat Boar and Roasting Ears all the Year long; these being the most excellent Food they can imagine."[5] In March 1541, though, Spaniards were neither amused nor forgiving. When they finally caught three of the Chicaza hog thieves, de Soto had two of them executed; the third suffered amputation of both hands and was returned to the chief as a warning. In the meantime, some of de Soto's officers, acting on their own initiative, had ridden about the countryside expropriating valuables from surrounding towns and incurring wrath sufficient, it seems likely, to unite regional networks under the Chicaza chief for making revenge.

The attack came at night while the Spanish were sleeping and their sentinels were inattentive. Chicaza warriors crept into the town from all four directions carrying firepots. Awakened by flames, smoke, and drumming that reminded them of Italian infantry, the Spanish never organized themselves, and few were able to mount horses. One Chicaza warrior died, lanced by de Soto himself. Twelve Spaniards, however, were killed by archers or burned alive, and no fewer than fifty-seven horses were killed, most with skillfully placed arrows. (The Chicazas understood that horses, more than firearms, were Europeans' principal military advantage.) Perhaps as many as 400 fat pigs burned in their sties, while an estimated 100 piglets wriggled out and escaped. (Conceivably some of these were ancestors to a huge feral population in the near future.) Soldiers and footmen who had not lost clothing and equipment at Mabila now were reduced to near-nakedness, unarmed or only partially equipped. The Chicazas planned to finish the Spaniards the next night, but a rainfall wet bowstrings and saved the surviving invaders. By April, though, having rested, repaired, and healed a bit, the diminished invaders moved on, now northwesterly.

In what is now called De Soto County, Mississippi, immediately below Memphis, Hernando de Soto and his men approached the lushest expressions of Mississippian culture then in existence. These chiefdoms and towns—Quizquiz, Pacaha, Casqui, Quiguate, and others—were gifts of the Mississippi River landscape. Fine loess soil, windblown from the west for thousands of years, settled here among the rivers' meanders. The great river being ever changing, especially here, many meanders became separated over time from the river channel, creating C-shaped oxbow lakes. Especially around these, Mississippian towns and extensive farms grew up. Such rich lands were flood prone, to be sure, but such friable soils, easily worked with wooden and bone tools by a people without draft animals and plows, were well worth seasonal risk. To the north, on a similar landscape in present-day

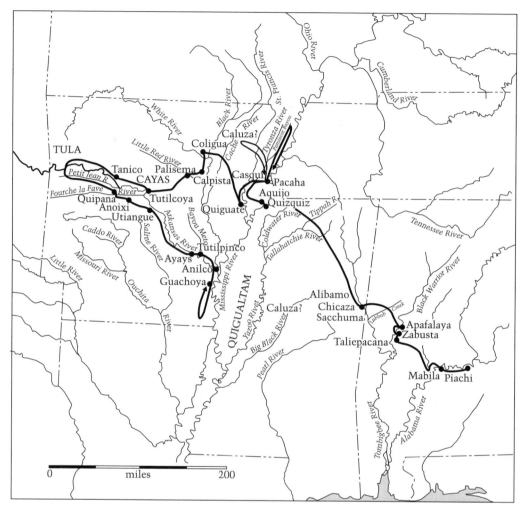

*De Soto's route from Apafalaya to Guachoya, 1540–1542 (from Charles Hudson,* Knights of Spain, Warriors of the Sun: Hernando de Soto and the South's Ancient Chiefdoms *[1997], courtesy University of Georgia Press)*

southeastern Illinois (opposite St. Louis), Cahokia, the greatest of all Mississippian sites, flourishing between ca. 1000 and 1250 C.E., had resembled a complex city of walls, enormous mounds, canals, fortifications, and perhaps 20,000 inhabitants. The onset of the so-called Little Ice Age, plus Cahokia's exhausting demands on surrounding forests, must have contributed to this remarkable civilization's decline and abandonment. Yet three centuries later—in warmer, more heavily forested locales on either side of the great river—more diminutive variations on Cahokia thrived still. Their prodigious crops of corn, beans, and squashes were more than sufficient, it seems, for the trading of surpluses for the few things the oxbow towns did not already possess—chert and flint, for instance, for arrowheads and cutting tools. Like the Cahokians, these sixteenth-century river peoples were farmers, hunters, builders, traders, players of games, heroic canoeists, and fearsome warriors.

Charging from one Quizquiz town to another, largely frustrated in his search for provisions and his demands of subchiefs for boats to cross the Mississippi, de Soto at last encountered the paramount chief, Aquijo. The Spanish were at labor building their own boats while de Soto strode about on a bluff, when Aquijo appeared on the river leading a flotilla of 200 large dugout canoes containing perhaps 7,000 warriors, all painted red with ocher and decorated with many-colored feathers. Archers, some bearing shields of cane woven tightly enough to withstand European crossbow bolts, stood at the ready between pairs of paddlers. Aquijo and native notables rode in the sterns of the largest canoes, shaded and protected by canopies. Closely massed, the fleet drew close to shore. Aquijo (through de Soto's translator) delivered a friendly sounding welcome and sent the Spanish gifts of fishes and fruit-bread. De Soto, ever treacherous, invited the great chief ashore, but Aquijo, unresponsive, ordered all his craft away. Spanish crossbowmen loosed their bolts and killed several paddlers, but the fleet achieved a safe distance with brave discipline. The Spanish then resumed their boat construction and, several weeks later, succeeded in crossing the river and landing in present-day Arkansas.

Here de Soto became entangled in the deadly rivalry between Casqui and Pacaha. Following a betrayal and bloody recriminations, de Soto left the riverine territory with the Casqui chief's daughter and one of the Pacaha chief's own wives, his sister, and another Pacaha noblewoman—all peacemaking gifts reflecting sensibilities that impressed the Spaniards as very European. They went north, following a rumor (yet again) of gold. Finding none, the Spanish returned briefly to Casqui and, reprovisioned, made their way south again, then westward through the Arkansas River Valley. The farther west they traveled, the more marginal were the inhabitants to Mississippian culture. Populations were more sparse, and corn was less cultivated. The Arkansas was an important trade route between the Mississippian farmers to the east and the buffalo and deer hunters of the southern plains to the west. Valley peoples, such as the Tula (whose town was located near present-day Fort Smith), were handlers and shippers of meat, hides, and tallow from the hunters, and salt, shells, beads, pottery, and fine copper adornments from the Mississippi and the Gulf. De Soto intended to winter among the Tula, but they resisted, shocking the Spaniards with their tactical ingenuity and ferocity. Knights of Spain were obliged to slaughter Tula women, who were as determined as their men to kill or die. Dead or alive, the Tula presented a frightening aspect. Practitioners of cranial deformation, their foreheads sloped backward from their eyebrows to the backs of their heads, and they tattooed their faces, including the exteriors and interiors of their lips. The Spanish happily departed Tula in October and marched southeastward, along the sunnier southern bank of the Arkansas.

A bit downstream from present-day Little Rock, de Soto and his men, slaves, and horses spent the frigid winter of 1541–42 in a populous Mississippian town called Utiangue. Local natives supplied (willingly or not) ample corn, beans, nuts, and fruits, but for meat the Spaniards relied on their native slaves to snare innumerable rabbits. Suffering extreme cold and deep snows, the invaders survived—except Juan Ortiz, de Soto's essential chief translator. So early in March, when they set out once more for the Mississippi, the expedition was effectively blinded and crippled. At Guachoya, on the western bank of the river again, de Soto fell ill while sifting conflicting information about distance to the Gulf of Mexico and the intentions of a great chief on the eastern shore named Quigualtam. According to the chief of Guachoya, there was no land route to the Gulf; one of de Soto's lieutenants reconnoitered and confirmed this. The chief also claimed that the ominous Quigualtam would visit in friendship, or he would attack any time. De Soto, furious and vindictive, ordered the razing of Anilco, a rival town, and the massacre of all its males.

Quigualtam, meanwhile, rebuked de Soto's invitation in a manner infinitely more insulting to the Spanish than Aquijo's silent withdrawal on the river. Quigualtam never visited anyone, he sent word, but expected all servilely to visit him. He was the Great Sun, who with his brother, Tattooed Serpent, ruled all absolutely, sacrificing enemies or his own subjects without objection or interference. Quigualtam's kingdom, a collection of southwestern Mississippi towns centered on the present-day city of Natchez, was doubtlessly the same polity known later as Natchez. A century after Quigualtam's time, the Natchez encountered the French and for a long period resisted subjugation. Generations of hostility near the vortex of Anglo-French trade rivalry, however, apparently fragmented the Natchez's hierarchy. A series of "rebellions" against the French between 1729 and 1731 culminated in the natives' defeat and diaspora. Some of the Natchez were enslaved on French Caribbean plantations; more fled eastward toward peoples allied with the British—the Chickasaws and Upper Creeks—with whom they apparently assimilated.[6]

De Soto never laid eyes on Quigualtam, for the Spanish leader died on 21 May 1542. His successor, Luis de Moscoso, fearing natives might find and desecrate de Soto's body, which had been secretly buried in Guachoya, had it disinterred, weighted, and dumped into the Mississippi by night. Moscoso told natives that de Soto was visiting the sky and would return soon.

Moscoso and his officers resolved to march westward in hopes of finding Mexico. All summer and into the early fall they passed over drier, poorer, landscapes, hoping to find Mexico just past the "River Daycao." There at last—perhaps "Daycao" was the Brazos—Moscoso's scouts found only a few poor and frightened people. So the Spaniards turned back, toward the hostile Mississippi country again, for at least there was corn beside the lush river. Winter found them passing through poor Anilco again, cold and wet in their deerskin shirts and moccasins, resembling the natives they had slaughtered. Moscoso and his scouts found two towns about a mile from the river. Both had provisions. They tore down one town to enlarge the other and begin construction of brigantines. With ingenious improvisation, craftsmen with experience in Genoa, Sardinia, and Fez transformed iron slave chains and collars into timber fastenings, indigenous plant fibers into caulk, pine sap into waterproofing, and so on.

On 2 July 1543 the Spaniards rowed their seven vessels, with canoes hitched behind, into the Mississippi's channel, leaving hundreds of native slaves, some of them Spanish-speaking and Christian, standing on a foreign and hostile shore. Two days later, downriver, they encountered at last the forces of Quigualtam. A fleet of perhaps a hundred canoes, some large enough to hold sixty or seventy men singing rhythmic songs of martial exploits, intercepted the Spanish, cut off a contingent in small canoes, and bashed or drowned most of them while Moscoso, caught in the swift current, watched helplessly. Quigualtam's sailors, still singing songs and insults, turned on the brigantines and let fly a blizzard of arrows. The pursuit continued through the night and into the following day, when the Spanish, battered, depleted, and without rest, passed beyond the chief's territory. But now another polity (its name unreported) was violated, and the fleet was beset by yet another flotilla of war canoes, this time numbering about fifty. Shortly after this frightening assault was broken off, a third, although smaller, group of canoeists engaged the Spaniards. When these finally withdrew, the exodus continued in peace to the Mississippi's mouth. Resting for the coming ordeal on the Gulf, however, the Spanish were confronted yet again, this time by natives who seemed huge in size—like "philistines"—and quite dark-skinned from the sun. These were fishers, not farmers, and they fought not only with bows and arrows but with spear-throwers that extended the range of heavy, pointed projectiles, and with war clubs studded with large fish teeth.

The Spanish escaped on 18 July and found Mexico, at long last, early in September. Of the 600-odd who had entered Tampa Bay in 1539, approximately 311 had survived. This number, probably a good estimate, presumably does not include a few men who deserted the expedition along the way. The black paramour of the Lady of Cofitachequi was probably not the only African slave who, smitten by a native woman, escaped with his love and disappeared, as it were, into an American culture. Likewise, one of de Soto's Spanish officers took up with a native woman in the next-to-last, western leg of the adventure and refused under threat to return to ranks. These were not the first Africans and Europeans to go "native," nor by any means the last. Disaster that the de Soto saga surely was, it had other consequences, too, and reveals much else about native civilizations.

🌸 Surely the Spaniards would have turned back to Cuba by mid-1540 or persisted in their expedition and starved to death had they not encountered one people after another who represented the Mississippian cultural tradition. Willingly or not, Apalachee, Cofitachequi, Coosa, Tascaluza, Chicaza, Quizquiz, Casqui, Pacaha, Quiguate, Utiangue, and others all fed the invaders from their often vast stores of corn, beans, squashes, fruits, breads, and "little dogs." Had the Spaniards instead encountered only early Woodland tradition folks—with their small villages, subsistence agriculture (if that), gathering, and hunting—the invaders might well have been fatally discouraged before they starved. On the other hand, it is difficult to imagine relatively primitive Woodland peoples inflicting such mischief, terror, wounding, and death upon the Spaniards as they suffered at Apalachee, Mabila, Chicaza, and Tula and on the Mississippi River. However disadvantaged militarily compared with Europeans, who had horses, armor, firearms, pathogens, and ultimate numbers, Mississippians were complex warring societies themselves that had for many centuries transformed landscapes to create and maintain security and comfort.

Archaic Americans, like archaic Europeans, Asians, and Africans, lived literally in darkness—that is, beneath the canopies of forests. Fire from the heavens opened the world to light and the opportunity not only to hunt small and large animals browsing in the so-called edge regrowth environments that fire created, but to begin the selection and encouragement of certain useful plants. The apparently universal lesson of the utility of lightning-fire seems inevitable: people could make, keep, and use fire deliberately to manage landscapes.[7] So in forested eastern North America (as in forested elsewheres), what is called the Woodland cultural tradition began ca. 700 B.C.E. or so. Firing the woods, hunting and fishing, and gathering and encouraging plants all supported cooperative effort and gendered subsistence roles. Men went forth with firesticks and the tools of hunting and fishing; women gathered, harvested, and made homes among villages consisting, we think, of clans of related people. Religion and ritual evolved to sustain the people and their system of subsistence.[8]

Then, not suddenly but approximately 800 C.E., some (not all) Woodland peoples began to disturb the earth with hoes and sticks and to plant corn. Squashes of many sorts seem already to have passed a primitive encouragement phase into cultivation. About two centuries after corn came beans, and the great Mesoamerican triad was in place in North America's Southeast. Now Mississippian civilization evolved relatively rapidly. Intensive agriculture—still supplemented by fishing, hunting, and gathering—was the foundation of most of the cultures that Europeans encountered in the sixteenth and seventeenth centuries. However gradually it evolved and however similar it was to late Woodland culture, cultivation must be called revolutionary in its effects. Now populations certainly leaped, and villages became what we must call towns. Surpluses of food and finished goods extended exchanges between different peoples often hundreds, even more than a thousand, miles away. (Cahokia's mounds contained copper and mica sheets and ornaments from the Appalachian mountains and carved shells from the Atlantic coast.) Larger populations placed demands on resources. Forests were scavenged for firewood and building materials as well as fired for crop fields and hunting parks. Growth doubtlessly necessitated management and leadership, so social hierarchy arose, along with more complex rituals connected with nobilities' legitimacy and ethnic loyalty and cooperation.

Ceremonial flat-topped earthen mounds, little known among Woodland phase peoples, characterized the Mississippians. The largest of these—for example, at Etowah in Georgia or Moundsville in Alabama—consisted of thousands of square yards of earth dug or scraped with tools pathetically ill suited by modern standards and carried sometimes considerable distances in baskets by hand. Meanwhile, rivalries for leadership as well as contests between peoples for resources encouraged war, which also marked landscapes. A Mississippian town typically had at least one mound but also a palisade around the mound, plaza, and houses. Palisades were typically composed of upright tree trunks stripped and anchored tightly together, sometimes also bound and buttressed with heavy plant fibers and daubed with clay—another demand on forests that exposed the earth to the sun. No wonder that the Spanish understood Quigualtam's title—and the French acknowledged that of subsequent Natchez superchiefs—as the Great Sun.

The astral sun itself, of course, figured large in natives' sense of power on earth. Still, it was a part of the "southeastern ceremonial complex," a system of signifiers evident from Texas to the Atlantic, from the Ohio Valley to the Gulf. Artists represented the complex in carvings, ornaments, and chiefs' dress with stylized mythic animals such as winged serpents and birdlike humanoids. Another important symbol, much noticed by European Christians, was a cross within a circle. This probably represented the cardinal directions, also large in native cosmology. Forces of nature, represented by mythic animals and by north, south, east, and west, must be recognized and reconciled by appropriate human behavior.

The annual Green Corn Ceremony, however, widely reported by Europeans before the eighteenth century, reveals late-Mississippian culture at its foundation. By mid- or late summer, as first corn crops approached maturity, all the clans in a polity would begin to prepare for the ceremony by purging themselves, fasting, and bathing. Then came dances and the recitation of town histories. Each town's communal fire would be relighted. Then women, who were the farmers, presented the new corn. Young people received their adult names. All crimes except murder were publicly forgiven, unhappy marriages were dissolved, and new spouses were taken. At last there was a feast. The people were thus purified, and communal harmony was restored. Corn was the center.

🌺 Europeans observed and wrote down much of native agricultural practices. Some, such as Jacques le Moyne de Morgues and John White, made sketches and watercolors of farms in Florida, North Carolina, and elsewhere. The woodcutter and engraver Theodore de Bry, not himself an observer, copied some of these (notably le Moyne's work) and famously imposed European features upon crop fields. De Bry added plow-point lines, for instance, to arrow-straight Timucuan corn rows in northeastern Florida. Contact-era natives were gifted artists, as already observed, yet they seem not to have executed representational portraits of their culture. Nor did they have written forms of language until early in the nineteenth century, rather long after Europeans' arrival and the disappearance of the Mississippian tradition. Europeans' and then Euro-Americans' recorded observations, while fascinating and essential, must be employed with caution and, wherever possible, corroborated. This may sometimes be accomplished with two additional sources: ethnographies compiled during the nineteenth and twentieth centuries (that is, recorded memory and oral traditions, along with studies of material cultures) and archaeological evidence.[9]

Unsurprisingly, archaeological remains of farming hundreds of years ago are scarce in the East. (In the arid West and Mexico, some ancient gardens and apparent fields are still visible.) Most crops are annuals, fields were abandoned, streams changed course and washed away sites, and forests returned, erasing generations of labor and nurture. Certain eastern gardens, however—not large fields—are an exception. A plausible reconstruction of late Woodlands and Mississippian domestic life explains why. All households have waste, such as broken pottery, worn-out fiber, the open skeletons of shellfish, and the bones and offal of fish and other animals. These and more were disposed of in pits, called middens (presumably rather shallow), not far from houses in every village and town. As middens were filled, lush vegetation appeared, signaling opportunity to establish kitchen gardens. So women weeded such household plots and tended them intensively, polycropping corn, squashes, beans, herbs, and medicinals. The forthcoming bounty, presumably, belonged to the woman who tended and harvested, for use in her own house and by whomever she chose.

Gardens, whether or not made upon middens, are the prototype for a long-lived narrative of *all* native farming. Indian agriculture was effectively the opposite of European. Fields were not permanently established squares and rectangles with evenly spaced rows. There was no tedious grain monoculture—or any monoculture familiar to, say Piedmontese, East Anglians, or Normans. Indian fields were temporary, shifting, as well as asymmetrical. Middens lost their fertility after a few years, so new ones were adopted. Or men killed trees by girdling in a portion of forest where tree species indicated rich soil; later they set fire to the dead trees, then reburned the fallen logs, virtually wading in ashes that were rich in phosphorus and calcium carbonate. Among big roots and blackened stumps, women made little hills (not rows) with hoe-blades of stone, rock, or shell. Then with fingers or planting sticks, they dropped several kernels of seed corn and covered them. As corn stalks arose, they planted beans, which later climbed the stalks, around the corn. Squashes and other useful plants joined the burgeoning vegetable jumble. Careful weeding and aeration with small tools was essential, but only for a short time. Squashes leached toxins inimical to weeds. Soon, too, the cornucopia grew simultaneously upward and outward, shading out competitors. Thereafter birds were farmers' principal concern, so little girls were assigned the serious (yet still playlike) task of acting as living scarecrows. Depending on the latitude of such garden fields and the vagaries of weather, harvests began as early as June. Often there were two or three crops of corn alone, each a different type, and harvesting of various beans and peas, gourds, plants for teas, medicinal herbs, and so on, probably continued well into November and later.

The genius of the system comports with modern, chemistry-savvy agronomy of the sustainable sort. Corn and tobacco (another ubiquitous cultigen in Native America) are notorious leechers of soil nitrogen. Beans and peas, however, supply nitrogen, complementing the calcium carbonate in wood ashes left by firing woods for cropland. Still, following several years of such farming, natives noticed declining yields and undertook preparation of a new patch of forest for firing. The abandoned farmland vegetation slowly succeeded again, through grasses, woody shrubs, conifers, and finally (in most places) a restored deciduous forest. Here, then, was "swidden" agriculture, also called "shifting" and "slash-and-burn." Peoples without dynamite, chainsaws, and bulldozers around the world, including Europeans, once upon a time, farmed in some version of the mode; a few still do. And as late as the nineteenth century (as we shall see later), most Euro- and Afro-southerners pursued an agronomy of woods-firing, polycropping, and abandonment, even though many owned land and draft animals and plows. White and black southerners' adoption not only of native staples but a large portion of the Indians' method surely strengthens this narrative tradition of Indian garden farming.[10]

Yet recently, scholars have brought the tradition under suspicion. Natives indeed gardened. The historical geographer William Doolittle has cataloged archaeological garden sites in southern Florida, northeastern Alabama, central Mississippi, and Kentucky (as well as in Cahokia and other midwestern places, plus in the Northeast and West). Early and later European newcomers mention gardenlike sites there and elsewhere in the South, too, but *also* large—sometimes very large—fields of corn. There were literally scores of white observers of extensive farming, many of them well remembered and generally credible—for example, Cabeza de Vaca, de Soto's chroniclers, John White, William Bradford, John Winthrop, and much later, William Bartram. So in addition to southern New England during the 1620s and 1630s, Europeans saw and recorded big, apparently communal (as opposed to household) crop fields in eastern Virginia (Powhatan federation), western South Carolina, eastern Tennessee, east-central Georgia, the Florida panhandle northeast and west, southwestern Mississippi (apparently Natchez), north-central Louisiana, and eastern Texas. Twentieth-century archaeologists, meanwhile, convincingly inferred large fields—some apparently for corn alone, others with corn and beans—not only at Cahokia but at great and lesser mound sites in Georgia, Alabama, and elsewhere. Native southerners, in other words, like Europeans, were both gardeners *and* farmers. The distinction is not only important in itself but comports with other known characteristics of Mississippian culture's sizable populations, polities, and hierarchy. Mississippians were so well organized and specialized that some actually maintained seedbeds for the early nurturing of tobacco and potatoes, before transplanting to sizable fields, apparently with no other plant under cultivation.

Doolittle also brings swiddens under considerable suspicion. True slash-and-burn agriculture includes burning forests, cultivation, and abandonment, plus an ultimate return to the same ground, repeating the process. Contemporary tropical practitioners of true swidden (such as in Belize and parts of southeast Asia) provide the model for ethnographers such as Doolittle, so farmers in temperate regions such as North America almost automatically disqualify themselves—particularly in the behavior of rotation to formerly slashed and burned farms. Climax forest cover returns to tropical fields in only twenty years, whereas the succession of grasses, bush, conifers, then mature deciduous trees requires up to 150 years in, say, North Carolina. Late-Mississippian populations were probably much too dense and demanding of resources to permit a century and a half's wait, as it were, to reuse farming sites.

A scholar with observational experience in the tropics, Doolittle perceives an important disadvantage in swiddens, too, even where the "true" version is practiced: Burning not only brings sudden exposure of former forest floors to sunlight but invites rapid infestations of weeds. Establishing food crops is arduous at best. For this reason and more, Doolittle argues that most Indians preferred permanent crop fields managed with brief fallows, or rests. After fallow, or each spring, natives carefully weeded each field, heaping grasses and brush, drying it on the site, then burning. In 1699 a Frenchman living among the Pascagoulas by the Gulf coast of Mississippi watched just this procedure. Doolittle catalogs additional scores of European documents of preparations of old fields for planting. What, then, of the tradition of the ubiquity of fire in native culture? Doolittle discovers only twelve documents referring to firing forests for crop fields, most famously John Smith's report in which Powhatan women plant around dead, still-standing trees. Smith has been endlessly cited, but his and the few additional written records that suggest—merely suggest—swidden hardly compare with the scores of documents presenting the preservation and nurture of old fields. Too, Doolittle reminds us, fire had many purposes other than creating open land for farming. We must not assume slash-and-burn wherever there is archaeological or documentary evidence of burning. Natives fired not only heaped and dried trash, as with the Pascagoula, but employed fire in hunting—to drive deer, for example, to bowmen, and to create grassy and shrubby browse for prey—and in warfare. They also used fire to encourage certain plants, creating growing space for fruit- and nut-bearers, for instance. And Indians were known to conduct what are now called controlled or prescribed burns, in which thickets and other understory are burned away beneath trees, clearing forests of low cover for human enemies, snakes, and vermin. "The notion of swidden," Doolittle concludes, "should perhaps be more appropriately labeled a myth."[11]

Still, the geographer almost concedes one significant exception, that being the sandy, acidic-soiled Atlantic littoral. A sixteenth-century Jesuit missionary among the Guale people of coastal Georgia, whom Doolittle acknowledges, wrote that "the land is so miserable, they move their huts, from time to time, to seek other lands that can bear fruit."[12] This may well have been the case the entire length of the coast, in fact, where if farming were possible at all, frequent shifting of fields, in addition to seasonal commuting to fishing and hunting grounds, was the rule. Perhaps John

Smith's famous observation of Powhatan planting time, hundreds of miles north of the Guale, represented swidden after all. Whether the swidden were "true" by Doolittle's lights remains problematic, of course. Nonetheless, late-eighteenth- and nineteenth-century white southerners' much-publicized difficulties in maintaining permanent fields in the tidewater country may reflect a virtually timeless condition. During the 1790s, John Taylor of Caroline perceived a crisis in European-style agronomy on permanent fields and prescribed revolutionary "green manuring" as recourse. The method failed. Three decades later, Edmund Ruffin (with the inspiration of an English chemist) finally discovered and described acidity and the fixing of nitrogen with fossilized shell (marl) in this same low Virginia landscape. Ordinary coastal farmers, however, seem typically to have practiced an untrue version of swidden within their own property lines, burning and reburning, say, 50-odd acres of a 600-acre farm over the course of a generation or so. Such is adaptation to local environment, ethnicity and technology notwithstanding. More of this in a later chapter.[13]

Much has been made, and properly so, of the transformative, destructive impact of Europeans, their animals, and plows upon the temperate landscapes of the Americas. Agriculture is surely the most savage and elemental disturbance of nature, and savagery is compounded elementally by technological power. Europeans' ultimately dense populations, their capitalist-mindedness, and their written system of legal protection of private property, as well as their guns, all produced a juggernaut agronomy that egregiously simplified the natural world, substituting what could justifiably be called a desert for a jungle. But the natives they supplanted, as we have seen, were also ambitious disturbers and manipulators of landscape—heroically so, one must think, given Mississippians' lack of draft animals, wheeled carts, and sharp, durable tools such as axes and plows. Equally important, one must also think, is Indians' ancient, preagricultural manipulations of landscape to produce food, medicines, and creature comforts. These explain the development of cultivation but also illustrate ingenious invention in certain environments that persisted well into the historic epoch alongside sophisticated gardening and extensive farming.

Consider the remarkable prehistorical career of the sunflower. Originally a wild native of the Colorado plateau (we think), sunflowers were at some remote time discovered as a valuable food deserving of protection— that is, they were not to be burned or cut or dug and discarded. Protection blended with encouragement, which included weeding and perhaps the pruning of tree branches competing for sunlight. Later, actual cultivation appeared—transplantation and reseeding. Thus sunflowers became cultigens and spread eastward, becoming ubiquitous in the humid East long before Europeans began to land on its coasts.[14] Tobacco and squashes were manipulated in form and locale, apparently, in similar fashion. Likewise wild grapes. The early Atlantic explorer Verrazzano observed encouragement of these on the present-day Delmarva Peninsula, where "the bushes around them are removed so that the fruit can ripen better." Later-arriving Europeans described arbors of grapes, representing a cultural stage approaching actual cultivation. William Bartram, traveling among the Creeks in Alabama in 1776, noticed not grape arbors but trees and shrubs "entangled with Grape vines" all of the same species. When the fruit ripened, Bartram wrote, "Indians gather great quantities of them, which they prepare for keeping, by first sweating them on hurdles over a gentle fire, and afterwards dry them on their bunches in the sun and air, and store them up for provisions."[15] The Creeks made raisins, in other words.

Natives also commonly encouraged favored tree species by not burning them for fields, by clearing competitors, and/or by pruning limbs so as to produce less but larger fruit. One of de Soto's chroniclers observed a large grove of walnut trees in an open field in eastern Arkansas. Cherokees in northern Georgia were all "nut growers," according to a later witness. And yet more Europeans recorded protected concentrations of plums, mulberries, peaches, pears, and nectarines. Plums were apparently the basis for "bread" natives presented to de Soto and his men along the Mississippi, and more than two centuries later, near the Tombigbee, Bartram remarked upon the "chicasaw plum," growing as a cultigen on abandoned large crop fields.

Among dozens of species of trees that Indians managed, though, the yaupon (*Ilex vomitoria*) seems the most extraordinary and revealing of native ingenuity. A scrubby evergreen native to sandy, salty South Atlantic shorelines, yaupon had become essential to coastal natives' medicine and ritual before the Spanish appeared in La Florida. Timucuans, the Guale, and other shore folk boiled yaupon branch tips, blossoms, and tender leaves to make a "black tea"—an emetic taken regularly to purge bodily (and probably social) imbalances and disharmonies. Jacques le Moyne de Morgues painted Timucuan men seated in a semicircle, women boiling water and diffusing tea before them, and the men drinking and projectile-vomiting. Natives imbibed their black tea from beautifully incised conch shells, representing the import of the substance and ritual. Two centuries later and hundreds of miles inland, the yaupon and black tea appear, astoundingly, in Bartram's *Travels*. William was among the Cherokees in the mountains when he "observed a little grove of the Casine yapon, which was the only place I had seen it grow in the Cherokee country." They "call it the beloved tree," he reported, "and are very careful to keep them pruned and cultivated, they drink a very strong infusion . . . which is so celebrated, indeed venerated by the Creeks, and all the Southern maritime nations of Indians."[16] By this time, one must expect, a tea derived from an oceanside desert landscape generally hostile to agriculture had become common and essential to the Green Corn Ceremony among late-Mississippian peoples living in lush farming subregions.

I am not suggesting that tea-drinkers or makers of beautiful drinking vessels and other art or ingenious rearrangers of landscape must necessarily be Mississippian. Long before any North Americans farmed, a people called Ortona undertook monumental civil engineering. Ortona is a small town in present-day Florida about fifteen miles west of Lake Okeechobee, just north of the Caloosahatchee River, which winds westward to the Gulf of Mexico at Fort Myers. The Ortona site, settled about 700 B.C.E. and lasting probably 1,500 years, approached its cultural and commercial peak between about 200 and 700 C.E., when its central town was two square miles large and fully realized with finely sculpted earthworks—one portion in the approximate shape of a crescent moon embracing a star—mounds, water impoundments, and geometric-designed main roads. About 250 C.E., the Ortona began to excavate canals down to the Caloosahatchee. The waterways were twenty feet wide and three or four feet deep—all excavated, of course, with wooden and shell digging tools and presumably woven baskets to carry out spill. For the Ortona were travelers and traders whose destinations, archaeologists now believe, included not only the Gulf coast but, via the Apalachicola and Chatahoochee rivers northward, ultimately over the mountains all the way to the center of the contemporary Hopewell culture in the Ohio Valley. Ortona architecture and ritual, only recently uncovered and dated, closely resemble those of the long-known Hopewell. Among the most curious artifacts found in southern Ohio mounds were alligators' and sharks' teeth and skins, and shells and bird feathers from Okeechobee. Their source in Florida now seems confirmed. Ortonans, in turn, seem to have taken flint, copper, beans, and perhaps effigy pipes back south, in exchange.[17]

The Ortonas' great successors in southwestern Florida, contemporaries of Mississippian peoples to the north, were the mighty Calusas. The Calusas politically dominated the Caloosahatchee Valley, the shores of Lake Okeechobee, the Everglades, and the limestone flats around present-day Miami, but their home bases, sites of their major and minor towns, were Marco Island, Pine Island and Sound, and Charlotte Harbor's shores. Here they engaged in intensive seasonal fishing, digging oysters and catching finfish (principally mullet) with nets made of palm fiber, with well-formed shell floats and sinkers. When not taking fishes, the Calusas hunted deer and other animals on the big islands and the mainland, and they gathered a large variety of fruits. For bread they relied on people who protected and encouraged a root plant by Okeechobee. The roots were dug, dried, and baked, and the Calusas took them as tribute or in trade. Calusa towns were utterly engineered landscapes facing water. There were elaborate defensive fortifications of shells, canals and artificial lagoons, sea walls and jetties, and handsome temples and housing, especially for their principal chief and aristocracy. Craftsmen's work—not only ingenious fishnet floats and sinkers and other tools—ascended to what must be called art. They created ornamentation to be worn, masks representing birds and animals, and wood carvings that some critics compare with those of ancient Egypt.

Calusa power was based first on their great numbers. In 1566, when Pedro Menéndez de Avilés (founder of faraway St. Augustine) visited, 4,000 natives attended a fete in his honor. Archaeologists believe that no fewer than 10,000 natives lived along Florida's southwestern coast about this time. By contrast, scholars estimate the population of the Ortona capital at 200 to 300, and even as late as the time of Menéndez's appearance on the coast, there were probably only about 1,500-odd fishers, hunters, and breadmakers by the shores of Okeechobee.

The Calusas exercised power through management and distribution of resources, which must have become scarcer in time as human population expanded. Chiefs and religious leaders governed, in effect, the seasonal fisheries, hunting, and plant gathering, and they controlled trade with other peoples for additional needs. We know more of the Calusa economy than of most others because of the seventeen-year captivity of Hernando Fontaneda, a Spaniard who was shipwrecked and captured in the Keys in 1549, then repatriated during Menéndez's visit. Fontaneda's account of his long experience with the Calusas includes detail on their cosmology's ritual connection to their most abundant and favored finfish. Each fall, mullet leave the coastal estuaries and return to the Gulf to breed. To assure their return, the Calusas conducted a gruesome ceremony centered on a human sacrifice. The victim—typically a nonrelated native or European captive—

was beheaded, and the head was presented to an effigy called an "idol" by a visiting Spanish priest. The idol, in turn, consumed the victim's eyes. Eyes were the supreme expression of immortal spirit, the last of three; the others were a person's reflection in still water and his or her shadow. When death comes, by whatever means, the Calusas believed, the second and third spirits pass into fishes or other animals that humans kill. When these die and are consumed, human spirits pass on and on, into other animals, until they are diminished to nothing. The eyes were not passed on but remained the soul in the mortal body after death. So was revealed the enormous value of such a sacrifice—and the symbiosis of the natural world and religion.[18] Fontaneda was a sagacious or lucky man, or both, to retire from Calusa with his immortal soul intact.

The Calusas were not the only North American natives ritually to sacrifice humans. Cahokia and Natchez noble ossuaries have yielded grisly evidence of slaughtered lessers buried with great chiefs. In Natchez the spouse of a Great Sun was required to accompany the paramount one into the afterlife.[19] Calusa ritual seems less revealing of hierarchy, then, than of the larger tradition of natives' respect for animals and of a profound understanding of the enchainment of life with life. It is logical that any people so dependent upon vast schools of mullet, for instance, would invest such serious collective effort in the resource's regeneration and return. The Calusas knew they did not possess the fish within a fence; mullet, like wild land animals, belonged to themselves and to the human commons, so the Calusas reacted accordingly. The behavior becomes more than logical when a culture's eschatology locates human souls within mullet, oysters, deer, wolves, raccoons, and birds, all of which possess agency in human affairs, however small their brains. For in most native myths of origins, distinctions between the beasts of the earth and humans are blurred. Indians' notion of human descent, then, was often expressed in references to bears, say, as grandparents, and native crafts and arts repeated effigies of humanoids—birdman and -woman, wolfman, and so on. Humans prayed for the commons' abundance, then, but also before killing, perhaps leaving a small (although still valuable) sacrifice, such as a bit of tobacco, in tribute and apology to catch and prey. Successful hunting and fishing proved that pursuers observed the divine harmonies and that animals and fishes were agreeable. And if humans respected the dead by using all of their bodies, then slain animals' spirits would communicate agreeably to the living, ensuring future hunts and catches. The frugality with which Plains peoples used the bison—they left nothing on the ground, using meat, sinew and fat, blood, bones and teeth, and hide—is legendarily illustrative.[20]

Thus Indians are set apart from the Europeans they encountered from 1492 onward. Europeans understood the notion of commons, but their laws of private property fated white men ever to compromise and then to despoil and eliminate common resources. For resources they were, sanctioned for appropriation by no less a power than Jehovah himself, as revealed in Genesis 1:26–31. Here humankind is separated from the rest of nature and granted "dominion over the fish of the sea, and over the fowl of the air, and over the cattle, and over all the earth, and over every creeping thing that creepeth upon the earth." Plant life is mentioned, too: "Behold," exclaimed God, "I have given you every herb bearing seed . . . every tree, in which is the fruit of a tree bearing seed; to you it shall be for food." In retrospect, or maybe even prospect, Jehovah not only separated humans from the rest of the natural world but invented the commodification of nature and capitalism. Most native Americans resisted Jehovah for a long time; some do, still, in great part owing to their cosmology's stunning incompatibility with the dominion-without-respect of Jews, Christians, and Muslims.

Here, then, is the frame and foundation for natives' legendary status as "ecological" and "conservationist." "Ecological" means not the interdisciplinary science established early in the twentieth century, but something similar and compatible: that Indians understood systemic relationships in nature. "Conservationist" means almost precisely what was meant by Euro-Americans who adopted the term about the same time that ecological science was established. Theodore Roosevelt and his friend Gifford Pinchot, chief forester of the United States, and many other elite eastern conservationists insisted that natural resources must not be wasted but used wisely, thus ensuring a future without want. Native Americans, then, may be seen as conservationist in that they not only had respect for the earth and all its features but that they did not waste.

An enduring exception is the legend of fish fertilizer in native agriculture. Supposedly the Plymouth settlers (early 1620s) were spared starvation not only by native generosity in the so-called First Thanksgiving but by the Indian Squanto's instruction to place a fish in each hill of corn. Here was a method of treating the littoral's notoriously infertile (as well as acidic) dirt. If indeed Squanto so instructed the English, he probably acquired the practice not from his own people but from the Spanish, with whom he lived during 1614–19. Several nineteenth- and twentieth-century ethnographers asserted a broader native tradition of fertilizing with a sort of herring called menhaden, however. Menhaden are intensely netted today, notably along the South Atlantic coast and principally for fertilizer, so a logical continuity is suggested that complements the recent consensus that Indians maintained large permanent fields. Yet thorough investigations during the last decades of the twentieth century reveal no evidence of natives using fishes in such a wasteful (not to mention disrespectful) manner. Fish bones found at sites throughout eastern North America were almost certainly household refuse, likely thrown into middens that became gardens.[21] Bones, then, may have been either inadvertent or deliberate—and chemically appropriate—fertilizer for kitchen gardens. The legend of whole-fish fertilization of large fields never made sense in a continent still howling with wolves and semi-wild dogs, not to mention raccoons and other varmints prone to dig about for nourishment. Imagine a native communal plantation, an investment in communal food security for a coming winter, ripped asunder, seeds and seedlings tossed about, broken, and ruined by scroungy eaters of rotten fish.

A more important controversy regarding native conservation, still unresolved after nearly four decades, is the palynologist and geochronologist Paul Martin's explanation of one of the Americas' most perplexing prehistoric phenomena: the relatively sudden extinction, about 11,000 years ago, of both continents' megafauna. Enormous tusked herbivores such as mastodons and mammoths (elephantlike creatures); single-humped camels; giant ground sloths, tapirs, and beavers; shrub oxen the size of bison; and others resembling nothing we have seen alive all disappeared, as did many carnivores, including dire wolves with huge, hyenalike heads; big cats with fearsome teeth of several shapes; and bears apparently capable of swift pursuit of prey. All came swiftly to oblivion, and according to Martin, "Man, and man alone, was responsible," during the approximately two millennia required for immigrants from Asia to walk from Beringia to the Atlantic to Punta del Fuego. Why—and how—could these people called Paleoindians have accomplished such slaughter, a "Blitzkrieg," as Martin termed it? Paleoindians brought big-game hunting experience and effective lances with longish "Clovis" stone points from Asia. There (and in Africa and Europe) animals large and small had shared landscape with predatory humans since all life forms had evolved. American animals evolved without humans for 2 million years, so they were innocent of hunters, perhaps even curious, and therefore the easiest of prey. Paleoindians fueled their progress southward and eastward with cheap meat, then, so abundant that much must have been left to rot after egregiously nonconservationist slaughters. Thus native American history began in waste and corrupted any future claims to moral authority—or so claimed some antienvironmentalists during the late 1960s and 1970s.[22]

Martin's version of Pleistocene extinctions would seem to merge neatly with much more recent archaeological evidence supporting monumental bison kills in western North America, especially at "Buffalo Jumps." Here peoples such as the Blackfoot drove great numbers of bison, sometimes hundreds of them, representing as much as 240,000 pounds of meat, over cliffs into ravines. A few scholars conjure estimates of efficient butchering; others calculate enormous waste. Natives effectively employed firing of prairie grasses in such hunts. When natives acquired horses from European intruders, beginning in the sixteenth century, their requirements for hides accelerated—they enlarged their houses—and hunts yielded proportionately yet more bison. There is some evidence, too, that even before Indians responded to white American and European markets for hides, they killed and sometimes took only favored parts of animals—humps, for instance, and tongues and fetuses. Some native ethnography denies this, but a Plains myth on the origins of the buffalo reinforces what conservationists must deem waste: Namely, many Indians believed that bison derived from great prairies below lakes, which nurtured limitless supplies. So because buffaloes came from another world, humans could never kill too many in this world. The lake prairies would forever yield more.

Humans seldom live by meat alone. As the anthropologist Shepard Krech observes, Martin and his supporters ignored not only small animals and birds, which also suffered massive late-Pleistocene extinctions, but the availability of many edible plants for convenient human sustenance. Archaic, Woodland, and Mississippian native cultures all gathered, even as they hunted and fished; so why not Paleoindians as well? Severe climatic change during the Pleistocene period might well have affected fauna large and small, with or without spear-carriers' carnage. On the other hand (as Krech also observes), well-documented parallel cases tend to support Martin. Even as Woodland cultures evolved into Mississippian in North America, Polynesian invaders came to Hawaii and New Zealand and utterly transformed both archipelagoes, where literally thousands of species, especially of birds, disappeared, long before Europeans arrived. Something comparable occurred, too, on the large island of Madagascar. Indonesian and East African settlers arrived—apparently during a long drought—and soon pressure on resources, the hunt not least among them, sent a stunning variety of animals to oblivion: great flightless birds, hippopotamuses, giant tortoises, and lemurs of perhaps a dozen and a half species, one the size of gorillas. It would seem, then, that even if there will never be conclusive evidence for Paul Martin's argument for exclusively human agency in American extinctions, persisting researchers cannot exclude bipedal hunters.

Bison roamed and foraged much of the Southeast, too, and Chickasaw ancestors, among other peoples, left bison bones in their middens. Whether native southerners killed bison excessively or wastefully, as Plains people apparently did, we know not. Perhaps the question is relatively unimportant, since bison were not the principal large animal prey in southern cultures. This was the white-tailed deer, which figured as large in southeastern landscapes, native lore and religion, and subsistence as the bison in the West and the beaver in the North. The importance of deer, indeed, can hardly be overestimated, and arguably (if perhaps ironically) their already huge numbers probably increased even as Mississippian peoples created substantial towns and ever-larger crop fields. This expansion occurred because Mississippians manipulated nature with fire, as had their predecessors, but now probably more so, and fire helped create edge environments and landscape mosaics called ecotones with more grasses and succulents for deer browse. Mississippians persisted in the Woodland practice of using fire to maintain grassy pastures — deer parks, actually — as well. Native uses for deer carcasses were the equal of western peoples' consumption of bisons' bodies: Venison was a major source of protein, and Indians believed eating deer meat made them strong and wise. Tongues figured in rituals, divinations, and feasts. Bucks' antler tips became arrow points. Hides were essential for bedding, covers, dresses, breechcloths and leggings, fringe, moccasins, and countless other domestic goods. In the Cherokee origins narrative, the deer was the most intelligent of animals (even smarter than the wily rabbit) and had led all creatures from the underworld, through the mouth of a cave onto the earth. Cherokees and Chickasaws named daughters after lovely does and cute fawns. Southern peoples were so numerous, though, and spoke so many languages that, except for Cherokees, we know little that is reliable, much less generalizable, about religion and ethics as possible constraints upon the waste of deer.

In the Cherokee myth, deer, bears, rabbits, and other animals spoke and interacted with humans, and rather equally, for a period, establishing respect even as humans hunted them. Later, however, humans grew in numbers, then became greedy and disrespectful, killing too many of their fellow creatures. Deer and bears held councils and made retaliatory war upon humans. A bear actually sacrificed himself so his guts might be made into bowstrings. Animals also inflicted rheumatism and other ills upon wasteful and/or disrespectful hunters. Humans allied themselves, in turn, with plants that became medicines for their ills. Ultimately humans acknowledged wrongdoing and the great truth that nature might strike back at those responsible for creating imbalance and disharmony. Peace was restored, and Indians undertook disciplined observation of rituals to ensure future peace. Thus hunters meditated or prayed before winter hunts, then asked forgiveness of slain deer. Little Deer, spiritual chief of deer and previous warmaker upon humans, policed hunts, inflicting rheumatism on hunters who failed to apologize.

Readers of this well-documented Cherokee ethnography might indeed conclude that these people—and probably Creeks and others, also known to sing and pray before and after hunts—would never waste, never kill "too many" deer or other animals. Yet nothing in the myth explicitly enjoins hunters from taking only part of a deer carcass or, exactly, from participating in market exchanges, whether with other native peoples or white strangers from across the ocean. Cherokee ethnography is derived first from Sequoyah's famous syllabary, from early in the nineteenth century, then from translations into English of "medicine books" composed in Cherokee after 1821. By this late date the whitetail population of the East had been diminished close to extinction by two long centuries of a deerskin trade initiated and conducted by Europeans (most successfully the British). Cattle diseases in Europe had crashed leather supplies. Then native Americans, in recorded instances even before the beginning of the seventeenth century, presented gifts of cured and uncured skins to European mariners, who seem immediately to have recognized a market potentially lucrative beyond imagination. No natives resisted, but Timucuan, then Tuscawaran, Powhatan, Chowan, Creek, Chickasaw, Choctaw—and Cherokee—rushed to accommodate, unrestrained by Little Deer and assisted, perhaps, by song and prayer. The Spanish in Florida, the French in Mobile and New Orleans, and the British from their great trading base in Charleston, sent agents hundreds of miles into the continental interior, bearing guns, powder and shot, iron pots and axes, beads and trinkets, woolen blankets ("duffel"), and later, an ocean of rum. Natives traded and consumed voraciously, becoming in short order, in the memorable words of the historian James Merrill, "discriminating shoppers."[23]

Mississippian culture was destroyed while native men became full-time hunters of whitetail as well as of native slaves, who were valuable as porters of deerskins and substitute laborers for town and village men now for-ever away. In the eighteenth century, declining deer populations sent hunt-ing parties farther and farther afield, into other peoples' territories, spark-ing intensified tribal warfare already encouraged by native alliances with rival European imperial powers. The scandalous near-extermination of the deer and the collapse of the skin market forced some native men—notably literate and privileged "half-breed" men—into farming, or "planting" big crops with native or African slave labor. More native men switched to a different occupation, from hunter-warrior to Euro-American-style stock-man, ranging herds of cattle and hogs through the forests and abandoned, overgrown old cornfields where native women no longer worked. Southern natives came also to live in log cabins separate from one another, like the whites, and to dress in cotton shirts and dresses, linen and woolen trousers, and shoes and boots made from the hides of cows.

My favorite view of native adaptation to the chaos of imposed Euro-pean biota and markets—because it fascinates without tragedy—comes from William Bartram. Having concluded his adventures on St. Johns River, William had returned to St. Augustine, where he decided to join a group of white traders headed westward toward Alachua. On horseback they rode through savannas, "through fruitful orange groves, and under shadowy palms and magnolias" and parklike pine forests. One of the traders, an agent for the governor of East Florida, hoped to buy "Siminole horses," probably descendants of Andalusians introduced by the Spanish and re-nowned for their smallish dimensions (compared with British- and French-introduced horses that dominated equine populations to the north and west) and their "lively and capricious" behavior. On the third day out, paus-ing in "expansive and delightful meadows," Bartram came upon "feeding and roving troops of the fleet Siminole horse." Most of these and several other "troops" were either tended or branded, but "our company," William wrote, "had the satisfaction of observing several belonging to themselves" —that is, they were feral. But then came something "remarkable . . . a troop of horse under the care of a single black dog, which seemed to differ in no respect from the wolf of Florida, except his being able to bark as the common dog." William marveled at the creature's diligence as shepherd to feisty hoofed "Siminoles." "He [the dog] was very careful and industrious in keeping them together; and if any one strolled from the rest at too great a distance, the dog would spring up, head the horse, and bring him back to the company." William discovered that the owner of the troop of horses and of the black dog was "an Indian in Talahasochte, about ten miles distance from" the herd, "who, out of humour and experiment, trained his dog up from a puppy to this business: he follows his master's horses only, keeping them in a separate company where they range; and when he is hungry or wants to see his master, in the evening, he returns to town, but never stays at home at night."[24] Here was a canine servant—conceivably a blend of the American and European—to render the fictional Lassie a slacker by comparison. And here also was a native man ingenious both as trainer and as gentleman of apparent leisure, yet at ease, too, in a world of commerce.

🐾 In the long meanwhile, trade—in deerskins and much else—was already ancient when Timucuans and others responded to Spanish interest in Florida during the 1560s and 1570s. As previously observed, throughout eastern North America, even in Archaic and Woodland times, people sought to exchange what was plentiful to them for the exotic and distant, and skins were an important commodity in such native trade, as well as a commonly used tribute paid to paramount chiefdoms by satellite towns and villages. Certainly among the most exotic (if not bizarre) commodities in long-distance exchanges between native groups, and before Europeans arrived, were the beaks of ivory-billed woodpeckers, which were natives to the lower Mississippi hardwood forests and the Gulf coast. The English explorer and naturalist Mark Catesby (writing in 1731) noted that Canadian natives and other "Northern Indians" coveted the beaks, which they strung together into coronets, points facing outward, for their nobility. Northerners paid lower Mississippi suppliers no less than two and occasionally three deerskins for each beak. Perhaps one should not be surprised, then, at the discovery (during the 1930s) of an ivory-bill, along with the beak of a pileated woodpecker, in a grave in Colorado. To some western peoples, woodpecker parts were not only aesthetically pleasing but instrumental in curing venereal diseases.[25] It may be likely that southern hunters who harvested ivory-bills and pileated woodpeckers took their feathers for their own decorative uses. Much of the rest of these beautiful creatures may as likely have been consigned to middens as waste, fit ultimately to fertilize domestic gardens. Birds as well as skins were private property, commodities, after all. The effect of the European-managed transatlantic trade in skins, then, was simply, albeit devastatingly, to accelerate the carnage.

Credible estimates of Creek skin-trading illustrate this effect. Before contact with Spanish and British traders, a Creek household required the killing of about 25 to 100 deer annually for its needs, which probably included some exchange as well as family use. Once the Creeks had virtually abandoned their Mississippian culture and thrown themselves into the getting of skins and European goods, the figure increased to 200 to 400 each year. Good estimates of exports from Charleston and other depots capture the enormity and international scope of the deerskin business: From about 1690 into the first few years of the eighteenth century, about 85,000 skins were shipped each year from Charleston and Virginia ports. In 1707 Charleston alone sent 120,000. By the mid-1760s, according to a British administrator, all American ports under national control shipped around 400,000. Add smaller but still quite substantial French and Spanish exports, and the total reaches at least half a million per annum on the eve of the American Revolution. Add the deer killed for domestic purposes, as the principal historian of the trade suggests, and the total approaches a million a year.[26]

No wonder that American colonial governments instituted the first hunting laws to restrict takes. Legislative leaders, often businessmen engaged in the trade as well as planters, understood threats to the commons. Virginia actually closed the whitetail season one year. This action was to little avail, of course, because to the west natives continued the slaughter. International tensions, war and disruption, and worsening intertribal wars over hunting grounds finally, early in the nineteenth century, effectively ended the trade. In another two centuries, throughout the East, huge deer populations would plague suburban gardeners and motorists, prompting the city of Princeton, New Jersey, to authorize in-town hunting with shotguns. Other localities, especially in the South, licensed night hunters with infrared scopes on rifles. In the long interregnum between the international trade and today's clashes between humans and deer over habitat, the whitetail, both ancient and modern factotum and staple, was a rarely seen creature.

Natives themselves faded into the netherworld of millions of deer. Before the first European set foot and loosed war, enslavement, greed, and pathogens upon North America, native clans, cultures, and polities had moved, merged, or disappeared. Recall that the very names of Chief Tazcalusa and his capital suggest a confederation using at least two languages, which probably evolved into the Creek Nation, so called in the late eighteenth and nineteenth centuries. But it was surely the Europeans who nearly destroyed the native peoples even as they certainly brought about the ruin of native civilizations, Mississippian and other.[27]

Hernando de Soto was not the first European to visit the continent. Juan

Ponce de Leon famously landed in northeastern Florida in April 1513. Later, down in southern Florida, Ponce's men were immediately attacked on at least two occasions when their longboats touched shore. And later yet, when Ponce met the Calusa chieftain Carlos (perhaps at Port Charlotte), a Spanish-speaking native appeared. Despite a translation that sounded friendly, Calusas attacked the intruders. These incidents suggest to many scholars that previous slave-getting expeditions from Cuba must have angered Floridian natives of several polities, who were prepared to resist. A generation later came the de Soto expedition that, begun in Florida, swept ultimately through hundreds of miles of the lowland, piedmont, and mountain South, encountering dozens of peoples. In another brief generation came Pedro Menéndez de Avilés's permanent settlement at St. Augustine, along with a French colony at the mouth of St. Johns River—a settlement rendered temporary by Menéndez at a place and by a river the Spanish named Matanzas, or slaughter. Shortly after Menéndez's success, in 1567–68 Juan Pardo led another Spanish expedition to coastal South Carolina, then overland to the mountains, to present-day Asheville, where he spent time with Cherokee-speaking peoples. Hardly a decade and a half later came John White and the English to Roanoke Island; in another generation came John Smith and more English to the lower Chesapeake and the French to the Gulf coast, Canada, and down the Mississippi, and so on. In sum, probably as early as 1500, Europeans and their pathogens were at least stopping briefly on the coastal mainland, then traveling far inland. If de Soto and Pardo had stayed home, native trade and war would doubtlessly have transmitted smallpox, measles, whooping cough, mumps, and other infections against which the Indians, having been isolated from the Eurasian landmass for many thousands of years, had no immunities.[28]

Late in the twentieth century, scholars and others argued passionately, almost violently, about pre-Columbian native populations. Estimates ranged from only half a million to all of 18 million, with 1 million more or less prevailing until the anthropologist Henry Dobyns, extrapolating the credible historical demography of Mexico and the Caribbean, declared that North America (north of the Rio Grande) contained 10 to 12 million inhabitants when Columbus first landed. Shortly after Dobyns published his figures in 1966, native Americans and many "Anglo" collaborators organized not only a civil rights movement but a burgeoning popular and political literature that was invested in Dobyns's and others' larger numbers. Buildup to the Columbian Quincentennial in 1992 represented a climax of politicizing historical demography, especially with the publication of a book actually titled *American Holocaust* (by David Stannard). The questions were, simply, Just how many innocent natives died as a result of European imperialism? Just how guilty should Europeans' numerous American descendants be? More recently, and hardly dismissing the scope of the American catastrophe of 1492–ca. 1800, a compromise reflecting good (albeit incomplete) archaeology and anthropology has emerged.

Shepard Krech, calmly synthesizing the "sensible" as well as recent research, suggests a figure between 4 and 7 million. Calculation of regional population densities, however, necessitates a low total of about 2 million, which can be reliably documented in detail. The higher numbers of 4 and 7 million require simply the multiplication by two or three of the following: Of a North American estimate of 1,894,000, the population of the Southeast in 1500 was about 204,000, with a density of 57 per 100 square miles. This figure was the densest in the eastern two-thirds of the continent. (The density in the Northeast was 49; the Plateau, 39; the Plains, 16; Great Basin, 10.) California had the densest native population, at 194; the Pacific northwestern coast followed at 140, then the Southwest with 73.

Thereafter all totals (whether or not multiplied by two or three) declined, occasionally in a terrifyingly short time, as virgin-land epidemics swept away thousands, destroyed polities, and forced evacuations of survivors and mergers with remnants of other peoples. Inexorable transformations of landscape doubtlessly contributed to natives' distress and pathos. Deforestation (by Indians and by Europeans), the elimination of game and trade animals, the manifold disturbances not only of Europeans themselves but of their trampling and routing animals, and then the invasions of European plants—wheat, turnips, and countless "weeds" now assumed native, such as dandelions—stripped the Indians of their places, cultures, orientations, and existences.

Surely European imperialism was as ecological as it was military and economic. Yet natives' cataclysmic diminution cannot simply be termed ecological. After all, European landscapes themselves had been deforested, overrun with fenced farms and hordes of animals, too. Yet in 1600, England's population density was 8,800 per 100 square miles; France's, 9,000. It was the killing of humans, by war and privation but primarily by diseases, that accomplished the horrific work. So in the South, where in 1685 the population was 80 percent native, by 1790 it was 3 percent.

🌿 Save substantial remnants of the "Five Civilized Tribes," most of them bound for exile in the Territory during the 1830s, the South was a country of Europeans and Africans, as it would remain. They (at least the Europeans) called it virgin land, a paradise, an Eden enchanting almost beyond expression. Not so, of course; for the Eden of Genesis was untouched, and we know that for thousands of years, the South had been both extensively and intensively managed by the first southerners. They brought their black tea trees from the coast to the mountains, created enormous granaries, practiced sophisticated medicine from plants local and exotic, created a thousand-square-mile deer park of the Shenandoah Valley, and much else. Now that they were gone, their landscape was, in Krech's words, "widowed —not virgin." In southern Florida, where nearly every human, Europeans included, was gone after about the 1760s, the landscape so long engineered by Calusas and their ancestors was, in David McCally's apt term, simply "derelict."[29]

*All I want in God's creation*
*Is a pretty wife*
*And a big plantation—*
*Way down*
*In the Indian nation*
—Popular ditty, especially in Georgia, ca. 1800

*It is you [planters] who have eaten up the land: the spoil of the poor*
*is in your houses; what mean ye that you crush my people and grind*
*the face of the poor.*
—From the "Ceremony of the Land," by Howard Kester for the
Southern Tenant Farmers' Union, eastern Arkansas, ca. 1935

2

## PLANTATION TRADITIONS

Before 1800, "widowed" landscapes throughout the western fringes of the Euro-conquered South became public land. During the Revolutionary War, beleaguered state governments made cession treaties with sickened and retreating native nations, principally to provide bounties for soldiers, war widows, and anyone who aided the cause of independence. Virginia reserved much of what became Kentucky plus an enormous slice of what became south-central Ohio for its veterans. And Georgia, by means of a remarkable lottery, distributed what amounted to nearly three-quarters of a big state to more than 100,000 men, women, and families. The lottery was "democratical" by design, and it evokes, somewhat, the enlightened purpose of Georgia's British founders, who aimed to make a slavery-free, white yeoman's colony. With the lottery, old Cherokee and Upper Creek farms, gardens, and hunting grounds were inherited (almost free), as it were, by land-hungry, independence-minded settlers.[1]

Georgians, most notoriously their governors and representatives in Milledgeville, the state capital, also became the most aggressive of white southerners in the acquisition of additional, remnant native preserves and then, at last, total Indian removal. Ironically, by the time President

Andrew Jackson and his successor effectively engineered this final solution, yeoman democracy was lost, and Georgia's vast lower piedmont was transformed into an empire of cotton dominated by planters, many of whom commanded scores, sometimes hundreds, of slaves, who toiled on estates of hundreds, sometimes thousands, of acres. The land lottery's democratic promise was undone by Eli Whitney's gin, invented on a coastal Georgia plantation in 1793, and three decades earlier, by the colonial government's capitulation to the institution of slavery. Whitney's (and other inventor-mechanics') gins made possible the cultivation of upland, or short-staple, cotton over the sprawling red clay landscape stretching southwestward. Chattels would plant and pick the cotton, feed the gins, and crank gin handles. Had there been no gin and no cotton kingdom, Georgia's frontier (then Alabama's and Mississippi's and onward) might have become Euro-Americanized like the emergent states of the Old Northwest. Instead, the piedmonts and black belts, and the black prairies and deltas, were to become the cotton kingdom and the heart of Dixie. Still, all this said of the reconfiguration of Georgia's landscape from "democratical" to plantation, the perversion is but a variation on a model already quite old by 1830.

🌸 "Plantation" entered the English language in a brutal sixteenth-century context: the beginning of the English conquest of Ireland. A plantation was, first of all, simply a conquered place and a colony. The conquerors might then plant their own people on the new frontier, having effectively weeded the original occupants of the space, or at least disinherited them, consigning the conquered to dependent laborer status. The conquerors might also plant a church, so a plantation could also be a religious mission, to benefit the colonized, the colonizers, or both. Francis Bacon employed "plantation" in this sense at least as early as 1605, two years before John Smith and company planted the first permanent English American colony, at Jamestown. Later John Milton also used the word, and the separatist Calvinists who arrived in Plymouth in 1620 called their settlement Plymouth Plantation. By the 1630s, nihilists and other troublemakers from Puritan Massachusetts Bay migrated or were banished to Providence Plantation.

Gradually and ultimately, though, "plantation" came to describe a conquered place where capital and labor were organized and applied to extractive industry—the production of agricultural commodities. This was so in Ireland, where early English law created reliable "plantation measures" instrumental to surveying and taxing land. This sort of plantation thrives best, however, in balmier climes than Ireland's, with growing seasons and soils appropriate to specialized crops for European and world markets: sugar (most important of all), tobacco, cacao, coffee, tea, rice, indigo, sea-island (long staple) cotton, upland cotton, mulberry trees (for silkworms), maize, and small grains—not to mention opium.[2]

Plantations resemble modern factories, and in fact plantations with processing facilities on the premises—mills for crushing and boiling cane sugar, for example, or special sheds for flue-curing tobacco—were literally factories within giant farms, without a hint of contradiction. These were early modern capitalist enterprises, after all, whether owned by individual entrepreneurs, groups in joint-stock arrangements, governments, or the church. Everywhere risks to investors were considerable: from hostile indigenous populations that had been displaced and/or enslaved; from exotic landscapes with dangerous climates; from strange (to Europeans) predators, vipers, and varmints; from wars with colonial rivals; from brigandage and piracy along shipping lanes to markets; and much else. Yet hopes of profit, even enormous profit, were often enough realized. No wonder, then, that by the eighteenth century many London merchants' coffee shops had evolved into insurance brokerages and banks. Financiers and insurers also stood behind Britain's emergent dominance on the west coast of Africa, which supplied the millions of laborers New World plantations ultimately required.[3]

If plantation production cannot be accomplished with machines, then it has ever been done with dependent, coerced labor of some sort. European Christian Crusaders encountered Muslim-owned cane sugar plantations worked by dark-skinned imported slaves on eastern Mediterranean islands such as Cyprus—this half a millennium before the English coined "plantation." By the mid-fifteenth century the Portuguese had finally attained their own sugar plantations—in the Madeiras. The horrendous labor of tunneling and digging irrigation systems through volcanic rock and then establishing terraced cane fields fell first to European, North African, and Guanche (from the Canary Islands) slaves. Later, dark-skinned Africans joined what was for a good while the Western world's premier sugar factory. Various European expeditionary forces spent much of the fifteenth century trying to conquer the Canaries and their ferocious Guanche defenders. The Spanish persisted and finally succeeded—and established their own cane plantations. Guanches were driven to extinction, like so many peoples in the Americas. In La Florida, the northern fringe of Spain's American empire of precious metals and sugar, Spanish soldiers and priests enchained large numbers of Timucuans and other natives to work huge farms devoted to food production. Then, as the natives disappeared (owing to flight or to death from overwork or disease), the Spanish, the Portuguese, and then the French, British, and Dutch turned in force to Africa's Atlantic littoral, which ultimately yielded the 10-odd million replacement workers who survived shipment to produce American staples.

After the abolition of slavery, governments nearly everywhere sent prisoners to sugar and cotton fields owned both privately and by states. Modern Australia infamously began as a penal colony. France shipped its (supposedly) most desperate convicts to the jungles of Guyana—one will recall the legendary escapist called "Papillon." All southeastern U.S. states practiced convict leasing of some sort from the late 1860s well into the twentieth century. A few set up huge state farms, Texas most egregiously, where African Americans (almost exclusively) worked mile-long rows. Elsewhere emancipation opened veritable floodgates of indigent, heavily indebted new immigrants, especially from Asia. Planters welcomed augmentations of poor populations that stabilized cheap labor markets in plantation regions. The Asian masses included Japanese, subcontinent Indians, and especially Chinese "coolies." Many of the last came from the province of Fujian, in China's rocky southeast, which was already famous (or pitied) by the mid-nineteenth century for its own shocking diaspora, which continues to this day. By late in the twentieth century, at least one of Fujian's packed counties contained somewhat less than the number of documented Fujianese living abroad. Some Fujianese migrants became merchants in southeastern Asia. Others mined gold in mid-nineteenth-century California. More were farmworkers, particularly after European investors drained parts of the Mekong Valley and other lush tropical places for sugar plantations. Fujianese farmers had grown cane sugar at home for at least a millennium. Now, in the nineteenth century, working for British, French, American, or Cuban masters, among others, they extended sugar culture into Indochina, the Philippines, and Hawaii and replaced African slaves in the Caribbean and other parts of the tropical New World.

After the emancipation of slaves in the United States, Mississippi planters expressed keen interest in replacement "coolie" labor, and a few hundred Chinese actually arrived. A generation later, a small part of the great Italian diaspora of ca. 1890–1915—indentured Sicilian and other Mezzogiornese peasants—was recruited to the lower Mississippi deltas to pick cotton and, their employers hoped, stabilize an increasingly restive black sharecropper population. Bad as they were, conditions in the deltas could hardly have been worse than those of the *colonia* in the Italian South. Yet most of the Italian newcomers ducked their contracts and fled to New Orleans in short time.[4]

Ultimately in the American plantation South, postemancipation immigrants were little more than local curiosities. The scheme of sharecropping with native African American labor actually supplied the insatiable requirements of a newly expansive cotton kingdom. Sharecropping evolved during the late 1860s and after as a labor regime specifically for freedmen. It superficially resembled tenancy or renting, but in actuality sharecropping was a labor system with neither tenant rights nor regular wages. Instead, croppers simply shared landowners' risks in future commodity prices each year, their reward being one-half the final market value of the crop produced—minus many deductions imposed by planter-owners (more of this below). Occasionally sharecroppers made handsome returns and improved their status. This tended to occur when prices were high and costs low— for example, on "new" ground in opening cotton frontiers that required no expensive fertilizers. More often than not, croppers were simply another version of powerless, dependent, and perpetually indebted laborers. Virtually all plantation labor, then, historically has been alienated—that is, only marginally at best invested in efficiency, much less in what has (since about 1900) been called conservation. At its very heart, then, the plantation tradition seems to present consistently, over at least five sad centuries, not only a purgatory (if not hell) for workers but a disaster for landscapes. Logically (although ironically, too), in the American South it was planters themselves who persistently proclaimed the intimate relationship between plantations, forced labor, and the breaking of the land.

More than a century before anything resembling a conservation movement appeared in North America, yet at a moment when coastal landscapes had been farmed plantation-style for more than a century and a half, Jeremiahs foreign and domestic began to decry American, and in particular southern, agronomy. The first important foreigner was a Yorkshire farmer named Edward Strickland, who arrived in the northeastern United States in 1794. Strickland's journey of investigation took him as far south as the Chesapeake states, and his summary findings appeared as a large pamphlet (published in London in 1801), *Observations on the Agriculture of the United States*. "Decline has pervaded all the states," Strickland concluded, yet unevenly. "Land in New-York, formerly producing twenty bushels to the acre, now produces only ten," he continued; but it was the Chesapeake region that approached actual ruination: "Virginia is the southern limit of my inquiries, because agriculture had already there arrived to its lowest state of degradation.... The land owners in this are, with a few exceptions, in low circumstances; the inferior rank of them wretched in the extreme."[5] Later European and Yankee sojourners in the rural South would be hardly less impressed than Strickland, but what may be more surprising, in Strickland's own time, is the receptivity of an American reader no less than Colonel John Taylor of Caroline County, Virginia, father, one could say, of American landscape Jeremiahs.

Born in 1753 near the falls of the Rappahannock, Taylor represented the fourth American generation of a distinguished, well-connected family. As a youth he studied at a private academy, the College of William and Mary, and in the law office of a famous uncle, Edmund Pendleton. Taylor's early adulthood, however, was given to soldiering and politicking on behalf of the Revolution. He rose to the rank of major in George Washington's Continental Army, served briefly in Virginia's wartime House of Delegates, then returned to the army (now as lieutenant-colonel) to defend Virginia against Hessian invaders and, finally, Lord Cornwallis at Yorktown. Taylor's patriotic service was rewarded by large grants of widowed land in Kentucky, yet Taylor himself was never an immigrant. He married, practiced law, and acquired more lands not far from his home estate, Hazelwood; he also served three unexpired terms in the U.S. Senate. Principally, though, after about 1789 Taylor's life was devoted to home, to legendary but unpretentious hospitality, to agronomic experimentation, and to political writing on behalf of agrarian interests threatened by a dozen years of Federalist rule in the nation's capitals. Alexander Hamilton's fateful 1791 economic plan included erection of protective tariffs to promote domestic industry at the expense, as it were, of agricultural commodity exporters. The Federalists never achieved Hamiltonian tariffs. Irony of ironies, it was the administration of Thomas Jefferson's Republican heir, James Madison, that turned its back on Taylor and other aging "conservative" Jeffersonians and adopted protection.

In *Arator*, his classic agrarian tract, first published in book form in 1813, Taylor took notice of Strickland's pamphlet early on. As an American (not to mention Virginian) patriot, he was obliged to express indignation. An Englishman, after all—a farmer but still an Englishman and a creature of the evil empire of manufacturing and mercantilism—had profaned with his presence and insults the very shores his government had attacked twenty years before. "Has Mr. Strickland forgotten," Taylor fumed, "that we agriculturalists had the sagacity to discover, that the English system of creating an order of capitalists, was leveled directly at our prosperity, and [that we had] the magnanimous perseverance to get rid of its authors?" (105–6). The real work of *Arator* was antimercantilist doctrine and especially agronomic observations dedicated to reversing the decline of farming in the coastal plain. The latter business compelled Taylor to admit that the arrogant Yorkshireman had been more or less correct in his conclusions after all, even though, Taylor confessed, "his veracity is insufferable" (105). Taylor insisted that his own experience and observations of "many farms for above forty years," combined with his mastery of available data ("general facts"), were more authoritative than a foreigner's observations. So he finally conceded that he "agree[d] with Strickland in opinion, 'that the agriculture of the United States affords only a bare subsistence—that the fertility of our lands is gradually declining—and that the agriculture of Virginia has arrived to the lowest state of degradation'" (72).

The essays that became *Arator* began to appear as early as 1803 in a Georgetown newspaper, soon, apparently, after Taylor had acquired and read William Strickland's work. Here, then, and again in book form in 1813 and in several subsequent printings over the following five years, the sage of Caroline pronounced a crisis of "our habit of agriculture, of which emigrations are complete proof" (68–69). Collectively, Taylor's essays contained historical exposition that led to the large questions of his day: If planter agronomy, modeled so consciously after the British modern farming "revolution" in East Anglia during the second half of the eighteenth century really worked, then why declining fertility along the South Atlantic littoral? Why decaying and abandoned villages in tidewater Virginia? Why were so many Virginians hastening to new lands in former Indian nations? Taylor was deeply vested in his native tidewater place—its society, its church, its history, and its dirt. In *Arator* he took his stand for conservation, for prosperous stability, and for civilization as he understood it. Thus, in making himself (however modestly) the evangelist of tidewater salvation, Taylor simultaneously rendered himself the first important southern declensionist historian.

Taylor's answers to the painful questions included, first and at length, unfriendly and unwise government. Then there was slavery: "Negro slavery is a misfortune to agriculture, incapable of removal, and only within reach of palliation" (115). Africans were ignorant, ineffective workers and dangerous potential rebels, as recently witnessed in "St. Domingo" (Haiti). The necessary evil of slavery might be endured (by white planters) only by imposing wise order and daily management of labor: "Slaves are docile, useful and happy," he declared, if treated kindly and firmly. Plantation overseers were essential to labor management, yet planters' management of overseers led inevitably to degradation of soils. Everywhere, planters offered overseers incentives to wring the most profit from plantations; then, having exhausted crop fields (and probably mistreated labor), successful overseers gained reputations that tempted envious neighboring planters to lure them to their own estates with higher salaries. Taylor also decried "the three shift system" of rotation—"Indian corn, wheat, pasture"—which amounted to "the massacre of the earth" (167). Grains large and small depleted far more nutrients from soils than might be restored by farm animals' scattered droppings in one season. Taylor dedicated no fewer than six essays to proper drainage of farmlands, and others dealt with various crops suited to an improved rotation system. He advised readers on animal husbandry and orchards. The fragmentation of *Arator*'s sixty-four essays nonetheless offered a grand scheme for the resurrection of the Chesapeake tidewater. This was "green manure."

By the time John Taylor was born, his father's generation of Chesapeake planters had happily married their fortunes to manure of another color. Cattle and hogs had been introduced to the countryside long before. Most ranged free and thrived in forests, marshes, and swamps. The English observed that swine multiplied rapidly while feeding upon heavy masts (nuts, seeds, tender shoots, and roots) in mixed hardwood and pine woods, and that cattle grew fat upon the reeds and grasses of expansive wetlands. For a long time, then, while European settlers and a small African population cleared forests and farmed tobacco chiefly with hoes—plows being virtually impossible to use in stump- and root-infested crop fields—"agronomy" and "improvement" through manuring were irrelevant. Trees were the barrier to civilization and to wealth, useful mainly in the construction of fences to protect crops from foraging cattle and hogs.

By the mid-eighteenth century, however, great planters had cleared enough land thoroughly and acquired sufficient African slaves (now approaching half the total population in Virginia) that they sought at last to farm like the most progressive Europeans. Their fields would be made permanent, with excellent fences (permanent ones, if possible); their animals would be placed under stricter control, so they might contribute more directly to farming's permanence. The ambition, techniques, and language of permanence came largely from the English southeast—East Anglia, especially the county of Norfolk. The Norfolk "system" included a five-part crop/land-use rotation that usually included turnips but also better and deeper plowing. Its real foundation, though, was grass and cattle manure. The most blessed of Englishmen, to paraphrase Galsworthy, were farmers who multiplied grasses. Grasses grow best in rich land maintained by carefully prescribed applications of cured cow manure. Cattle eat grass, and the alimentary cycle ensures the miracle of permanence.

Great planters of Maryland and Virginia absorbed the gospel and became devoted practitioners. Before the Revolution, most had wisely decided to forsake tobacco culture in favor of grains, both maize and wheat, huge surpluses of which were readily marketed in the Caribbean. The Chesapeake countryside, meanwhile, became overrun with cattle, not so much for beef as for their manure. Colonel Landon Carter, prince of Sabine Hall on the Northern Neck and vast holdings to the west, was arguably the king of Chesapeake cattlemen. A close reader of English agronomy, he raised clover, already a known restorer of tobacco and corn land, and carefully herded cattle in order to use their droppings. Carter (and apparently many other tidewater planters) devised movable pens, or corrals, to contain and concentrate cattle where their manure production was required. Some of his slaves were full-time herdsmen and -women; others filled farm carts with manure for storage and application to fields. Carter himself was consumed with record keeping—as must be any modern farmer—especially the tallying of his carts of manure.[6]

Then came the Revolutionary War and American independence from the British Empire and its protected markets. Grain-exporting businesses such as Carter's and George Washington's were thrown into protracted disarray. This was John Taylor's world of stress, worsened for him and other tidewater planters, doubtlessly, by the utter shift of still-profitable tobacco culture to the piedmont. By comparison, commercial grain culture seemed indeed to be in dreary decline. Thus to Taylor's analysis and prescriptions.

According to Taylor, between 1607 and about 1800, settlers in the Chesapeake tidewater had managed to remove three-quarters of the region's vegetative cover. Chemical reactions between soil and atmosphere had become impoverished. Late in this era of vast crop field formation, applications of dung had been ameliorative, to be sure, but obviously inadequate. Taylor hardly entertained reforestation as a logical solution. Instead, he reasoned that farmers needed desperately to produce enormous quantities of corn, especially, but also clover and other green crops and, instead of processing them through animals, return "green manure" (or "offal") to the soil. Cattle, indeed, must be "inclosed"—"Inclosing" was the title of four consecutive essays in *Arator*—to prevent them from consuming invaluable

vegetative resources. Landon Carter's generation had herded and especially penned cattle, demonstrating a managerial modernism that boded
ill for persistence of the open range. Now Taylor's more formal usage of
"inclosing" doubtlessly inspired the precocious attack upon Virginia's old
field-fencing laws led by Edmund Ruffin during the 1830s. In the meantime, though, Taylor declared green manuring a success, and Edmund Ruffin, then not quite twenty years old, newly married and newly a farmer, read
*Arator* and tried Taylor's principles on his own weary James River plantation. Other tidewater readers must have, as well.

Much later, when Ruffin himself was a full-time editor and writer in
Petersburg, he published a fine seventh edition of *Arator* in his agricultural
journal, *Farmers' Register* (31 December 1840)—this despite Ruffin's own
failure with the doctrine of green manure more than two decades earlier.
The young Edmund had even put his estate, Coggins Point, up for sale,
hoping to emigrate. Finding no buyers, he persisted in reading, past *Arator*
and older British agronomic works, but he found these mostly inapplicable
to South Atlantic conditions. At last he came upon the first important modern organic chemistry, Sir Humphry Davy's *Elements of Agricultural Chemistry, in a Course of Lectures for the Board of Agriculture* (published in London in 1812, then in Fredericksburg, Virginia, in 1815). Taylor's chemistry
was primitive and wrong, like that of the pre-Davy British agronomies. It
was Davy's fourth "lecture" that electrified young Ruffin. In Lincolnshire,
the professor had observed soil of apparent excellent texture and color, yet
"steril." Davy's test revealed that the sample contained "salt of iron," an
acidic matter that could be reversed simply by "application of quicklime."
Ruffin contrived equipment and materials to test his own soils—there were
no commercial suppliers or experts within his reach then. At first he failed.
His soils were not salty. Despairing but briefly, Ruffin then experienced
a sort of epiphany, which he described much later in his autobiography:
"Though not a salt of which one of the component parts was an acid, might
not the poisonous quality be a *pure* or *uncombined acid*?" Ruffin had discovered the problem of acidity, actually quite common to tidewater soils,
whether long farmed or not. The problem's cure was lime, or some other
form of calcium carbonate. This was located on his own property. One of
Ruffin's elderly slaves took him to an old, overgrown excavation, a relic of
a discontinued experiment by an ancestor. What young Edmund saw was
deposits of marl lying just below the ground's surface. Marl is fossilized
shells left from advancing ancient coastlines; the shells are often so des-
iccated by time and the earth's upheavals and subsidences that they are

barely recognizable as shells. Europeans knew marl well through long experimental use. No one, including Edmund Ruffin, understood just yet that calcium (whether lime or marl) fixed nitrogen in manured soils and that, thus fixed, nitrogen would feed plants instead of evaporating into the atmosphere. How much marl per acre should be applied on soils in various conditions? This became Ruffin's ongoing experiment in applied science. In 1821, when he was all of twenty-seven years old, Ruffin's account of his discovery and first applications appeared in the *American Farmer* of Baltimore, then the nation's most prestigious agricultural newspaper. Ruffin hesitated another eleven years before publishing his magnum opus, *Essay on Calcareous Manures*, which he would edit, update, and republish in new editions (five in all) over the next two decades.[7] Dung and green manure were hardly disrespected—the colonels Carter and Taylor had their worthy points—but now calcareous manures earned the imprimatur of modern science, and hope now dawned that tidewater plantations, and eastern civilization, might be saved after all.

At thirty-seven (in 1833), Ruffin started his *Farmers' Register* in a shed on his second farm, inevitably named Shellbanks. Shortly the master farmer quit his profession and took his paper to nearby Petersburg, where he persisted through 1842 as editor, writer, and exhorter to brother southern planters. The *Register* attracted about 1,400 subscribers by 1835, then somewhat fewer, and finally less than a thousand by the journal's final year. This readership consisted principally of influential and engaged male members of the elites, particularly in Maryland, Virginia, and both Carolinas, plus a few from trans-Appalachia and the Gulf states. The *Register* offered them a few "exchange" reprints from other papers, but much fewer than customary then. Ruffin himself contributed many general and specialized articles and was probably author of nearly all the small and substantial unsigned pieces. All the while he persisted as avid reader of European chemistry and agronomy, learning French to extend his grasp and becoming an important American vector for practical Continental learning. When, for instance, an English translation of the German baron and professor Justus von Liebig's *Organic Chemistry in Its Application to Agriculture and Physiology* appeared in 1840, Ruffin bought and devoured the book, then proclaimed Liebig's genius in *Farmers' Register*. Liebig had already (during a visit to England) shocked British scientists by attacking the "humus theory" of soil improvement and plant growth. An inventor of modern inorganic chemistry, Liebig offered instead what the British called a "mineral theory." Liebig argued that organic fertilizers such as dung were largely superfluous, because plants receive nitrogen essential for growth from the air, via rainfall, and from phosphorus and other minerals present in soil already. Ruffin, himself a champion of marl, an inorganic manure, may have been charmed by apparent vindication, but one must remember that the American remained in theory and practice a consistent advocate of *all* manuring —dung, green, and calcareous. This combination of organic and inorganic management of soil fertility would be validated after Ruffin's death, at the Royal Agricultural College at Cirencester.[8]

Meanwhile Ruffin became a minor celebrity. One of his most receptive distant readers and correspondents was James Henry Hammond, an innovative planter by the Savannah River. Hammond happened also to be governor of South Carolina when Ruffin was closing down *Farmers' Register* in 1842. So Ruffin eagerly accepted Hammond's invitation to conduct a geological survey of the Palmetto State. The Virginian never quite completed his planned tour—weather and illness intervened—yet he submitted a substantial report that (hardly unexpected) demonstrated acidity in South Carolina soils and identified several good native sources of marl. Now Ruffin returned to farming, this time at the Pamunkey River's navigable head just north of Richmond, on a plantation he inevitably (again) named Marlbourne. There was now private work to be done: Marlbourne was inadequately drained and (of course) marled. Yet Ruffin still found time to travel, observe, correspond and advise, and promote scientific agriculture as a public writer. In 1851, a western admirer, J. D. B. De Bow, editor and publisher of the influential *De Bow's Review* in New Orleans, printed a laudatory biographical sketch (written by one of Ruffin's Virginia admirers) that declared Ruffin the South's premier "agriculturist."

During the 1850s Ruffin also became one of the nation's most aggressive and tenacious defenders of slavery, white supremacy, and "southern rights." He was a "fire-eater" for a separate slaveholders' republic who at last, early in 1861, accepted another invitation from South Carolina. This was the courtesy of honorary membership in the state's militia at Charleston, and there, in April, after a warning flare sent up by regular Confederate artillerymen, Ruffin apparently touched fire to fuse and sent the first hostile projectile hurtling toward Fort Sumter. The old man had a famous photographic portrait made of himself about this time, with his straight white hair falling on the shoulders of his coat, his expression implacable, and his rifle at hand. Now his celebrity was magnified enormously. Sixteen months later, when Yankee gunboats stopped by the plantation of Ruffin's eldest son on the James, from which the elder Ruffin himself had fled just in time, among the graffiti soldiers left on walls was "You did fire the first gun on Sumter, you traitor son of a bitch."

Edmund Ruffin's two celebrated personae—premier agriculturalist and architect of slaveholder independence and war—were by no means illogical or incongruent. Ruffin the white supremacist and holder (with family members) of up to 200 enslaved people consistently asserted not only his class's interest but an elaborate vision of a southern landscape so manipulated, so well maintained, as to be unthinkable without slavery. The vision is most clearly presented, I think, in an address Ruffin delivered to the South Carolina Institute in November 1852. Titled "An Address on the Opposite Results of Exhausting and Fertilizing Systems of Agriculture," the paper might be overlooked as a dull précis of a reprise of his *Essay on Calcareous Manures*, then two decades old. Indeed Ruffin seldom tired of redundancy on the subject of marl, but there is more here. Ever obsessed with drainage as well as with calcium, Ruffin had long been an advocate of what is called reclamation, in this case the drainage of wetlands large and small. A decade earlier, he had proposed (as had others before him) clearance of the Great Dismal Swamp. Now, to a South Carolina audience, he urged extensive and cooperative drainage of the entire Low Country. "Lower South Carolina," he said, "might possess the peculiar facilities of Holland for extensive inland navigation. These connecting canals, by diverting some of the superfluous supply of fresh waters of some rivers, to others where it is deficient, might perhaps serve to extend greatly the present area of tide covered land, capable of being flooded for rice culture." The Ashley, Cooper, Edisto, and Santee would thus become an efficient and profitable network. As an additional benefit—surprise—digging the canals would doubtlessly uncover vast quantities of marl. Other (and earlier) writings, combined with this address, suggest an ambition to rearrange landscapes that was hardly less monumental than the grandiose schemes of water-mad early-twentieth-century California ranchers. Ruffin, foe of federal power, seems to have anticipated New Deal public works gigantism. Lacking dynamite, bulldozers, and big diesel-guzzling trucks, Ruffin and other southern "improvers" of his generation required slaves to perform the arduously disagreeable labor of landscape manipulation. They, and mules and horses, then, would extend and improve corn-wheat, rice, and cotton cultures from the Potomac to the Pamlico to the Cape Fear, the Santee, and the Ashley—and yes, conceivably to the Savannah, Flint,

Chattahoochee, Coosa, and beyond, to that most interesting lower Mississippi system.[9]

✾ A slave-remade South Atlantic region was not to be, of course, nor was an enduring slaveholders' republic. Ruffin, seventy-one years old and ailing, committed suicide in June 1865. In his own later years and in recorded memory, however, Ruffin's reputation as a brilliant pioneer of agro-ecology has become canonical. He was "father of soil science" in the South (if not in all America) and savior of long-farmed, "exhausted" tidewater landscapes. Thirty years after Ruffin's death, the librarian of the U.S. Department of Agriculture (USDA) wrote in the agency's yearbook that the *Essay on Calcareous Manures* was "the most thorough piece of work on a special agricultural subject ever published in the English language." (More important than Davy's work on chemistry?) In 1904, Richmond's venerable *Southern Planter* offered a long article on contemporary leading southern agronomic scientists and educators but reminded readers "that the South produced the first man (Edmund Ruffin) who, in this country, endeavored to apply science to the advancement of agriculture." One of Ruffin's grandsons, Julian, still farming the marled fields of Marlbourne, supplied the photographic portrait of Edmund that accompanied the article, to which was appended a reprinting of the 1895 USDA yearbook's extravagant declaration of Ruffin's genius.

In those days, federal-state agricultural experiment stations connected with such college-based schools of agriculture as Virginia Polytechnic Institute's seemed monuments to Ruffin and other antebellum improvers who had long advocated formal agronomic education. Likewise Congress's creation of the Cooperative Extension Service in 1914 could be viewed as overdue justification of southern improvers' advocacy of expert outreach to farmers. Sponsors of the enabling legislation were, after all, Senator Hoke Smith of Georgia and Asbury Francis (A. Frank) Lever of South Carolina. The Smith-Lever Act served every American farming county, but everyone understood that the new Extension Service was built on an older, entirely southern, organization that had been fighting the cotton boll weevil for years. One can hardly imagine Edmund Ruffin inviting federal agents onto private farms, but honorific memory was attached more to scientific agriculture than to the mechanics of delivery. Finally, in 1932, the centennial of Ruffin's own magnum opus, the first scholarly biography of the great man appeared. This was the work of Professor Avery Odell Craven of the University of Chicago: *Edmund Ruffin, Southerner: A Study in Secession.* By this time Craven, like many of his historian contemporaries in the United States, had become consumed with analyzing the origins of the Civil War. So while the biography provided a brief albeit vivid account of Ruffin's discovery of soil acidity and advocacy of calcareous manures, it was chiefly a political narrative in which its subject became destructively obsessed with other matters. Craven's first book, the tediously titled *Soil Exhaustion as a Factor in the Agricultural History of Virginia and Maryland, 1606–1860* (1926) is actually the pioneering exercise in agro-ecological history in which Ruffin's first celebrity, as agronomic improver, is featured. Craven was certain that, despite Ruffin's own repeated protests that hardly anyone followed his advice, the Chesapeake states were saved by Ruffin's science and relentless proselytizing.

Now, however, one must doubt that the Chesapeake country was ever lost or needed saving. If indeed this and other long-used American landscapes were saved late in the antebellum period, it was not progressive science wisely applied but a new, foreign (albeit organic) agricultural input—guano—that contributed to the East's relative productive successes. Alexander von Humboldt was apparently the first European to spot enormous deposits of cormorant droppings below cliffs on a series of islands off the coast of Peru. The guano (an indigenous word for the droppings) was eons old yet still accumulating, intact, dry, and laden with nitrogen and phosphorus. By the 1840s British and American companies had claimed the islands and organized labor to extract the resource and ships to carry it to Atlantic ports. By the mid-1850s, with Peruvian stores diminishing, the U.S. government sanctioned development of guano operations near the Hawaiian group and nearby islands in an emergent American territorial protectorate in the Pacific. By this time U.S. consumption of guano had grown to 140,000 tons a year. Guano was expensive—about $50 up to $90 per ton—before the Civil War, but farmers and agronomists alike conceded that, compared with local animal manure by weight or cartloads, a small fraction of guano would "dress" an acre magnificently. So—this conclusion may be difficult to exaggerate—progressive, "improving" agronomy was short circuited, and a view of our own era's big-expense, big-debt, farming-for-the-few began to materialize.[10]

🌿 Avery Craven, meanwhile, had a distinguished career and lived long, publishing his last book during the 1980s. His rural Iowa youth and especially his graduate education, beginning at Harvard with Frederick Jackson Turner, had naturally colored his early work. Like Turner, he hated what open frontiers seemed to do to land; farmers felt no need to maintain fertility in settled places, since there was always fresh land to the west. So the process of European settlement of the American landscape was one of exhaustion, migration, exhaustion, migration, and so on. Finally there was no more frontier, as Turner famously announced in Chicago in 1893. Now American farmers (and their governments) had to face consequences. These seemed obvious enough: Improving science or utter ruination and defenseless dependency on imported food and fiber. Edmund Ruffin and his enlightened contemporaries became instructive historical voices, crying from their own exhausted wildernesses—except that Ruffin had actually demonstrated success in the oldest, most worn-down place in America.

Ruffin himself denied this claim, but Craven and many scholars after him dismissed the denial. Surely some of Ruffin's private and public self-deprecations and complaints must be taken with proverbial grains of salt. He assumed a cloak of modesty in the face of praise. He was also the depressive crank, tirelessly pronouncing himself a failure as a reformer. When Ruffin protested that there were precious few practicing marlers in Maryland, either Carolina, and even his beloved Virginia, however, he reported the truth. This is confirmed by a careful British historian (from East Anglia, of all places), William M. Mathew. Mathew's relentless search for active disciples of Ruffin's agronomy yielded but a few hundred, virtually all of these with accessible deposits of marl on their properties and sufficient labor readily to exhume and spread it. Elsewhere—nearly everywhere—marl's inaccessibility, its costly weight in shipment, its labor intensiveness in application, and variabilities in application to specific fields (notwithstanding Ruffin's repeated updates of instructions) precluded widespread acceptance and practice. (A few wealthy planters along James River and elsewhere bought barges of lime from New England quarry merchants.) Other scholars suggest that there was never a "crisis" in late-eighteenth- and early-nineteenth-century agriculture, anyway. The relative prosperity of Virginia and Maryland as agricultural states, late in the antebellum era, cannot be attributed either to Ruffin's truly important discoveries of acidity and calcium or to guano. Certainly some farmers were careless, feckless, or cynical and "exhausted" their croplands. Yet somehow, the Chesapeake states and the rest of the greater South, by 1860, managed not only to feed itself quite well but to export (to the North and West and overseas) grain and livestock surpluses as well as fleet-loads of cotton and other commodities.[11] How can we account, then, for half a century of rhetorical gloom?

Southern farmlands, owing to landscape morphology, forest clearance practices, and other reasons (some to be explored later), often were not neat, symmetrical, and aesthetically pleasing, especially to travelers from outside the region. Most important of these sojourners, toward the end of the antebellum period, was the landscape architect Frederick Law Olmsted, who wrote hundreds of New York newspaper sketches about the rural South during the mid-1850s that were shortly collected into widely read books. A trained agronomist and ex-farmer himself, Olmsted opposed slavery not so much on moral grounds but because it was inefficient and wasteful in ways we might call anticonservationist. This he demonstrated repeatedly in his travel writings, persuading many readers then and since that only smart proprietors and free laborers do good work and save the land. Just as important, Olmsted-the-aesthete found most of the South rather ugly. Ugly here includes most architecture, city streets, and poorly maintained farms; ugly also implies poor, unproductive, and perhaps exhausted. In this reaction Olmsted joined legions of European visitors, who came and went away despairing. Disaffected German Romantics had decried Americans' *Bodenlosigkeit*, which Simon Schama translates as "a willed rootlessness, embodied in the flimsy frame construction of [their] houses."[12] But Olmsted, I think, was mostly wrong, too.

Ugly and exhausted were doubtlessly actual, here and there, now and again. But the terms, and persistent discourse centered on them, divert us from what Ruffin and his reformer contemporaries were *actually* engaged in. This, simply and profoundly, was serious consideration of the possibility of stable civic culture, community, and civilization, in a frontier country. (No wonder they resonated with Frederick Jackson Turner and Avery Craven.) John Taylor, then Ruffin, spoke for a part of the South Atlantic. James Henry Hammond and especially William Gilmore Simms, the worthy novelist, poet, essayist, historian, and Low Country South Carolina planter, represented another. Yankees had their great worriers, improvers, and spokesmen, too—notably Jesse Buel of Albany and John Lorain of Philadelphia. All were easterners who perceived an eastern crisis, namely, the region's ruin and abandonment by youthful and talented populations. Buel, Lorain, and other northeasterners essentially addressed those migrating to the northwestern states and territories; Ruffin, Simms, and other southern improvers tried to speak with actual and potential migrants to Alabama, Mississippi, and the trans-Mississippi Southwest. If the discourse were also a dialogue, would-be and actual westerners were relatively passive and indifferent. It was the East that was ardently voluble, its tone and substance tensely shifting between imminent triumphalism and doom.

There was much, indeed, for committed easterners to feel gloomy about. Their kin and friends were departing for faraway places not to be served by railroads for years. Immigrants faced a hard fact that they would never see the Old Country again, and vice versa. Immigrants and those left behind also rightly feared that westering would lead to serious illnesses and premature death. This was probably truer among southern migrants, whose destinations were more likely to be malarial wetlands. But perhaps as much as mourning and sympathy, easterners' rhetoric gave vent to resentment. Old states seemed to stagnate and to lose representation in the national House, absolutely or at least relative to astounding gains by new states. Ruffin and other Virginians were preoccupied with federal census data that revealed the enormous numbers of the Old Dominion–born in Ohio, Indiana, but especially in the Gulf states. He and other easterners seem to have assumed that migrants represented loss—of good farmers, engaged citizens, and potential statesmen. And there was good reason, of course. Recall that Andrew Jackson was born in South Carolina and buried in Tennessee. Senator Thomas Hart Benton of Missouri was born in North Carolina, sojourned in Tennessee, and so on. Virginia-born men were prominent in the founding of the Texas Republic.

Westering was a "fever"—the descriptor recurs with both despair and enthusiasm. Eastern reformers who would have everyone—at least "good" people—stay home and improve soils were helpless to stop it. So roads south and west, such as they were, and every navigable river were clogged with migrants. In the South, many of these were planter families and their slaves. The great Scottish geologist Sir Charles Lyell observed the fever and the flowing crowds during his second fossil-hunting trip to Alabama, in 1846. Traveling from the coast of Georgia inland, Lyell and his wife shared roads, boats, accommodations (such as they were), and campgrounds with South Carolinians and especially Georgians heading west. Travelers were ever merry, it seemed, even on a rainy night, when one group kept a fire of pine roaring despite the wet. Once inside Alabama, Lyell discovered that people who had just come, a few years before when he first visited, were already about to move farther on, this time probably to Texas. The correspondence and diaries of planter migrants themselves affirm the ambitions and the conflicts that propelled so many to new countries: To make one's own economic way, and grandly, of course, but also to escape a family patriarch's tyranny back east or to find political opportunity in a state not yet dominated by an entrenched elite.

Such hopes ever compel migrants to separate themselves from the secure and familiar. At least this was the case for men, who ruled; women were often less eager migrants. But altogether, migration, discontinuity of people-in-place, and a fragility and tentativeness of community characterized antebellum America. This would be hardly less so after the Civil War and through the twentieth century. Consider a recent sociohistorical profile of William Faulkner's home county of Lafayette, in northern Mississippi—that which Faulkner called Yoknapatawpha in four decades of fiction. The historian Don Doyle has revisited Lafayette with grand imagination and scrupulous, microscopic research. Among the most important of Doyle's findings is the persistence of flux in Lafayette's human history. "The mobility of the population suggests a people who rarely put down roots or congregated often enough to form what we think of as genuine communities," he writes. "The peripatetic people of Lafayette County sometimes appear as little more than an assembly of migrant strangers scattered across a remote land covered with woods and cotton fields." "Migrant strangers" might well suggest something more sinister than wanderlust, too, recalling Faulkner's Rosa Coldfield railing about pretentious newcomers in *Absalom, Absalom!* "And the very fact that [Sutpen] had had to choose respectability to hide behind was proof enough . . . that what he fled from must have been some opposite of respectability too dark to talk about."[13] But generally, and magnified to virtually everywhere, Lafayette County, Mississippi, may also explain sentimental myths of home-sweet-home, stability, continuity, "old families," and obsessive land-loving in the South and perhaps over the continent. Sentiment, in other words, has compensated for homes and communities dreamed of but hardly realized. In *Gone with the Wind*, Scarlett's daddy, Gerald O'Hara, the Irish immigrant, counsels holding onto the land; much later, after poor Gerald is gone, a momentarily despairing Scarlett determinedly declares, "I'll always have Tara!" But had she herself not already commandeered an Atlanta lumber business, ordered the clear-cutting of Georgia hills to rebuild the city, and become a permanent migrant? Perhaps it is time we stopped confusing Stephen Foster songs with historical reality—except "Oh, Susannah!" which is of course about migration.

🌺 Humans have always moved, voluntarily and involuntarily. We describe migration within parameters called pushes and pulls that have been canonical in demography for more than a century. The Fujianese, for instance, were pushed from Fujian by population in excess of the carrying capacity of the landscape and pulled to southeast Asia, California, the Caribbean, and elsewhere by business and especially laboring opportunities.

*Ruins of a plantation house near Marshall, Texas, 1939. Photo by Russell Lee.*
*Courtesy Library of Congress (LC-USF34-032788-D).*

Millions of West and Central Africans were victims of the cruelest of pushes, across the Atlantic. In the Americas, millions were migrants yet again. An African arriving late to Brazil's northeastern sugar plantations may have ended her life tending coffee trees a thousand miles to the south. Likewise, many enslaved South Carolinians came to clear forests and plant cotton in Mississippi and then Texas.

White southerners, their population (like the rest of America's) finally burgeoning in the nineteenth century, were pulled in droves to widowed western landscapes. The West's widowhood appeared at a remarkable demographic moment. For at least a century and a half, southeastern families had barely survived. Men outnumbered women for a long time. Parents died early and had no or few children. Neighbors raised unrelated orphans. Family lines disappeared. Edmund Ruffin's Virginia line illustrates both this and the Malthusian revolution to come. Edmund and his wife, both born during the 1790s, were orphan survivors of families long in Virginia yet who barely escaped extinction. Amazingly, they became parents of eleven children, nine of whom survived to adulthood. Typically, the young Ruffins considered heading west; untypically, they remained at home.

What was called the South in the decade of the Ruffins' births—the coastal states below Delaware through Georgia, plus Kentucky and Tennessee—contained fewer than 2 million people. Mountain Virginia, western Kentucky and Tennessee, and nearly all of Georgia were unorganized, unsettled, and practically vacant. By 1830 Appalachian Virginia and North Carolina averaged close to ten persons per square mile, as did the upper and central piedmonts of Georgia, and Alabama's south-central black belt approached twenty. In 1860 the South's total population was about 12 million. Georgia's lower piedmont as well as Alabama's black belt, southwestern Mississippi, and adjacent eastern Louisiana were all relatively crowded, with densities of at least thirty persons per square mile. Southern Missouri, Arkansas, eastern Texas, and northern Florida were settled and growing fast. This sixfold increase in population and the constant movement—the fiery reclamation, as it were, of old native landscapes—led to four years of war fought principally on these same landscapes, followed by reconstructions of several sorts, then the creation of a second and much larger cotton kingdom that endured well into the twentieth century. One begins to appreciate the discontinuity, the disruption-as-norm, and the chaos, perhaps, that is the history of the South.[14] Yet this is not what is remembered.

When the Civil War got under way, along the banks of the rivers James,

*Soil erosion, Stewart County, Georgia, 1937, later the site of a state park popularly known as Georgia's Little Grand Canyon. Photo by Arthur Rothstein. Courtesy Library of Congress (LC-USF34-025215-D).*

*Loading cotton, Natchez, Mississippi, 1935. Photo by Ben Shahn.*
*Courtesy Library of Congress (LC-USF33-006096-M5 DLC).*

Neuse, Ashley, and Cooper (among other seaboard, long-settled places) there were plantation mansions already old. Most were constructed of brick and had been rebuilt and/or enlarged several times. Their masters were progressive farmers proud of fields both expansive and productive. Such men, with their wives, were usually aesthetes, too, and supervised not only neat kitchen gardens but manicured greenswards that stretched down to beaches, and ornamental plantings of trees, shrubs, and flowers in the styles of the English and the French. Olmsted himself admired James River mansions and lawns from a steamboat bound eastward toward Norfolk in 1852. Many of these places endure to this day, sometimes in possession of the same families who planted the properties in 1860 or even long before. (One thinks of the descendants of John Tyler at Sherwood Forest, on the James.) Somewhat younger mansions survive farther inland, beside great rivers that served the first big cotton frontiers—the white-columned neoclassicals of Macon, Georgia, by the Ocmulgee, for instance, and the Twickenham neighborhood of Huntsville, Alabama, near the mighty Tennessee. Twickenham's proprietors proudly open their doors to visitors each year in an event called Pilgrimage. The wealthiest Americans on the eve of the Civil War lived in and around Natchez, Mississippi, and across the river in Concordia Parish, Louisiana. Many of their mansions, too, remain and are regularly admired by the public during Natchez's annual Pilgrimage. Predictably, though, nearly all these notable western estates were young, new, or still unfinished when the Civil War began. Now they are old, by American lights, anyway. Interesting and valuable as all these domestic monuments may be as architecture and artifacts of self-indulgent living by the few, they misrepresent the region profoundly.

Most southern architecture, even "big houses," was constructed of wood. Such as these were, if Yankees did not burn them, friendly fire did, sooner or later, and if fire did not destroy them, termites did. Builders of such places often abandoned them to move, too, and if there were no buyers or squatters to maintain them, big houses succumbed to rot and the weight of encroaching vegetation. Mobile, ever-westering planters often never got around to constructing mansions. The dogtrot (or open-hallway) house was the nineteenth-century double-wide that suited slaveholders on frontiers well enough. Built of logs or, later and well into the twentieth century, of sawn boards, dogtrot houses were usually two rooms on the same foundation separated by a covered but otherwise open "hall," through which a dog (or almost any creature) might trot. For a year or two or three, a planter and his white family might live in one room, with slaves in the other. Once forests were cleared, cotton harvested, and money made, perhaps more distant slave quarters might be constructed, or slaves might take over both sides of the dogtrot as a larger separate house, perhaps two stories, was constructed for whites. Or perhaps the planter would instead invest in more slaves rather than domestic comfort (much less grandeur), then move before there was ever anything resembling a manse. This was the plantation landscape—temporary, in process, abandoned, repossessed, and so on, seldom pretentious, manicured, or lovely. Yet altogether it was home to millions, economically productive, and the subject of scorn *and* passionate sentiment. This landscape was not *nature* as virgin untouched, even though patches of wilderness persisted all over the South. Native landscapes had not been unmanipulated either, and plantation landscapes do bear important resemblances to Mississippian ones: very large fields as well as vegetable gardens, colonies of plants far removed from their places of origin, and expanses of girdled forests, burned and reburned, later to be abandoned or at least idled for years. Both were landscapes made, reshaped, abused, and often as not, as best we can tell, used well, too. They were vernacular landscapes.

Then came the planters' war. Edmund Ruffin, brother fire-eaters from the lower South, and their clerical and other intellectual allies had succeeded in galvanizing the great majority of white southerners to defend slavery and white supremacy. Ruffin most of all welcomed the war, fired his famous shot at Fort Sumter, kibitzed on eastern battlefields for a couple of years, and sacrificed a teenaged grandson in 1862, then his favored son, Julian, in 1864. Skirmishes and full-scale battles were fought on plantations, including Ruffin family properties. Yankees vandalized Edmund Jr.'s estate and stole Edmund Sr.'s library and correspondence; they also mistakenly burned the house of Edmund Sr.'s neighbor by the Pamunkey, thinking it was the old fire-eater's. Robert E. Lee's family estate on the Potomac became Arlington National Cemetery. U. S. Grant made Dr. Richard Eppes's big house at the confluence of the Appomattox and the James his headquarters during the siege of Petersburg. Earlier, Grant's soldiers had laid waste to Tennessee, Louisiana, and especially Mississippi plantations. Then William Tecumseh Sherman's midwesterners scourged northern Georgia and South Carolina. Photographers following the troops relished capturing images of blackened brick chimneys standing sentinel over the ashes of once-proud plantation big houses.

Gone too were millions of livestock. Horses and mules were taken for war service, and cattle, hogs, and fowl were carried off and consumed by soldiers of both sides in the conflict. Fences, the ubiquitous necessity in a region where the range remained open, were torn down by soldiers (on both sides, again) to make way for traffic, but especially for firewood. Most important, the fires of war consumed also the institution of slavery. Nearly 4 million human chattels were appropriated by the federal government with no compensation of their monetary value to previous owners. The white southern class that had made the war suffered consequences indeed —as they indeed should have.

Adult males of the planter class were a minority of the South's 1860 population. In 1862 the Confederate Congress, enacting the nation's first conscription legislation, exempted from military service heads of households with twenty or more slaves. The law's rationale included that home security and food production were best left to planters accustomed to commanding servants, yet the law embittered the nonslaveholding majority of white southerners, who may have invented the caustic, always applicable declaration, "It's a rich man's war and a poor man's fight." Nonetheless the planter class suffered enormous mortality in the war, as did other white classes. Mississippi presented the most gruesome unbalancing of the sex ratio. During midsummer 1865, no less than 45 percent of the white male population between the ages of fifteen and forty-five were dead, maimed, or still missing, months after the war's end. Immigration from abroad presumably righted the northern sex ratio imbalance within a few years. But the former Confederacy endured something approaching the European experience following the 1914–18 holocaust—a generation of women without men, without prospect of marriage, companionship, and progeny. We know that upper-class white women descended from pedestals to direct plantations and businesses—not unlike the fictional Scarlett O'Hara. Others became clerks, teachers, writers, and editors. Other women became, simply, farmers on lands where once, before widowhood, all farmers had been female.

Yet for all the carnage, loss, grisly death, and dislocation, the plantation tradition of extensive commodity production with less-than-free labor persisted. Surviving and new planters with cash and/or access to reasonable credit maintained centralized estates with black wage labor. This was the case in Louisiana's sugar country as well as among many Chesapeake grain plantations. Dr. Richard Eppes, for example, returned to Appomattox Manor after the war to find it a shambles. His fences were long gone, his outbuildings had been stripped of siding, and his livestock were gone except for a few animals secreted from the Yankees by his neighbor Hill Carter of Shirley plantation across the James. General Grant's cabin still stood on Eppes's once-magnificent lawn. His mansion (where Grant's staff had lived) was uninhabitable. Yet Eppes was determined not to practice medicine, which he had done only briefly, for the Confederates, but once again to farm—if he could borrow money to rebuild. Here Eppes was fortunate in having a Philadelphia-born wife whose family were glad to assist him.

Among Eppes's astute managerial strokes during his personal reconstruction was the purchase at a bargain price from the federal government of Union barracks that had been constructed on his property. These became Eppes's workers' quarters, a pull, as it were, to homeless, wandering freedmen and their families—and a bargaining tool and weapon (if need be) to control labor. By the beginning of January 1866, Eppes, John Seldon of Westover plantation, and the redoubtable Hill Carter, among others, were conspiring on Turkey Island (up the James in Henrico County) as a James River Farmers association to fix wages according to classes of labor (i.e., men and women), to determine terms of employment, and especially to reestablish planters' authority to discipline. This was no return to slavery, but a golden opportunity for planters to rationalize labor without slavery's "welfare" obligations to the young, old, and infirm.[15] Sugar planters' transition to free (yet repressed) labor was complicated by flood damage and discontinuities of plantation ownership, but altogether theirs and the world of Virginia grain planters must be said to have improved.

Elsewhere, especially in the sprawling interior cotton-corn belts, cash and credit were hard to find, and sometimes U.S. army agents persisted in trying to represent and protect freedmen's rights. Here a new labor system for plantations evolved tentatively and with difficulty. Finally (to generalize) a deal was made: Freedmen wanted their own farms but had no money. Planters wanted to drive labor in gangs at their discretion but had no money for wages, either. Freedmen seem to have initiated the solution to cashlessness in some places. In order to claim discrete "farms" and homes and to work as individuals and families rather than in gangs under constant supervision, they would share half the market value of a cotton crop with a planter willing to fragment his estate and forgo central management and gang labor. Planters—now as often called landlords—would also be obliged to provide sharecroppers with animal power (usually mules), harnesses, tools, and other farming equipment. Landlords (who were literate and usually experienced in business) would market crops and deduct from sharecroppers' halves their shares of fertilizer costs, shipping, insurance, and brokerage fees. Thus began a vast reorganization of most plantations, plus the beginning of decades of struggle between labor and business. Some planters were doubtlessly relieved to turn over production to a collection of hard-working men and women on their separate plots. Most, we suspect, were ever scheming to recentralize their estates and rationalize operations to suit themselves.

In the meantime, though, the initial deal was incomplete. How were croppers to subsist for a year before crops were sold? Here entered the third element: "furnishing" merchants who established country stores throughout the broad region. With credit of their own, they stocked the cheap clothes, tobacco, kerosene, coal, whiskey, and bibles required by ordinary people, and they extended to each cropper household a line of credit based on guesses at cotton and corn futures and local knowledge of workers and soils. Clerks kept accounts of each debit, which included an interest charge. Interest rates charged croppers were secret, actually, but are calculable from many surviving merchants' ledgers. They were high, as risky long-term agricultural private banking has always demanded. Late in the nineteenth century, a young white editor of a North Carolina farm journal summarized: interest rates, he wrote, "ranged from twenty-five percent to grand larceny." No wonder that planter-landlords could not resist entering the business themselves, and they often established "commissaries" on their own properties. At the end of each calendar year came settlement time. Planters sold crops and presented croppers' shares. Croppers went to merchants to pay their bills. Often they knew their store totals no better than their crop share values, since both planters and merchants preferred to keep records private. Because of their color and lack of civic power, often compounded by illiteracy, croppers were usually too powerless to demand transparency.

In the long run, then, high interest charges, new international competition in the cotton trade, the long downward trend of cotton prices, and simple larceny undermined croppers' initial hopes for private initiative, decent earnings, accumulation, and finally proprietorship for themselves. Instead, tenancy of all sorts, especially sharecropping (which merely resembles tenancy) grew with the postbellum era's enlarged cotton kingdom. A vast (even international) chain of exploitation had taken shape: Metropolitan bankers charged usurious rates to regional and local banks, which passed their costs to merchants and lending planters, who robbed sharecroppers, who themselves had nothing to rob but the earth. No wonder that croppers were mobile workers, moving and deserting or avoiding landlords with mean and greedy reputations, but especially looking for better ground to exploit, probably in some new delta or blackland prairie.[16] Here are the origins of the notoriously benighted South of the 1920s and 1930s, the subject for perplexed sociologists, economists, nutritionists, and not least, conservationists.

🌿 Yet the plantation system's postbellum stage was a very long one, from ca. 1865 to about 1960, when croppers and sharecropping had at last faded away and production of most of the South's great staples was either thoroughly mechanized or abandoned. Within these several generations, and here and there, a few redeeming, at least ameliorating, practices existed. One was the persistent practice of intercropping corn with beans of some sort, usually climbers. (Cotton, like all machine-harvested field crops today, seems to have been universally a monoculture enterprise.) Even planters (and ordinary farmers) who were unaware, say, as late as 1900, that beans are legumes that impart nitrogen, religiously intercropped. Maize and beans both were picked by hand, for domestic and market use. When the corn was finished and the bean vines began to wither, hogs or cattle might be turned into intercropped fields to feast and fatten—and to deposit their droppings in preparation for a crop of cotton the following year. Velvet beans were a favorite of both humans and beasts well into the twentieth century. A twiny climber, velvets (we now understand) contained significant amounts—3 to 9 percent—of L-dopa, a natural compound until recently used to treat Parkinson's disease, and parts of the plants probably contained other toxins, including mild hallucinogens. Precise analysis of the composition of velvet beans is now impossible because cultivation of the bean drastically diminished and then disappeared after about World War II—a casualty, probably, of cheaper inorganic fertilizers, farmers' massive switch to soybean monoculture, and machine harvesting of corn.[17]

Another conservationist practice (whether intentional or not) was the long fallow system pursued not only by small landowners but by large planters, especially in the East. Hardly any landowner had all of his or her property under cultivation and pasture. As fertility declined, then, owners cleared sections of their woods by burning—a version of an ancient practice on the same ground. After an initial blaze among deadened trees, workers "rolled" logs that were not yet completely incinerated and reburned them. Soil preparation with hoes and shallow-draft "stump-jumping" plows then took place in knee-deep ashes. These ashes, depending on the sort of wood burned, contained as much as 60 percent calcium carbonate, as well as phosphorus and other elements. This source of nitrogen-fixing dissolved faster than marl or lime, of course, but for a few years, supplemented by other manures, the residues of wood ashes helped production on the oldest plantations and farms.[18]

Yet another New South conservationist practice represented antebellum plantation management carried over—for a while, anyway—to fragmented sharecropper properties. This was simply that workers should feed themselves from garden plots worked in their own time. In the beginning, then, croppers had their own cabins and nearby, well-maintained vegetable gardens that, resonant of American Indian middens plots, became jumbled cornucopias of intercropped comestibles. Slaves had often produced surpluses from their gardens and entered local markets as sellers. Many croppers with sufficient family labor doubtlessly fed themselves and others well too.

Over time, however, especially on the largest riverside and lower Mississippi delta plantations, the trend in New South planting reflected the growing power of owner-managers to reduce croppers' independence. Eager, too, to rationalize and to recentralize their operations, planters and their riding bosses imposed the "through-and-through" system of plowing and cultivating. Multimule teams with large plow and cultivator rigs swept over entire plantations twice (in perpendicular directions), as though the supposedly fragmented estate were one unit. Cropper families typically picked cotton on their respective plots, but they had obviously lost much autonomy. This was brutally evident in the twentieth-century practice, usually associated with through-and-through, of plowing and planting virtually to the foundations of croppers' cabins. So now croppers' garden spaces were sacrificed to increased commodity production. Of course the principal advantage to planters in this instance was forcing croppers into planters' own closed, high-interest markets for food. Commissary business picked up.[19]

Now poor peoples' diets, degraded by increasing dependency since the Civil War, devolved to the pathological. From voluptuous private gardens supplemented by fishing and hunting, croppers and others now consumed the notorious three M's: meat (i.e., fat pork), meal (i.e., corn), and molasses. Thus by the 1930s, the South was home not only to malaria, hookworm, and pellagra but the "hypertension belt." Nowadays associated with obesity, high blood pressure was another morbid aspect of malnutrition and thinness. Examine the faces and bodies Walker Evans photographed in Hale County, Alabama, in July 1934 while he and James Agee were preparing their remarkable documentary book, *Let Us Now Praise Famous Men* (1941). Or study Margaret Bourke-White's portraits in Georgia three years later, when she toured the piedmont plantation belt with Erskine Caldwell, who made up captions for the photos in their work, *You Have Seen Their Faces* (1937).

The rest of the enormous pictorial archive of the Great Depression yields more than faces and bodies, of course. There is also the degradation of human shelter and clothing and especially of the landscape itself. The cumulative *environmental* effect of the conversion of garden plots to cotton monoculture seems quite impossible to estimate. The last southeastern cotton kingdom had such enormous geographic reach, not only into new plantation-country deltas in Mississippi, Arkansas, and Missouri, but into hilly, marginal, nonplantation places such as northwestern Georgia and northwestern Arkansas. Both flat and hilly landscapes suffered lasting mischief. Still photographers placed despondent human subjects before backdrops of deeply, often irrevocably eroded farmland that should never have been cultivated. Most memorably, Pare Lorentz's motion picture documentary *The River* (1937) dramatically captured the connectedness of human poverty and soil erosion in the lower Mississippi country with deforestation and cultivation in Appalachia and the Midwest. Lorentz's sonorous narrator intoned, "Poor land makes poor people."

The systemic ecological thinking that *The River* represented so well was also propaganda for the Tennessee Valley Authority (TVA). Authorized in 1933, the TVA not only constructed dams and hydroelectric operations but supervised reforestation projects that complemented federal subsidization of the retirement of farmland. By the 1960s, the "mid-South," as the huge TVA-served part of the region was called by then, had become industrialized and urbanized to a greater degree than ever before. By this time, too, the southeastern cotton kingdom was reduced to a few earldoms in the deltas.

The rest of the New South's plantation complex died in protracted stages, beginning a half-century before mechanization of cotton, corn, and soybeans and elimination of sharecropping and most other sorts of labor.[20] In 1910, southern cotton production approached its zenith. More territorial expansion was already under way or in the offing—in Texas's Blackland Prairie, eastern Arkansas, and the Missouri bootheel. By 1930–31 a staggering production of more than 15 million bales prompted Louisiana's Governor Huey Long to lead a heroic but failed attempt to persuade cotton growers to take a year off. By that time, however, both the cotton kingdom and the plantation complex were already doomed by three momentous developments.

First was a silent, little-noticed "management failure," as the geographer Charles Aiken names it. The term assumes (correctly, I think) that

sharecropped plantations, no less than centralized ones, required interested, resident managers. For a variety of reasons, reported anecdotally and
inferred, planters were beginning a massive withdrawal from the countryside by about 1910 and becoming absentee landlords or simply divesting.
Why? Plantation management is tediously repetitive yet, considering the
increasing mobility of croppers and tenants, consumed with stress. Too,
the planter class was generally an educated one, and remote places offered
members little society among their peers and less-appealing opportunities
for professionals among them than in towns and cities. Idle wives famously
preferred town life. Middle-aged and elderly planters discovered that their
sons and daughters preferred to take their own college credentials to cities,
even faraway northeastern ones. The cumulative effect was a dramatic reduction in the numbers of plantations. In 1910 the Bureau of the Census
counted 39,073 plantations in the eleven former Confederate states. Only
thirty years later—in 1940 and before the South felt the full impact of tractors, much less the chemical and harvester revolutions to come—there
were only 19,498, a reduction of slightly more than half.

Second was the massive exodus of labor, both black and white, which
began in 1915, as American industry responded to Great War market opportunities. Between then and 1960, 9 million southerners (about half of
them black, half white) decamped for other parts of the country. These included 300,000 so-called Okies (actually from Texas, Arkansas, and Louisiana as well as Oklahoma), who streamed west in only five years, 1935–40.
Most of them were, first, farm laborers in Arizona and especially California,
but they shortly went to work in war industries. The great bulk of southern émigrés became industrial workers in the Northeast and Midwest. Yet
more millions of southerners moved within the South, almost always from
rural to urban places. Even Texas became statistically an urban state, and
with startling rapidity.

Third was the juggernaut emergence of cotton culture on the West Coast.
Cotton had been tried at least twice before in California—in Los Angeles
County during the 1850s, with "coolie" labor, then at the turn of the twentieth century at the bottom of the state, in what was newly called the Imperial Valley. Both these experiments failed, the latter owing mainly to the
unruly geology of the Colorado River delta. Then in 1917 the United States
entered World War I, and war planners decided that the army's flying corps
desperately needed secure supplies of long-staple cotton for covering the
wooden and metal frames of airplanes. The USDA sent its best cotton man,
Wofford B. "Bill" Camp, out to Kern County, in California's Central Valley,

*Florida migrant workers bound for New Jersey, Currituck County, North Carolina, 1940.*
*Photo by Jack Delano. Courtesy Library of Congress (LC-USF34-040820-D DLC).*

*Migrant construction worker and his family, Portsmouth, Virginia, 1941.*

*Photo by John Vachon. Courtesy Library of Congress (LC-USF34-06492-D DLC).*

to persuade fruit ranchers to switch to cotton. Camp had been raised on an up-country South Carolina cotton farm and educated at Clemson, the state's agricultural college. Accustomed to southeastern farmers' curmudgeonly unreceptiveness to science and innovation, out west Camp discovered communities of entrepreneurial farmers (they preferred "ranchers") already legendary for their willingness to invest, band together, and exploit state and federal institutions—not to mention brutalize labor as brazenly as any Mississippi planter. So Camp succeeded easily in establishing cotton in Kern County, just as the war emergency suddenly ended. Curiously, the USDA's program continued. A new, improved strain of long-staple cotton from Mexico flourished in El Norte, and Camp and his sons became prominent cotton (and potato) ranchers. Over the next two decades, California cotton culture spread northward in the Central Valley past Sacramento, as well as southward, again, through the Imperial Valley. Ranchers enjoyed cheap, subsidized irrigation and abundant and mostly manageable migrant labor. And their desert environment was hostile to the boll weevil that had wrecked swaths of the humid Southeast since the 1890s. Ever progressive, too, the Californians leaped at new chemicals and machines as soon as any were offered. Already tractorized by the 1920s, they were also first to buy en masse the first cotton harvesters, just after World War II. Delta planters in the Southeast, still owners of thousands of mules and rulers of still-substantial numbers of resident croppers and tenants, dawdled at full conversion to machines, through the 1960s.

About 1971, H. L. "Mitch" Mitchell (1906–90), just retired from a long career as a farm labor organizer and human rights champion, returned to eastern Arkansas, where he had cofounded the Southern Tenant Farmers' Union in July 1934. Mitchell was well aware that both agriculture and landscapes were utterly transformed from the time of his youth. Yet driving around in Poinsett, Lonoke, and other counties once crowded with impoverished black and white cropper and tenant families, Mitch was astounded. Irreconcilable images still swam in his head a few years later as he composed his autobiography, but one set in particular struck him: On one large, well-remembered property that once supported (after a fashion) a hundred families, by the early 1970s only *three* men conducted all farming operations from their giant machines.[21] Such a property, almost without people, cannot be called a plantation. The old labor-intensive complex had finally been broken, by pre- and postemergent herbicides, petroleum-based pesticides, anhydrous ammonia (a superfertilizer that discouraged soil conservation), and huge tractors and harvesters. Hardly any workers were required, so call the place a farm, then, a big one, certainly, and a gear in the great wheel called big agriculture, or "big ag."

There remain, however, two southern geographies where chemicals and machines have yet to solve the problem of harvest, and where human hands are necessary. The smaller and more discrete is the burley tobacco culture of the mid-South, especially Kentucky. Eastern, flue-cured tobacco was subjected to mechanical harvesting, finally, at the beginning of the 1970s, but air-cured burley continues to defy inventors and engineers. Burley begins to ripen, or cure, in the field, as leaves turn a blazing yellow. Then workers move in, cut whole stalks, tie them to sticks, and hang them in well-ventilated curing barns. Hand labor is required again to take the sticks down and to strip and sort leaves for the auction houses. Tiny burley crops are still managed primarily with family labor. Larger fields, which grew in size and number with consolidations of tobacco allotments during the 1960s, require crews of nonrelated laborers. For a long time these were typically neighboring and dependent poor black folk. When those workers found opportunities elsewhere, burley farmers turned to the migrant stream from Mexico and Central America, the same workforce that supplies labor to meatpacking plants and other loci of the most disagreeable work in the country. Since the migrants are not citizens, and since many of them are "illegal" transients and/or do not speak English, they are as vulnerable as sharecroppers ever were. So plantations of a sort may be said to survive in southern places not historically associated with plantations.

This is also the case in the larger rural landscape that extends along the South Atlantic coast, from reclaimed fringes of the Everglades up through Georgia, the Carolinas, the Delmarva Peninsula, and beyond. Here lies an old citrus and vegetable "produce" belt as well as an old migrant route. Harvests of oranges, watermelons, strawberries, cucumbers, and dozens of other products remain unmechanized. So crews of workers continue to follow picking seasons northward every year. Once, these workers were overwhelmingly Afro-southerners, many of them runaway, as it were, croppers. More recently, though, migrant crews look like burley workers; they are Mesoamericans. In North Carolina, which has the largest population of legal Mexican residents in the region, a Mexican man tried to form a union among cucumber pickers to bargain collectively with a pickle-bottling company in 2002. This (thus far) failing effort may portend much, however, because these perverse shadows of plantation-style labor relations recall unhappy aspects of the last strife-torn decades of sharecropping and—perhaps more—doleful episodes in California's agricultural history.

The appearance of Spanish-speakers among the rural proletariat does not contradict our generalization about the end of the plantation complex. The new brown proletariat is a tiny one, and everywhere else, farmworkers are hardly visible. In the lower Mississippi deltas, where cotton still flourishes, many ex-plantations are now also devoted to soybeans or to rice culture, both utterly mechanized. What workers remain in this heart of what was once called the American Congo are more likely to be employed in light industries, service businesses, or casino gambling than cotton or any other agricultural commodity.

In piedmonts and hillier places across the South, plantations and all other agriculture have simply disappeared. Once-thriving ginnery compounds by rail sidings are closed, bulldozed, or rusting. Farmhouses, outbuildings, and rural general stores by the thousands are long vacant, falling in upon themselves and crowded or covered by trees. Countless rural cemeteries behind deserted churches are forgotten, nearly buried in vines and brush, with markers toppled and human remains exposed by surging tree roots. Fifty- and sixty-year-old forests stand on old crop fields, their straight "hills," or rows, still discernible to those who venture into the woods. But the piedmonts are also scenes of the most extensive (and ongoing) post–World War II suburbanization. What are now "greater" Richmond (or "the Richmond area"), Raleigh-Durham, Charlotte, Columbia, and most spectacularly, Atlanta, for example, overlie old tobacco, corn, and cotton landscapes.

Whether abandoned or suburbanized, these are principal settings for the much-heralded "greening" of the South since World War II. The expression celebrates establishment of stabilizing cover and protection for long-bare and eroded ground. If such ground is converted to suburban housing, then suburbs will be green, too, since people as well as ground must have shade, not to mention beauty. The problem with "green" for such ex-plantation country is, first, pavement—foundations, driveways, sidewalks (although these are not popular in a car culture), roads and highways and bypasses, and many more to come. There is more paving, too, for gas stations, stores, and malls. I fancy that the fictional Tara, along with a number of historical plantations in Georgia's upper piedmont, now lies beneath Hartsfield-Jackson International Airport, which has been expanding nonstop for four decades. A second problem with suburbanization is suburbs' squandering of water, a subject to be taken up in a later chapter.

Finally, much of the hilliest, most eroded landscape in the benighted South of the 1930s was indeed greened, and healed, by a storied exotic plant: kudzu. First imported from Japan at least as early as the 1920s, kudzu became popular as a quick-growing forage crop and nutritious hay. Then it proved itself an excellent bandage over wounded ground. Government agencies set crews to planting settings throughout the TVA domain, and inspectors confirmed that kudzu slowed and halted erosion, preserving what was left of sometimes jaggedly cut hills. Private individuals set out kudzu, too, and sometimes fretted that it climbed and covered utility poles and wires in short order. Once, while walking at night in a residential neighborhood near downtown Atlanta, I myself stumbled on kudzu vines streaming from a vacant lot over a public sidewalk. No wonder "Kudzu" became a long-running cartoon and comic subject for novelists and stage performers. Still, any Alabama farmboy or -girl knows that a couple of cows might easily control a three-acre field of kudzu, while the field itself remains lush and stable. What could be finer?

*There were eight of the pigs. The first thing I heard every morning at daybreak was the whole outfit crashing under the fence and rushing under the floor of my bedroom for a matutinal rubbing of backs against the crosspiece. The rubbing ended, and the grunts, my room stopped shaking. . . . [Then] the happy congregation moved on to the trays of biddy-mash, the skimmed milk and the fluffy-ruffle petunias.* —Marjorie Kinnan Rawlings, *Cross Creek*, 1942

*[My work in North Carolina] asserts a proposition which must ultimately be at the base of forest preservation in this country: namely, that it is not necessary to destroy a forest to make it pay.* —Gifford Pinchot at the Biltmore Estate, 1892

# 3

## COMMONERS AND THE COMMONS

The very first history of Virginia—Robert Beverley's, published in London in 1705—glimpses the delights of great planters' domestic lives and much else of nature and the countryside. At William Byrd's Westover on a warm day, Beverley luxuriated in Byrd's honeysuckle-covered gazebo, hummingbirds fanning his face. Beyond Byrd's carefully fenced big house and crop fields, though, there was wilderness-apparent, plus innumerable packs of swine running at large and amok. "Hogs swarm like Vermine upon the Earth," Beverley wrote, "and are often accounted such, inasmuch that when an Inventory of any considerable man's Estate is taken by the Executors, the Hogs are left out, and not listed in the Appraisement." Counted or not, "the hogs run where they list, and find their own Support in the Woods, without the Care of the Owner." Twenty-three years later, Byrd himself, on the North Carolina side of the Great Dismal Swamp, supervising the survey of a dividing line with Virginia, scoffed at the laziness of locals: "The only Business here is raising of Hogs," he observed, "which is manag'd with the least Trouble, and afford the Diet they are most fond of." Only five years later (in 1733), the governor of North Carolina reported that in good mast years, 50,000 fat hogs were driven through his colony to Virginia ports, suggesting that supposedly indolent Carolinians not only subsisted on range swine but were engaged in a well-organized and lucrative market. Planters were not the only southern white folk in business.

More than a century later, toward the end of 1852, Frederick Law Olmsted, riding alone in Prince George County, Virginia (downriver from Westover, in Edmund Ruffin's old neighborhood), experienced scenes hardly unlike Robert Beverley's: sparse human populations, seemingly endless pine forests, and squadrons of hogs darting across his trail as though, he wrote, on a fox hunt—all this in a tidewater countryside settled by Europeans for almost 250 years. By this time, federal census takers were trying, at least, to enumerate farm animals, including pigs. In 1850 and again in 1860, there were at least twice as many hogs as humans in the Virginia "Southside" (i.e., below James River) tidewater and adjacent northeastern North Carolina. The count was probably low, especially of swine belonging to the middling classes of white and free black farmers and herders. Planters were not only disciplined record keepers, but some of them had already begun to confine their animals. In Prince George County's riverside precincts, for instance, Edmund Ruffin had initiated creation of a "ring fence association" more than a decade before Olmsted's sojourn. The ring fence enclosed all cooperating and contiguous plantations, so their masters might pen their cattle and hogs instead of their crop fields, saving enormous expenses for fencing and permitting close management of livestock. Still, this was an exceptional practice.[1]

Everywhere else the open range prevailed and would long endure. Owners of hogs made some attempt to keep track of the animals. They rounded them up each fall, usually, sometimes with herding dogs; checked their identifying marks (usually notches cut in ears); and marked new litters. Bigger hogs were held for fattening and winter slaughter, and the rest were set at large once more. In what were called "good mast" years, sows gorged on acorns and other nuts, pine seeds, and plant shoots and roots and probably dropped larger litters. By any account, though, swine, and often cattle as well, were the foundation of the cultures and economies of the masses of white southerners and not a few free Afro-southerners.

If good estimates of the number of swine versus humans in the longest-settled parts of the South surprise, figures on newer Euro-southern locales in the nineteenth century may amaze. Grady McWhiney, the most authoritative chronicler of southern herding, reports that in 1840, in twenty-five of Mississippi's thirty-two southern, piney-woods counties, hogs and beef cattle outnumbered people four-to-one; in Greene and Perry counties the ratio was thirteen-to-one. At the next federal census—after Mississippi's south had become more populous—twenty-three counties still had four times as many cattle and hogs as humans. So it was throughout the piney coastal regions by the Atlantic and the Gulf, but hardly less so in piedmonts and other upland places on both sides of the Appalachians. Southern farms (not plantations) were nearly twice as large as average northern ones—384 versus 203 acres in 1850—but typically worth less than a quarter of the value of Yankee farms. This was owing to southerners' economy of minor cultivation (relative to farm size) mixed with extensive range herding. Most southern farms consisted overwhelmingly of woods, which collectively, along with planters' woods and publicly owned forests, comprised an enormous land commons. Ordinary southern farm owners' crops may or may not have included surpluses for market, but in meat-for-market they were massively engaged participants. A substantial minority of southern herdsmen owned no land at all, yet they were men of substance nonetheless. McWhiney identifies a number of landless Alabamians—one, for instance, with 160 cattle and 250 hogs worth $2,104, another with 200 cows and 70 swine worth $1,390, and a third owning 15 cattle plus 300 hogs at $808. Such numbers indicate much more than capacity for family subsistence. Like landowning and farming herders, the landless were also marketers. In 1849 alone, 124,000-odd swine passed through Cumberland Gap and Asheville, North Carolina (along what was called the "Great Kaintuck Hog Highway"), on their way to seaport markets. McWhiney calculates that during the last fifteen years of the antebellum era, southerners drove and/or marketed no fewer than 67,026,000 hogs, an annual average of 4,468,400. Compare this with the much-better-known postbellum (1866–80) cattle business centered in Texas: The annual average was 280,000; the grand total, 4,223,497.[2]

No wonder that typical farms seemed carelessly, even sloppily, operated and that the southern yeomanry (as small and middling owners have ever been called) were, with few exceptions, viewed as the great obstacle to improvement. Edmund Ruffin and most other agronomic reformers ignored them, generally, as hopeless. Outsiders such as Olmsted deemed them intractable. Nonlandowners were everywhere condemned by the privileged and educated, who actually knew little of the scope of the meat market and nothing of the culture of herding folks.

Consider another famous commentator, Frances Anne "Fanny" Kemble, and her informants among the island plantations of Georgia. A celebrated leading lady of the English theater, Kemble was touring the United States during the 1830s when she met and married the fabulously wealthy Philadelphian Pierce Butler. Butler's fortune rested in part on his family's hundreds of slaves and huge rice and sea-island cotton plantations on Saint Simons and Butler islands. Fanny went to live on Pierce's Butler Island estate, then Saint Simons, for fifteen weeks, from the end of December 1838 into April 1839. There she delighted (for a while) in engaging company, gardens, and walks along edges of fields and forests. She was morbidly curious about rattlesnakes until house slaves brought her a freshly killed specimen. Meanwhile Fanny, already deeply committed to the international abolitionist movement, grew more appalled at the institution of slavery from her daily exposure. So she began a journal (in the format of letters) that frequently gave expression to her mounting disquiet. Decades later, divorced from Butler and at home in England, her *Journal of a Residence on a Georgian Plantation* was finally published, in 1863, the very year of Abraham Lincoln's proclamation. Kemble's book brims with fascinating minutae as well as reflective thought on coastal Georgia, slavery, and much else, including nearby rustic folks called "pinelanders." Here she absorbed and perpetuated a compelling myth that dissolved social stratifications among what the aristocracy perceived as the lower reaches, revealing a persistent outsiders' blind spot to the real economy and culture of the piney woods.

One evening "after dinner," Kemble wrote, she had "a most interesting conversation with Mr. K," Roswell King Jr., who was Pierce Butler's plantation manager, a shrewd and learned gentleman and an agronomic improver. "Among other subjects, he gave me a lively and curious description of the yeomanry of Georgia," she went on, "more properly termed pinelanders." Fanny carried British conceptual baggage, naturally, and properly associated the word "yeoman" with "well-to-do farmers with comfortable homesteads, decent habits, industrious, intelligent, cheerful, and thrifty[.] Such, however, is not the yeomanry of Georgia." Slavery had degraded all labor, so white men without slaves refused to exert themselves, choosing their own degradation but compensating with racial pride and bluster. The poorest among them "squat (most appropriately is it so termed) either on other men's land or government districts—always near swamp or pine barren—and claim masterdom over the place they invade till ejected by the rightful proprietors." Their shelters were abominable, and "their food [was] chiefly supplied by shooting the wildfowl and venison, and stealing from the cultivated patches of the plantations nearest at hand." Pinelanders' "clothes hang about them in filthy tatters, and the combined squalor and fierceness of their appearance is really frightful." Such was her summary take on King's revelations. Later, speaking for herself, Fanny declared "the so-called pinelanders of Georgia . . . the most degraded race of human beings claiming Anglo-Saxon origin that can be found on the face of the earth—filthy, lazy, ignorant, brutal, proud, penniless savages, without one of the nobler attributes which have been found occasionally allied to the vices of savage nature."[3]

The characterizations—both King's and Kemble's—are ignorant and reflect, among other things, fear of fundamental disorder and a loathing of the countercultural in brother Anglo-Saxons that had perplexed and disgusted the planter class for generations. William Byrd II is usually credited with invention of the "poor white trash" stereotype when he encountered shiftless "lubbers" (as he termed them) in the Great Dismal Swamp. It was Edmund Ruffin, however, who first published Byrd's *History of the Dividing Line* in his *Farmers' Register*. This was the era of a wild Southwest much celebrated and joked about by learned sojourners from more civilized places —Davy Crockett in his outrageous *Autobiography*, for instance; Augustus Baldwin Longstreet in *Georgia Scenes* (1835); and later, Joseph G. Baldwin in *The Flush Times of Alabama and Mississippi* (1853).

Fullest elaboration and confirmation of Byrd's disdain for human trash actually awaited the twentieth century and the best-sellerdom of novelist Erskine Caldwell. Crockett, Longstreet, Baldwin, and other antebellum tale tellers and sketch writers may have condescended a bit, but mainly they celebrated a rowdy, disordered southern backwoods filled with male characters—poseurs, cheats, innocents (usually "Virginians"), and boasters— who anticipate the works of Mark Twain. Baldwin's Ovid Bolus, Esq., is emblematic owing to his theatrical mendacity. As Baldwin wrote,

> Some men are liars from interest; not because they have no regard for truth, but because they have less regard for it than for gain: some are liars from vanity, because they would rather be well thought of by others, than have reason for thinking well of themselves: some are liars from a sort of necessity, which overbears. . . . Bolus was none of these: he belonged to a higher department of the fine arts, and to a higher class of professors of this sort of Belles-Lettres. Bolus was a natural liar. . . . Accordingly, he did not labor to lie: he lied with a relish: he lied with a coming appetite. . . . He lied from the delight of invention and the charm of fictitious narrative.

Of course Ovid Bolus was a lawyer; our eagerness to mock the profession is timeless. But Bolus is also a representative backwoods white southerner.

He is a "cracker," actually. The expression, about 400 years old in English popular usage, means one who boasts, cracks wise, exaggerates, and lies for the sheer story-making joy of it.[4]

Expressive narrative traditions as well as certain economic behaviors —such as ranging hogs and cattle and neglecting farming—often bleed past conventional categories of social class. Bolus the fictional lawyer was brother to other Alabamians, roughly dressed, who waxed outrageous in speech by campfires along the hog trails to Mobile. Daniel R. Hundley, an Alabama gentleman and soon to be a Confederate officer, in 1860 became the region's first serious sociologist with publication of *Social Relations in Our Southern States*. Crackers as herders and cultural types are hardly seen, but Hundley devoted large chapters both to "The Middle Classes" —townspeople, storekeepers, craftsmen, and clerks—and to "The Southern Yeoman," who while modestly prosperous to "poor," bore more resemblance to the English yeomanry than Fanny Kemble's pinelanders. Hundley devoted other chapters to a sort of moral typology overlying economic standing. "The Southern Gentleman" was ideal; "The Cotton Snob," a disgusting failure of restraint and responsibility. "Poor White Trash" received thirty-two pages of mostly reflective, indirect treatment but finally a sad resignation to heredity and God's will—Europe and the North had their poor, too, after all. "The Southern Bully" approaches aspects of the cracker tradition in his violence and braggadocio, though little else.[5]

Considering the enormous volumes and values of the antebellum pork and beef markets, one might guess with confidence that herders were roughly the equivalent of what twentieth-century sociology would call middle- and lower-middle-class folk. These included yeomen who were serious, perhaps even improving, farmers, plus the legendarily "careless" farmers who preferred ranging and droving to cultivation, but also numbers of the landless who, if not even moderately well-off, were comfortable enough by their own lights, from the animal business alone. These last were hardly "trash," save in the eyes of the comfortably ignorant, whose loathing was ever mingled with fear. So what then, of the ecology of these masses of white southerners and their culture?

Eurasian domesticated animals—horses, cattle, hogs, but also sheep, goats, dogs, and cats—were from the beginning great disturbers of New World environments. Their hooves and feet, whether shod, hard, or soft, trampled, compacted, but especially stirred the earth, providing opportunity for a variety of Old World plants to establish themselves. These were sometimes purposefully introduced—seeds and seedlings for familiar European field crops, kitchen gardens, and ornamentals—but most species were introduced inadvertently, clinging to bedding, clothes, and bagging, but also clinging to domestic animals' hides or surviving journeys through animals' alimentary canals. One visualizes cows browsing among American tidewater marsh grasses, simultaneously plopping European plant seeds in their meandering paths, or swine rooting and devouring tender shoots on forest floors, leaving behind in hog-plowed ground a variety of foreign plants buried in fertilizer. What emerged, principally, was "weeds," that is, opportunistic, fast-growing plants that healed an earth much disturbed by teeming herds, squadrons, flocks, and packs. The weeds soon became ubiquitous, as they remain today: dandelion, plantain, nightshade, black henbane, white clover, Saint-John's-wort, barberry, corn cockle, cress, and a host of others, including a grass later (and imperially) named Kentucky bluegrass. One can hardly visualize the stunning conquest by Eurasian flora throughout humid eastern North America and on to the plains and deserts of the West and Mexico without the agency of invading domestic animals.

All the animals listed above figured in transformations of southern landscapes. Many country people kept at least a few sheep, for instance, for wool, and a few spots of the region supported considerable numbers, with predictably resulting bare, gnawed-away hills. Goats were not much favored. Cattle were, as already seen, very important. But the South was really the region of the hog. Their numbers amaze, still, and are reflected well in human culture. Until recently, "meat" in the South meant pork. (Beef was beef.) To be in "hog heaven"—an old southern exultation—suggests every sensual gratification. "High on the hog" is ambition—not that pigs' feet were scorned. Best of all was the whole skinned and cleaned hog, cooked for many hours outside over an open pit filled with the charcoal of hickory and basted lovingly with a perfect sauce of vinegar and red peppers. The next day entire extended families or neighborhoods or congregations or hordes of sovereign voters might "pull" the pork in celebration. The meat would be tender—some juicy, some ("outside meat") crisp—all of it sublime. This was, of course, "barbeque," the European and African American-ization of a native Caribbean word and grilling apparatus imported, in all likelihood, by the Spanish. The word, the fuel, and the peppers essential to basting and sauce are native—unless the peppers are of African origin; the animal and vinegar are European, rendering the most magnificent hybrid imaginable, beyond the blending of the three peoples themselves. Barbeque is pork (never beef, unforgivably never chicken), and it is as much as anything the unifying substance of that pesky abstraction, the South. Long before the mule, hogs were the icons and factotums of southern being.

Meanwhile, swine have ever been interesting and not unproblematic creatures. Stigmatized as filthy at least as long as they have been regularly confined, pigs are not necessarily so. Since they cool themselves by sweating through their nostrils, not pores in their skin, swine trapped in hot pens will wallow in mud to protect themselves. Their natural habitat is the shady forest, where they are comfortable and (relatively) clean, and where feral hogs' strong, long legs propel them toward food and other pleasures at surprising speed. Their snouts, ending with tough, cartilaginous rooters, are perfect for disturbing even compacted soils. The range (or wild or feral) hogs of the sixteenth through the nineteenth centuries bore scant resemblance to swine bred and confined during the late nineteenth and twentieth centuries. The first of these new hogs, many of them engineered in the Miami Valley of Ohio—most famously one called the Poland-China—were enormous creatures, slow-moving on relatively small trotters, their tusks removed for their own and humans' safety. Much more recently, in obeisance to a weight-conscious market, hogs have become slimmer and leaner but still only remotely resemble the "razorbacks" of old. These were (as the nickname suggests) high-backed animals, tall on legs not only long and swift but capable of jumping fences. They were quite hairy, with snouts longer than contemporary pigs', tougher rooting instruments, and long and menacing tusks. Gordon Grice, biographer of predators, not only counts swine critical among the causes of the extinction of the dodo in Mauritius about 300 years ago but claims an angry adult boar might actually amputate a man's arm with his tusk.[6]

Often thought vegetarian, swine are actually vigorously omnivorous. Dodos, flightless birds related to doves, which had never encountered predators, were easy pickings for the hogs Europeans deposited on Mauritius and thousands of other islands and mainlands over the centuries. Hogs will also take frogs, lizards, and snakes—even rattlesnakes. Grice watched a litter of piglets devour a road-killed skunk thrown among them. More famously, everywhere farmers have confined hogs, there are stories of the elderly farmer who went to feed his pigs and did not return. His wife searches the pen but finds only his bloody hat. The unfortunate man had suffered a stroke or heart attack, fell helpless among his rooting property, and was eaten, dead or alive. The legend, which persists in our era, extends a good (although hypothesized) explanation for the prohibition of pork-eating in the holy texts of Jews, Christians, and Muslims, namely, that in the

Holy Land, where some people buried their dead in caves, swine broke in and consumed corpses. How then, did European Christians diverge? Medievalists conjecture, to put it simply, that Christians ate pork to demonstrate their non-Jewishness in times of anti-Semitic hysteria—not to mention the pig's ubiquity in European forests as a source of protein.

Whatever, modern Christians of the American South not only consumed mountains of barbeque, but as we have observed, the great majority of the white population—nonslaveholding or owners of very few—built a thriving economy on swine. The economy, in turn, was founded on colonial era laws, beginning with Virginia's, establishing the open range. Forests, great enemy of civilization and light, would provide not only the countless miles of fencing to protect crops but endless shelter and nourishment for animals ranging freely. Any forest—or unfenced creek bank, meadow, savannah, swamp, or other wetland—no matter if privately held, was part of the vast commons. The commons and the pig (sometimes the cow, as well) were in turn the ordinary person's, especially the poor person's, wealth. This was so because one did not have to devote cropland to feeding stock, except a small portion, perhaps, before slaughter and home use of pork. By the 1830s and 1840s, the range had been closed in the Northeast and most of the Old Northwest, imposing reapportionment of farm resources on small farmers and, among the smallest among them, outright privation. Not so in the antebellum South, despite Edmund Ruffin's best efforts to "reform" fence law in Virginia, during the 1830s. In this sense the South was clearly the more democratic region. Ruffin and legions of other planters raged that poor neighbors' beasts perennially damaged their fences, crops, and pastures. When planters took owners of intrusive animals to court, juries were usually unsympathetic to the planters. Ruffin and his ilk took no pleasure in the knowledge that many landless, shabbily dressed men actually possessed modest wealth in animals—sustained on other men's property. That such men had the franchise, too, meant that the range was likely to remain open.[7]

Aside from their frequent damage to fences and crops, swine surely affected the commons profoundly, given their numbers. Like cattle, they fouled watercourses and their banks with wastes. They consumed plant seedlings or killed plants by devouring their roots. Native squirrels had gathered nuts of oak, chestnut, walnut, and other mast trees immemorially before Europeans deposited the first pair of pigs on a North American shore. Now swarms of thousands of hogs—whether galloping freely or herded through forests—scooped up uncountable nuts. Conceivably hogs

*Marjorie Kinnan Rawlings at her garden fence, Cross Creek, ca. 1940s.*
*Courtesy Florida State Archives.*

contributed to the "degradation" of forests, reducing the proportion of hardwood deciduous species in relation to pines. Ruffin, among others, shared this bias against conifers but blamed excessive fencing requirements on reductions of deciduous trees, not on hogs' browsing. Pines probably did gain in proportion to deciduous trees over the long term, but it seems more likely that burning forests to clear land, then reburning a decade or two or three later, was more responsible than hungry swine. Pines generally grow faster than deciduous trees, taking over disturbed places and quickly forming canopies that retard competition until the next burning.

The more plausible victim of hogs-on-the-range is actually a pine, the longleaf, most magnificent (in my opinion) of all southern conifers. Fire is friendliest to longleaves, whose outsized seeds, nestled in large fallen cones, require heat to pop them out onto ashes covering fire-disturbed ground. Unique among conifers, however, longleaves, once sprouted, experience a prolonged infancy—sometimes as much as a decade—called their grass stage. The expression refers to very young seedlings standing only a foot or two high but already festooned with leaves (or needles) at least twelve inches long. At the top center of a grass-stage longleaf protrudes the plant's bare, almost milky-white terminal bud, about the size of an adult human's index finger. When conditions are right—when the taproot has reached a safe depth and when rains and sunlight are sufficient—the tree takes flight, ultimately, if all goes well, reaching 175 feet. Meanwhile, though, the grass-stage longleaf is vulnerable to fire and to hogs. For that terminal bud, virtually pure protein, stands at eye-level to the typical foraging pig, a treat perhaps to be compared to barbeque.

So, one might figure, in 1733, when the governor of North Carolina reported that 50,000-odd hogs were herded from his colony's interior northeastward to Virginia ports—presumably Smithfield (already a pork-packing town on the James), Portsmouth, and Norfolk—the horde marched through the northernmost range of the longleaf, especially through Southampton, Isle of Wight, and Nansemond counties. If each hog found but one grass-stage tree along the way, then 50,000 longleaves were not to be, chawed-in-the-bud. A century later, the hog drives to James River and Hampton Roads continued, now from south-central and southwestern Virginia as well as North Carolina—all this atop the considerable local ranging population that browsed the forests year-round. But by 1843 (as the traveling New York poet and editor William Cullen Bryant reported), the longleaf was extinct in Virginia.[8] Multiply the too-conservative estimate of longleaves killed in one hog drive to Virginia in 1733 by McWhiney's figures of annual drives the last fifteen antebellum years—to other Atlantic and to Gulf ports—and the diminution of many thousands of square miles of longleaf forests becomes overwhelming. No wonder the species is gravely endangered today, its ultimate extinction predicted annually.

This scenario may be true enough, but not quite true. First, near the Blackwater River in far southern Isle of Wight County, well into the twentieth century a stand of longleaves was found by lumber and paper industry cruisers. Nearby were barely visible remains of turpentine stills from the 1930s, and stumps of long-ago-cut trees revealed marks showing that the trees were "boxed" to tap resin for turpentine distilling. There were also grass-stage longleaves scattered about. The tree had survived, if barely, in Virginia after all. During the 1980s the lumber/paper company (Union-Camp) gave the little grove to Old Dominion University, which in turn chartered the Blackwater Ecologic Preserve. Managers regularly burn the forest floor so longleaf regeneration may be assured. Meanwhile, the remains of turpentine distilleries and the old slash wounds on stumps of long-cut longleaves suggest a different cause for longleaves' near-demise. The crackers' hogs had their day, but it was naval stores entrepreneurs who must bear major responsibility for prolonged, massive depredations of the magnificent longleaf pine.

🌿 The naval stores industry is at least as old as sailing ships. Wooden hulls bore up better if protected with tar and pitch, which with caulking not only sealed out water but discouraged shipworms. Miles of roping to manage sails needed protection, too. No wonder that sailors handling lines and climbing rope ladders were called tars by English-speakers. During the seventeenth century, as England became deforested principally from the building of its own navies, Scandinavian naval-stores producers achieved, collectively, near-monopolistic control over the industry. The mercantilist response of the British, new imperialists, was promotion of tar, pitch, and resin production in America. So was born the first and longest-lived "First Wave" southern industry, especially in North Carolina, where a northeastern river is named the Tar and whose people, even now, are known as Tar Heels.

In America the naval stores industry had an up-and-down history, starting before 1700 and persisting through the colonial era. Production was outrageously wasteful there. Workers made open, elongated pits of clay, piled the pits with pine logs and limbs, and set them ablaze. As the wood disintegrated, its liquid remains drained into catchments; workers collected the muck and, with little processing or cleaning, poured it into barrels—the making of which, incidentally, enormously enlarged a cooperage trade and business already devoted to tobacco hogsheads and brandy casks. One of the reasons for the instability of the American naval stores business was the vagaries of demand, particularly from the British. Another was the recurring complaint that American tar and pitch were bad—trashy, inconsistent in viscosity, and spoiled from over-long storage in hot sun. Scandinavians may have been independent of British control and thus a national security worry, but they made good naval stores and were much less wasteful.

After American independence, tar and pitch production persisted, albeit mostly on the unreliable national market. It was a new pine product, also diffused from European ingenuity, that revolutionized the industry. This was turpentine. By the 1830s and 1840s, turpentine had become an early, hugely successful commercial medicinal. It was used as an external analgesic, taken orally for a host of complaints, and employed as an enema. Turpentine also became an illuminating fuel, set to rival whale oil, and an industrial chemical with ever-multiplying uses—for example, in paint manufacturing. Carolina entrepreneurs rose to the demand and in a generation radically altered the coastal countryside.[9]

Like Virginia's tidewater, eastern North Carolina possessed a few strands of rich earth along tidal rivers that attracted planters and built wealth on slavery. For the most part, though, soils there are sandy and acidic, and the forest cover is predominantly, often exclusively, conifers—sure signs of not-good farming country. It was turpentining that converted such a countryside into something very much like plantations. By the 1830s, enterprising capitalists with slaves (owned and/or leased) bought up or leased the vast "groves" (also called "orchards") of longleaf pines between the coast and fall line. White and sometimes black riding bosses supervised hundreds of slaves, overwhelmingly men, in the boxing of tree trunks and collection of dripping resin. Conventionally, a mature tree was to be tapped via two boxes, which were chevron-shaped cuts first made fairly close to ground level. Crude, portable distilleries, operated usually by white journeymen, followed the progress of the harvest. Markets were almost consistently good, prices were rising, and turpentine men could resist neither new technology, such as larger, more efficient, and stationary stills nor extending the slashing of bark from two to four or more boxes.

Throughout the 1840s, travelers such as William Cullen Bryant and a host of local people not directly connected to the industry, decried "over-boxing" and wanton killing of longleaves. The predicted, calamitous collapse of the North Carolina industry came soon enough, in a space of only a couple of years at the end of the decade. Its suddenness seems unreasonable, but the historian Robert Outland has provided a plausible combination of factors that renders the sudden death of so many longleaves understandable enough: boxing, certainly overboxing, strained the trees. Boxes opened the trees to massive parasitic invasions that further weakened them. Unfavorable weather, low numbers of bird predators of invading insects, and other serendipitous elements finished off the longleaves. They never recovered, since longleaves almost always coexist with another conifer, the loblolly, that regenerates easily and more rapidly, shading out grass-stage longleaves. So-called "old-field pines," ubiquitous in abandoned croplands, were almost certainly loblollies.

Beginning about 1850, the North Carolina turpentiners simply went south and restarted their businesses in South Carolina and especially in Georgia and northern Florida, where they boxed slash pines as well as longleaves. The Civil War was an inconvenience; mostly the new turpentine groves underwent, in about the same amount of time, the disastrous experience of the North Carolina longleaves. By the 1880s the new groves were ruined and dying, too, so the turpentiners spread westward along the Gulf's sandy plains. The turpentine market had become weaker and less enriching, though, with the appearance of competitors in the medical, illumination, and chemical industries. The development of government-sponsored research and professional forestry forced turpentiners to moderate their wasteful ways. French turpentiners, meanwhile, had demonstrated not only successful conservation of pines but a far more efficient ceramic cup to catch resin. Charles Herty, Georgia-born chemist and entrepreneur, modified and patented his own cup for manufacture and sale to the southern industry. Still, the industry, now old and running out of resources, was slowly dying.

One must say, in retrospect, good riddance. Much of the enormous expanse of the piney-woods southern commons was compromised. And then there was the industry's cruel record with its laborers. After emancipation, turpentiners became principal lessors, especially in Georgia and Florida, of state and local prison populations. These men were overwhelmingly freedmen and were treated, not unexpectedly, worse than slaves, since their labor cost so little and was so easily and cheaply replaced. Other "free"

*Overboxed turpentine pine near Valdosta, Georgia, 1936.*

*Photo by Carl Mydans. Courtesy Library of Congress (LC-USF34-006714-D).*

workers the industry ensnared by debt to company stores no less hopelessly than contemporary coal miners. It seems entirely possible that more turpentine workers became de facto slaves—that is, caught in debt peonage—than cotton sharecroppers. Yet even as these doleful postbellum decades dragged on in the forested South, the commons suffered other wounds, the commoners' elemental economy was restructured, and the region was reformed ecologically and politically. The reformation seems unthinkable without the manifold destructions of the Civil War.

First, of course, the war reduced the white male, mostly young adult, population by more than a quarter-million, unevening the sex ratio and connubial and other opportunities for women for perhaps a generation. Many of the dead were victims of disease, often "old" maladies that Europeans had inflicted on natives long before yet were still capable of killing Euro-Americans. Scarlett O'Hara's hastily married first husband in *Gone with the Wind*, one will recall, perished not in battle but in camp, of measles, as did many nonfictional men on both sides. The United States remained an overwhelmingly rural nation in 1861, the South somewhat more so than the North, and isolated people, brought together in masses for induction and training, exchanged pathogens, sickened, and sometimes died. Southerners became, temporarily anyway, an urban and a seriously ill people. Existing industrial cities such as Richmond and Augusta grew enormously, along with new production sites, in response to war. So newly crowded civilians suffered as well.

Horses and mules also perished by the thousands, as eastern military fronts drew essential cavalry mounts, artillery caisson- and wagon-pullers, and pack animals from virtually the whole continent. Horses and mules, too, were congregated en masse from relatively isolated and disparate places and paid the price. Equine glanders, a killer apparently unknown in Virginia before 1860, became a plague persisting to the end of the war. Late in 1864, on a single day at a northern Virginia depot, a Union captain ordered the shooting of 311 poor horses. They amounted to a pittance among many thousands of glanders victims who perished more slowly. Survivors, meanwhile, were maimed and killed by the thousands in battle, if not worked to death carrying troops and supplies to battle sites. Since the carcasses of mules and horses are so much larger than men's, their remains presented daunting sanitary challenges after battles. Onsite burial was usually hasty and incomplete, and nature, according to some observers, was little help in disposal. Edmund Ruffin, for instance, kibitzing on Virginia fronts during the first half of the war, reported that vultures, previously ubiquitous, were nowhere to be seen. He conjectured that they were frightened away during battles by the noise, particularly of artillery. Perhaps the only blessing derived from the war's equine carnage was what may be termed the real beginning of modern veterinary medicine, especially the etiology of glanders.[10]

Hogs massed in pens came down with hog cholera during the war, and cattle, sheep, and other food creatures suffered as well. What was worse was simply the mass consumption of cattle, hogs, and sheep by soldiers of both sides, wherever the war was fought. Usually the animals were simply appropriated as troops marched and camped. Some were confined; most, presumably, were at large in the same forests occupied by units on the move or encamped waiting for battle. Here and there are officers' reports that enumerate the casualties. Most famous, perhaps, was Union general Philip Sheridan's account of his 1864 scourge of the civilian population of the Valley of Virginia. In addition to the 3,772 horses and 545 mules Sheridan's men appropriated without compensation to Shenandoah owners, he reported the confiscation of more than 11,000 cattle and calves, 12,000 sheep, and 15,000 hogs. The last three groups were doubtlessly consumed by Yankee troops. Overall, though, we cannot count the animals lost, except by comparing figures in the federal censuses of 1860 and 1870, the latter, of course, taken after five years of peace and (presumed) recovery of populations. In seventeen counties of eastern Virginia and North Carolina—a section of the immense piney-woods South long settled and with many hogs, albeit not nearly so many as, say, southern Mississippi—in 1870, swine still numbered somewhat less than half the total of 1860. The war's crippling of the region's ability to feed itself, indeed, seems almost permanent. For succeeding censuses through 1920 reveal that the late antebellum hog population *never* recovered. (We shall return to this subject.)

Meanwhile the war destroyed something else associated with hogs, cattle, and the commons: farm fencing. Hundreds of thousands of soldiers living in the field seldom found ready-made housing with stacks of firewood just outside. More often soldiers were relentless woodsmen and scavengers. They downed and trimmed countless trees for log winter quarters, gun emplacements, and combat shelters. Desperate need of fuel for heating and cooking led troops on both sides virtually to strip the South of thousands of miles of split-rail fencing. The phenomenon complemented the

*Massachusetts soldiers carrying away fence rails, North Carolina, 1862.*
*Courtesy North Carolina Collection, University of North Carolina Library, Chapel Hill.*

near-eradication of cattle and hogs in combat zones: no ranging animals to speak of, no need for crop field protection.

Certainly the war marked the beginning of the end of the open range. This would require decades of political struggles. In some states these grew heated by the 1880s; in others the dispute continued until the second decade of the twentieth century, when the authority of professional agronomists and foresters, who all favored closing the range, added irrepressible weight to the argument for confinement. Edmund Ruffin and other improving planters would have been delighted. Even then, some states' county-option scheme for closing the range left pockets of the old world of razor-backs as late as World War II—in remote rural Appalachia, for instance, and in Marjorie Kinnan Rawlings's Alachua County, Florida.

The long view of these protracted struggles over the range, however, might be that they were more about ordinary and poor men's traditions and dreams of renewal than about substance. Not only were meat animals massively slaughtered in wartime, not to recover in absolute numbers until well into the twentieth century, but the broad region's human population growth surged quickly, negating war losses and an unbalanced ratio between the sexes. Fewer animals, in other words, supported far more middling and poor folks. Enormously worsening the postbellum ratio between animals and humans, one must also calculate, was the sudden and massive augmentation of the free, but generally quite poor, population at the close of the war. Black southerners never realized their dream of a stake in society as recompense for their enslavement—the "forty acres and a mule" for every emancipated household. Instead they were thrown into the labor market helpless, for the most part. Two centuries and more before, penniless Europeans had come to America as indentured servants, served their five or seven years, and became free. Whether or not they received from the crown a "head-right" of fifty acres (as in Virginia), such men and women might and could secure themselves in the vast commons. Typically they bought, begged, or appropriated a few range hogs, marked them, and let them gorge on whatever nature presented. The ambitious and lucky might ultimately thrive. Most, it seems, rose rapidly to the cracker sub-classes, content to work (or not) when they wished yet participate in markets near and far that provided cash enough. Beginning with the Civil War, and more direly after 1880 or so, poor white men lost out and became dependent. Few black folks ever saw such an opportunity. Instead, they were swept up in dependency from the start, becoming mere grubbing operatives in the stunning recovery and expansion of the cotton kingdom and other, new, industrial principalities.

✿ For all the devastation of war—to people, animals, farms and plantations, cities, and forests—the so-called New South not only burgeoned rapidly but made important contributions to U.S. westward expansion. First, the South not only remained an agricultural region of global significance, but it expanded commodity production and exports during the postwar decades and long thereafter. Astoundingly, southern cotton harvests at the end of the nineteenth century were *triple* the production of 1860. The expansion was accomplished in part by reconstruction of antebellum farms and plantations, but more by territorial expansion: the clearing of swampy forests, notably in the Yazoo-Mississippi Delta, then across the Mississippi in northeastern Arkansas and southeastern Missouri; the deforesting of upper piedmont and low mountain landscapes (e.g., in northwestern Georgia and parts of Ozark Arkansas); then an invasion of cotton culture into the subhumid Southwest—central Oklahoma and Texas—and later, during the twentieth century, onto the southern high plains themselves. A few postbellum cotton growers were newcomers, Yankee and foreign opportunists; most, however, were white and black southerners, mobile people, some rich but most poor, scions of large families that survived the war and produced yet larger families of their own. The postbellum population boomed, labor was cheap, and the war's great losses were no impediment to vast growth. Likewise the supply of agricultural power—horses and especially mules—recovered quickly and expanded. Missouri, Kentucky, and Tennessee, as in antebellum times, were the great postbellum breeders and sellers, to be joined by Texas early in the twentieth century. Railroad construction propelled everything, sometimes following but usually leading territorial advances of cotton and corn.[11]

The Civil War's destruction of countless trees—relentless harvests by soldiers as well as burning both intended and inadvertent—was not to be fixed in less than a generation, as was cotton production. The ravages of war, though, must be considered within the very large chronological context that forest history nearly always requires. The holocaust within the 1864 Battle of the Wilderness, for example, was a horror uncomfortable to revisit: wailing, wounded men trapped by fire, and horses and mules screaming, roasting alive. Yet this burned-over patch of north-central Virginia after the battle hardly compares with alterations of forests wrought by at least a thousand years of human management (and carelessness). Native southerners were, after all, deliberate and systematic arsonists. They cleared countless Mississippian crop fields this way, and they and their Woodlands ancestors cleared much more land to open deer and bison pastures to sunlight. Throughout the Appalachians and Ozarks, mountain-ridge "balds," a mystery to white travelers later, were almost certainly native fire-managed hunting spots. And the great Valley of Virginia, scourged by Sheridan's troops during the summer of 1864, had already been an ancient—and giant—pasture and hunting park created by natives. European settlers were hardly less addicted to fire, employing the torch to create their own crop fields and, after some years of abandonment—fallow, really—returning to burn again. As ever, too, sometimes fire got out of hand. Altogether, the millennium-plus of fire must have yielded landscapes much more coniferous than would be "natural" without human intervention—and this long before antebellum planters' complaints that hardwoods were becoming scarce and expensive because of demands for "good" wood for fencing.

Still, one must be awed by what remained of the South's forests—deciduous as well as piney—ca. 1865, 1895, up to about 1920. Before an introduced blight doomed American chestnuts, for example, these huge and noble trees almost dominated the canopies of much of the southern Appalachian chain. Other species of hardwoods still thrived in the foothills and lower piedmonts, too. And the ongoing destruction of longleaf pines in the coastal plains notwithstanding, the piney woods remained relatively healthy and enormous, albeit clearly less diverse than before. The loblolly pine was doubtlessly the reason. Loblollies are the great weeds of the piney woods and piedmonts. In the eighteenth and nineteenth centuries, they were more often referred to simply as "old field pines," reflecting confident observation that when crop fields were abandoned, the first woody plants to appear, other than barberry and other shrubs, were prolific loblollies. These grew quickly and created canopies that discouraged competing plants. Left alone indefinitely, such old fields might produce taller deciduous species, too, that could shade out pines; but such fields were usually burned again, while loblollies still prevailed, the burning perpetuating the cycle of loblolly dominance. During the twentieth century, loblollies became the principal raw material for a new southern pulp- and paper-manufacturing industry, and they were harvested early for this purpose. In the nineteenth century and even today, however, loblollies may grow to great heights, almost as tall as longleaves, and make respectable lumber for building. This indeed was the loblolly's fate—and that of every other marketable species of tree—with a vengeance, beginning about 1890.

Logging is a very old business. Throughout eastern North America, most rural, farming households engaged their strong men and draft animals in logging every winter. Typically, men kept mental inventories of saleable trees while hunting. The great obstacle to taking many specimens, though, was a tree's location. A big, straight white oak, say, towering over a deep creek or beside a road would be ideal—that is, easy to strip and float or drag to market. Trees in boggy swamps, in steep ravines, or in other difficult and distant spots were problematic, and they would not be harvested for a very long time. A good stripped log might be chained to a harnessed ox, horse, or mule and dragged out of the forest, but only a fool would risk an animal essential to farming, much less himself, to log in the most dangerous places.

After the war this changed, as timber entrepreneurs applied technology that could subdue any forest, no matter how wet or high and rugged. Most important was the light, portable Shays steam railroad engine. Men laid down track atop mats in wetlands and used dynamite to blast rail beds along mountain ridges. Then locomotives pulled up with flat-bed cars waiting for the logs to come. In swamps, piedmonts, and mountains alike, the new timber men also employed long cables (as much as a thousand yards), strung out from giant spools with winches atop rail cars, to grapple distant logs and haul them to the railroad for loading. In very steep places, they built portable water transport for logs: wooden flumes filled with fast-moving water diverted from a spring or creek. Frederick Weyerhaeuser, among a few others, built a lucrative empire using such technology, combined with aggressive purchase or leasing of woodlands. These entrepreneurs began in the upper Midwest, cutting off the tops, as it were, of Michigan, Wisconsin, and Minnesota and shipping millions of board feet down to Chicago, then west onto the virtually treeless high plains, where farms, towns, and cities were under construction everywhere new transcontinental railway lines were built.

By about the 1880s, the upper Great Lakes states were bald, yet the growing nation, especially the West, demanded more lumber, more telegraph and telephone poles, and more railroad ties. Now Weyerhaeuser and other midwestern operators turned to the South, where lumber production in 1880 was a mere 1.6 billion board feet. This had been accomplished the old-fashioned way, without railroads or steam-powered tools, by such men as Anderson "Devil Anse" Hatfield of Logan County, West Virginia, soon to be a world-famous feudist. Patriarch of a clan who farmed little, Hatfield and crews of male relations devoted winters to the labor-intensive task of getting logs and floating them downriver. Tradition has it that the Hatfields were done in by righteous state and federal prosecutors and judges, who forced the conclusion of the feud with the McCoys. Actually, Hatfields lost their freedom and their logging business because outside rail and mineral interests coveted the coal seams beneath Logan County's forests. It was they who won the feud—and who introduced dynamite and steam technology to logging in southern Appalachia.

Other native southerners fared better in the great cut-down. The brothers Paul, James, and Robert Camp are sterling examples. Sons of a Southampton County, Virginia, farmer, in 1875 they founded a steam sawmill at Franklin, then set about not only leasing and buying up enormous acreage in Virginia and nearby North Carolina but buying out native and Yankee competitors. Camp Manufacturing Company ultimately employed light rails, long cables, and winches to log much of the Great Dismal Swamp, and during the early twentieth century, the Camps expanded landholdings and mills into South Carolina, Georgia, and Florida, bypassing Philadelphian John Roper's and the Weyerhaeuser company's huge acreage in northeastern North Carolina. During the 1930s Camp entered the papermaking industry. Another southern native, John Henry Kirby, watched Williamsport, Pennsylvania, lumbermen move into western Louisiana and eastern Texas during the 1890s, as Kirby worked the same territory negotiating petroleum prospecting leases. The Texan plunged into the wood business himself, founded Kirby Lumber Company, and by the 1910s owned 15,000 acres in Louisiana, 365,000 in Texas, and timber rights to another 690,000 acres of the Houston Oil Company's fee-held land. Kirby was as friendly to steam technology as any Yankee, and he modestly named his principal lumber camp and mill, in extreme southeastern Texas, Kirbyville.

The great business successes of the Camps, Kirby, and a few other native southerners notwithstanding, the great cut-down of southern forests was still largely the work of northern American and British entrepreneurs. They bought up the greatest part of the millions of acres sold so cheaply during the late 1870s and 1880s, and their land and lumber companies and especially their consolidating and expanding railroads accomplished most of the carnage, milling, and shipping. Concentrations of enormous landholdings were densest in the Gulf states, but Weyerhaeusers were everywhere, independently or interlocked with allied companies. The Norfolk and Southern Railroad Company was among the largest identifiable woodland owners, as was the Florida Coast Line Canal and Transportation Company. With few exceptions, lumber companies by any name operated on the business policy of "cut out and get out," just as they had in the Midwest. In the meantime, collectively, all these individuals and corporations raised southern lumber production from 1.6 billion board feet in the 1880s to 15.4 billion in 1912. The stunning figure for 1912 represents the regional zenith. Lumber production in Virginia peaked in 1909; in other states, a bit later than 1912. Generally, while lumber and other forest products continued to dominate southern industry through at least the 1920s, the great wave begun during the 1880s had crested, and a profound reconfiguration of southern landscapes was under way.[12]

First, massive clear-cutting not only removed forest canopy but, of course, destabilized watersheds everywhere and geometrically increased the propensity of rivers to flood in spring. The great Mississippi deluges of 1913, 1927, and 1937 doubtlessly came in large part from deforestation, both near the river and far away. Congress's Weeks Act of 1914 aimed to re-stabilize watersheds through government land acquisitions and reforestation programs. Restoration of landscapes demolished for private gain proceeded slowly yet deliberately and momentously. The Weeks Act should be seen as a triumph of the maturing American conservation movement—and of professional foresters, who were then, arguably, the soul of the movement. Conservationists were typically urban northeasterners. Theodore Roosevelt and his friend Gifford Pinchot were exemplary. Both were vigorous outdoorsmen and ambitious policy makers who clearly perceived national security and prosperity as dependent on self-sufficiency in "natural resources." To conservationists, soil, water, trees, and air were all just that, resources. Water draining into an ocean, for example, was "wasted," Roosevelt once famously declared. It should be "used," and "wisely," just as trees, also essential to national well-being, had to be used with wisdom.

"Wise use" was the mantra of both crusading editors and politicians and degree-bearing foresters. Pinchot, chief forester of the United States during Theodore Roosevelt's and part of William Howard Taft's administration, was educated (after Yale) at the famous French school of forestry at Nancy. Later his wealthy family funded a forestry school at Yale. Federal foresters worked in a division of the USDA—an appropriate association in the important sense that foresters applied to their work principles similar to modern, "progressive" agronomy: Trees, like corn, must and will be harvested, but humans must assume stewardship of forested landscapes just as farmers must maintain fertility in their soils. Selective cutting is conservationist, not clear-cutting, and harvested woodlots must be replanted and protected. Forestry's first canon, indeed, was protection of woodlands from fire. Protection would be accomplished by construction of watchtowers and fire roads, by providing for the mobilization of forester-led firefighters in emergencies, but first by the criminalization of firing forests.[13]

This was the second part of the great reconfiguration. Federal and, more important, state legislation outlawing the firing of woods was simply revolutionary and countercultural in the South. Forest arson was, after all, historically oxymoronic. How else to clear land for crops? How else to hunt? How to open a seemingly endless forest canopy to sunlight so grasses and other forage for range animals (especially cattle) might thrive? How to clear out viney, shrubby, snake-infested understory so people might walk or ride through forests in ease and safety? Many plain southerners, white and black, apparently believed that cotton boll weevils, a crippling scourge since the 1890s, wintered in woods adjoining crop fields and that firing the woods killed them, along with other summertime pests. Yet throughout the Progressive Era, but especially during the second decade of the twentieth century, urban conservationists, foresters, and agronomists organized, lobbied, and campaigned for fireless forests and, incidentally, the closing of the range wherever it remained open.

The battle in North Carolina, where the swampy eastern plains counties remained defiantly a region of rambling hogs and smoky skies, was emblematic. By the opening of the twentieth century, eastern North Carolina was less the Tar Heel State's chic, moss-draped "colonial" center— one thinks of New Bern and Tryon Palace—than the most troublesome and backward section of an urbanizing and industrializing queen of the so-called New South. City editors, agricultural editors, improving planters, and the recreational-minded urban conservationist class impatiently urged fire protection. In this they claimed allies at William Vanderbilt's Biltmore estate in the mountains near Asheville, where the mogul engaged the elderly landscapist Frederick Law Olmsted, the young Gifford Pinchot, and a corps of young forestry students to manage and conserve Vanderbilt's vast grounds and forests. The Biltmore Forestry School was ignored during the massive clear-cut, but its graduates numbered among the foresters who would oversee reforestation in the near future. Meanwhile North Carolina's state legislature finally created a forest bureau charged with fire protection but appropriated few funds—typical of most southern lawmakers at the time. Citizens' groups formed and lobbied for adequate funding. While this slowly accumulated, agronomists attacked ignorant country people for burning the woods to kill boll weevils. Southern reformers, including North Carolinians, had sought the improvement of the quality of animal stock for decades. Now the foresters, a lumber industry trade group, urban recreationists, editors, and college and USDA agronomists fastened on the interrelated behaviors of one (apparent) class of people who both burned the woods and ranged their animals. County governments and especially courts were embroiled in open-range controversies for years, as improvers sought county-option means for reform. In 1918 the state's department of agriculture stigmatized eastern counties via a quarantine to "prevent the spread of hog cholera." Soon, long-deferred state legislation won the day for reformers and drove the last nail into the coffin of old rural rights and traditions. The last of the range was closed on New Year's Day in 1922. Thereafter, Carolina's woods sometimes still blew up via human mischief, but most citizens came to accept the notion of forest arson. New Deal suppression programs, followed by the World War II fear of enemy sabotage of forests, produced a national regime approaching absolute fire suppression. State-sponsored "Keep Green" and federal "Smokey the Bear" fire safety publicity campaigns, too, seemed to foreclose any resurgence of antique attitudes and behavior.

But such was not the case. Throughout the twentieth century, forest arson persisted in the South, perturbing and perplexing forest professionals and their urban/suburban fellow travelers. The least perplexing yet most ironic instances appeared during the Depression. By this time most southern states maintained funds to pay emergency forest firefighters to suppress blazes in state forests. Virginia's wage was fifty cents. The federal wage for fighting fires in national forests, however, was seventy-five cents. Little wonder, then, that Virginians living near the Jefferson National Forest often predicted fires, which seemed inevitably to flare up, then volunteered to work at the federal wage. There were very few fires in state preserves. During the war there were few fires anywhere. Perhaps patriotism prevailed, but it seems more likely that country folks found themselves in the armed services and away from home, or at war jobs that paid better than woodsy firefighting.

As soon as peace came, however, southerners returned to their old pyromaniac ways — sufficiently so to provoke federal and state forest officials to organize a Southern Forest Fire Prevention Conference, which attracted 1,200 attendees to New Orleans in 1956. Three decades later, a writer for *American Forests* (the popular journal of the American Forestry Association) dated a "growing arson epidemic" approximately from the time of the New Orleans conference. The American Forestry Association, whose large membership includes professionals in state, federal, and private corporate service, as well as many recreationists who also subscribe to *American Forests*, has ever been the principal publicist of forest arson, openly in league with government forest bureaus and rural police. Back in 1936, a U.S. Forest Service officer named John P. Shea had published his scholarly study of the southern phenomenon of forest arson. Reread today, Shea's conclusions on the motivation of arsonists seem a shocking trivialization: Fire-setters, he averred, lived in environments of "low stimulation," so they "craved excitement." Forest fires merely served this end, so the task of conservationists was simply to locate alternative amusements for the bored rural ignorati. One must wonder if the brilliant composer and singer Hank Williams (1924–53) knew of Shea's report when he wrote one of his rare joyous songs, titled "Settin' the Woods on Fire." The piece celebrates, well, celebration:

> You talk loud
> 'n I'll talk louder
> We'll be settin' the woods on fire!

The title line probably should be construed metaphorically—having a rousing good time; yet I think the line's specificity is plain enough, too. It is bloody great fun to torch the woods! Pyromania lies within many of us, especially if we are drinking, dancing, and shouting. Shea, middle-class ignoramus that he surely was, had been onto something, even if only superficially.[14]

By 1956 and the New Orleans forest arson conference, emerging statistical trends and mounting insurance claims and police reports all compelled a deeper look. The perspective of another half-century reveals, I think, why the foresters needed better ethnography than Shea's. First, by the 1950s, the cumulative effects of the closing of the range, the criminalization of woods-firing, the huge cut-down of forests ca. 1890–1920, and the subsequent creation of vast state and especially federal protected forests and national parks were becoming clear. Access to and use of what had once been a commons was effectively closed, except to privileged hikers, climbers, hunters, fishers, and vacationers, and also to influential lumber companies that were able to log in government forests with permits. Add to this the emergence, by about 1960, of the South as the nation's premier papermaker. Pulp and paper manufacturers bought and leased many thousands of acres, mostly in the old, coastal piney woods, but some in piedmonts and the mountains. Nearly everywhere they grew loblollies (sometimes slash pine) like any agricultural crop; it was monoculture of vast proportion, maintained chemically to prevent deciduous trees (now, in effect, "weeds") from competing with the pines. Thousands of small woodlot owners across the region who did not sell or lease their trees to the companies were relentlessly drawn into the papermaking complex so they might earn from this newest of Dixie's extractive industries. The companies and woodlot owners, meanwhile, cherished the assistance of professional foresters, police, and game/wildlife commissions in suppressing fire and regulating fishing and hunting. A great vise squeezed the rural poor—men, first of all, who seldom held full-time jobs but cobbled modest livings from cutting and selling wood and hauling logs in their rusty trucks. This was mostly winter work; in warm weather they did part-time road- or construction work. Always such men were hunters and fishers.

The observations of Jack Camp, president of Camp Manufacturing, on his 40,000-odd acres in the Dismal Swamp during 1952–53 illustrate a new departure and a much larger dilemma. Camp and his lawyers had just settled a long-standing boundary dispute in the swamp with a corporate neighbor. With property lines finally established—and Camp nearing a merger with New York City's Union Bag—Jack Camp recalled that his company was eager to "get the hunting established so that we would have everything organized in hunting clubs who in turn would be responsible for fire control." Camp's organizers, typically, excluded local, working-class men from their clubs, provoking outrage. One local whose family had lived on the swamp's fringe for generations confronted a company lawyer, declaring (as Jack Camp repeated him), "Look, don't bother me about hunting. I hunted here, and my father and my sons, and we're gon' hunt here as long as we want to hunt here. You can forget trying to tell us what not to do." Camp himself reflected, later, on "how rugged a lot of the people were around the edge of the Swamp. If people got upset with you, they'd set your woods on fire. That was their retaliation, you couldn't catch 'em. . . . Boy, once they get something against you, they'll burn your woods, or shoot you, or something like that. Pretty rough crowd."

In 1956 there were 55,000 forest fires in the South. In 1981 there were 76,000, an increase of 38 percent. Improved suppression reduced actual acres burned, but the greater incidence of fires, especially those apparently set intentionally, was profoundly troubling. Remembering Shea's 1936 attribution of arson to boredom, foresters and wood products company officers observed that by the 1970s, after all, the poorest rural folk owned automobiles and television sets and, thus adequately stimulated, should no longer be incendiarists. A new scholarly study was in order, then, and Alvin L. Bertrand and Andrew W. Baird produced one that remains a credible model.

Constrained by a small pool of informants—arsonists are not often apprehended (just as Jack Camp had declared two decades earlier) and are seldom convicted when caught—Bertrand and Baird still developed a working set of motivations. First, they offered, was a traditional folk aesthetic: the sight, sound, and smell of burning woods pleased many people (men, women, and children). Forests with burned-away underbrush looked better and cleaner to them. Second was comfort and safety: burning killed and/or frightened away snakes, varmints, and insects. Third was (to the authors) a surprising persistence of the open range: poor folks unwilling (or more likely unable) to raise or buy feed for cattle burned other property owners' woods in order to admit sunlight and induce growth of pasture grasses for free-ranging cows and steers. Fourth was revenge, a big category of behaviors both traditional and quite modern: quarreling neighbors fired each other's woods. Hunters resentful of exclusion from forests now posted by clubs protested with the torch. Squirrel hunters resented pine monoculturists' killing of nut-bearing deciduous trees. Bertrand and Baird discovered a 1950s ditty from Livingston Parish, Louisiana, long an arsonists' haven, sung to a popular tune:

You've got the money
We've got the time
You deaden the hardwoods
And we'll burn the pine.

Other fire-setters lurked in national forests out of resentment for Forest Service policies. Yet more arsonists had employment grievances against wood products companies. During the 1970s, for instance, three men set thirty-six fires around Drip Rock, Kentucky, when a tree-planting firm declined to rehire them for another year. And two Florida women spent a day setting fires on the plantations of a paper company that would not give jobs to their sons. Finally, Bertrand and Baird presented a model "community" of potential and actual arsonists: Formally ill educated and "identif[ying]" with lower social classes," members disliked foresters, and they open-ranged livestock.

Such communities were, statistically, most likely grouped in Louisiana, the epicenter of American forest arson. According to the Forest Service, between 1974 and 1978 there were no fewer than 5,195 woods arsons there. Other Gulf states followed: Mississippi, 4,388; Alabama, 3,602; Georgia, 3,575; South Carolina, 2,554. The Sabine River must have been the western border of forest arsonists, since Texas had only 425 cases. The upper South, too, was less a concern for foresters. Virginia had a mere 400 arsons. Yet the geographic distribution of arsons seems less a matter of latitude and longitude than rural poverty. For the Forest Service's data correlate very well with the Southern Regional Council's maps of Dixie's enormous "po' country."

Meanwhile the firing persisted. The *année horrible* of forest arson was 1985. A deep January freeze followed by drought and high winds to fuel and drive wildfires leveled a quarter-million acres in the South. In the blackened aftermath, investigators classified no fewer than 60 percent of the conflagrations as arson. This marked what was actually a three-year-long holocaust in which 224,549 fires burned more than 5.5 million acres in the region. Lightning and careless burning of debris by humans apparently accounted for most of the disaster. But by 1985 almost 98 percent—another breathtaking statistic—of all American forest arson took place in the Southeast. And by then, too, another element had entered Bertrand's and Baird's arsonist profile.

This was the era of a burgeoning, violent, and expensive government "war on drugs," dramatized on TV by the Armani-fashioned detectives of *Miami Vice* but in reality a grittier, more mean-streets and down-home tragedy. In remote rural Florida, drug dealers set signal fires to guide delivery planes; sometimes the fires got out of hand. So the new federal Drug Enforcement Agency found itself in alliance with federal and state foresters. More significantly, cultivators of cannabis across the nation took to the woods, and rivals not infrequently burned one another out. An *American Forests* map prepared from Drug Enforcement Agency data revealed that arboreal marijuana planting was most common in regions with the most widespread rural poverty: the desert Southwest, the Pacific Northwest, the northern Great Lakes, and of course, the Southeast, especially Appalachia and Ozarkia. It was an updated but familiar story, for here was also the old territory of the moonshiner, before, during, and since Prohibition. Early- and mid-twentieth-century illicit whiskey making had taken place in cities, in the company housing of piedmont textile mill towns, but most famously in the woods, the deeper the better. Few southerners were big-time moonshiners; I have discovered neither a remote counterpart to Al Capone nor to Latin American drug growers and dealers there. Typically, southern moonshine makers and marijuana farmers were ordinary country people (not always men) who made modest livings in hard times. A bit like the followers of legendary Robin Hoods in medieval Europe, moonshiners and most pot growers of recent times resorted to risky business within shelter of a commons now taken away. The sheriff's men—and deputies and revenuers—pursued them relentlessly. Unlike medieval forest rebels (in legend, anyway), American moonshiners and cannabis growers were often apprehended and sent to prison.[15] There they are likely to languish forever, awaiting a just and merciful king who will return them to the forest.

🌿 Government-controlled forests and parks have been, since their creations, scenes of loss and contention as well. Many people—the natives and then European and African Americans—once lived on the landscapes, after all, and for many centuries. Now human habitation is forbidden. We may visit, hike, work, drive through, but always leave. Most of the forests and nearly all the national parks happen to be in mountains, for reasons arbitrary, maybe peculiar, yet (I think) very revealing of human imaginative traditions. For decades before the National Park Service was created (in 1916), while a doctrine of protection evolved into something approaching consensus, government officials and private advocates of wilderness preservation wrangled over the criteria for nationalization of various landscapes. Yellowstone (mostly in Wyoming) was the first national park and ultimately the model for qualification: spectacular peaks, rock formations, broad valleys, and a spouting spring. Yosemite (in California's Sierras) followed: more soaring mountains and gorgeous river valleys. Among others there was Sully's Hill in North Dakota. The Hill, it was later decided, was insufficiently transporting, aesthetically and spiritually, so it was demoted from park status. Meanwhile, as the Park Service assumed administration of the growing system, the automobile was already prominent in calculations of park visitorship and required amenities. The service and its outdoorsy lobbies decided also that mountains would ever be their most popular venues.[16] And so it has been, despite mountains' forbidding and uneconomic challenges to road building and construction.

Yet the greater the challenge—the most inaccessible pinnacles and the most unstable valley floors—the greater the reward in inspiration. Mountains are spiritual metaphors, first of all. From mountaintops one gains vision, literally and figuratively. Thomas Jefferson would doubtlessly have been a sage if he had lived in a swamp outside Williamsburg, but no, he was the Sage of Monticello, wealthy enough (or in possession of a good enough line of credit) to afford the carting of all his building materials, books, and cases of wine up the hill. (Poor animals—and slaves!) Moses received Jehovah's law atop rocky Mount Sinai; Noah's ark returned to earth upon Ararat, and Jesus' most famous sermon was delivered on "The Mount," an elevation worthy of the timeless message. No wonder that John Muir's language about Yosemite and Hetch Hetchy was so biblical—mountains are "cathedrals"; prominent rocks and valley floors, "sacred altars." Muir has had much referential company, too. During the 1920s, in a faraway part of another Europeanized world, the South African general and statesman Jan Christian Smuts was famously photographed atop his favorite spot, Table Mountain, which towers above Cape Town. There, during years out of political favor and office, he had befriended young botanists, conducted his own research, and emerged as a sage himself, the Philosopher on Table Mountain. The reputation derived from Smuts's critical participation in a British Empire–wide discussion of plant communities. The general created a new, holistic ecology with ambitious political purpose, namely, the reconciliation of hostile Europeans within the Union of South Africa, plus justification for the segregation of Coloureds, Indians, and Bantus. Such was Smuts's version of "thinking like a mountain." Another version, with opposite aspirations, is an Afro-Cuban song, "Bruca Manigua," presented most recently by Ibrahim Ferrer, the charming lead singer of Buena Vista Social Club. *Yo soy carabali*, the song begins, "I'm from the Carabali coast," referring to the slave coast of Nigeria, *negro de nacion*. "This hostile world" of slavery has made the singer bitter: "I'm crazy within." Then comes a chorus: "In the mountains lies the answer," and the singer responds, "Show me the paths of freedom / Mountains." The lyrics remind us of more recent Cuban history, too: that Fidel Castro's revolution began in the Oriente highlands and swept down onto corporate sugar plantations worked by dark-skinned campesinos. Simultaneously, West Virginia's government and corporate interests persistently blended mountains and liberty in branding the state's identity, without suggesting abolitionism or communism. Before this poor economic colony in southern Appalachia was "Wild and Wonderful" (the current highway greeting and license plate slogan), West Virginia proclaimed, "Mountaineers Are Always Free." It's a nice notion, as is the idea that mountains are clean and spiritually uplifting. Certainly everyone seems to agree that mountaintops induce clarity of vision, ambitious hopes, and wisdom.[17]

Yet except for the wealthy few and perhaps weird holy people, actual mountain people have not lived on top. These include the first human residents of the Appalachians, ancestors to the Cherokees. In the Cherokee creation narrative, the mountains were made not by a violent albeit imaginative old white man but by the Great Buzzard, who, wearying of long flight over a wet, level Earth, finally alighted and, to keep himself from becoming mired, flapped his gigantic wings, stirring the uninteresting terrain into mountains and valleys. Later humans, once they became separate from bears and other animals, climbed to ridges and peaks to burn balds for hunting pastures. The natives lived below, however, where there was water and arable land. Their European successors did more or less the same, for a long while. They maintained the fired spots as high summer pasture for domesticated animals. Mostly they lived below, by rivers, creeks, and coves. Cove land was farming land, close to water for drink and transportation. The tops of mountains were, well, difficult—strenuous to reach and sometimes dangerous to descend. They were to be used only seasonally, as commons.[18]

Weather in the Appalachians is unsouthern, usually ten (or more) degrees colder than the piedmonts and plains to the east and west. Within the mountains, too, weather may vary drastically between 5,000- and 6,000-foot summits and valleys below. As to rainfall, mountaintops may get as much as eighty inches annually, while valleys get sixty inches or less. Then there is the simple but profound consequence of living on coves or in valleys, far below high ridges and peaks: Depending on season and the predicted risings and settings of the sun, mountaineers have ever been deprived of light. Admiring the gorgeous scenery of the neighborhood of Grandfather Mountain, in northwestern North Carolina, in high summer, I have been dismayed that, where I stayed, the sun did not clear the ridge to the east until 10:30 A.M., then passed below the western ridgeline before 4:30 P.M. I am tempted to hypothesize that light deprivation among typical below-ridge-living Euro-Appalachians helps (at least) explain their stark morbidity and the brutal forthrightness of their acknowledgment of death—this even today, when death is, if not denied, sanitized. Consider the "ole-timey" musical score to Joel and Ethan Coen's brilliant 2001 film *O Brother, Where Art Thou?*[19] The film is set in the Yazoo-Mississippi Delta, but the music that drives and tones the silly plot is overwhelmingly Appalachian, and death-oriented fare indeed. Little girls sing, joyously anticipating becoming angels doing roadwork in heaven. A grown "Man of Constant Sorrow" will soon be "in my grave." "I'll Fly Away" means the singer can hardly wait to die. Another title, "Keep on the Sunny Side," urges mindless optimism despite a repetitively gloomy "dark side of life." Most spectacular is Ralph Stanley's reprise of the traditional "O Death." (More of this remarkable film, in a different context, in the Epilogue.) Low-country southerners, white and black, share highlanders' evangelical Protestantism and demographic and medical history: many children, many of them dead early, and the survivors poor and expecting early demises. But flatlanders rarely express life's sorrows and inevitabilities in such a fashion. Musical behavior—not to mention geological morphology and wonderful biological diversity—invite discrete and emphatic attention to the mountains.

🦋 The Black Mountains of western North Carolina, above Asheville, are a useful localized case of upland experience. The range was effectively doomed as wildlands and commons because among the Blacks is the highest peak in eastern America, Mount Mitchell. As recently as 1957, when I was a teenaged soldier stationed in Massachusetts, some New Englanders were still asserting that the highest peak in the East was Mount Adams or Mount Washington. By coincidence, 1957 was the centennial of the death of Professor Elisha Mitchell, who had measured the highest pinnacles in the Blacks more than twenty years before his demise, who endured a long and bitter controversy with a former student over just which of the peaks was highest, and who, climbing alone and at night (and in his sixties), fell from the very mountain that would bear his name and, a few years later, would bear his grave. Mitchell was born in Connecticut in 1793 and well educated in chemistry and mathematics at Yale. The University of North Carolina recruited him for its science faculty in 1816. There Mitchell promptly made himself into an excellent field botanist and geologist. He was heroically disciplined and felt called to explore Carolina, which still seemed to him a vast wilderness. Late in the 1820s the state legislature commissioned Mitchell to conduct a geologic survey. The labor took Mitchell across the state, east to west, measuring and prospecting. Legislators hoped that he would discover valuable minerals, identify rich new farmland and timber sources, and indicate the best routes for future roads that would speed economic development—that is, to find means somehow to reverse the flow of out-migration and increase public revenues. This political context—understood and agreeable to Mitchell, himself capitalist-minded—enveloped all his visits to the Blacks, his designation of the tallest of them, and even his death and burial.[20]

Returning to the Blacks for more hiking, climbing, and measuring in 1844, Mitchell experienced a Romantic moment. He and his two local guides traveled all a July day on foot, beyond trails, at one point crawling on hands and knees through a thicket of rhododendron. At this point, Mitchell noted later, he "could not help thinking . . . what a comfortable place [this] would be to die in." A bit later, as they reached the summit already named for him in one popular atlas, a rumbling thunderstorm approached suddenly, and the men scrambled back down. The revelation of his mortality—

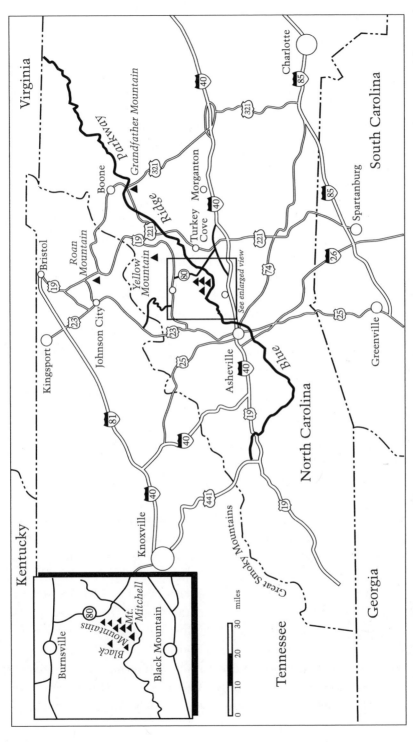

*Black Mountains of Western North Carolina (from Timothy Silver, Mount Mitchell and the Black Mountains: An Environmental History of the Highest Peaks in Eastern America [University of North Carolina Press, 2003])*

in "a comfortable place" notwithstanding the exhaustion required to get there—resembles Henry David Thoreau's reaction to reaching the difficult summit of Mount Ktaadn, in northern Maine, two years later. Namely, a beauty so dangerous as to be sublime—an "Earth," as Henry famously wrote, "made out of Chaos and Old Night." Thoreau relished the wild release from reason, but Mitchell suppressed chaos, preferring the illusion of civilization and its engineered development. In his first published reports on the Blacks, Mitchell had welcomed the prospect that tourism would likely change the mountains and local people for the better. Indeed, as Timothy Silver, intimate biographer of the range, concludes, "Mitchell never wavered from his progressive plans for the region."

Mitchell's earliest news of the Blacks induced visits from other scientists, professional and "gentlemen," the latter including Thomas Lanier Clingman, the former student, now a Whig politician, who during the 1850s declared that his former mentor had identified the wrong peak. The public dispute contributed to an already growing volume of visitors, not least the hugely popular writer David Hunter Strother (Porte Crayon), whose caricature appeared in *Harper's New Monthly Magazine* in November 1857. By that time summer and fall tourism was a substantial business in the Blacks, and a corps of local men, most famous of all Big Tom Wilson (who hosted Porte Crayon), had developed thriving guide and hostel businesses. A well-maintained horse trail permitted tourists to visit Mount Mitchell's peak and return to quarters in one day.

Wilson's hostel and the horse trail were but the beginning of what Silver ominously terms "Modernity." The Civil War halted cattle and hog drives and temporarily all but halted agriculture in the valleys, and tourists were no more. By 1880, though, Morganton, the mountain town just to the south of the Blacks, had regular train service. This accommodated a newly emergent social phenomenon: a craving among urbanites for "wilderness" experiences. The Appalachian Mountain Club—hiking and climbing scientists and professors—was founded in Cambridge, Massachusetts, in 1876, and in a few years many members made their way south. Mount Mitchell disappointed them, lacking as it did the cragginess of New England peaks. But birders, also now organized and traveling, delighted in Mount Mitchell and the Blacks. (Many were collectors who shot birds and carted them to taxidermists for preservation-in-death.) Most visitors met and admired Big Tom Wilson, by now an aging Confederate veteran but still physically imposing and garrulous. Wilson himself was probably the best of the Blacks' wilderness experiences for visitors, since even as a young man he was the legendary tracker and killer of bears, the pathfinder and trailmaker. Wilson died peacefully at age eighty-three in 1909.

By that time, the great timber cut-down in the South approached its climacteric, and the Blacks were not unaffected. During the 1890s the newly organized Southern Railway established a hub in Asheville, with branches into the backwoods territories of Tennessee and both Carolinas. This accelerated the taking of timber north of Asheville, even though logs still had to be hauled by wagon over bad roads to the railhead. Then in 1909—the year of Wilson's death and the state forester's first assessment of marketable timber in the region—several outside timber cutters from Pennsylvania, Ohio, and Illinois suddenly gained leases or purchased thousands of acres in the Blacks, including a swath of Mount Mitchell itself. They brought in their own light rails, locomotives, and harvesting gear, and their assault on the range was a blitzkrieg. In a few years, previously unreachable stands of spruce, pine, and hardwood were gone and steep ridges were laid bare to erosion. Discarded treetops, limbs, and branches (collectively known as slash) lay bleaching in the sun—volatile stuff awaiting the first lightning strike, live cinder from a locomotive's stack, or discarded cigar. The mountains had always known fire, but now a new and terrible fire regime was under way, annihilating soil and surviving flora and fauna alike. Had Big Tom survived a few more years, still fit for the climb and hunt, there would have been nothing for him to do. The deer and bears—Wilson killed some 115 of the latter himself—were gone. The range (Wilson and his contemporaries were herders, too) was effectively closed by the clear-cut and fires several years before North Carolina's fencing reform. Farmers' cropland, always tiny, barely fed the people and could never support big herds. And despite eager talk of an inclined rail to the top of Mount Mitchell, tourism was badly compromised by fire-blackened ridges and endless (and ugly) piles of slash along railroad tracks. What to do? What else but make a park for hikers, climbers, birders, and general nature seekers. Tourism—Elisha Mitchell's now-old dream—would redeem the Blacks.

Asheville's business and political elite had been campaigning for an Appalachian National Park in western North Carolina since the 1890s (even as the great cut-down began). Governors and upland members of Congress got nowhere with the proposal, though, and by mid-1914 a timber company was advancing toward the summit of Mount Mitchell. But now Asheville's most prominent son, Locke Craig, was governor, and he proposed an emergency appropriation to buy Mount Mitchell (beginning with forty or so acres) and create a state park. Early in 1915 the legislature responded, and the highest of the Blacks was saved, such as it was.

Now relatively secure from the companies, the mountains' vast and ancient stands of American chestnuts shortly began to blister and die from an enemy more insidious. Decades earlier, U.S. nurserymen had inadvertently imported from Asia chestnuts infected with a fungus. Identified in Pennsylvania at the beginning of the century, the "chestnut blight" appeared in piedmont North Carolina at least as early as 1913 and reached the Blacks between about 1917 and 1920. By midcentury the American chestnut was effectively gone—as a beauty, as a source of excellent lumber, and as a critical supplier of mast to forest squirrels, turkeys, deer, and bear. Mitchell and the Blacks, meanwhile, were reforested, albeit without chestnuts; fire protection was established; and hunting and fishing were regulated or prohibited. Later, a long-awaited federal project, the Blue Ridge Parkway, wove near the Blacks, and a hard-surface spur led to the pinnacle of Mount Mitchell. The state park remains a popular tourist and sportspeople's destination.

More recently, though, trees are dying again—this time conifers and deciduous alike. A pest is responsible for much of the affliction of firs, but the greater blight is toxic air, blown eastward as clouds from factories and electrical power plants. So now tourists driving along the parkway or, farther north, Skyline Drive near Waynesboro, Virginia, might stop for a view of a valley but find a sky turned artificially gray. The Park Service has provided a glass-cased photographical exhibit of air pollution. Farther south, on Mount Mitchell, views are occluded, too, as they are on down into the Great Smokies. One must wonder if mountaintops' metaphoric tradition will die, too, along with the reality of views from summits.

🌿 Meanwhile the South's (and the East's) largest and most popular national park took shape. This was the Great Smokies, formerly a contiguous expanse of far western North Carolina counties combined with a swath of Tennessee reaching toward Knoxville. By the end of the 1880s, as timber cruisers estimated stumpage and outsider companies prepared their Shays locomotives for the great cut-down, a few locals and more middle-class visitors were establishing little summer resorts and proclaiming the Smokies' salubrious benefits to body and spirit. The cut-out proceeded anyway, around and beside the resorts, and ironically, excursionists experienced the grand beauties of steep ridges and rushing creeks far below, from timber-getters' railcars. Still, as late as 1900, about 7,000 people still lived

*View of a farm from Blue Ridge Parkway, Virginia, 1940.*

*Photo by Marion Post Wolcott. Courtesy Library of Congress (LC-USF34-056359-D DLC).*

in at least a score of communities throughout the area of the cut-down and future park: in Big Cove; in Noland, Deep, Baskins, and Mill Creeks; and in Cataloochee, Sugarlands, Junglebrook, and Cades Cove, among others. The communities represented generations of Euro-southern settlement, with the expected farmsteads, churches, schools, and cemeteries. Since living adult males could vote, it comes as no surprise that influential promoters of a national park—principally in Asheville and Knoxville—repeated over and over that a park would never displace communities filled with descendants of pioneers. The campaign and the promise persisted almost unabated from the 1890s into the 1920s.

During less time than this, the timber operators clear-cut fully 60 percent, or 300,000 acres, of the Smokies, taking away about 2 billion board feet of lumber. Meanwhile the predictable fires came, further degrading the cut-over mountainscape and burning down yet more trees. Now that the range had become in substantial part a ruin, progress was made toward federal purchases and creation of a southeastern Yosemite.[21]

The Park Service and a host of New Deal agencies constructed the park during the Depression. The Civilian Conservation Corps established fire protection and planted seedlings to reforest cut- and burned-out swatches. The corps also helped build trails for horses and hikers, plus other amenities Park Service officers deemed necessary and appropriate. Others built roads. Then President Franklin Roosevelt came to dedicate the park in 1940. Shortly the nation was at war, and another federal power in the region, the TVA, demanded a new dam and lake along the southwestern perimeter of the park, to supply electricity to the war effort. An addendum to TVA's imperative was more than incidental to the Park Service's mission: While Fontana Dam's turbines fed the power grid, Fontana Lake offered a marvelous recreational opportunity to park patrons. Unfortunately, the dam/lake area was mostly good cove land and had long been populated by humans as well as wildlife. The people were moved and the site was flooded, but not without ugly exercise of legal and police power. Fontana communities merely followed others within the new boundaries of the park. For the old promise of leaving resident humans inside the park was reneged upon early on. Eminent domain ruled as law, and police executed the law. Both expulsions came hard on 1930s removals of rural folks who lived on sites planned for the first TVA dams and lakes.

Like Yosemite and the other famous western parks, the Great Smoky Mountains National Park was to serve the automobiling public. Paved highways entered the park from all convenient directions, and "bear jams"—

cars gridlocked as drivers and passengers disembarked to feed panhandling bears—became daily events in summer. Cherokee, North Carolina, the principal eastern entrance, became a bizarre roadside strip of souvenir stands offering plastic native artifacts manufactured in the remote home continent of natives: Asia. Many of the Eastern Band Cherokees shilling the souvenirs wore Plains Indian attire, most obviously big chieftain's headdresses. At the main western entrance, the hamlet of Gatlinburg quickly grew into a nightmarish version of Las Vegas—nightmarish because Gatlinburg had the neon but no blowzy sex shows, much less gambling and hardly ever the substantial architecture and confident self-mockery of Las Vegas. Inside the park's domain, the Park Service consciously promoted the Smokies as Yellowstone or Badlands. Promotional photography emphasized large rocks in the park, evocative of, say, Utah. Horseback opportunities for visitors seemed indigenous enough but also suggested a western experience. More blatant was the remaking of an old community, Cades Cove, into "one big farm" crowded with cattle. Margaret Lynn Brown, the Smokies' own most intimate visitor and biographer, observes that hereby a defunct aggregation of small farms was transformed into the Ponderosa of fond TV memory.

Meanwhile, too, as in the West but more egregiously so, the Park Service, working with game and fish experts and managers, early began to manipulate and "improve" wildlife amenities. There would be no predators in the park, humans or other. Bears, being cute, were a fine attraction providing one does not mind traffic jams in so-called wilderness. Certainly fishing might be improved, following the enormous damage loggers had caused watersheds, creeks, and rivers. Native catfish were disdained, however, being bottom-feeders and boring to serious anglers. So western trout, nonnatives, were introduced. If a certain stream deemed prime for trout already contained a competing native fish, managers were not above poisoning the stream to make way.

Later—during the 1960s, 1970s, and 1980s—when Americans had changed their mind about predators, or at least the idea or principle of predators, the service permitted reintroduction of red wolves to the park. Red wolves, relatively small and furtive, once abounded in the mountains where farmland and burned spots maintained an edge environment that, in turn, encouraged high prey populations of rabbits and raccoons. The wolf introducers and Park Service were obliged to abandon the project, however, once they figured that surviving animals had left the park, apparently looking for food. By the 1980s most of the Smokies had again become a climax, high-canopy forest, not a home to lowly bunnies and 'coons. Meanwhile, and curiously, the service had a predator preoccupation before the failed wolf episode. This was, of all things, feral hogs. Back about 1920, before the park was created, a number of European "wild" boars escaped a private hunting preserve and adapted themselves to the cut-over mountains, multiplying rapidly as hogs are prone to do. Half a century later, a young park superintendent devoted himself to getting rid of the beasts. Their rooting snouts had "strip-mined" forest floors, he declared, and worse, the hogs were rapidly devouring wildflower bulbs. Local hunters relished chasing the boars, but the superintendent decided studies should be conducted; then he called in contract hunters. Protests stopped the slaughter, in favor of live trapping and deportation. Essentially, though, the superintendent was checkmated by organized hunters in at least two states. The interest of the episode—the significance—is that a struggle over hogs could happen at all, in a place once part of Hog Heaven and in a park presented as wilderness.[22]

In all the East, arguably the closest thing to a real wilderness experience is not the "windshield" one in parks but the autoless serenity of hiking and camping along the Appalachian Trail. The trail was the brainchild of Benton MacKaye (1879–1975), a politically left visionary, big-scale landscape planner, and early champion of wilderness refuges from noisy cities and congested, smoke-befouled roadways. MacKaye began to conceptualize a hiking trail that linked the Appalachian chain from Maine to Georgia as early as the late 1910s; then he published a brilliantly realized plan in an architectural journal in 1921. The West had its refuges. Ordinary people in the more populous East and Midwest were not yet able to reach the high plains and Sierras. So a protected forest corridor, arching from Ktaadn toward Atlanta, with cooperatively maintained rest stops and camps along the way, might simultaneously interrupt automobility's propensity toward sprawl and provide blessed peace to ordinary folks in the eastern third of the United States.[23]

MacKaye's disdain for "motor slums" in part propelled his thinking and planning about human development within well-planned landscapes. Contemporary outdoor recreation had its benefits but was merely escapist and discouraged reflection. MacKaye wished to promote an "outdoor *culture*" that raised consciousness. Successive articles he published on these subjects and the prospective trail drew him into welcome contact with hiking clubs from New England and New York to Tennessee—and also with congenial intellectuals who fed and expanded his own thinking. These included Aldo Leopold, the forester, game manager, and elegiac nature writer, and Bob Marshall of Johns Hopkins University, the already legendary climber and hiker with firsthand mastery of every truly wild place left in America. During 1934 the three, along with Robert Sterling Yard, founded the Wilderness Society.

MacKaye lived long enough to inhabit the Appalachian Trail. Slight of build, graying, bespectacled, and pipe-smoking, the elderly MacKaye became iconic and beloved in his slouch hat and gaiters, resting on a ridge or telling stories in camp. He is remembered, too, by hikers born since his death. Among these are a succession of my former students, children of prosperous midwestern suburbs who have traversed substantial segments of the trail, all in the South, and all in the MacKayeian spirit of outdoor culture as opposed to braggardly athleticism. They had all read Thoreau's *Maine Woods*, too, most eagerly the "Ktaadn" section, which has the best climbing tale and some of the more fascinating observations on interior Maine's native remnants. Several of the students were eager to write ethnographies of the trail's Virginia or Tennessee segments.

But from these and casual conversations about their trail experiences, I learned something disturbing. Hikers were warned of hazards beyond the "natural," namely, the danger of fishhooks suspended over trails from tree limbs overhead, intended to snare hikers' eyes. Here was a scenario of hostility better associated with the Mekong Delta of the 1960s and early 1970s. But according to trail advisories, southern Appalachia of the 1980s and 1990s had its own Viet Cong, youths from nearby who resented the presence of the hikers from the suburbs, who were perceived as privileged interlopers. One student told me he encountered a suspended fishhook in Tennessee. The others had not, but they related the warning stories.

Dirty tricks on the Appalachian Trail may be only another urban legend. Dismiss it we might. But I think that the legend's persistence relates at least two important things: First, upper-middle-class hikers, however humble and sweaty on the trail, are well aware that they move through a corridor of persistent poverty, where foreigners and Yankees extracted timber, coal, and other minerals and departed with nature's bounty. Second, there is the irony of creating a new commons, a fine one in the MacKayeian ideal, where once there was a commons of a different sort.

*The cat, with huge leaps, clambered up a tree; and now he had reached the very pinnacle, and as he gathered himself up to take a flying leap for a neighboring tree, I caught up my gun, and let slip at him in mid-flight. The arrowy posture in which he made his pitch, was suddenly changed, as the shot struck him to the heart; and doubling himself up, after one or two wild gyrations, into a heap, he fell dead, from a height of full fifty feet, into the very jaws of the dogs! It proved to be a female, smaller than the first cat, but beautifully spotted.*
—William Elliott kills a "wild-cat" in *Carolina Sports*, 1859

*That's what the companies call feed conversion. It's the amount of feed you need for the weight gain you want. Obviously, you look to use as little food as you can. That's why you don't want them moving around. It just wastes a bunch of calories.*
—A Maryland Eastern Shore chicken farmer explains production, 2003

*These [demons] have power to shut heaven, that it rain not in the days of their prophesy, and have power over waters to turn them to blood.* —Revelation 11:6

# 4

## MATANZAS AND MASTERY

In the opening scene of the film version of *To Hell and Back*, a slight, wiry, teenaged version of Audie Leon Murphy (1924–71) stalks prey in the scrub of the Texas Blackland Prairie. Murphy carries a single-shot .22-caliber rifle loaded with his only bullet, and he must succeed in the hunt. His father has deserted Audie's mother and their dozen children. They are cotton sharecroppers without credit or sufficient family labor—most of the children at home are too young to work. Audie (then called Leon), the oldest boy remaining and bitter about his father, assumes responsibility and brings home a rabbit cleanly killed; then he quits school and takes a job with a neighboring farmer. By 1941 his mother is dead and his siblings have dispersed. Now a war is on, too, and soldiering, he is persuaded, is a better opportunity than farm labor to help his younger brothers and sisters.

Universal-International writers composed that scene from a reluctant Murphy's musings in 1954, as the studio polished the film script. Baby-faced Audie would be the new Sergeant York—another poor southern boy handy with guns, intimate with landscape (as great hunters must always be), and now the most decorated hero of another world war. Alvin York's added attraction to the adoring public, in 1919 and again in 1941, when Hollywood made *Sergeant York*, had been York's deep evangelical Christian belief. Murphy was problematic on this theme, freely admitting that he had been virtually an atheist-in-a-foxhole: he was, he allowed, "close to never having any religion at all." So World War II's most decorated hero would be presented as Dust Bowl poster child; he had, after all, grown up even poorer than York. He had adored his mother, too, and his abstinence from tobacco and booze complemented the boyishness that in turn made his combat exploits the more astonishing.

The first scene, however dubious in detail, nonetheless surely represents truths about an American childhood deprived of childhood: no bicycle, no baseball, no carefree play, hardly five years of schooling, and relentless labor in cotton fields. Murphy's own 1949 war memoir (with the same title as the movie) has no such scene, merely a riff on his family's misfortune blended with a funny conversation about soldiering with a World War I veteran while chopping cotton. Elsewhere, though, another story of Murphy from Depression-era Texas—and a better one—seems true. One day a young man home from college spotted young Leon heading out with his slingshot. He called to the boy, offering the loan of his single-shot .22 rifle, along with eight rounds of ammunition. A few hours later, Leon returned the rifle and four of the shells with thanks, then walked home with his four dead rabbits.

When he was seventeen, Murphy saw *Sergeant York* twice. He tried desperately (early in 1942) to get into the Marines but was turned away. Who would sign for an orphaned, underaged volunteer? More problematic was his size: five feet, five and a half inches tall, 112 pounds. As soon as he turned eighteen, in June 1942, though, the army took him, and after basic training he insisted on a combat job with the infantry. He trained more and shipped out with the Third Infantry Division for Casablanca early in 1943, barely missing the end of the North African war; but in Sicily he and his comrades were bloodied soon enough. One day Audie was with a group of scouts in front of their company. Suddenly they "flush[ed] a couple of Italian officers. They should have surrendered" but rashly "mount[ed] two magnificent white horses and gallop[ed] madly away." Murphy described his own "instinctive" response: "Dropping to one knee, I fire[d] twice. The men tumble[d] from the horses" dead. A green American lieutenant came up and reproached the young soldier: "You shouldn't have fired." Murphy's answer was a precociously mature soldier's: "That's our job, isn't it?" Oddly, the boyish figure who dropped two galloping targets had scored merely "marksman," the least of three qualifying ranks, on shooting in basic training. The explanation his old friends and family members offered to Murphy's biographer was that stationary targets were boring to him and that even when Murphy was small, he preferred moving ones. One acquaintance declared that young Leon was deadly even when firing from a moving automobile.[1]

By the time he was nineteen and fighting in Italy, Murphy was a sergeant with the first of his Purple Hearts and a Bronze Star. Just twenty, he was fighting Germans in southern France and won a Distinguished Service Cross and the first of his Silver Stars. His fifth-grade education notwithstanding, he received also a battlefield commission as second lieutenant. Then, on a frigid January afternoon in 1945, at the Colmar Pocket near Strasbourg, Murphy sent his company into retreat in the face of an overwhelming German attack. Alone, he climbed atop a burning tank-destroyer with a functional .50 machine gun. Firing the gun at wave after wave of enemies, he simultaneously called in American artillery on his own position. The few German survivors finally withdrew, and moments after Murphy walked away, the tank-destroyer exploded. In his Medal of Honor citation, the official estimate of enemy Murphy killed, in the space of an hour at most, was 50. And in two and a half years of combat, Murphy likely killed, by himself, 240. By the time he returned to the United States during the summer of 1945, just before his twenty-first birthday, the still slight, wiry, and babyfaced Murphy had become the most decorated American soldier ever.

Murphy's World War I counterpart was Alvin York, the other celebrated poor boy from the rural South and another skilled subsistence hunter. York (1887–1964) was a child of the Cumberlands, from Fentress County, Tennessee, hard by the Kentucky border and present-day Daniel Boone National Forest. His large family owned but fifty acres and struggled, especially after York's father died in 1911. York, like Murphy, was the oldest son at home and assumed greater burdens on the farm, a duty not very agreeable to him. But his chief responsibility was feeding the household fresh meat from the

*Audie Murphy displays his medals, ca. 1950s. Universal Studios promotional photo, courtesy The Audie Murphy Research Foundation.*

hunt. This enterprise was young York's great calling and delight. He had become an excellent shot while still quite small. His father, York wrote much later, "threatened to muss me up right smart if I failed to bring a squirrel down with the first shot or hit a turkey in the body instead of taking its head off." [2] By the time Alvin reached his twenties his marksmanship—and drunken scuffles—were becoming legendary in his part of the mountains. He swilled moonshine and flipped cards in rustic Kentucky-border "blind tigers" and rode his horse home, swaying in the saddle yet looking for targets. The sheriff came when, on a drunken bet, Alvin shot a neighbor's goose. Another time, when Alvin was also drunk but testing his steadiness, he killed six domestic turkeys with six shots. Deadly when inebriated, a sober young York was apparently unbeatable in shooting contests. He favored "pony purse" matches in which each participant ponied-up a quarter (while onlookers made side bets), and the most accurate marksman won the purse. A more formal contest was "shooting for beeves." Men would pay in advance for chances at a target, the cash going to purchase of a steer. Then came the contest, careful measurement and accounting for accuracy, and usually a division of the beef into five parts for the five best marksmen, the best part going to the top shooter. On one such occasion, Alvin York won all five awards and went home with his beef on the hoof. Turkey shoots, too, remained as popular ca. 1910 as they had been throughout the previous century. Here a turkey was secured by its feet behind a substantial object (often a log), with only its bobbing head exposed to riflemen standing forty yards distant. The first to decapitate the turkey with a ball or bullet won the remainder of the animal's corpus. Most country males excelled at shooting things still and moving, but York may have been the top gun.

This he would remain, but at last, in his mid-twenties, Alvin became exclusively the sober gunman. He got religion and quit drinking and gambling. His spiritual home was now the Church of Christ in Christian Union, a fundamentalist sect with roots in nineteenth-century midwestern Methodism. This was 1915. Two years later, Alvin had still not backslid. He was working hard, reading his Bible daily, and courting a young lady from a neighboring farm when he received notification that he must register for the draft. On advice from his pastor and mentor, he sought conscientious objector status: "Don't want to fight," he wrote on the form. County and state draft boards refused; so with grave misgivings, Alvin reported for army training at Camp Gordon, Georgia, toward the end of 1917. When he was assigned to an infantry unit of the Eighty-Second Division, York repeated

*Alvin York posing in uniform back home, Pall Mall, Tennessee, 1919. Note the Medal of Honor and Croix de Guerre on his chest. Courtesy Sergeant York Patriotic Foundation.*

his moral doubts to his company commander, who took him seriously and sent him to talk with the battalion commander, a New England Protestant and master of the Bible. The major and the private conducted disciplined argument, the private almost surrendering to the older man's clever citations and repetitions of the Allies' propaganda about German war crimes in Belgium. Then the major sent York home on a leave. Alvin still agonized and finally retired to meditate and pray alone—where else but on a mountaintop, where he remained a day, a night, and part of another day. When he descended, all doubt was gone, and Alvin York would be the Lord's killer, utterly confident of mission and his own safety, no matter the danger.

The Eighty-Second was finally moved into combat in September and October 1918, at the St. Mihiel Salient and in the Argonne Forest. The war was ending, and German and Austrian soldiers were weary and disheartened. Yet even as the Central Powers began to collapse, there was bloody fighting and chaos as trenches were overrun, forces were surrounded, and units were "lost" behind shifting lines. Corporal York's remarkable day, 8 October, dawned in this context. His company had advanced so quickly it became surrounded and pinned down by machine gun fire. Plunging bravely ahead, York's platoon came upon enemy soldiers at leisure, most of whom surrendered; but one fired, and York killed him. Then another German machine gun opened up, and the Americans were pinned down again. Still guarding prisoners, York attacked. He could see enemy heads bobbing up and down, like Fentress County turkeys, but bigger, easier targets. York gobbled, turkeylike, to encourage the bobbing. Dangling a big .45 Colt automatic pistol from one finger of his right hand, he fired at first with his Enfield rifle, popping one head after another. Then York saw a group of German infantrymen running in his direction in single file—another scenario resembling the Tennessee backwoods: When hunting rambling wild turkeys or birds in flight, the smart shooter never guns the leader first, warning those behind, but kills the last in line, then the new last one, and so on. This York did, with bolt-action rifle and pistol, until both his barrels were hot and his ammunition was low. Then he shouted for survivors to surrender. They did, and York and a handful of wounded comrades began to march a large column of prisoners out of the wilderness to American lines. York, soon promoted to sergeant, was credited with capturing 132 and killing, with icy calm precision, 25. There were to be more days of combat, and York was nearly blown up once; but he survived to return home a hero. He won the Medal of Honor, a Distinguished Service Cross, a Croix de Guerre, and many other medals. He married and became a father and pillar of his community. In 1941, gray and a bit portly, he was invited to hang out with Gary Cooper while Cooper prepared to portray him in *Sergeant York*.

Later that year, Audie Murphy saw the movie twice. Then he impatiently volunteered with the army. Soon he would be a soldier himself, more than a decade younger than York when he was drafted and hardly two-thirds his size. In less than two years he shot men from their saddles in Sicily rather as he would drop bad guys in Hollywood westerns during the 1950s and 1960s. In Italy Audie favored the light, rapid-firing carbine, although he usually slung an M-1 rifle, too, and packed a .45 pistol for good measure. For all his steely expertise as a sharpshooter, Murphy loved sheer firepower and gravitated toward Browning automatic rifles, tommy guns, and most fatefully at Colmar Pocket, the big .50 machine gun. He understood industrial-scale killing. Finally, having miraculously survived the war, Audie returned to Texas in his beribboned summer tan uniform to see his scattered brothers and sisters and to acknowledge honor and thanks in a series of public ceremonies. These made the still-shy man anxious, but in Dallas he met his favorite movie star, Gary Cooper. Cooper asked if Murphy wanted to hear just how Alvin York captured 132 Germans. Audie declined with thanks; he was much more interested to know how the actor had re-created York's gobble at the turkey shoot.

York and Murphy, lonely and purposeful marksmen as boys, lived long enough to witness the disappearance of common hunting grounds that made subsistence possible for the poor and near-poor. They had been exemplary individuals, hunters, and soldiers, yet their publicized exploits—their own and their admirers' conscious connection of hunting with soldiering prowess—served also, and ironically, to illuminate the end of the long, long era of shooting for the table. Within fifteen years or so after World War II, the rural South was virtually depopulated. Agricultural land was either consolidated or abandoned. Sharecropping succumbed to machinery and chemicals, and huge mountain families gave up trying to farm on a pitiful fifty acres. Old rural worlds dissolved before the cash nexus. California filled with migrants from Texas and Oklahoma, people not unlike the unfortunate Murphys, who did not leave because they had no adult male with a car to pull onto U.S. Route 66. Alvin and other Yorks remained in Fentress County, but hordes of other "hillbillies" engorged the Midwest during Alvin's own time.[3] And poetically, I suppose, Daniel Boone, archetype of the Euro-southern frontier marksman, was memorialized in a national forest near Fentress, where hunting was restricted.

It is easy to sentimentalize subsistence hunting, even while acknowledging the desperation young Audie Murphy and many boys and men like him took to the task. Subsistence hunters killed to supply essential protein and hides for themselves and their kin. They used what they took, and they took no more than they needed. Many must have prayed for good fortune rather than the prey's forgiveness, like their native predecessors on these landscapes. But subsistence hunters seem altogether justified and honorable, and public memory has smiled on them. The boy or man alone, with one ball or bullet, out to feed himself and kin is a great trope that ennobles the American poor and working classes.

During the 1930s, Marjorie Kinnan Rawlings created such a late-nineteenth-century hunter, her fictional Penny Baxter, modeling him after a composite of men she knew in northern Florida. Desperate as Penny often was, he was principled in his relationship with animals, notably in his refusal to employ cruel leg traps, like the neighboring Forresters. Penny thought animals ought to have an even chance, at least, and in this respect he closely resembles elite European and American "sportsmen." Penny actually sympathized with his nemesis, Ole Slewfoot, the marauding, human-hating bear, because of the trap disfigurement that gave him his name. But because Slewfoot threatened human subsistence in the hammocks, he had to die—albeit cleanly and humanely. Penny's ultimate manly accomplishment was his dispatch of the bear in this hard and personal way, and his reward (in addition to poor Slewfoot's hide, meat, and oil) was approval and admiration by his community—even the Forresters. Such admiration would live on, too, doubtlessly. For in fiction and in vast historical experience, hunting makes stories that last longer than the men and animals featured.[4]

The problem with the sentimental portrait of subsistence hunters is that —while doubtlessly true here and there—lonely necessity and economic use of animals does not capture the more important context of hunting. This was social: hunting as pleasurable entertainment for men singly but especially in groups, as an essential venue for the socialization of boys, and not least important, as that inexhaustible wellspring of stories both picaresque and epic. One cannot underestimate the necessities and pleasures of the table. Yet hunting should be viewed as but one aspect (albeit an important one) of men's relationship with animals in general and with one another.

Grady McWhiney, historian of antebellum cracker culture, devotes little space to hunting but rightly subsumes the subject within an encompassing chapter titled "Pleasures." Southerners embraced leisure, fun, and self-indulgence. They adored dancing, drinking (rum, brandy, and whiskey of all sorts, good and bad), tobacco (cigars and pipes, the chew, and dipping snuff), gambling (cards, sporting events, and billiards), rough sports, riding horses (instead of walking), the company of many dogs, and talking (as endlessly as the Irish) about anything. And boys and men fished and hunted, often (it was widely reported) to the neglect of farming and business. A concerned father, for instance, sought to discourage his son from constant hunting and trapping in the forest—in lieu of school and punctuality at suppertime. Finally the father baited one of the boy's traps with an arithmetic text, but the boy was unpersuaded by the rare snare. Travelers in the rural South remarked on the extreme youth of expert marksmen, often mentioning the trick of "barking off" squirrels—that is, firing at a tree limb close to the animal's head so that the creature would die from the concussion of flying bark rather than a bullet wound.

Such mercy (if that be its name) did not prohibit, apparently, such hunters from the "pleasure" of blood sports. These included bearbaiting, the teasing and often wounding of chained or caged bears; dog fighting; and especially cockfighting.[5] I myself recall a caged bear outside a South Carolina tavern and take-out as recently as 1960. When I emerged from the business with a six-pack, my companion, an inebriated ex-army buddy, was provoking the bear. On opposite sides of the cage, man and bear had climbed several feet off the ground, growling at each other and shaking the cage dangerously.

Dogfighting may seem too ordinary and ubiquitous to be called sport, but men have trained dogs to fight one another—out of pride and in order to bet—for a very long time. Late in the twentieth century, when blood sports had become illegal as well as abhorrent to most people in the Western world, a well-known essayist and fiction writer, Harry Crews, Georgia-born and a professor in Florida, relished his notoriety as a practitioner of falconry and an admirer of fighting dogs. Cockfighting, meanwhile, enjoyed enormous popularity among all social classes well into the twentieth century. In Alex Haley's *Roots*, one of Haley's enslaved ancestors is called Chicken George because of his skill at raising, training, and handling ferocious gamecocks—all belonging to his North Carolinian master, of course —for high-stakes derbies. Almost a century later, the wealthy businessman and planter E. R. Alexander of Tuskegee, Alabama, employed a black man comparable to Chicken George throughout the 1920s and 1930s, and the Varner-Alexander Papers at the Alabama Department of Archives and

History include (in addition to much paper) a heavy box of assorted steel spurs for gamecocks. Resembling miniature sabers and daggers, such instruments were intended to slash arteries or penetrate hearts and lungs. Poor and middling men had their chickens and betting circuits, too, continuing long past the criminalization of cockfighting in nearly all states.

Then there was gander-pulling, a rollicking contest that appalled northeasterners and even some urban southerners in antebellum times. A. B. Longstreet brought picaresque vividness to one event that took place on a fringe of Augusta, Georgia, in 1798. The organizer, a petty merchant, announced a venue strategically located between rival settlements and attracted an eager crowd of participants and spectators. Here a small, circular track "of about forty yards diameter" had been laid out. At one point along the course, tall poles had been sunk into the ground on either side, "with a strong cord" connecting overhead. From the center of the cord was suspended a gander, its neck thoroughly slick with grease, "to vibrate in an arc of four or five feet span, and so as to bring the breast of the gander within barely easy reach of a man of middle stature upon a horse of common size." Mounted competitors circled the track at a gallop, grabbing at the gander's slippery head as each passed between the poles. Longstreet doted upon the quirks and physiques of both men and horses, the spectators' cheering, and the surprise conclusion. "Bostwick . . . broke the neck." "Now Odum must surely have it" (i.e., the gander's detached head). "When lo! Fat John Fulger had borne it away the second before." Fat John dismounted, crowed his victory, and taunted all his doubters, reaching into the merchant's hat to collect his cash prize. John quashed his own provocations, however, by spending all his winnings on liquor for the crowd. He was, after all, as Longstreet reported, "really 'a good-natured fellow.'"[6]

Bostwick, Odum, and Fulger, competitive and bibulous, were (to borrow the title of a recent study of southern hunting culture) "bathed in blood." And they represented the broad majority of white southerners, with their convivial contests, their subsistence trapping and shooting, and yet more gruesome, their part in the slaughters and extinctions that mastered nature so that agriculture and towns might thrive in safety. They were elemental to the Old South and the New. Even as market hunting nearly extinguished white-tailed deer populations before the end of the eighteenth century, settlers set out to exterminate large predators—wolves especially, but also bears, panthers and other cats, and foxes. Cats and foxes were objects of frolicking rituals pursued on horseback and on foot. Wolves were trapped in baited pits and then shot or lanced to death, until they were unknown east of the Appalachians, then east of the Mississippi and beyond. Much the same occurred with eastern panthers and wildcats. Bear hunting was a prestigious sport everywhere. But farmers, resenting bears' treating crop fields as cafeterias, rigged muskets or shotguns with trip wires connected to bait. Many bears—and doubtlessly raccoons, opossums, and squirrels—were thus blasted, in absentia, in a fashion resembling more the industrial than the woodlands hooliganism of booze and male bonding.[7]

Southerners ate all sorts of birds. Slaves in the Carolinas windrowed brush late in the year, in effect inviting songbirds, among others, to nest and become victims of blinding by torchlight at night, gathering and killing, and the making of festive stews. Children (usually white boys) killed the most colorful songbirds one by one using nets and sticks and traded them for toy tops and candy at country stores. Thus youth were initiated into market hunting. Storekeepers packed the dead birds off to milliners in northeastern cities—all this as early as the 1830s, well before the late Victorian peak of the fashion rage for hats adorned with egret feathers as well as the complete bodies of smaller avians. In the fall, adults and older boys flocked to open fields, where they gunned down clouds of passenger pigeons. Many of these they ate, although unused excess kills were justified as riddance of a nuisance. The very last passenger pigeon died in the Cincinnati zoo early in the twentieth century.

Some southerners may have consumed Carolina parakeets, but this lovely bird's massacre to extinction (by about 1900) was desperate and deliberate. The Carolina parakeet, vividly green, yellow, and red and about a foot long, bore little resemblance to today's tiny tropical creature in a cage. Like passenger pigeons, the big parakeets nested and migrated in enormous flocks, feeding on seeds and berries opportunistically. Then came Euro-American settlers, crackers and planters alike, who ritually established fruit orchards, usually of apples. Fruit, consumed fresh or dried for storage, is of course an important human food. But it was also currency on frontiers and on almost every nineteenth-century backwoods farm and plantation. In 1809 Rachel Jackson (wife of Andrew) had slaves plant no fewer than 9,000 apple trees. Her objective, doubtlessly, was to feed the cider press and distillery. Liquor, often apple brandy, could always be sold in a countryside where children drinking watered booze with breakfast was not unknown. The Jacksons had many commodities under production at the Hermitage, brandy being only one. Small farmers and herders, however, often produced few field surpluses for market, so they depended on their orchards not only for private imbibing but for cash to pay taxes, school fees, and church dues and to buy coffee and other things their climate would not permit them to grow. Clouds of parakeets descending ravenously on heavy orchards, then, provoked no expressions of awe at the birds' plumage. Country folk netted and killed, blasted with scatter guns, and poisoned, usually with arsenic concealed within bait, which was becoming a common method, by the 1830s at least, for coping with pests. Carolina parakeets were, to millions, as menacing as Ole Slewfoot. Market hunting of many sorts of mammals and birds, meanwhile, is difficult to separate from the more ennobled subsistence hunting, because the line between the two was often invisible. Daniel Boone, honored model for marksman-soldier-pioneers, was also a market hunter from youth into advanced age. At fifteen Boone and a companion delivered many bundles of deerskins from the Virginia mountains to Philadelphia buyers. A few years later, settled in North Carolina's Upper Yadkin Valley, he reportedly killed ninety-nine bears in a single season, a stunning statistic hardly comporting with pot or subsistence activities. In those days Daniel, like the natives, was a "fire hunter," too. At eighty, in Missouri, Boone and his male offspring spent winters checking leg traps in the woods.[8] Another hunter, more typical than Boone, might kill one bear or so a year, keep most of the meat and oil, and sell the hide. He and his family needed food *and* some cash. A shooter of fifty passenger pigeons or doves might exchange twenty-five for cash or something else needed or simply desired.

But by the 1850s, market hunting, especially of waterfowl, presented a distinction quite clear. Rapid metropolitan population expansion in the coastal Northeast, the improvement of guns, and the ease with which migrating waterfowl might be harvested at the birds' regular stops combined for a seasonal carnage that persisted well into the twentieth century. One of the prime shooting locales was Back Bay, a coastal section of Princess Anne County, Virginia, just north of the Outer Banks of North Carolina, where enormous convoys of canvasbacks, redheads, and mallards also rested and fed during their heroic journeys south from Canada. Local watermen and farmers had for a long time shot and packed the migrants for local markets—Norfolk, Portsmouth, and probably Baltimore as well. But by 1857, a single Back Bay farmer employed twenty gunners who in a single season "consumed," as a Virginia newspaper reported, "twenty-three kegs of gunpowder with shot in proportion." Gunners and other workers packed the kill in barrels, which went overland to the Norfolk waterfront and then in speedy packets to Baltimore, Philadelphia, New York, and Boston.

A few booster urban editors, steamboat owners, and commodity traders celebrated such enormous expansions of market hunting. Most men of substance and influence, however—especially those who identified themselves as gentlemen sportsmen—were outraged. Market hunting of all sorts, especially that of Back Bay scale, would surely cripple animal populations, depriving the gentlemen of their sport. The most enlightened of late antebellum sportsmen—usually the most articulate, as well—understood what would later be called ecology and game management. Habitat must be protected, hunting and fishing regulated (including temporary prohibition, if warranted), if field and stream were forever to provide healthful, character-building sport. Elite hunters and anglers, then, began to champion conservation more than half a century before Gifford Pinchot, Theodore Roosevelt, and others borrowed the word from the British and made it a crusade in the United States. Roosevelt and others had founded a national gentlemen's hunting organization in 1887—the Boone and Crockett Club—to promote protection of forest and wetland habitat and regulation of hunting. Ducks Unlimited came somewhat later. But earlier elite men, fathers and grandfathers of the first conservationists, had all but defined and organized a class war on subsistence pot-hunters, drunken killing-bingers, and market hunters of all sorts.[9]

The South had many gentlemen sportsmen, of course. Among them, however, no one was more charmingly gifted as raconteur and writer, more scholarly, more precocious in defining conservation, nor more spectacularly accomplished as hunter and fisherman than William Elliott (1788–1863). Elliott was scion of rice and sea-island cotton planters on Port Royal Sound and Beaufort, South Carolina, below Charleston. A well-educated cosmopolite, Elliott and his family moved several times every year, according to season as well as business, among several agricultural estates, Beaufort, Charleston, and the Northeast. He read and wrote Latin and contributed to newspapers and literary journals. Elliott also served conscientiously as a state legislator, resisting states' rights extremism almost to the brink of secession. In the meantime, he became a legendary sportsman well before middle age and, during the 1830s and 1840s, provided accounts of his exploits to various periodicals. These and a philosophical addendum, "Random Thoughts on Hunting," were gathered and published as a book in 1859. At this late date, with Elliott in his early seventies, a visiting British journalist invited to fish with the old gentleman was agog at the planter's fishing vessel. Long, elegant, and equipped with masts and sails, the sporting boat lay heavy in the water because it carried extra servants to attend the party, bountiful provisions, and no fewer than six slave oarsmen dressed in red flannel jackets and straw hats with broad "ribands." Elliott had been a handsome man when Thomas Sully painted his portrait in 1822. He was ever stylish and—in light of his class, color, sex, and time—principled.[10]

The random thoughts that conclude Elliott's wonderful volume, *Carolina Sports by Land and Water*, illustrate and define the attitudes of the gentleman sportsman. All of history, he began, demonstrated that "man" required "amusement and recreation." "Ascetic innovators, who would make life as unjoyous as their own natures; who would reform society, by denouncing dancing as a sin—the theatre as an abomination—and all amusements, however innocent, as a waste of time unworthy of immortal beings" live in a narrow "valley" without perspective, he declared. "Field [and aquatic] sports are both innocent and manly" simply because they are "amusements that employ the senses, are needful to restore *their* worn bodies, and revive their wasted spirits"—not to mention that sportsmen "are happier and better for the relaxation" (247–48). Men who endeavor to become proficient in such sport actually become more virtuous, Elliott averred: They tend to be punctual, considerate, resolute, and sagacious (therefore excellent potential soldiers), and they become disinclined to gamble. He did not mention the getting of food, much less hunting or fishing to get money in markets.

Elliott's lasting regret in old age was the retreat of habitat and the diminution of game. As planter as well as sportsman, he could not, he wrote, "regret the destruction of the forests, *when the subsistence of man is the purpose*." History had ordained "that the hunter should give place to the husbandman." What he abhorred in this context was "the wanton, the uncalled-for destruction of forests and of game" (252). Sportsmen such as he were never wanton. Rather, "professional" market hunters and local rabble (black and white)—fire hunters—who blinded game at night and executed them without sport were hastening animals to extinction in the Low Country. Here Elliott gave vent to a rage against the commons as ferocious as Edmund Ruffin's. "The right to hunt wild animals is held by the great body of the people, whether landholders or otherwise, as one of their franchises, which they will indulge in at discretion; and to all limitations on which, they submit with the worst possible grace!" (254). Elliott wished for all his estates to be private hunting preserves. But since he owned so much and traveled so often, he could not police it all, and he often found "his" game killed off when he returned from an absence. "Hunter's law," Elliott was unsurprised to hear in court from a fellow landowner, overruled property rights when men and dogs pursued deer through another's property, taking down fences on the way. The judge seemed outraged, but jurors "are exceedingly benevolent in such cases" (258–59). Elliott hoped ultimately to thwart "the throng of destructives who seem bent on the extermination of the game; rather than attempt the difficult, and unpopular, and thankless office of conservators!" Some sweet day in future, beyond his own time, he hoped, "there will be reform . . . the juries will have no interest in construing away the law . . . [and] men may, under the sanction of the law, and without offence, or imputation of aristocracy, preserve the game from extermination—and perpetuate, in so doing, the healthful, generous, and noble diversion of hunting" (260).

This last extended quotation fascinates for two reasons: First is the precocious (if self-interested) declaration for conservation—perhaps more because the word "preserve" appears, too, suggesting more than wise use of nature but something approaching the love expressed by Elliott's contemporaries George Catlin and Henry David Thoreau. Second, however, is the internal contradiction of his denial of "aristocracy" before the declaration that hunting is "generous." *Generous?* In a conservationist future, under rule of law, would not the *privilege* of generosity be gone, too, along with poaching, night hunting, market hunting, and the knocking down of private fences? The rest of *Carolina Sports* suggests otherwise: namely, that gentlemen hunters and fishers, not themselves needing more to eat, engaged in sports for amusement, to be sure, but principally for the exercise of power—over slaves, certainly, but also over lesser classes of free people and all women.

🌸 Wealth (and power) that yielded leisure in endless coastal South Carolina summers also offered opportunity for high adventure. William Elliott came from a vigorous, adventure-seeking tribe that eagerly took opportunities that were exceeded, he once suggested, only by pith-helmeted European tiger hunters in tropical India. One hot day on Port Royal Sound, in the halcyon days of his grandfather, Elliott wrote, two enormous manta rays approached the water fence beyond the beach before the old family mansion. First merely disporting, then apparently frustrated by the fence moorings, the "devil-fish" (as these generations named them) began to batter and pull at the fence. Ah, provocation—and justification for adventure! The fabled grandfather ordered his "barge" and enslaved crew of men, with "May," "his favorite African slave," in the bow with a harpoon. They quickly approached the first of the pair of mantas, and May, "grasping his staff in both hands . . . sprang into the air, and descended directly on the back of the largest devil-fish, giving the whole weight of his body to the force of the stroke!" As the manta accelerated and the harpoon line tightened, May leaped in the direction of the boat and was safely pulled aboard "by his fellow-blackies, who were delighted at his exploit" (Elliott reflected that had May "belonged to the Saxon or Norman race, he had probably been knighted, and allowed to quarter on his shield the horns of the devil-fish") (18–19). Elliot, shield-bearer of the first Port Royal hunter-prince, was unwilling (obviously) to emancipate May post mortem but celebrated him in print, instead. The unusual tribute, sad to say, merely perpetuated simultaneously the narrative ritual and raison d'être of sport and another master-class litany of loyal servitude. Meanwhile the grandfather and his merry crew had a ride. The manta towed the barge and men. Someone sounded a bugle, and neighbors scrambled into their own vessels and tied up alongside the Elliott barge. At one point, as the caravan approached the beach under manta power, the master "ordered a bowl of arrack punch to be prepared and sent on board." It was a community frolic, until at last the manta, exhausted, rose to the surface, succumbed to spearing, and was drawn to the beach for observation and celebration. Its pectoral fins—the batlike "wings" that also suggested the name Vampire of the Sea—came to twenty feet.

Much later, in August 1837, William himself spotted eight devil-fish as he sailed across the sound to Hilton Head. Inspired to resume the Elliott maritime legend, he ordered a harpoon and forty fathoms of half-inch rope. Soon he set out in unpromising weather with a teenaged son and a crew of six oarsmen and a steersman. William would permit no one but himself at the bow, with harpoon, and after several attempts at the elusive manta, he succeeded in lodging his weapon in its back. At last he also experienced the fabled ride—"driven by the most diabolical of locomotives"—with friends' boats now also in tow. William reclined under an umbrella, eating melon, watching "the hammocks of Parris Island grow into distinctness," as grand frolic proceeded. The manta remained well below the surface, resisting Elliott's and the crew's attempts to coax it up for spearing. The manta persisted despite a bent spear and a broken bayonet embedded in its flesh. A fresh crew with more weapons came on from another boat. Finally, after many more thrusts, the manta escaped. Shortly, though, the Elliotts and their neighbors returned to the sound with more satisfying results—that is, kills with capture, redeeming the disappointment of the first hunt's conclusion. Thereafter William engaged in other pursuits and abandoned devil-fishing for six years, but he returned with a vengeance in the summer of 1843.

That season the mantas were abundant; the strikes, rides, and kills, thrilling. Elliott's bloodlust, however, seems appalling. Fearing loss of a harpooned manta, the intrepid sailor blasted its head with his shotgun, producing "a jet of blood . . . cast several feet into the air" (55). Nonetheless the manta surged on, thrashing, bashing its head against the boat's bow. Finally it surfaced, writhing on its back, its "feelers thrown aloft above his head, like giant hands upraised in supplication. There was something almost human in the . . . expression of his agony." Elliott had a moment of sympathy: "a feeling quite out of keeping with the scene stole over me while I meditated the final blow." But "it passed away in an instant" (56–57). The poor manta was relieved of its torture and, with a great deal of difficulty, towed to shore. The following summer Elliott, ailing, went to the shore to recuperate—and to continue devil-fishing. At the conclusion of one of his lengthy June 1844 diary entries there finally appears a justification for killing manta rays—that is, other than amusement: "the highest relish (it is, in fact, whale-fishing in miniature)." Certainly it was not "objectionable on the score of cruelty; it is not killing in mere wantonness," he offered lamely. Rather, the manta's "liver yields an oil useful for many agricultural purposes"—he did not specify which—"and the body cut into portions convenient for transportation, and carted out upon the fields, proves an excellent fertilizer of the soil" (61). Gentlemen sportsmen have ever required comparable practicality in defense of their amusements—that is, anything but the feeding of themselves. Devil-fishing in Carolina took sparingly from the sea and returned generously to starving soils, we are to understand. The argument compares with the stalking and killing of predators on land, which provided relish while protecting humans and their domestic animals and crops.

Similarly, if any American needed blessings upon the absurdity of foxhunting, there was available to him the great bard of English field sports, William Somerville (1673–1742), author of "The Chace" (1735), which A. B. Longstreet reproduced at length to begin his picaresque "The Fox-Hunt" in *Georgia Scenes* (1835):

But yet, alas! The wily fox remain'd
A subtle, pilfering foe, prowling around
In midnight shades, and wakeful to destroy.
In the full fold, the poor defenceless lamb,
Seized by his guileful arts, with sweet warm blood
Supplies a rich repast. The mournful ewe,

Her dearest treasure lost through the dim night,
Wanders perplex'd and darkling bleats in vain.

In his own self-mocking narrative Longstreet, as "Hall," is inexperienced and hapless, riding a geriatric steed unable to jump a fallen log. It is December, freezing, and Hall is underdressed as well as underhorsed. The fox, barely glimpsed, proves wilier than the experienced militia officers who own the packs of hounds: the smartest of the hunters deduces that the prey left the ground and walked a fencetop for 300 yards, outsmarting the smartest of the dogs, too. Some hunts will fail, after all, and their narratives must allow for humor. Elliott was witty on the subject of his own and brother-sportsmen's bad luck and failures, too. Still, the fox's wiliness, as vampire to precious lambs as well as evader of noble dogs, necessitated more hunts.[11]

Other explicit justifications were charity to sportsmen's lessers and gifts to one's more-or-less equals, especially female. On the subject of drum fishing, for instance, William Elliott observed that Port Royal "planters . . . succeeded in taking, during the last season, at least twelve thousand of these fish; and . . . except the small number consumed in their families, the remainder were salted and distributed among their slaves, not in lieu of, but in addition to their ordinary subsistence, [so] you will perceive that this is a case wherein the love of sport, and the practice of charity, are singularly coincident" (112). Elsewhere he justified killing more than a family might consume as opportunity to initiate or reciprocate kindnesses among neighbors, especially the infirmed and widows. Ultimately, however, but never quite explicitly admitted in *Carolina Sports*, elite hunting and fishing rituals and stories demonstrated power and mastery. For these one reads especially the conclusions of narratives of expeditions that were not only thrilling but successful.

Elliott's rather tense recounting of a devil-fishing expedition in July 1844 is, for example, fascinating in detail and amazing—sixty-odd pages after his thrilling account of his grandfather and the African hero, May. Four crowded vessels set out to harpoon mantas. William's son, Tom, commanding one boat, was the first to overtake and strike a prey. Immediately, the "fish made a demi-vault in the air," William wrote, "and, in his descent, struck the boat violently with one of his wings." The blow sent the vessel suddenly backward, tossing the steersman and oarsmen forward—and Tom into the air and onto the back of the resurfaced manta. There Tom remained for a few endless seconds, then he leaped off, swimming toward relative safety in the boat. William's "henchman, Dick" was alert and tossed out a coil of rope and extended an oar. Tom, brought onboard again, stood and "gave three hearty cheers," assuring men in the other boats of his survival. William was furious, however, that oarsmen in the other boats were so intent upon the spectacle of Tom atop the manta that they neglected to row hard to the rescue. Simultaneous looking and rowing, William decided, "was expecting too much from African forethought and self-posession!" (71–72). However sagacious, Tom was no May, and grandsons and great-grandsons of May's black generation were not, either.

A less complex scene, redolent of European elite hunting imagery, was the finale to Elliott's "Wild-Cat Hunt in Carolina." He, his companions, horses, and servants had a remarkable day, killing a fine male before William's wizardly one-shot kill of a female in midair, fifty feet up, as she attempted to leap from one tree to another: "I . . . let slip at him in mid-flight. The arrowy posture . . . was suddenly changed, as the shot struck him to the heart," and the "beautifully spotted" creature, shortly to be identified as female, fell to the dogs. Now it was late, the sun was sinking, and they "had more than five miles to ride to our dinner." The party galloped for about two miles to a prearranged rendezvous where they were met by a large, luxurious carriage—a "barouche." From that point, "in high spirits, we dashed into town, our horns sounding a flourish as we approached—and our wild-cats, flanked by the raccoon [an incidental kill], showing forth, somewhat ostentatiously, from the front of the barouche" (151).

William Elliott was surely a lucky hunter. On another occasion he killed two bears with one heavy load of shot. He intended the first kill; the second was a fluke of that bear's standing position behind the first. The second bear crawled a short distance and died. The first must have died instantly, for William recorded that it slumped against a tree and remained upright, imitating life, but motionless. The bizarre scene evoked a memory of a large specimen, taxidermied upright, standing in the entrance hall to a fellow hunter-planter's big house (194–200). Elliott would have been the first to deny that flukey, merciful hunting was the norm, however. Indeed, he relished and repeated the most sanguinary of woodland slaughters.

On a jolly day at Chee-Ha, not far from Beaufort, horsemen converged on a shotgunned deer apparently downed by young "Tickle," a novice. Out came a knife, the deer's throat was cut, and the novice "bathed his face with the blood of his victim. (This, you must know, *is hunter's law* with us, on the killing a first deer)." The young hunter arose "from the ablution, his face glaring like an Indian chief's in all the splendor of war-paint" (155). Elliott assured his reader that the triumphant hunter, by custom disdaining to wash his face, was warmly welcomed by his young wife at the end of the day. On another occasion at Chee-Ha, William and his companions enjoyed a capital hunt among thickets of myrtle and mallow, firing from horseback, standing, and crawling on their knees, as men and prey converged. At one point a leaping deer almost joined William on his horse but, twisting itself in midflight, brushed Elliott's knee on its descent. William flipped down his gun, "pistol-fashion, with a rapid twitch, and sent the whole charge through his backbone." The deer writhed on the ground by his horse's feet. The hunter dismounted, wrestled the animal into exhaustion, and dispatched it with his knife. Still clutching his bloody blade by its handle, William heard a friend's gun, and suddenly "another deer was upon me!" By the time he recovered his gun from the underbrush, this deer had disappeared, but not for long. Crawling among the myrtles, William spotted the creature, "and to my joy and surprise, *another deer is mine!*" (170–71). Later, the dogs still scattered, men exhausted, and William covered in blood, one of the hunters sent a slave for a cart. Four dead deer needed transport, and a twenty-five-pound wild turkey hung from the saddle of one of William's companions. William exulted: "How pleasant to eat! Shall I say it? —how much pleasanter to give away! Ah, how such things do win their way to *hearts*—men's, and *women's* too!" William could not resist a bit of Carolina chauvinism, either, taunting Long Island sportsmen obliged to restock and manage game on protected club grounds. "Ours was no *preserve* shooting! . . . They were wild deer, of the wild woods, that we slew, this day at Chee-Ha!" (171–72).

Yet the image of blood-covered men celebrating charity sits with me uncomfortably. Elliott himself once declared that a "sportsmen, who gives a true description of his sports, *must be an egotist. It is his necessity*" (162). He referred to participants' perspective (as well as self-interest) in the making of hunting narratives. In *Carolina Sports*, charity—whether fish or venison given to the enslaved (people and dogs) or classy neighbors, especially women—seems simply more egotism of the masculine sort, and a bit dishonest. Slaughter for glory seems the better construction.

What a contrast to the brutal transparency of the imperial Spanish, whose term *matanzas*—massacre or slaughter[12]—remains the name of certain spots around the world: a zone (now industrial) outside Buenos Aires, a province of El Salvador, a bay in Cuba, and on this continent, a river in northeastern Florida and a creek in California. From about the mid-seventeenth century until their departure in 1763, the Spanish maintained enormous cattle ranches along the coastal plain east of Rio San Juan (subsequently St. Johns River). Logically, they may have named one of the smaller streams between San Juan and the Atlantic Rio Matanzas, as site of cattle butchering. More likely, though, Matanzas got its name from much earlier butchery—of French soldiers in 1565 at the hands of the founder of St. Augustine, Pedro Menéndez de Avilés. A French fort had been established to the north, near the mouth of the St. Johns, to intercept Spanish shipping bound from the Caribbean for home and also to menace if not capture St. Augustine. The little French force had terrible luck, however. A storm wrecked their ships and enfeebled survivors, who happened to be overwhelmingly Protestants and who offered their surrender to Menéndez. Menéndez seems deliberately to have saved perhaps half a dozen Catholics among them and then ordered the cold-blooded execution of the rest of the lot.[13] Today the Matanzas River still flows past the oldest city in the United States, hard by the restored Castillo de San Marcos, under the Bridge of Lions, on southward past the restored Fort Matanzas, and through Matanzas Inlet. In St. Augustine, Avenida Menéndez, perhaps the most prestigious street in the historic district, on the Matanzas waterfront south of the bridge, honors Don Pedro, the butcher. No one seems to mind; rather the opposite.

When William Elliott died, in 1863, an enormous slaughter of southern livestock—not to mention men—was well under way, as we have seen. Another of the war's lasting contributions to the South was the littering of the countryside with still-working firearms. The surviving poor, especially black southerners, likely gained easier access to weapons than ever before. Inevitably, whites (always of the upper classes) began to describe an epidemic of pot-shooting. Pot-shooting (also pot-hunting) meant originally the taking of wildlife for the pot, at home. Well before the Civil War, though, the term came also, and more usually, to mean casual, purposeless shooting, such as idle target practice. Precipitous declines of bird populations were everywhere attributed to pot-shooters—boys of both colors and drunken adult white men, especially. As early as 1838, Edmund Ruffin had printed in his *Farmers' Register* a long, anonymous article protesting the shooting and poisoning of birds. The author hinted at the instrumental value of birds to farmers—their consumption of insect pests—but concluded with a Christian doctrine of birds' intrinsic worth, an extraordinary suggestion for the time: "Every thing, however diminutive it may be, is formed for some end." By 1860 the *Southern Planter*, published in Richmond and representative of white elite opinion, printed a long letter from "C," self-described as a very old man from the piedmont county of Cumberland, widely familiar with the countryside, and a hunter. "C" asked, "What has become of our birds?" and proceeded to answer his question: habitat destruction for agriculture, of course; conceivably climatic change; but certainly farmers' systematic killing, and the idle, wanton shooting for "sport." "C" went on to defend not only woodpeckers and songbirds but bats and crows, reminding readers that decades earlier, the eccentric but wise John Randolph of Roanoke had forbidden the killing of crows on his plantation, preferring to put out a bit of food for them at planting time, until crops were up and crows might assist in controlling insects.[14]

Such enlightened, conservationist sentiment grew after the war, in the South as well as the Northeast. But—ever the sad case—conservation came loaded with class and racial biases heated by Reconstruction. Here is where white fear of armed freedmen joined elite sportsmen's long-announced desire to end market hunting and restrict subsistence and recreational hunting. The end of slavery, in other words, multiplied enemies of conservation—real or imagined—and thus fueled the cause. Southerners were slow, apparently, to join northeastern organizations, but gradually, toward the end of the century, there were southern Boone and Crockett clubmen and, early in the twentieth century, Audubon Society chapters and avid Ducks Unlimited members. By this time so-called fencing reform was complete or nearly so, foresters and agronomists campaigned for criminalizing woods-firing, and the broad stage was set for climactic battles for the future of men and animals.

The battles—the term does not exaggerate—were initiated by women and by their allied cultural agents, principally evangelical ministers, who were men. In 1915, one will recall, it was pious women who at last converted Alvin York from the wild ways that had made him a hero among rowdy boys and men. (His bloody mature international heroism was Christian and biblically sanctioned.) Alvin's patient mother and his young romantic interest on the larger neighboring farm (whom he married when he returned from France) disapproved of his carousing and led him to their pastor, who became Alvin's spiritual adviser. The conversion was no small accomplishment. York was a creature of an old southern world in which a man's status, often termed his honor, derived from manly regard, or how one was perceived by other men. To embrace instead an inner-directed code of discipline, restraint, and piety, doctrine almost universally understood as feminine, was serious business indeed. So in microcosm, Alvin's salvation represents a small yet significant feminine victory in a protracted, elemental confrontation.

Ted Ownby, historian of the cultural forces within modernization, has imaginatively construed much from women's and preachers' struggles against masculine "recreation," which (as we have seen) included hunting and a range of boisterous, violent entertainments that usually included animals. These struggles provide much of the context for the emergence of women's organizations and presuffrage political engagement, and for the temperance and prohibition movements. Prohibition and the Nineteenth Amendment, the national successes of women and their allies, may be, arguably, no more important than less well-known reforms, including child protection, hunting regulations, decorous county and state fairs, the humane treatment of animals, and other issues related to sanguinary male behavior.[15]

Evangelical complaints had substance. Tales of drunken gangs of males hunting all night—not infrequently binge-killing animals—surely offended many ears; but such amusements were male-only and took place outside civilization, as it were. Often as not, however, all-night shooting carousals were concluded by noisy returns—horns blowing, shots fired, and voices yelling. And since Saturdays were typically the beginning of such binges, disturbances of Sunday morning church services were not unknown. The movie *Sergeant York* opens with a nighttime country church service that is aborted by the shouting and pistol-firing of three drunken men on rearing horses outside—one of them Alvin York. Outside, the congregants (including Alvin's pious mother) notice that the initials *A Y* are shot, in perfect form, into a tree trunk. Mrs. York and other church members cannot resist expressing admiration for the signature. Other disrupters of church services were more disturbing and never tolerated. They created not only alarming noise but reckless, intentional intrusions; rocks were thrown at walls and windows, and horses actually barged into sanctuaries. When drunken hunters finally came home, they were merely drunks. Infamously abusive, sometimes physically, to their families, drunken heads of household were infamously impecunious, too, wasting wages on "bust-head" and gambling away property. Christmas, whatever day of the week it fell on, seems to have been drinkers' all-favorite holiday for bingeing.

In towns, Saturdays were occasions for men to gather—and drink—at stores, in the street, and before stables. Foul language, open gambling, and fighting were commonplace. Women and girls, wanting Saturday town diversions themselves, were disgusted and dismayed—often led away or forbidden in towns by their husbands and fathers. The same prevailed at special events such as fairs, especially when traveling circuses arrived. Both fairs and circuses provided a mixture of educational and lurid attractions. Freaks, fraudulent marvels of the animal kingdom, and scantily clothed women dancing or riding horses either intrigued or put off decent folks. Circuses' exhibitions of genuinely exotic animals, usually African and Asian, were enormously popular with southerners. Since everyone in this culture was so intimately connected to animals already, children, preachers, women, and indeed men longed to lay eyes upon elephants, lions, tigers, rhinoceroses, zebras, and giraffes. But could they avoid the lurid while visiting an educational marvel?

Home and church, as Ownby writes, were literal and figurative redoubts of decency. The task of evangelicals, simply put, was to extend them to the woods, to Main Street, and to the fair and the circus. In the instance of hunting, they had influential allies, of course, in elite sportsmen, who were well organized by early in the twentieth century, and in the new and growing corps of professional foresters. Bingeing hunters, after all, careless of animal welfare, were notoriously careless with fire. A Southern Baptist weekly paper actually endorsed conservation, which included fire suppression as well as game protection. By 1906, nearly all North Carolina counties had restricted hunting. Deer season was restricted to two or three months; seasons for quail, turkey, and other game birds lasted three or four months. Some counties prohibited the taking of squirrels and opossums. State law prohibited the killing of nongame birds. (There was an active Audubon Society, founded in 1902—apparently the South's first—at the North Carolina College for Women.) Bag limits were becoming common, too, throughout the region, and—the dead heart of William Elliott must have quickened —states or counties came increasingly to require hunters on any private grounds other than their own to obtain landowners' written permission. Old laws prohibiting fire-hunting at night were now enforced. Fishing with dynamite and market-style nets were outlawed.

In towns, ministers, organized women, some reformist editors, and supporters from business communities succeeded early in segregating rowdy sin spots and districts—from churches, from near schools, and from the emporia decent people wished to patronize. Chapters of the Woman's Christian Temperance Union participated in such moral "zoning" codes, even as they conspired and paraded to ban saloons altogether. At home and in church, too, women led (or persuaded or bullied) their menfolk to sign temperance or abstinence pledges. (One of my grandfathers, a South Caro-

*Alvin York (front center) at a community turkey shoot, early 1930s. Note that all the shooters used muzzle loaders. Courtesy Sergeant York Patriotic Foundation.*

lina Baptist born in 1879, loved to be reminded that he had once signed such a pledge, especially as he and my father had a nip before supper.) The famous South Carolina "Dispensary" of the 1890s was an early attempt to substitute a state agency for too-influential private distributors of liquor. Ultimately, though, every southern state abolished the saloon—first, usually, in county local-option elections, and then in what were usually raucous statewide referenda. The entire region was "dry" before the United States entered World War I, and southerners were essential in pushing national prohibition down the throats of northeasterners.

The reform of public entertainments such as circuses and especially county and state fairs proceeded apace, too. Localities, sometimes states, attempted to prohibit fraud, gambling, and nudity in traveling circuses and at least put show companies on the defensive. Fairs, being county- and state-sanctioned institutions, were more successfully restructured. Here again, evangelical forces were allied with emergent professions, in this case county agents employed by foundations and states and then (after 1914) the federal government, to demonstrate scientific agronomy to farmers. The addition of female home demonstration agents hugely complemented the corps of reformers dedicated to extending home and church to public venues. Early on, the agents promoted boys' corn clubs, cells of minor agronomy students who eagerly submitted to supervised production contests, as well as a variety of girls' clubs and especially the 4-H rural youth movement. Fairs became the annual summer celebration of modern achievements of many sorts: for male farmers, the display of prizewinning crop samples and livestock; for their wives, demonstrations of superior cooking, home crafts, and dairy production; and for children, the junior versions of the above. By the 1920s, fairs local and statewide were utterly committed to "progressive" farmers and their families. The lurid became rare, and even where horse racing still took place, it seems to have been (relatively) sober and well regulated.

In the parallel universe of the black South, county and home demonstration agents, along with supportive institutions such as churches and especially the colleges, pursued similar agenda at separate fairs and conferences. A noble and long-term program called Ham and Eggs was closely associated with Fort Valley State College in Georgia. Agents and their allied teachers and preachers promoted the propagation, sharing, and cooperative distribution of hogs and chickens. A patron might begin with donation of a boar and sow or rooster and hen to a worthy family, with the obligation to present a portion of litters to another family, and so on. In such a manner black farmers, the huge majority of whom were tenants or sharecroppers, might begin to establish not only better diets but the first important measure of independence from landlords and their commissaries. Communities of successful participants were celebrated every summer at Fort Valley's Ham and Eggs Week.

White agents and receptive farmers were not concerned so much with subsistence and independence as with productivity and markets. The experience of Agent E. W. Gaither of Hertford County, North Carolina, demonstrates a new and, ultimately, portentous departure. Hertford is a coastal plains county in the poor, sandy-soiled, and "backward" region of the state that was the heart of resistance to so-called fencing reform and fire suppression. Gaither arrived for part-time work in 1911 and became Hertford's full agent in 1917, toward the climax of North Carolina's battles to close the range and suppress fire. Acutely aware of this political context, Gaither campaigned to improve now-confined livestock, beginning with an anti–hog cholera program and installation of a dip vat to eradicate cattle fever ticks. About 1920 he decided to make a seemingly outrageous public gamble that he could win—or lose and be run out of Hertford. Gaither told a group of farmers that a hog, to be profitable, ought to weigh 200 pounds at six months of age. His audience apparently guffawed. With much ceremony, the agent found a "demonstration" farmer with a sow and seven piglets. Gaither supervised the feeding and care of the animals and then their exhibition at the county fair, where on average they weighed 225 pounds. Fairgoers, the agent wrote later, loved the demonstration pigpen as much "as any side show," and he "was allowed to remain" in Hertford County.[16]

Gaither was but one of many heroes of modernization across the South. White and black, men and women, the agents labored throughout the difficult interwar decades. These were economically stressed times, during which the farming population generally declined. Poor commodity prices, floods, droughts, dust storms, and tractors combined to drive out the landless, the small owners, and the unlucky. Agronomic experts aimed to help surviving farmers become more efficient—witness Agent Gaither's miracle with confined hogs. Efficiency included conservationist soil restoration and soil building and capital investments (conceivably from better livestock sales) in better production equipment and machinery, which were instrumental in increasing production on expanded fields. County agents favored large, influential farmers, who in turn might expand agents' influence. But in the South (perhaps more than other regions), during hard times state and county agricultural experts counseled farmers to "live at home." The slogan was actually an old maxim representing the ideal of self-sufficiency: Farmers should produce on their own places as many of their needed commodities as possible, beginning with vegetables, fruits, grains, and meat. Ironically, before the Civil War, the great bulk of southern farmers, including the poor ones, had already been self-sufficient. Even slaves had enlarged their welfare with cabin-side gardens, fishing, and hunting. Then, as we have seen, black southerners began freedom in dependency, and a large proportion of whites gradually slipped into dependency themselves in the decades after the war. Then came the climax of the long wars against the commons. After that, among those still farming, came the age of gasoline and a mass culture of consumption fueled by print and radio advertising. Rural Americans, in other words, were encouraged to motor off to town to buy any number of products, even food. It seems likely that hard times were more effective than county and home demonstration agents in persuading rural folk once more to try, at least, to live at home.

Women, in particular, succeeded at this and thus saved many family farms. Responding to demonstration agents' and others' initiatives in creating "curb markets" in towns, farm mothers and daughters sold eggs, butter, garden vegetables, and other produce for cash. At home they enlarged poultry flocks and increased production to make more money. Some operations became extensive, with women entrepreneurs sending shipments to more than one town, even relatively distant ones. The cash these women made in new markets was often the only money seen by farm families for years on end. Meanwhile, the chicken and egg business generated another enterprise. Since more chickens required more feed, women engaged in markets bought feed from millers, who shipped in bags. Feedbags were never thrown away but were fashioned into diapers, table linen, aprons, shirts, skirts, and dresses. Milling companies responded to this market by offering feedbags in patterns and colors. Some women actually went into the business of buying and selling bags. Only when men effectively took away from women the now-lucrative production of chickens and eggs, after World War II, did these remarkable female rural enterprises disappear.[17]

🌺 Once upon a time, chicken was a treat. Among Christians it was the centerpiece of Sunday dinner, especially if the preacher were coming. As early as the 1920s, though, a few urban-based feed and seed sellers developed means to increase supplies by distributing biddies to hard-pressed farmers, who would raise them on contract and return the broilers to the salesman for distribution in city markets. Farmers on the fringes of the

agricultural heartlands of the South were particularly receptive. Atlanta job-
bers always traveled north and northwest from town, understanding that
on the margins of Appalachia, cotton had always been a risky crop. Likewise, apple growers in northwestern Arkansas, after suffering two successive failed harvests, were eager to do contract work with feed men from
Fayetteville and Springboro. The first major expansion of chicken production took place on the Delmarva Peninsula, however. About 1923, a daring
woman raised several thousand birds, sold them all to advantage in Baltimore, invested her profits in many thousands more biddies, and so on.
Feed-mill company managers (all men, presumably) took notice and set up
contract operations with local farmers, and as early as 1926 the peninsula
produced more than a million broilers a year for the markets of Baltimore,
Philadelphia, and New York.[18]

The Delmarva ascendancy persisted through the 1930s. All this time
eating-sized chickens were still sold, live or plucked, in traditional meat
markets, and most buyers were urban folk. Yet the success of Delmarva
broiler growers in the largest urban markets prompted, or coincided at
least, with other developments. One was the creation of the so-called supermarket, a revolution in retailing and consumerism that permitted customers to wander about surveying products and even touching and handling them, instead of seeking the assistance of a clerk who stood between
merchandise and buyer. A southern chain called Piggly Wiggly was founded
by a Tennessee owner of a traditional country store who, driving one day in
the country, observed a litter of piglets meandering freely over their enclosure, picking and choosing their desires as they found them—a legendary
entrepreneurial inspiration. The second, complementary new thing was a
tendency in food marketing that mimicked industry: offer attractive, stan-
dardized, and reasonably priced products that customers might personally
examine. To this end the National Poultry Improvement Plan was created in
1935. The plan was a collaboration between industry and government dedicated to the eradication of poultry diseases, especially pullorum—chickens are sickly birds—and to the creation of high standards of breeding
and nutrition for the mass market. The ideal was a large-breasted creature,
tender, pinkish-white, and without dark feather quill marks after plucking. One of the earliest supermarket chains, the Great Atlantic and Pacific
Tea Company, announced in 1946 a Chicken of Tomorrow contest offering $5,000 to the breeder of such a superbird. The first contest finals were
conducted on the Delmarva Peninsula in 1947; the winner was a Californian. A second contest, in 1951, was revealingly held in Arkansas. By that

date, the Delmarva ascendancy had been dashed by its own success: The War Food Administration had closed the northeastern market and made the federal government principal buyer of poultry, for the armed services. Later, peninsula producers would recover, albeit in a different structure, but in the meantime, lower South entrepreneurs made their move.

Among them the most daring was Jesse Dixon Jewell, a modest fertilizer and feed dealer in Gainesville, Georgia. Like Atlanta farm supply men, Jewell and some Gainesville banker associates had been promoting broilers among marginal farmers in northern Georgia for years. Then in 1936 Jewell introduced a plan to integrate broiler production vertically. Four years later he owned a large hatchery; distributed chicks, feed, and medicine to contracted farmers in several counties; and collected the broilers after about two months, paying the farmers for their time—minus the costs of biddies, chicken feed, and medication. Jewell also owned his own processing (or "disassembly") plant, where the birds were killed, plucked, eviscerated, portioned, and packaged. Packages of chicken (whole as well as parts) were then trucked down to Atlanta distributors. In 1951 Jewell decided to sell all his chicken frozen, providing more flexibility and security in distribution— that is, shelf life.

Jewell became wealthy and famous as the first significant integrator. He owned and controlled his product virtually from egg to dinner table, and he inspired other integrators across the South: John Tyson of Tyson Foods and Harold Snyder of Arkansas Valley Feed in northwestern Arkansas, and a small group of entrepreneurs who founded Holly Farms in Wilkes County, North Carolina. Perdue Farms, a family corporation (like Tyson's), finally integrated vertically the old chicken business of the Delmarva Peninsula. Chicken became cheap, tasty meat for any day, every day, whether the preacher was coming or not. But at what a price.

First, today as fifty years ago, the presence of chicken farms almost invariably signifies a countryside's economic subjugation and dependency on powerful corporate entities. At first "chicken farming" had seemed a blessing. Cotton culture was moving west, and rural landowners occupying uncompetitive ground—especially on the fringes of the Appalachians and Ozarks and on coastal plains—were eager to work for guaranteed cash. But soon contracting with the integrators evolved into something else. In the early years, Jesse Jewell himself drove around and inspected the progress of his chicks, renewing ties with country people. As his business grew, though, he was obliged to hire inspectors. In a short time these men (and their counterparts in other companies) became de facto bosses to supposedly independent farmers. New feed formulas and medicines were not just suggested to but required of contracted farmers, as were new, larger, expensive buildings, ventilation systems, and automatic watering apparatuses. If a farmer refused, he (or she) would lose the contract and be left with investments and debts. Specialized buildings and equipment for growing broilers were suitable to no other enterprise, not even turkey farming. So farmers became ensnared, mere laborers on their own properties.

By the 1960s there was a great wave of horizontal integration in the chicken business. The great midwestern grain companies Pillsbury, Ralston-Purina, Central Soya, and others, many of them already with mills in the South, now acquired many southern broiler operations outright, along with their contracted farmers. Meanwhile, too, ongoing research involving industry and agricultural colleges yielded accelerating efficiencies not only in poultry breeding and nutrition but in the architectural details and functioning of chicken barns. By 1969 practically all American poultry was produced on such farms, in virtually uniform industrial detail. Broilers were by then the most important farm product in Alabama, Arkansas, and Georgia and second only to tobacco in North Carolina. These four states together led the nation in poultry production in 1980; Mississippi ranked fifth, Texas was seventh, and Virginia was tenth. Even before this date, fierce price competition had already squeezed farmer-operators even more. Economists finally recognized that "farmers" had actually become laborers and undertook to measure the wages they were earning. In 1967 an early USDA study revealed that northern Alabama chicken farmers earned on average *minus* thirty-six cents an hour. In 1970 the chicken corporations made record profits, but the typical farmer in the business made only about $2,000 from broiler sales.

Another aspect of the chicken house in the countryside is the literal squeezing of chickens. Confining animals may seem a natural progression from so-called fencing reform. Natural it is not, however, utterly to separate domesticated animals from the rest of nature. Fenced chicken yards permit sky, rain, and dirt as well as movement and species society. Once the government and retailers had created a new-model chicken, however, the logic of taking larger and larger numbers indoors became compelling: indoors is safer, healthier, and management friendly. Confinement, in turn, necessitated the universal practice of removing chickens' beaks so the birds could not damage one another. And as competition grew ever fiercer in the industry, it seems inevitable that just as farmers were squeezed, so were chickens. Animals in motion burn energy and reach broiler weight more slowly; they also require more feed, water, and medicines. So industrial designers made (and farmers were obliged to build) factory-barns in which birds were not only debeaked but nearly immobilized. Light stimulates, so the barns were dimmed to a torpor-inducing twilight. Each broiler was confined, too, as hens in egg factories are—in about forty-eight square inches, half the area of a conventional piece of typing or printer paper. (Egg producers within the European Union must allow each hen 120 square inches, plus a perch and a nesting box, by 2012. In the United States, there is not even discussion of interfering with industry standards.) No wonder then, that when men come in tractor-trailer rigs to gather the chickens for the slaughterhouses, the animals are relatively docile and easy to carry by their feet in groups of three or even four per hand (if the men are well-sized themselves). "They can get to throwing those birds around a bit," said a Maryland chicken farmer of the pick-up crews. "It's a tough job."[19]

Chicken slaughterhouses and packing plants are notorious not only for their low wages, miserable working conditions, and high employee turnover rates but for the senselessly cruel manner in which they end chickens' brief lives. Typically, the animals are tied (or clamped) live, by their feet, overhead at the beginning of the disassembly line. Their throats are quickly slit with workers' knives. But decade after decade, workers and inspectors have observed that chickens are often still alive when submerged in scalding water to begin the defeathering process. Other than the late Harry Spira, who campaigned against unnecessary slaughterhouse cruelty of all meat animals and, more recently, People for the Ethical Treatment of Animals (PETA), few Americans, and perhaps fewer southerners I would bet, have concerned themselves. Our distance from these creatures has so lengthened that one might say there is no relationship between consumer and meat animal at all, save consumption.

Poultry process workers are different, of course. PETA had long collected anecdotal evidence of undue cruelty (that is, other than killing) in chicken plants and, in October 2003, managed to place an undercover investigator on the disassembly line at the Pilgrim's Pride unit in Moorefield, West Virginia. Pilgrim's Pride is the second-largest poultry processor in the United States and a major supplier to Kentucky Fried Chicken, which buys some 700 million chickens per year. Somehow the spy was able to videotape much of the activity along the line, and soon after he left the Moorefield plant in May 2004, PETA posted the video on its website, sent out print news releases, and made the anonymous investigator available for interviews. In (blessed) brief: The spy observed workers jumping on, drop-kicking, and slamming live chickens into walls. He also saw workers plucking them (again while alive) to "make it snow," squeezing them to shower feces on other chickens, suffocating them with latex gloves placed over their heads, and tearing off heads in order to write graffiti on walls with blood. There was more—the spy said he witnessed "hundreds" of acts of cruelty—but enough! Allowing for the grim and onerous working conditions and poor pay of slaughterhouse workers, everyone from the investigator himself to PETA, reporters, and the general public wanted to know why. The spy simply declared that drop-kicking and slamming were for fun; the rest was done "to alleviate boredom or vent frustrations."[20]

If one wonders whether social classes a few rungs above the bloodied slaughterhouse proletariat display more sympathy with animals that are to be consumed, I suspect the answer is negative. A demonstration presented itself on 11 May 2003, when I happened to catch a segment of a cable TV Food Channel program on a little Texas town's celebration of the local turkey industry. The festival's highlight, apparently, was a contest called "Bowling with Turkeys." I stared in astonishment as succulent white people, men and women, tossed and rolled frozen, shrink-wrapped turkeys, outdoors, down an alley of artificial turf carpet toward bowling pins. With every minor knockdown, the competitors jumped, squealed, and high-fived one another. Pathetic. No sympathy, no respect.

PETA, arguably a southern, if only marginally so, radical animal rights organization, would abolish such obscenities. English-born Ingrid Newkirk founded PETA more than two decades ago in suburban Maryland. She has provoked outrage on several continents with her guerrilla warfare on fur and leather clothing—PETA once managed to serve a dead raccoon to the editor of *Vogue* at the Four Seasons restaurant in Manhattan—as well as on cosmetic and medical researchers who experiment on animals, and on the meat industries. In 1996 Newkirk had enough contributions to buy a steel-and-glass building by the Elizabeth River in Norfolk, Virginia, and PETA persists onward in battle.

Meanwhile, the industrialized chicken has also signified one more horror for the landscape. That is the fouling of water. Once upon a time, animals were assumed essential to conservationist agriculture. Before that, shifting culture in places with a low population may have repaired farming's degradation by the long fallow, or simple neglect. But when farmers began to stay in one place and tried to make crop fields permanent, applications of animal manure were central to maintenance. Exogenous commercial fertilizers—especially guano in the mid-nineteenth century—cer-

*Headquarters, People for the Ethical Treatment of Animals, Norfolk, Virginia, ca. 2000. Courtesy* PETA.

tainly lessened animal manure's place in the soil-improvement gospel, but early-twentieth-century "progressive" agronomy treasured manure, still, for the independence it conferred on poorer and "family" farmers. So when such farmers contracted with, say, Jesse Jewell during the 1940s, it was assumed that the ton of manure accumulating with each two-month cycle of broiler breeding would go onto the farmers' corn and cotton fields—another benefit.

In short time, though, chicken houses grew—up to 300 yards long by the end of the twentieth century. Even if poultry droppings had been appropriate fertilizer for northern Georgia's clay, now there was a mounting superfluity. Chicken farmers, already economic captives of the integrators, became violators of 1960s and 1970s clean water legislation. Fertilizer applied in a rainy spring almost inevitably leaches into watercourses; toxic creeks and annual fish kills are predictable. Great dumps of chicken waste, left by farmers or by cleanup contractors, are certain polluters. Add to this wastes from the companies' processing plants, too often improperly disposed of.

Tyson Foods had, by the 1990s, become the most notorious of polluters. The explanation lay partly in the poultry pioneer's sheer size. Don Tyson, son of the founder, like his father worshiped the doctrine of "grow or die," and after Tyson's acquisition of North Carolina–based Holly Farms in 1989, Tyson became the largest producer and processor of poultry in the United States. Complaints of watercourse pollution were already legend in Arkansas. Now the federal Justice Department charged a Tyson processing plant with dumping in the Missouri River. Simultaneously Tyson was infamous for the merciless competition and cost cutting associated with what could justly be termed a slaughterhouse labor syndrome. In Iowa, the aggressive new-era meat processor, IBP (formerly Iowa Beef Packers), had already established a regime of recruiting desperate workers from afar—southern black migrants, then Chicanos, Guatamalans, and even East Africans— willing to labor under dangerous and debilitating conditions. In the South Tyson, having exhausted local labor pools dominated by poor black women, connected with Mexican and Central American "coyotes" and filled assembly lines with Mesoamericans. Many of them were illegal, some were also too young, and a few used their U.S. positions to import and deal illegal drugs. In 2001 Tyson narrowly failed in a risky bid to buy IBP; Tyson lost to another southern giant, Smithfield Foods of Virginia. And notwithstanding Tyson's close ties in Little Rock and Washington, D.C., with both Democrats and Republicans, the company was beset with indictments and fines for violations of child labor and immigration laws as well as the Clean Water Act.[21]

🐝 Water pollution is hardly new. The term apparently appeared in English North America in the eighteenth century. In Virginia and Maryland (and doubtlessly elsewhere), people living downstream from sawmills and tanneries complained of sawdust and toxic wastes flowing past their properties and sickening people and domestic animals. Another human-caused phenomenon, obvious at least as early as the eighteenth century, was siltation of creeks, rivers, and estuaries. Siltation clouds water, filtering or shutting out the sunlight that nourishes subaquatic vegetation, which is the origin of the maritime food chain. Subaquatic vegetation feeds phytoplankton, which are fodder for larger creatures, and so on, to us. Great storms have loosened soils hundreds of miles from Chesapeake Bay and the Mississippi —from all watercourses—and carried loam, clay, and other terrestrial debris down tributaries to the principals, disrupting wildlife sometimes for more than a year. More often it is agriculture that pollutes in this fashion. Seventeenth-century hoe cultivation of tobacco and grains may have bared enough tidewater and upland landscape not only to cloud rivers but to change rivers' boundaries. Introduction of plows and slave labor, both intensive by the first quarter of the eighteenth century, hugely enlarged cultivated landscapes and, doubtlessly, increased siltation. By the time of the Revolution, any number of early tobacco ports along the upper Chesapeake system were isolated by receding shorelines. Everywhere, but especially in lowlands with high water tables, privies must have leached into shallow aquifers and then into watercourses. Where populations were concentrated —Baltimore, Norfolk, and Charleston in early times—leaching and simple dumping of many sorts of wastes were concentrated, too.

English riparian law, adopted everywhere in eastern North America, conveyed rights to use watercourses to all who dwelled by them. Individuals might construct next to rivers parallel "traces" to power mills but were obligated to permit streams to flow onward and supply people downstream. In this sense every creek, river, bay, and sound was a commons as vital as the South's vast forests. Fishing the commons was no less a common right than hunting, even though, of course, there was a protocol to obtaining permission to line-fish on a bank belonging to someone else. Commercial fishing with seines was more problematic and best conducted on open waters.

Industrial-scale fishing came late and most disastrously (and famously) to Chesapeake Bay. At the beginning of the seventeenth century, explorer

John Smith had effused over the plenitude and sizes of edible aquatic life in the bay—oysters a foot long—despite substantial populations of indigenous people who fished with nets as well as hooks, spears, and arrows. European and American denizens of the bay followed suit. They angled for many species, for sport and table. They strung huge seines across rivers to trap migrating shad. And elegant little boats, called skipjacks, sailed the bay gathering oysters, most of them the hard way. This was the muscular business of tonging on an oyster bank, filling the boat, and sailing back to a town to sell by the bushel. Regeneration of oysters requires maintenance of banks of shells in the water. Skeletons of the dead harbor the life of the future: infant oysters, or "spats," which cling to the banks and feed. We know of few skipjack captains or river tongers returning with shucked shells. These accumulated in great piles by docks and packing houses, to be spread on paths and roads as paving and, later, to be ground into grit for chicken feed supplement. So two centuries of oystering by Euro-Americans surely reduced the banks. Then came industrial technology.

Shortly after the Yankee invasion that destroyed fences, cattle, and hogs, but preceding that of the industrial lumber operators, came the dredge boats. Steam-powered craft pulling large iron- or steel-toothed scoops, or dredges, had already raped the oyster beds of New England and Long Island Sound. Now their migration carried them southward, to Delaware Bay and to the Chesapeake. Chugging up to ancient shell banks, the dredgers scraped up and dumped on their decks loads of oysters unimagined by local watermen. The harvests were in turn dumped at canneries, especially in the new town of Crisfield, Maryland, where some oysters were shucked and packed in tins, while others were shipped in-shell. The Baltimore and Ohio Railroad gained good business, while midwesterners and Plains folk savored undreamed-of *fruits de mer*. Hoosiers took up the custom of eating oyster dressing with their Christmas turkeys, and oyster-shell paths began to appear in inland gardens.[22]

In 1871 the first in a series of "oyster wars" began when dredge boats steamed into rivers where dredging was against the law. River tongers, frustrated with Maryland's failure to enforce the prohibition, took up arms. Both Maryland and Virginia finally established fisheries police; but some dredgers persisted, and local tongers again took the law into their own hands. Meanwhile, in 1878, a U.S. navy engineer began the very first survey of the Chesapeake's bottom. In Tangier Sound, always a rich and contested oyster ground, the engineer found on average only one oyster for every three square yards—evidence confirming long-held suspicion that the bay was becoming exhausted. Despite decreased yields, dredging and tonging went on, and the 1880s were actually the shippers' most prosperous decade. Only when the banks were nearly gone, in the early 1890s, with dredgers absurdly competing for dregs, did Maryland and Virginia begin to consider regulation. Early in the twentieth century, Maryland tried leasing grounds. Both state governments favored programs to rebuild oyster banks, but watermen, dredgers, and tongers alike were uncooperative.

Finfishers were no less greedy and resistant to restraint than the oystermen. During the 1890s, for example, the typical harvest of shad from the Chesapeake was 14 million pounds. By the 1930s it was 0.5 million. Crab populations fared a bit better, but their numbers fell, too. Ironically, by the time William Warner's elegiac, Pulitzer Prize–winning *Beautiful Swimmers: Watermen, Crabs, and the Chesapeake Bay* appeared in 1976, pure crabmeat approached the prohibitively expensive.

Meanwhile urban development and suburban sprawl throughout much of the bay's immediate vicinity and hundreds of miles into its 64-million-square-mile drainage area brought other ills: untreated or ill-treated sewage from metropolitan Baltimore, Washington, Richmond, and Norfolk; oily runoff from millions of autos and trucks; air pollution (including acid rain); and increased siltation of the bay and its feeder rivers from forest clearance and wetland filling, both of these to make new suburbs. Subaquatic vegetation was sparse and dying. In the decades after World War II as well, both farmers and suburban gardeners became addicted to petroleum-based herbicides and pesticides; these, too, washed into the rivers and the estuary. Then in 1997 a particularly deadly "red tide," a toxic algae, appeared in a tributary of the Pocomoke on Maryland's Eastern Shore. The substance of the tide was quickly identified as *Pfiesteria piscicida*, a recently discovered dinoflagellate that, in one of its many forms, inflicted brutal lesions on finfish, consumed them, and worse (to us), produced skin lesions and neurological damage in humans who touched affected water or breathed air from concentrations of *Pfiesteria*.

Panic ensued as dead fish surfaced in huge numbers. Before November's chill winds finally canceled the tide, tourism was stopped cold, virtually all fishing in the upper bay ceased, and packing plants closed, leaving thousands unemployed. The governor produced a half-million-dollar fund for study and problem solving, largely, it seems, to calm panic. The fish-killer tide had certainly been triggered by so-called nutrient-loading: the dumping or leaching of nitrogenous matter into the water. There were any number of candidates, but the most likely culprit was the 6,000-odd chicken farms and associated processing plants on the Delmarva Peninsula. Such probable causation obliges us to return once more to land animals and the industrial-scale production of meat.

🦟 *Pfiesteria* had been discovered and named in Raleigh by a young aquatic biologist named JoAnn Burkholder at North Carolina State University. Intensely engaged in her own research and still struggling for tenure, one day Burkholder took a call from across campus, from the veterinary school: the fish specialist there complained that his specimens kept dying in his tanks, no matter how well he and his assistants cleaned and checked; would she help? So began an amazing and horrifying story. Burkholder and her assistant, especially the latter, suffered disorientation and memory loss from working over an infested tank. Later, reports of many thousands of dead fish floating up with dreadful lesions came in from eastern Carolina's sounds and rivers, along with reports of watermen and swimmers with lesions on their hands and arms. Burkholder, at her microscope, finally saw her dinoflagellate as it morphed through an astounding number of shapes when, stimulated by oxygenated nutrients in its environment, it was aroused to mass as a red tide and attack fish and all other flesh.[23]

After Burkholder's research was confirmed and published, she was hailed by environmentalists and some representatives of the tourism-recreation industry as heroine and savior. A few businesspeople along the coast cursed her for prolonging bad news, which (they profoundly hoped) might simply go away. Unambiguous fury came from a new and powerful group in North Carolina: big pork, since that industry happened to be the leading suspect, among a slew of polluters in eastern Carolina, as a trigger of *Pfiesteria*. By the early 1990s North Carolina was challenging Iowa as the nation's leading pork producer. (It had succeeded by 2001.) There were about as many hogs in the state—most of them in the east—as people in New York City: about 8 million. It is disgustingly fascinating, too, that pound for pound, hogs generate approximately twice as much feces and urine each day as humans. Coastal Carolina's geologic morphology is unsuited for such intensive industrial husbandry. It has a high water table and wetlands everywhere, between rivers great and small: the Chowan, the Tar and Pamlico, the Neuse, the New, and the Cape Fear. What to do with these oceans of swine waste, then? Spread or spray it on nearby crop fields. Before it can be disbursed, though, the waste accumulates so rapidly and enormously that it must be stored somewhere. So Carolinians resorted to an old midwestern solution to handling the effluvia of great concentrations of animals: creation of storage "lagoons" of considerable proportions. Even in the Midwest, where many soils are semipermeable clays, lagoons are usually well lined with heavy plastic to prevent leaching into aquifers and watercourses. No such regulations existed at the time in North Carolina, and many hog confinement operations excavated lagoons and never lined them, although they were positioned directly atop aquifers and/or along-side swamps (through which waters move), pocosins, creeks, or rivers. Leaching proceeded apace. Then came storms, and some lagoons burst. Great spills went directly into the Neuse, New, and Cape Fear rivers. One spill alone consisted of 25 million gallons of swine wastes.

Darkened hog farms with millions of fat occupants drowsily eating their way to oblivion smelled bad already, everyone agreed. A study sponsored by Duke University (during the mid-1990s) confirmed that foul odors indeed included toxic fumes—ammonia, most obviously, and worse. In 2003 a Stanford University physician found permanent neurological damage in a middle-aged, middle-class couple who lived half a mile from a confinement hog farm in Ohio.[24] In eastern North Carolina, however, the biggest hog operations exist in the poorest and blackest rural neighborhoods in the state—notably in Duplin and Sampson counties—where simple justice lags and so-called environmental civil rights were long unimaginable. The lagoon breaks, however, plus mounting evidence of wastes leaching into aquifers and streams, affected all classes. Burkholder's discovery confirmed that the wet commons were scarily imperiled; creeks, rivers, and sounds were plied by poor and working-class watermen, by businesses, by wealthy summer people and vacationers—by virtually everyone. An industrial-environmental struggle was under way, then, and along the way, North Carolinians (and many others) began to reconstruct just *how* so many hogs appeared, in such a short time, in this unlikely and inappropriate part of the state.

Coastal Carolinians, along with more remote rural mountain folk, had long resisted enclosure and by-the-book animal husbandry, demonstration agent Gaither's 1920–21 triumph in Hertford County notwithstanding. Ultimately, though, hard times and the relentless campaigning of other government-sponsored scientists and educators succeeded in converting "backward" down-easterners, as coastal plain folk have long been known. According to Michael Thompson, ethnographer of hogs down east (and a native himself), the beginning of North Carolina's great changeover to modern pork production was the appointment in 1918 of William W. Shay to head the state department of agriculture's new swine division in Raleigh. Shay himself was an experienced midwestern hog breeder. He and his wife moved to a western Carolina mountaintop after they were diagnosed as tubercular. (Mountains, we will recall, allegedly promote health as well as wisdom—rather the opposite of lowlands.) The Shays, natives of a regional culture long devoted to purebred farm animals, systematic feeding, sanitary penning, and careful attention to markets, were shocked at animal husbandry, southern style. In Raleigh, Shay became principal evangelist for midwestern-style pork production, taking his commonsense Shay Method to demonstrations throughout the state. He took a particular interest in eastern counties, where there seemed no method at all to raising hogs, and where cotton culture was weevil-infested and crumbling. Shay readily adapted his program to the Depression-era USDA emphasis on self-sufficiency: the safety-first, live-at-home premise for careful husbandry. Thus Carolinians were gradually persuaded toward a rural business culture that more resembled that of Iowa and Shay's native Michigan. Later, and again like midwesterners, once the opportunity and technology appeared, such folk might require little persuasion to move beyond mere enclosure to confinement, then industrial-scale confinement.

By 1965 eastern North Carolina had a state-sponsored Swine Development Center near Rocky Mount. State officials, anticipating a growing assault on tobacco use and ultimate attacks on the New Deal–era tobacco subsidies that farmers relied on, hoped to develop a profitable alternative in hogs. Carolina husbandry still lagged far behind the Midwest, however. There, some farmers were already abandoning the wet, cold (or hot) outdoor work of raising pigs and turning to brilliantly designed new confinement operations, where mastery was more comfortable and science was more easily administered. The model for hog confinement was hardly foreign but as southern as Jesse Jewell: the chicken business, of course.

The most portentous, now-legendary, initiative in North Carolina, however, came not from government but one individual, down in Duplin County. There, in 1961, Wendell Murphy was a vocational agriculture teacher at the Rose Hill high school. As such, he was a poorly paid minion at the bottom of the system of modern agronomic education, founded back in 1914. Murphy was ambitious to be in the private sector, though, and with his own modest savings and his father's guarantee of a bank loan, he bought a feed mill. Now he followed Jesse Jewell's path by entering the market animal business as a sideline. By 1968 Murphy had given up both teaching and the feed mill to concentrate on hogs. At that point his method was conventional: he stuffed swine with corn in his own open-air feedlot. Then calamity led to innovation. An outbreak of hog cholera in 1969 forced Murphy to close his operation. USDA officials ordered the destruction of infected animals and quarantined others that may have been exposed. Unwilling to wait out the quarantine, Murphy figured out a way to raise hogs on others' property, beyond the quarantine. He contracted with small farmers to raise his pigs. Murphy supplied fencing, and the contract farmers provided the labor, for which he paid one dollar for the raising of each animal. Murphy collected the grown hogs and marketed them.

Shortly he created Murphy Family Farms, which led the national trend toward confinement and an ever-larger scale in production. By the mid-1990s Murphy Farms was the biggest pork producer in the country, meaning it owned more than a quarter-million sows and 6 million pigs in progressive stages from farrow to what is morbidly called finish. By this time Murphy himself had served in the state senate (with a particular interest in environmental regulations) and become known as "Boss Hog." In 1997 he was featured in *Forbes* magazine as "The Ray Kroc of Pigsties."[25] Stunning business success by an individual or corporation, however, has consequences.

By the 1990s, Murphy Family Farms, Smithfield Foods, the Cargill agriconglomerate's Swine Products Department, and a few others had made contracting and confinement virtually the *only* way to be in the pork market. (In Jane Smiley's 1992 Pulitzer Prize–winning novel, *A Thousand Acres*, poor Ty, the ambitious son-in-law of the Iowa patriarch, is ruined in his attempt to become a confinement operator by himself.) Bankers and agricultural economists colluded to discourage individuals from entering the business on a small scale. Persisting family-size hog farmers are driven out of the market by conglomerates' low pricing. A few Carolinians and southeastern Virginians I happen to have heard of—all of them now old—raise a few pigs for their own and their friends' delectation. They think hams and barbeque made from hogs that have trod the earth and seen the sun taste better. One must doubt, however, that their conviction and tradition will be carried on.

Another consequence is the revolution in pigs' own life circumstances. Their fate, of course, has become that of chickens, except it is arguably a more brutal one, given that swine are mammals with sizable brains and considerable intelligence. Sows, whose purpose is to drop litters as efficiently as possible, are confined (within confinement buildings) so tightly they cannot turn or bow to nuzzle and manage their own offspring. (This practice was banned in the United Kingdom in 1998 and will soon cease throughout the European Union.) Once weaned, farrows are confined, not unlike broilers-to-be; kept medicated; and are encouraged to feed almost continuously in gloomy semidarkness until in a short time they are ready for the slaughterhouses, which are themselves a well-documented horror for workers as well as animals.[26]

Then there is the industry's cumulative effect on air and the waters. The first is rendered dangerous, and the latter is "turned to blood," just as threatened (or promised) in the terrifying last book of the New Testament. Murphy and other confinement integrators resisted regulation. By the mid- and late 1990s, the government finally imposed moratoriums on construction of new pork operations, and North Carolinians, black and white, had organized themselves to force fume abatement. Whether Wendell Murphy, a native of the region, after all, ultimately would have responded constructively became moot in 2001, when he sold Murphy Family Farms to Smithfield Foods. Smithfield is of Smithfield, Virginia, where Pagan Creek empties into the James, not far west of Hampton Roads and the bottom of Chesapeake Bay. Smithfield Foods' chief executive, a native of this low landscape so similar to eastern Carolina, lives and works in Manhattan. His corporation, meanwhile, has been one of the most flagrant scofflaws in the region. It is the Tyson's of tidewater, Virginia, dumping slaughterhouse wastes into the Pagan, silently daring the state's environmental protection agency to act, then paying relatively modest fines if officials are paying attention. That Smithfield will be a better corporate citizen in North Carolina seems a possibility as dim as the atmosphere in a chicken or hog barn.

🦋 Thirty years before Smithfield took over Murphy Farms and North Carolina became premier pork producer, Audie Leon Murphy, near-mythic successor to Daniel Boone, was killed in a small plane crash near Roanoke, Virginia, just short of his forty-seventh birthday. An old buddy observed that it took a bad pilot and a mountain to do him in. Since his picture had appeared on the cover of *Life* when he came home from Europe in 1945, Murphy had become a Californian, starred in B+ westerns, married twice, and fathered two sons—all despite unending nightmares and flashbacks from the war, a taut edginess that led to fights and lawsuits, and a reckless propensity to gamble. But then he failed as a movie producer and, apparently, lost all his money. Aside from his many medals, his personal effects included a huge collection of firearms, military and others, suggesting continuity to his dangerous ways. And he had carried a pistol (licensed in Los Angeles) throughout his postcombat years. Odd, then, remembering that first scene in his movie autobiography, that some time before the crash, a friend had invited Murphy to go hunting and Murphy had responded, "I don't like to hunt animals. But if you want to hunt some people, I'll go with you."[27]

*I am convinced that Christianity as practiced is an*
*attenuated form of nature worship.*
—Zora Neale Hurston to Langston Hughes, 30 April 1929

*You'd love a Florida rain-storm. Raindrops huge and pelting. The*
*sky ripped open by lightning, the heavens rocked by thunder. Then*
*a sky so blue that there is no word to name its color, and birds*
*bursting open with song.*
—Zora Neale Hurston to a New York City friend, ca. 1932

*The ecosystem is greater than the sum of its parts.*
—Eugene P. Odum, 1953

# 5

## ENCHANTMENT AND EQUILIBRIUM

During the 1970s—the decade of jogging and tennis—
Americans began to put on weight. Three decades later,
public health officials declared an epidemic of obesity. The
phenomenon is national. Midwesterners, ever stereotyped
as husky, are now bulky; even Californians have added heft,
but Mississippians are the fattest Americans—yet another
doleful ranking for the Magnolia State. This vast succulence
Americans have layered upon themselves corresponds, of
course, to the suburbanization of the population. Americans drive more than ever and walk and climb probably
less than ever. Very few American cities are walking ones.
New York, however, the borough of Manhattan best of all,
is among the premier walking metropolises on earth, and
New Yorkers are among the slimmest and fittest Americans.
Case explained, then.

Yet, must sedentary lifestyles necessarily, and alone, produce obesity? Could the etiology of the suburban plague be
this simple? Michael Pollan, a gardening and nature writer,
argues no. Obesity is caused by consumption of too many
calories, and recently Pollan has accumulated what seems
an incontrovertible case against corn as source of those
calories—*corn*: the blessed gift of ancient Mesoamericans

to the world and the grain that waves most gloriously across North America still.[1]

Between 1977 and the beginning of the twenty-first century, the typical American added at least 10 percent—200-odd more calories—to his or her daily diet. During the same years, Coca-Cola morphed from eight-ounce bottles into twenty-ounce jugs, the fluid counterpart of the great burgeoning of serving sizes of restaurant food (both sit-down and take-out) and the gargantuan multiplication of so-called snack foods. All these augmentations remained relatively cheap, too, and herein lay the real source of the new plague.

The United States is overwhelmed by its own grain production, especially corn. Some is dumped abroad, further hardening the lives of struggling farmers in poor countries in the Southern Hemisphere. Some is refined into a fuel called ethanol. Most, however, is ingeniously (and insidiously) converted here at home into "added value" processed food and beverage components. Corn becomes chips and other snacks, it coats and/or binds chicken "nuggets" and other ersatz foods, and as high-fructose syrup—replacing cane sugar—it sweetens Coke and a host of other soft drinks, even so-called milk-based products vended in schools.

Corn's sudden ubiquity in American diets dates from a strange domestic political crisis. In 1972 the Nixon administration brokered a stunning grain deal with the old Soviet Union, whose agricultural expansion schemes of the previous decade had flopped miserably. American farmers would feed their fearsome Cold War enemies, and Nixon had scored a great coup, or so it appeared, both abroad and at home. On the latter front, however, the coup turned on the deal-maker in short order. Enormous shipments to the Soviet Union reduced domestic stores, and prices for not only bread but meat and milk soared. Consumers demonstrated against suddenly rising food prices outside supermarkets, boycotted meat, and threatened to throw out the Republicans. Nixon ordered his secretary of agriculture, the midwesterner Earl Butz, to do something, and quick. Senators and representatives from farm states eagerly lobbied for the secretary's dramatic reversal of national agricultural policy established in 1933. The new departure encouraged and rewarded with lavish subsidies *not* the restraint of production via subsidized retirement of acreage into "conservation" but an enormous expansion of grain culture, wherein every farmer would "plant from fence row to fence row." Soon food prices at home came down again, even while Soviet demand persisted. Some farmers of my acquaintance in the Midwest adopted a business plan called "continuous corn." The plan meant, of course, no crop rotation and the abandonment of any pretense of "conservation farming." Foreign purchases and government support rationalized expensive chemical "inputs" to grow corn on the same land, year after year. The result was more anhydrous ammonia for enfeebled soils and more petroleum-based herbicides and pesticides to protect vast man-made deserts consisting of but one species of plant. And while food and drink still seemed a great bargain at the stores and restaurants, by 2003 tax-payers were contributing no less than $19 billion a year in direct payments to farmers. Toward the end of 2005, the USDA projected a subsidy approaching $23 billion.[2] The ecological companion to the obesity epidemic, then, is an enormous rural landscape saturated with chemicals and—as ever with extensive agriculture—windblown, gullying, wasting soil.

The contemporary plague of corn is not unprecedented. Another occurred centuries ago and much farther from the birthplace of maize culture. It was an epidemic outbreak of a chronic, sometimes fatal dietary disorder later named pellagra that in deep retrospect seems a supremely ironic spin on the storied Columbian Exchange. The Americas, having been isolated from Eurasian people, animals, plants, and pathogens for so many thousands of years, were, beginning with Christopher Columbus and the Spanish, simply overrun with Europeans and European cattle, hogs, honey-bees, wheat, smallpox, measles, and a host of other invisible conquistadors.[3] In return—so goes the simplified version of the cataclysm—other than precious metals and a few novel specimens of plants and animals, the original Americans sent only syphilis. Actually Europeans sent home many tree seedlings intended to reforest their homelands, plus many practical, edible plants, including potatoes, tomatoes, and maize. Most Europeans seemed to have thought corn unfit for direct human consumption, but finally, in northern Spain and northern Italy, well before the end of the sixteenth century, they adopted extensive corn culture in order to feed swine, which tasted quite good when fattened with maize. Later, after the French national horticultural society vigorously endorsed maize culture in 1829, extensive corn planting diffused to southern France, then to northern Egypt, southern Africa, and parts of temperate and tropical Asia. Pellagra also appeared in all these places, first in southern Europe.

In 1735 a physician to the Spanish court recorded the first known epidemic of a "disgusting indigenous disease" among Asturian peasants. Victims' exposed skin reddened, then broke out with lesions and blisters. In advanced cases a distinctive butterfly pattern of darkened blisters appeared on their faces, across noses. The affected peasants also suffered severe diarrhea, lassitude, and melancholia. Dementia was common in advanced cases. Some died from dehydration and possibly secondary, opportunistic pathogens. The Spanish doctor published his record twenty years later, with the unhappy observation that the malady was incurable. Italian peasants suffering the same symptoms, meanwhile, were observed and treated (without success, apparently) by Dr. Francesco Frapolli, who named the disease during the 1770s. The heartbreaking malady was subsequently identified in Austria and elsewhere in Middle and Central Europe, where big corn estates had also been established, and then, by late in the nineteenth century, in Egypt, South Africa, and China.

Yet as late as 1902 an Atlanta physician was perplexed by a country patient who almost certainly suffered from pellagra. The disorder—if it appeared at all in American medical texts—was unfamiliar, confused with other ills (such as beriberi) or dismissed as an inherited degenerative condition. Within five years, however, U.S. doctors not only identified pellagra in the South but declared an epidemic. The timing was simultaneously fortuitous and embarrassing. Hookworm (yet another "European" malady) had recently been detected in the South, and the plutocrat-philanthropist John D. Rockefeller had donated $1 million to fund its eradication. Then came the discovery of pellagra—another poor people's distress, another "lazy" disease (to be added to malaria), and yet another peculiarly southern ill. The antihookworm program certainly facilitated the long search for a remedy for pellagra. Southern physicians became public-health-minded and learned to recognize pellagrins (as sufferers are called), and state governments and especially the federal Public Health Service mobilized laboratory studies. The national press also took notice, sometimes with little sympathy if not actual malice toward the region. Four and five decades after the Civil War, southerners were still capable of presenting an embarrassing mirror image of the prosperous, healthy United States. Articulate southerners' response was often angrily defensive, so public ad hominem exchanges were distracting and counterproductive.

Pellagra, we know now, from early-twentieth-century research in the southeastern United States and elsewhere, results from an extreme deficiency of a B vitamin known as nicotinic acid or niacin. (Nicotinic acid was renamed niacin in 1942 because baking companies who agreed to enrich bread with the vitamin feared scaring consumers with a label so similar to nicotine.) Well-off people have been known to suffer from pellagra, but they are rare, probably victims of deranged, usually alcoholic, self-neglect.

The world over pellagra has ever been an illness of the poor, both rural and urban, whose diets center on corn. Maize, whether local and fresh or imported and suspect, lacks an amino acid to unlock its own niacin. Somehow Mesoamericans learned long before recorded history that corn must be soaked in lime and water before grinding and cooking. The lime not only separates husks from kernels but unbinds niacin available in the corn itself. Later, we also know, Mesoamericans cultivated citrus limes and commonly supplemented maize dishes with the juice of lime. More important, Mesoamericans always consumed corn along with the other two parts of the great American triad, beans and squashes, which also supplied the niacin-releasing amino. The triad is not only an ancient system but a perfectly balanced foodway. Maize becomes a plague, then, only when its companion foods are, for whatever reasons, lacking, and the world is out of balance.[4]

The most common causes of the crippling of the triad seem to be two: economic dependency and the alienation of dependents from land that might produce food with niacin-releasing properties. When Dr. R. M. Grimm traveled through Georgia, South Carolina, and Kentucky during 1911–13 observing pellagrins, he discerned a clear-enough pattern. Hardly any sufferer had a garden. Instead, virtually all pellagrins purchased their food (usually on credit) in company stores or plantation commissaries. Practically none of this provender was fresh but dried, canned, or packaged. Practically none was of first quality, either, rather the opposite.[5] Eighteenth-century Spanish and Italian peasants were similarly deprived of access to gardens and balanced diets, even as they labored in maize fields to produce food for animals. Workers' own rations consisted principally of mealy maize leftovers. Italian peasants in mid-eighteenth-century Lombardy labored under the *mezzardria* system, which closely resembled post-bellum sharecropping in the American South. For a long while, many southern sharecroppers had gardens and kept chickens, milk cows, and hogs. But Lombardian peasant plots were so tiny that their occupants devoted all their arable space to the commercial crop that would pay their rents. Maintaining milk and meat animals was out of the question, too. So they ate principally polenta—the yellow version of grits—made from old and/or substandard corn.[6] When maize culture expanded southward to the region of Lazio (surrounding Rome) and beyond, pellagra followed, for similar reasons.

One early educated guess at the source of pellagra, both in Europe and America, was spoiled cornmeal, badly processed and old. Very poor rural people who were deprived of access to land for their own gardens, and perhaps also denied access to game meat from aristocrats' forests and streams, may have *always* suffered from pellagra. The disease as epidemic, however, seems intimately associated with industry—with mining and manufacturing worker villages without gardens and with concentrated, industrial-scale agriculture, where owners and bosses also discovered extra profit in depriving workers (here sharecroppers, mostly) of garden plots and forcing them to depend on company stores. This phenomenon was relatively new in the American South toward the end of the nineteenth century—like pellagra itself—and it became morbid during the twentieth century.

The great British epidemiologist Fleming Sandwith, who worked in Egypt during the 1890s and then traveled through Italy and compared his own experiences with pellagrins to other physicians', observed and publicized the international correlation of pellagra with corn. Peasants in Upper (i.e., southern) Egypt ate millet and were free of the disease; peasants in Lower Egypt depended on corn, and there was an epidemic of pellagra. When he wrote to American physicians in 1893, though, Sandwith met only silence or puzzlement. And after 1907, when American public health doctors swarmed over the South, few if any seemed to be aware of Sandwith's or other Europeans' work. Many persistently assumed that pellagra originated with a germ that was transmitted by aerosol or physical contact among the laboring poor. A few early eugenicists attributed pellagra to bad genes. To settle the debate, the U.S. Public Health Service assigned one of its finest medical detectives to the region, in 1914.

Dr. Joseph Goldberger (1874–1929) was by no means alone in confirming Sandwith's conviction that pellagra was a dietary disorder, but there is justice in Goldberger's celebration as principal hero of pellagra's ultimate defeat, years after his premature death from cancer. A son of eastern European Jews who brought him to New York when Joseph was nine, Goldberger grew up in the fabled jumble of the Lower East Side and graduated from the Bellevue Medical College in 1895. He tried private medicine in New Jersey but found the work unsatisfying, so in 1899 he joined the Public Health Service. A few years later he met and married Mary Farrar, who was a grandniece of Jefferson Davis. The couple would be posted to the lower South, home of Mary's ancestors, for most of their married lives, but they also made periodic excursions to spots tropical and foreign while Goldberger waged one good war after another. He fought yellow fever in Louisiana, Mississippi, Puerto Rico, and Mexico; typhus in Mexico City; and dengue fever in Texas. He contracted but survived each of these diseases while earning a reputation for professional directness, modesty, patience, and remarkable powers of listening and observation.[7]

Between 1914 and the early 1920s, Goldberger either invented or confronted a string of hypotheses on the source(s) of pellagra, then tested each. Among the first was the theory that diet *within institutions* caused pellagra, since the illness was first confirmed at a hospital for the insane, then at similar institutions in other southern states, and in orphanages. Told that nurses and kitchen staff ate the same food as inmates or patients, Goldberger noticed that not a single staff member suffered from pellagra. Certainly they had other food sources, away from institutions, but Goldberger insisted on watching everyone eat. Observation confirmed his suspicion that staffs ate first and took better portions for themselves. Likewise, patients not suffering from pellagra and those in the early stages took food from the plates of advanced pellagrins, who were weak, despondent, and compliant. Goldberger found federal funds to supplement institutional food with milk, eggs, beans, peas, and fresh meat and ensured that every patient received appropriate portions. Nearly all who consumed these foods improved; some walked out of hospitals in good health within a few weeks. A bit later Goldberger conducted an experiment by supplementing diets with legumes alone—here was a cheaper, more accessible theoretical treatment. Once more he was successful, and he wrote exuberantly to Mary, "It seems probable that pellagra can be wiped out in our South by simply getting the people to eat beans, Beans, BEAns, BEANs, and BEANS!!!"[8] Two of the Mesoamerican triad's three legs would do, of course, although neither Goldberger nor any other researcher yet knew just why.

Next, and most famously, Goldberger tested the germ hypothesis. Having already observed that professional staff and institutional food and cleaning workers among pellagrins virtually never had pellagra themselves, he was confident that volunteers who ingested pellagrins' skin scales, nasal mucous, urine, and feces or who submitted to muscle injections of pellagrins' blood would not come down with the illness. So in 1916 Goldberger organized what he called "filth parties" for sixteen volunteer subjects, including himself and his wife. (The others were principally medical people scattered between New Orleans and Washington, D.C.) Goldberger injected himself with a sufferer's blood as well as swallowing a fat "pill" containing wastes. Like the other volunteers, he felt pain in the tissue the needle penetrated, and he suffered bowel disorders for a while after taking the filthy pill. All recovered in short time, and of course none contracted pellagra. Some doctors criticized the experiment: the volunteers were too few; the trial was mere grandstanding. But the germ theory was discredited.

Goldberger labored on in the South through most of the 1920s, and his medical comrades continued through the Depression and beyond. These decades were fruitful in humanitarian fieldwork but also in laboratories. Nutrition was a new science when that first-known pellagra sufferer appeared in Atlanta in 1902. Thereafter scientists separated and named one vitamin after another. Among these were brilliant and persistent biochemists and epidemiologists in Germany and at the University of Wisconsin, who during the 1930s confirmed that nicotinic acid, among the B group of vitamins, was the missing element in pellagrins' diets. Renamed niacin and added to virtually all store-bought bread since 1942, the mighty amino conquered pellagra, at long last, in relatively short time.

Perhaps as many as 100,000 Americans actually died from the disorder. They were overwhelmingly southerners, more were women, and black southerners suffered disproportionately to whites. Conquest of pellagra was spotty and interrupted, too. In 1940 — three years after distribution of nicotinic acid pills — 2,040 pellagra deaths were recorded. In 1945 — three years after the introduction of niacin-enriched bread — there were 865. Few cases and hardly any deaths were reported after the 1950s. This triumph-apparent exceeds that of the nineteenth-century French version of Joseph Goldberger, the great Dr. Théophile Roussel, who defeated pellagra by persuading the national government to distribute wheat to corn-plagued peasants.[9] (Distributing beans, one must think, would have been yet more successful.) Normally, or canonically in medical history, scientific understanding of cause and practical application of a cure trumps experimental and humanitarian fixes, such as Roussel's and Goldberger's. But perhaps not. The ancient triad — or merely corn and beans without squashes — had prevented pellagra for millennia, and Roussel, Sandwith, Goldberger, and many others demonstrated that it could cure pellagra quickly and relatively inexpensively. Important as beans and information were and remain, however, the real causes of pellagra were and remain poverty, dependency, and alienation from garden- and animal-sustaining land. Goldberger and his cohort understood this well enough. They were humanitarians and publicists, at best saving a few lives here and there, giving temporary reprieves, and knowing all along that only structural changes would ultimately end the epidemic. Sure enough, post–World War II migration and prosperity eliminated pellagra. Niacin-laced store-bought bread seems more like insurance. Meanwhile, the course of pellagra in the South between the two world wars demonstrates the marginality of public health programs and laboratory discoveries.

In 1917, as the United States entered the Great War, everyone feared that teeming southern army camps would compete with already undersupplied towns for food, and that pellagra, already epidemic, would increase geometrically. Instead, the government managed to organize better food distribution and fed its servicemen well. Wartime labor shortages drove up wages even for cotton-mill hands, who spent more money on better food. Pellagra abated. Goldberger warned, meanwhile, that peace and demobilization would unleash another epidemic, and he was right. The 1920s were a horror.

Then, amazingly, between 1930 and 1934—the very depths of the Great Depression—pellagra abated once more. The USDA claimed much of the credit. Its county agents (especially in the South) had been campaigning among ordinary farmers, tenants, and sharecroppers on behalf of "living at home"—that is, keeping vegetable gardens and raising one's own eggs and meat. During these years, too, the women agents of the home demonstration program taught countless rural women about not only gardening and poultry raising but preservation of produce by canning. Canned beans and tomatoes, opened in late winter and spring, could carry a household past that starving season when pellagra typically broke out.

A complementary explanation is that with commodity prices so low in these years, farm owners opted for gardens and hogs on land previously planted entirely in cotton and corn. Also, some landlords, who had in earlier times forced sharecroppers to plant cotton up to the foundations of their cabins, now permitted gardens.[10] But probably just as important, many thousands of southerners, black and white, were on the road during these years, migrating within the region and beyond it, almost always to cities. Difficult as life was in urban places during such hard times, particularly for the down-and-out, food supplies were better there than in the country, and food was absurdly cheap.

But then pellagra resurged. Explaining this doleful phenomenon, at the height of Franklin Roosevelt's New Deal social welfare programs and after the laboratory proof of nicotinic acid's relation to pellagra, is not easy. One obvious target, however, is southern planter-landlords: Hugely disproportionate beneficiaries of the Agricultural Adjustment Act's acreage-reduction and subsidy program, they evicted tens of thousands of tenants and sharecroppers, many of whom became stranded on rural roadsides. Simultaneously, the adjustment act succeeded in stabilizing and then raising commodity prices; so the 75-odd percent of farmland still under cultivation became too valuable to subdivide into gardens. A reduced and desperate rural workforce—sharecroppers were legally the same as laborers—meant that landlords were also emboldened to forbid gardens again and to reopen or persist with their stores and commissaries.[11]

The New Deal and the organized chaos of the war brought about the structural changes that ultimately erased pellagra and other ills of the South's grossly unbalanced postbellum system. Federal regulations and subsidies and the introduction of tractors, cotton-harvesting machines, and combines rendered big agriculture in the region more like California's than the dying sharecropping regime. By 1960, too, more than 9 million southerners had left the South, and a roughly comparable number had moved from rural areas or mill towns to southern cities. Southerners, at home or abroad in the land, had become an urban people at last. And cities (and, later, suburbs too) are where the food is.

Finally, pellagra's place in southern history may be properly viewed, I think, as yet another long-reaching result of defeat in the Civil War, which (as we have already observed) led to an overreliance on production of commodities extracted from the earth, the overrunning of the old commons by the powerful, and the enormous expansion of the poor population. The era of pellagra, ca. 1890–1950—also the era of Jim Crow and of Dixie demagogues, among other pathologies—was a long storm of disequilibrium in the South's history, the worst altogether since Europeans infected the natives and created the derelict landscapes of 1800. Pellagra and complementary ills of diet were not inevitable, not unpreventable, and hardly the norm, rather the opposite.

🐦 Eighteenth- and early-nineteenth-century southerners, on the trails to resettle former native countries, often outran bountiful supplies of food. They depended on game, bread from meal brought along, and whatever new frontier landscapes presented. Depending on their circumstances and the time of year emigration took place, migrants' provender may have been monotonous and unbalanced, notably by the absence of fresh vegetables. Southerners have always loved vegetables, the more variety the better. Sweet potatoes (rich in vitamin C) thrived in southern soils and climate, and they were ubiquitous in fireplace or campfire ashes or simmering in boiling pots. Southerners loved peas and beans of every sort and, like the natives, commonly planted them among corn. Turnips, both the nutritious green tops and the tubers, were also popular. Yellow summer squashes were common, too, and beloved, as were eggplant and okra. Partly because stoves did not become common in the region until after the Civil War, frontier and antebellum southerners were universally fond of stews, which were made in iron pots suspended by fireplaces or at outside cooking sites. Turnips, tops and bottoms, were often bases, along with sweet potatoes and legumes; the whole was seasoned with peppers and whatever meat was available—bacon, most commonly, but also chicken, squirrel, and rabbit. The liquid in such stews was called pot-likker (i.e., liquor), and it was never thrown out but drunk with relish or saved to soften yesterday's cornbread, crumbled into the pot-likker. Such variety and such taste, not to mention such good nutrition, must have haunted every migrant's dreams. Reestablishing gardens, plus cow and hog pens and chicken yards, surely motivated wayfarers to work hard to reestablish old comforts in new lands.[12]

Still, notwithstanding two centuries of warfare on deer, relentless killing of bears, and the diminution of dark forests where bears lived, migrants reported the hunting and eating of both venison and bear meat. Certainly deer and bear were much scarcer, though. Land clearance for farms and the ranging of European animals (not to mention generations of market hunting) had reduced large-animal habitat while hugely enlarging the brushy "edge" environments where quail, opossums, raccoons, and rabbits thrive. The latter thickened stews for wayfarers. Far from salt coasts, migrants found freshwater fish—catfish was ever a favorite—but few travelers seem to have had equipment for fishing. For vegetables in early spring, however, there was pokeweed, an early emerging wild plant long known to be sweetly edible. Indeed many southerners preferred poke salad (often rendered "poke-salat") to any other greens, long after frontier stages. (Poke was Elvis's favorite green.) Others, especially folks in the highlands, found another wild green, cress, and ate "cress's salat." Migrants found a variety of other wild provender as well: nuts of many kinds, wild grapes, plums, and "Indian" peaches.

Back in the old parts of the South, then in the expansive, newly settled places that collectively became the antebellum South and the Confederacy, folks of just about every class ate from a staggering variety of foods. Wealthy whites, in cities and on plantations, particularly in the East, ate mutton and lamb as well as beef and pork and game. Sheep were almost ubiquitous across the broad region, but ordinary people kept them for their wool rather than meat. In Florida, southwestern Louisiana, and Texas—cattle country —beef was the principal domestic meat. Everywhere else, pork was king, making at least two appearances each day in the ordinary household. There were many more, minor and seasonal, foods of substance, too. On frontiers chickens fell prey to predators despite their capacity to fly into trees, but on settled landscapes chickens thrived and eggs were plentiful—except in winter, when most hens stopped laying. Chickens were not so plentiful to be common meat, however, but were reserved for special occasions. Even then, it was usually tough old roosters and aged hens who succumbed to the axe, and their flesh was usually better devoted to stew pots for extended tenderizing. Virtually all families owned a milk cow or two, although southern stock was notoriously scrubby. The cows usually ranged about, to be brought home for milking or calving. Milk seems to have been common, however, if not so abundant or reliable by modern standards. Venison and small game were common, too. In addition to rabbits, turkeys, quail, opossums, raccoons, and squirrels, southerners black and white shot or snared pigeons and, in spring, robins (among the easiest of catches). Then there were fish. Coastal southerners always caught and consumed many shell- and finfish, and settled inlanders acquired poles, line, hooks, and nets, adding quantities of catfish, especially, to their diets.

Haute cuisine was rare in the Old South. Instead, everyone, it seems, from great planter to yeoman farmer to herder to slave, tried to present great quantities and as much variety as possible at the afternoon meal called dinner, especially when there was company. A visitor to an Alabama big house was astounded by the plenty helped upon many platters yet complained of dissimilar meats on the same plate: "always roast turkey and ham, a boiled fowl here, a tongue there; a small piece of nondescript meat, which generally turns out to be pork disguised." But these were hardly all. Table and sideboard groaned with "hominy, rice, hot corn bread, sweet potatoes; potatoes mashed with spice, very hot, salad and radishes, and an extraordinary variety of pickles." The enslaved women who cooked such a meal likely enjoyed some, if not a lot, of it. Their fieldhand sisters and brothers did not, but except in rare cases of irrational abuse or neglect, the black proletariat of the Old South had sufficient and healthy food. Nearly always sufficiency and surplus alike were owing to slaves' own initiatives— at gardening, hunting, fishing, trading, and appropriation.[13]

For practically everyone in the late antebellum South, there was a cornucopia of vegetables. In addition to bread in many forms made from corn, hominy and grits from corn, wheaten biscuits, turnips, and sweet potatoes, there were several varieties of peas in the family called cowpeas, including blackeyed and crowder, and many beans, the favorites called string (green beans to Yankees) and butter, a small, light green (sometimes speckled) lima. There were also velvet beans grown among the corn, most beloved by one of my grandmothers (born 1884 near Lake City, South Carolina) and, she said, all her American ancestors. In tropical America, velvets are known not only as a valuable legume for humans and livestock but for their mild hallucinogenic effect. Whether velvets cultivated farther north, in USDA zone 8, say, possessed much of this enchantment is unknown, because unlike string and butter beans, velvets seem to have disappeared. Southerners also relished cabbage, beets, onions, and okra—there is no gumbo without okra—that is, practically every European, native, and African edible plant we enjoy today. For washing all this down, there was little beer in the South, and few except the elite had wine. The typical table (with company or not) offered water, milk, and whisky, all consumed in volume by men, women, and children.

🐾 The era of pellagra, so well documented by public health officials, the press, still- and motion-picture photographers, novelists, and commercial moviemakers, may have led many, including historians, to project the pathological South of the early twentieth century backward, chronologically. The Confederacy had been doomed (among other reasons) because of the Old South's gross inefficiency and the poor nutrition and health of most of the people. What may have remained of such a thesis should have been wrecked in 1972 with the appearance of *Hog Meat and Hoecake: Food Supply in the Old South, 1800–1860*, by the historical geographer Sam Bowers Hilliard. Here and in his *Atlas of Antebellum Southern Agriculture* (1984) a decade later, Hilliard demonstrated not only that southerners fed themselves quite well, but that on the eve of the Civil War, they made 60 percent of the nation's corn, exported wheat (mainly from the Chesapeake states), and ranged, consumed, and sold huge surpluses of pork, of course, but also beef. Hilliard's findings were based principally on federal censuses of agriculture but also on a large number of published and unpublished accounts of food, eating, and food supply by travelers, visitors, and locals at home. Late antebellum censuses were early marvels of statistics and are still considered reliable. No matter how many anecdotal sources are consulted, however, as Hilliard warned, it is impossible to discover just how well food distribution functioned or (among other shortcomings) if every social class and subclass benefited from the South's bounty.

One must wonder, especially, about the nutrition of the large number of herdsmen in the population. Some farmed little, as we have seen, whether landowners or not, and spent weeks away from home on roundups and long winter drives to markets. The fictional Forresters in Rawlings's *The Yearling* may illustrate a historical reality several ways. Herdsmen were men, after all, and the Forresters are an overwhelmingly masculine clan illustrating practically every genteel objection to piney-woods crackers: Their grooming and dress are scraggly at best; they are loud-talking boasters, gamblers, and drunken joy-makers. When not lounging, they are on horseback, wreaking havoc for play or engaged in the serious and probably lucrative business of roundups and drives. Such men, one might logically calculate, spent cash from cattle, pig, or horse sales on meat (read pork), meal, and molasses—the notorious three-M diet of the age of pellagra. The youngest of the Forresters, the crippled boy, Fodderwing, dies young, although there is not a remote suggestion of pellagra. Fodderwing's older brothers, however, might have been candidates for dietary distress and disease, given their high mobility and disinclination to dig in the earth. But no, the Forresters are actually quite robust. Rawlings does not detail the Forresters' provender, but I think it significant that this herdsmen's household was (de facto) headed by a woman, the matriarch who, like Rawlings herself and almost all southern women, beginning with the original ones, was very likely a gardener. Women almost certainly produced and prepared the vegetables that balanced and enriched the meat, meal, and molasses for many generations. Historians have written much of such peoples' very masculine public economy but little of their private, feminine, and sustaining one.

❧ As much as shelter, the garden is home, another room, as it were, extending from kitchen and hearth. Open to the sky, such rooms nonetheless required walls to protect plants from foraging varmints, deer, bear, cattle, and hogs, not to mention meandering dogs. Walls might have been similar to palisades of wood or cane among natives and then frontiering Euro- and Afro-southerners. Later they would be more conventional fences, like the one the fictional Jody heightened against Flag, the yearling, in Rawlings's novel. Later still, when varmints were scarce, deer and bear were gone or distant, and domestic animals were penned, more gardens were unfenced. Yet rooms many of them remained, by design, especially among black country folks.[14]

West African people maintained protected exterior spaces near their houses, for gardens and for outdoor chores and relaxation. These may or may not have been remembered by descendants of forced migrants to North America. Certainly the climates of the southeastern United States invited rich and poor, black and white, outside. (The mountains' longer and colder winters were much less encouraging, but lower piedmonts and especially coastal plains were delightful places to be outside nine or more months of the year.) Poorer people, having lesser shelter, were logically more likely to expand their houses outdoors. Vegetable gardens, including winter crops of greens and a few roots, needed tending practically year-round. Laundry, the slaughter of farm animals, and the cleaning of fish catches and dead game were better done outside, as was maintenance and repair of household and farm equipment. Shade from mature trees was prized for such chore-doing sections of yard, then, and Afro- and Euro-southerners generally kept the bare ground swept clean. Nearby, very likely, would be chairs for resting and benches or tables for holding work projects, drinks, and plates. Such spaces as these would also be decorated—with flowering shrubs, small fruit trees, climbing vines, and perennial flowers sometimes set (particularly in the twentieth century) inside found objects such as old tires from cars, trucks, or tractors.

By the 1920s, some home demonstration agents, all middle-class women themselves, promoted grassy lawns and other suburban bourgeois notions of homestead landscaping among poor farm women, but their attempts usually failed. Other agents, however, caught on not only to the poverty of their clients but to their decorative sensibilities. Such agents, usually led by country women, began to scour nearby woods for natural, indige-nous flowering plants. These served more than well enough to define and beautify outdoor spaces, even those rented by tenants and sharecroppers. Nearby, preferably close to the kitchen and its overlooking window, would be the garden room, in full sun. "Garden," indeed, has ever meant vege-tables rather than flowers, self-provisioning rather than ornamentation—among the multitudes of ordinary folks, anyway.

Members of the elite established ambitiously decorative "pleasure gar-dens" early in the Europeanized South—witness the restored formal ("French") exhibits before the governor's palace in Williamsburg and Tryon Palace in New Bern. The wealthiest of eighteenth-century Chesapeake planters also indulged themselves in enormous private gardens, all in the symmetrically perfect mode. Townsmen such as George Wythe, law profes-sor at the College of William and Mary, laid out more practical versions in the deep lots behind their big homes. On either side of Wythe's graveled central garden walk were borders of ornamentals, and beyond them there were rectangular sections of currants, vegetables, gooseberries, figs, and raspberries, plus a large grassy lawn with a square seat under one spreading tree, with a view of a nearby apple tree. Beyond a screen of more trees were Wythe's carriage house, a stable, and a big cornfield.

There is much to recommend right angles and straight lines in the cultivation of vegetables and other food plants. How to distinguish between young desired plants and weeds, otherwise? How else to cultivate, fertilize, and protect one's designs? The perfect circles, half-circles, triangles, and other geometrical fancies common to French-style pleasure gardens are another matter. Before Thomas Jefferson was born, Alexander Pope lacerated the French gardening fashion and campaigned for decades to create a distinctively English design for gardens. Ultimately the English garden evolved as studied asymmetry, the best examples set on large scales, where broad landscapes are rearranged to imitate nature. Thereafter, I think, it was impossible to view a formal French-style garden without feeling the design mocked nature with hubris. We humans are masters of all—science of every sort—and capable (given sufficient labor) of reforming nature to reflect Enlightenment perfection. Jefferson loved the French and spoke their language, but he read his Pope (and others), visited English gardens, and over many years created at Monticello a combination of practical, right-angled vegetable gardens among contoured, vista-oriented, almost asymmetrical ornamentals.[15]

Later, nineteenth- and twentieth-century planters and businesspeople created informal "English" gardens on their properties, displaying their curiosities and powers of procurement with trees from Asia and the American tropics as well as native and European specimens. Humans seem incapable of leaving nature alone but must transport plants (as well as animals) and test them in new habitats, for profit or novelty or both, and much more. Pleasure gardens are one version of what Michael Pollan and others have called "second nature"—the first being wilderness.[16] All versions of second nature, vegetable patches no less than the formal gardens of Boboli, Versailles, and Tryon, are arranged and tended intensively. Design signifies much, as already suggested, of human ambition and attitude. The Indian midden and, later, the kitchen gardens of African slaves and the wives of herdsmen and yeomen—great jumbles of corn, beans, peas, squashes, and herbs by harvesttime—would seem the opposite, aesthetically, of the symmetrical French pleasure garden. The English-style park-landscape, offering the illusion of nature's asymmetry if not the seeming chaos of the midden, was, it seems to me, a pleasant compromise. All were brilliant and useful human accomplishments, all with fine aesthetic virtues. Too, one might argue that all were conservationist in that, whether for ornamentation or provisioning, gardens were created for permanence (even though they constantly evolved) and demanded not only design but diligent attention.

Men have been and are gardeners, designer-creators of pleasure parks and provisioning cornucopias alike. Thomas Jefferson was exemplary at late-eighteenth- and early-nineteenth-century Monticello. And among the twentieth century's most celebrated southern white male gardeners was Eugene P. Odum (1913–2002), a giant of international science and a principal developer of ecosystem ecology. Odum (to be visited again, below) was the older son of another famous academic man, Howard Washington Odum, founder of the sociology department and the Institute for Research in Social Science at the University of North Carolina. The elder Odum was also a farmer, renowned in the Carolina piedmont for raising dairy cattle on his well-ordered place west of Chapel Hill. Eugene spent his own academic career in his father's native state, Georgia. There he was principal creator of the university's Institute for Ecology, trained generations of graduate ecological scientists, wrote the first undergraduate textbook in ecology, and gardened on a quarter-acre plot outside Athens. This last activity was, he wrote to friends, a "reduced tillage, chemical, and water usage vegetable garden." Every fall he rototilled the entirety and planted a winter cover crop of crimson clover, then kale and collards for winter greens, which would all be picked before spring. The clover fixed nitrogen and left a "green mat." In spring, then, without further tillage, he planted his warm-weather crops directly into the mat. As his rows of tomatoes, potatoes, pole beans, squash, and blueberries began to grow, Odum bought a pickup-truck-load of mulch and bales of wheat straw. These reduced moisture evaporation and weeds while supplying more soil nutrients as the mulch decomposed. He hoped to avoid pesticides, but in emergencies he would apply "only short-lived" ones. He hoped also to avoid irrigation but prepared for regular late-summer droughts with an underground " 'jug irrigation' system used for centuries in arid countries." (Odum added, parenthetically, that "we have a lot to learn from traditional agriculture practiced in underdeveloped countries.") His jugs, or pots, were permanently installed at root-zone depth, so he watered only directly into the root zone. Such little reservoirs would conserve moisture while it percolated or evaporated upward, directly on target. He also added "small amounts of mineral fertilizer" only to the roots. Finally, he kept a tall, latticed bamboo fence around his beans to protect them from the massively resurgent deer population of the late twentieth century.[17] One mourns Odum now, perhaps not least for the passing of his garden, a model for us all, constructed on knowledge ancient and modern.

One might also turn to the work of two other southern men: Edmund N. O'Rourke Jr. and Leon C. Standifer. Natives, respectively, of Louisiana and Mississippi and now in their seventies, both are retired professors of horticulture at Louisiana State University in Baton Rouge. Their university permitted them to keep their offices, equipment, laboratories, and outdoor research plots, however, so O'Rourke and Standifer might complete their joint valedictory, a big, chatty, detailed, and illustrated book, *Gardening in the Humid South* (2002). The authors suggest that their readership might be confined to the Gulf states, but their necessary preoccupations— abundant rainfall, excessive pests, and sandy, acidic soils—apply well up the Atlantic coast, where USDA zone 8 extends, narrowing as it proceeds northward, all the way to Hampton Roads. I myself, who gardened with my father just south of the James where it enters the Chesapeake, recall too well most of the challenges and pleasures that O'Rourke and Standifer address. Drainage is decisive, so "beds," or rows, must be raised. Acidity must be addressed, nitrogen fixed, and so on. At one point late in the volume, the authors respectfully but briefly address the philosophy of organic gardening, its instrumental vagueness (even as the federal government was beginning a certification program), and their preference for applying yard and garden wastes to gardens rather than hauling them to landfills. Mostly they are engaged with many details, many of them presented in amusing, mock-cantankerous exchanges with each other. One author believes a gardener should buy the best watering hose available; the other recommends the cheapest, since one is just as likely to run a lawn mower over an expensive hose. They jointly describe an underground watering system, but it is not composed of simple jugs. The book's great virtue (aside from the authors' wit) is its application of the very broad field of academic horticulture to home gardening. O'Rourke and Standifer know, for instance, pests of every sort, and while they admonish gardeners to use pesticides sparingly, there is much of chemicals with many applications.[18]

Then there was A. L. Tommie Bass, born in the hills of northern Alabama early in the twentieth century, a poor man only basically lettered. After working for another family for many years, Bass lived alone, never married, and might have passed from the earth with no more than a fleeting local remembrance. But because the historian Allan Tullos happened upon Bass near Centre, Alabama, during the 1980s and referred a Duke University historian of medicine to him, Bass became a minor celebrity—at least among folklife devotees—with publication of his reminiscences, which included recipes for plain meals and his personal catalog of valuable wild herbs. Bass in old age collected and sold junk, but he also peddled containers of herbs, many for the making of teas that improved digestion and mitigated, at least, a host of ailments. In earlier times he had been a farm laborer, a cotton picker, and a timber getter, but at all stages of life Bass was a gardener, a cook, and a relentless seeker of herbs. Surely there was no copy, white or black, of Tommie Bass, but the hardscrabble, self-sufficing world that somehow produced him must have yielded many like him. These will likely never be known to us.[19]

Among early-twentieth-century Afro-southerners, Booker T. Washington (1856–1915) relentlessly promoted self-sufficiency among the rural masses, and Washington was not infrequently photographed, in suit and tie, in his own garden, chicken yard, and pig pen at Tuskegee. And among Tuskegee's longtime faculty, during Washington's time and for years after, was the tireless laboratory genius and writer of agricultural experiment station pamphlets, George Washington Carver (1864–1943). Carver was famously preoccupied with soil building and conservation and with money crops that might save the South from cotton. The best-known and enduring of these was peanuts, and Carver is immortalized for his inventions of a remarkable number of uses of peanuts, as a means of increasing demand. All the while Carver was also the humanist-agrarian whose talents were devoted to the elemental subsistence of the region's poor.[20]

The best-known black farmer-gardener of the era, however, was Neb Cobb, who is called Nate Shaw in Theodore Rosengarten's *All God's Dangers* (1974). Cobb was illiterate and became a sharecropper while still very young, then a tenant farmer, and finally a farm owner. All the time, too, he was a gardener determined to provide for himself, his large family, and his cows, chickens, mules, and hogs. "I didn't never want for no vegetable, what I had I growned em," Cobb declared. "Okra, anything from okra up and down— collards, tomatoes, red cabbages, hard-headed cabbages, squash, beans, turnips, sweet potatoes, ice [Irish] potatoes, onions, radishes, cucumbers —anything for vegetables." And there were also fruits, watermelon, cantaloupes, and more. Cobb declared he wished he could abandon cotton and grow only vegetables, but the latter were so plentiful and the markets so mediocre; he generally persisted with self-provisioning while sustaining his lifelong battles with boll weevils.[21]

Tommie Bass spoke of sharing garden produce, and sometimes milk when a cow went dry, with neighbors and friends. Ned Cobb was not only provident but generous, too. And Gene Odum, his beloved dog Phoebe (and all her predecessors) at his heel, happily supplied his friends' tables as well as his own for many years. So have other men, we must think, with the important proviso that women probably undertook the crucial and grueling tasks of processing, preparing, and preserving all the bounty. Such was the case in my boyhood home, where my mother, dripping sweat in her unair-conditioned kitchen, all four stove burners blazing, shelled, cleaned, sliced, chopped, and boiled, boiled away. Later, say in February, when she appeared from the pantry with a Ball quart jar of tomatoes, butter beans, or corn, perhaps the family's joy compensated and she forgot the endless steamy days of September and October, much as women are said to forget the pain of childbirth. One hopes so.

Indeed, throughout the long era of pellagra, epidemic that it was, most southerners, even the poorest, gardened and largely escaped the disorder. The earliest black home demonstration agents found tenant and share-cropping women with vegetable patches, a few chickens, maybe hogs, and a scrawny milk cow. The agents encouraged the gardeners and began the great task of helping them accumulate equipment and the know-how to can their little surpluses. So it was, too, with the white mothers of the South. During the late 1930s, amid the terrible resurgence of pellagra, Margaret Jarman Hagood, a young demographer and social statistician recently graduated from Howard Odum's graduate program in Chapel Hill, undertook sixteen months of travel, surveys, and interviews in 254 white tenant households across the piedmonts of both Carolinas, Georgia, and Alabama. Some places she visited twice. White, a woman, and a mother herself, albeit a member of the upper middle class, Hagood was kind and receptive and seems to have readily earned the trust of her subjects. Her resulting study, *Mothers of the South: Portraiture of the White Tenant Farm Woman* (1939), was a striking rebuke to the then-prevailing pathography in the region, particularly to the condescending portraiture in Erskine Caldwell's novels and Caldwell's and Margaret Bourke-White's so-called documentary book, *You Have Seen Their Faces*, which had appeared two years earlier. Hagood's women were smart, articulate, strong willed, and competent. Seven-eighths of them told Hagood that they actually preferred fieldwork to housework. Many of them produced tobacco, the most labor-intensive of all Dixie's commodities, and they bragged of their prowess at "priming" (picking leaves), curing, tying "hands" (bunches), and grading. Well into the New Deal, with tobacco prices now stabilized, some of these women caused

*Working in a school garden, Gees Bend, Alabama, 1939. Photo by Marion Post Wolcott.*
*Courtesy Library of Congress (LC-USF33-030360-M3 DLC).*

Hagood no small concern: the smartest and most aggressive among them seemed too much like men, being more interested in commercial crops than in self-provisioning. Yet overall, the statistician discovered that tenant women had been and continued to be the principal feeders of their families, from their kitchen gardens, flocks of fowl, and cows.[22]

One of Hagood's subjects, a single mother of five, was so extraordinary that she deserved four pages of text in *Mothers of the South*, yet she illustrated much of the social scientist's general findings. Forty-nine years old when Hagood interviewed her and spoke with her neighbors, the tenant farmer, unlike most, was neither born nor reared on a farm but in a textile mill village. After minimal schooling, she went to work in the mill at age eleven, finally marrying late, at twenty-five. A bit later, her husband was reported killed in France in the Great War. He reappeared, like Enoch Arden, after her remarriage. The woman chose to stay with the new husband because, as she put it, at least he "*would* work sometimes." They set to farming about 1919, but the husband's health began to fail. She took on more and more farmwork while he stayed home with their baby, drinking liquor. After the husband sank into full-time self-medication, the wife sent him off to a government sanatorium and divorced him. This was about 1929. By then there were five children under twelve and no man to seek a tenancy contract. But the mother found a kind landlord with a vacant three-room log cabin on his property. She set her oldest boy to plowing, while the other children contributed what they could at home and in the field. As other tenants left, the mother became principal tobacco grower on the landlord's farm. All the while she and her children voluntarily, and without pay, performed labor in the landlord's garden patches. All the while, too, she maintained her own garden, canned, and kept animals. Beetles were her bane the year Hagood met the mother. There would not be enough preserved vegetables to last the coming winter, and the one hog she was able to slaughter would not quite provide enough meat, either. Yet except for her oldest child, who was nineteen when Hagood visited and had had rickets and become unfit for farmwork, all the children were healthy. By then the youngest was twelve, and the mother felt more at ease, even though Hagood fretted that her blood pressure was high. The mother was nonetheless happy. Her children were nearly raised, she was indispensable to her employer, and she had even acquired a used automobile — "my car"!

My own favorite gardeners from this era are not anonymous. There are three, and I first met each of them in luminous print while looking for things remote from vegetables, canning, and ornamental plants. The first (alphabetically) of these self-nourishing writers was Bernice Kelly Harris (1894–1973). Born on a large farm in Wake County, North Carolina, Bernice Kelly grew up a beneficiary not only of her parents' status as landowners but of what is remembered as a golden age of agriculture, when weather and commodity prices were so good that, forever after, farmers and their advocates benchmarked them, hopefully, as "parity." Bill Kelly, her father, grew cotton, tobacco, corn, and other crops. Bernice herself remembered the Kelly farm, including its woods and edges, as a cornucopia—all this in the age of pellagra. Her memoir, *Southern Savory* (1964), drips with nostalgia for "gooseberry bushes yield[ing] tart purplish fruit for mouth-watering pies and preserves." Also for "currants and figs, scuppernongs and black grapes," not to mention "white mulberries and purple damsons, black walnuts and hickory nuts, every kind of orchard fruit." Her family harvested "cane patches" for sorghum and sage bushes for sausage seasoning and "tea for chills and fever." Then "there were plump chickens and pigs and milk cows to supply fowl and meat and dairy foods for the table. There were garden vegetables winter and summer."[23]

A bookish child, Bernice decided she wanted to be a teacher, and her parents sent her to Meredith College, a Baptist institution for women in nearby Raleigh. Then she was off to her first post, down east in Duplin County, then to another rural school in western North Carolina, and finally, when she was twenty-five, to the little town of Seaboard, up in Northampton County near the Virginia line. In the meantime she had encountered the new "folk drama" movement in Chapel Hill, where she took a summer class with Professor Frederick Koch. Koch and other advocates of a grassroots theater encouraged teachers and other privileged people to promote and facilitate playmaking among ordinary country folk, who would create drama from their own stories and traditions. Back in Seaboard, a transformed Bernice Kelly began to help her students and then their parents compose and put on dramas. Ultimately she was principal founder of the Northampton Players, and her young playwrights were frequent winners of annual state prizes. Food and the natural world figure large in much of this drama, reminding Bernice that she would ever be a farm girl, a rural person at heart, irretrievably connected not only to crops and gardens but to brambles, meadows, and woods.

In her thirties Bernice Kelly married Herbert Harris, an older man and a member of one of the powerful families of Northampton. With his brothers Harris owned farms, rental housing, timberlands, a cotton ginnery, and a fertilizer business. Bernice ended her school-teaching career and moved into the brick house her husband had built for them. Now a prominent matron, she could not resist the countrywoman's imperative to plant a big vegetable garden. She gloried in the "bounty"—one of her favorite words—although, like many women before and after her, she came to regret the egregious scope of the garden in a good year, come canning time. Her husband made things worse: ever the competitive businessman, he insisted that they outdo friends, family, and neighbors, filling not only the pantry but the cellar. Nonetheless, many years later, her husband long dead and Bernice herself approaching eighty, she still had her "little acre" plowed and, with a little help, grew her vegetables.

In the meantime, Bernice had found brief employment in 1939 with the New Deal's Federal Writers' Project. Traveling about Northampton, mainly among people (white and black) well known to her, she interviewed a variety of rural subjects, men and women, representatives of every social class, collecting their life stories, typing them up from her notes, and sending them off to Chapel Hill, headquarters for the project's southern region. Because Bernice was married to a big man in the county, she had access to practically everyone, and indeed, Herbert usually drove her to interviews. But Bernice was a kind person, sympathetic and approachable; she also had been a beloved schoolteacher, a Baptist churchwoman, and a tireless and celebrated local playmaker. Now she demonstrated a receptivity to the poor that was the equal of that of her younger contemporary, Margaret Jarman Hagood. But Bernice Kelly Harris interviewed Afro- as well as Euro-Northamptonians, a few of whom offered shocking indictments of big white bosses, men not unlike Herbert Harris. A number of Bernice's life stories have been collected in print. I read all her typescripts years ago, while wading through the 1,400-odd Writers' Project southern stories then available in several libraries and archives. Bernice's are not only the best-framed and contextualized and the neatest, but they are fearlessly honest in reproducing human voices in many life situations, without condescension.

This intense vicarious experience of others influenced Bernice Kelly Harris's fiction writing for years to come. Her first novel, *Purslane* (1939)—also the first fiction ever published by the University of North Carolina Press—is a rural southern Romeo-and-Juliet tale in which young lovers are ill fated not because their respective families are feuding but because they represent different white social classes. The boy/young man is the equivalent of "trash," although Bernice herself would never employ such a term. Instead the doomed protagonist and his sort are represented by nature—in Harris's title, purslane, a common weed. Typical of all plants called weeds, purslane (also rendered "pusley" in speech) appears suddenly wherever there is sun and disturbed soil; it is opportunistic, prolific, ordinary, and therefore not welcome. Harris continued the botanical allusion in her second book, *Portulaca* (published by Doubleday in 1941), a thinly disguised autobiographical novel in which a naive farm girl, Nancy, becomes a writer and sophisticated town-dweller. Nancy had appeared with a slightly different, countrified name in *Purslane*. Now, having become cultivated in the urban and urbane sense, she has changed from weed to portulaca, which is a domesticated ornamental plant, a cultivar derived from the wild purslane. Readers and reviewers who were gardeners must have recognized the author's meaning immediately.

Then there was Zora Neale Hurston (1891–1960), a force of nature and gardener extraordinaire. Zora was born in eastern Alabama, but her father, a carpenter and Baptist preacher, found new roots in Eatonville, Florida, a new, all-black town in Orange County, near Winter Park and Orlando. So there she grew up, in a big house full of siblings. Outside were palms, pines, and live oaks; a lake with alligators; exaltations of colorful birds; and lush gardens by every house. Like Bernice Kelly, she rambled, played, and absorbed nature. And when she eavesdropped on elders telling stories, she was surrounded again by nature and all its critters. Much later, in her 1942 autobiography, she exclaimed, "It did not surprise me at all to hear that the animals talked." Observing nature's own genius for recycling, too, she declared—in the context of her doctrineless religious beliefs—"I know that nothing is destructible."[24]

Zora's childhood idyll ended in her teens, when her beloved mother died and her father married a disapproving woman. Zora was sent away to school in Jacksonville. But when her father's support failed, she fled to Memphis to live with an older sister, then—now and almost forever after on her own—to Baltimore and, finally, New York. In her twenties but pretending to be younger, she finished high school and began college. She studied at Barnard under the tutelage of the great American anthropologist "Papa Franz" Boaz and graduated in 1928. Now she would collect folkways, folksongs, and folklore, not in the southern Pacific islands or Asia but in her own old country, among southern black people, who remained rural and isolated— "primitive," as described by the terminology of the white world at the time. Zora needed a car and money to go collecting, however, and decades before the appearance of foundations and agencies that supported research, this was no small problem. On the other hand, she was magnetically attractive and voluble with a genius for friendship, and she won the financial support of a wealthy, white, Upper East Side matron.

In 1928, then, she was off to Florida, first to Eatonville. This had been her home, of course, but Zora's rationalization of central Florida as prime prospect for accumulating southern black lore was valid: Florida was booming in the 1920s, not only its fabled housing and land market but its phosphate mines, its timber operations, and its ever-lengthening railroads. So Orange and Polk counties were new homes, or mere pass-throughs, for countless immigrants from throughout the South. Florida was a semitropical melting pot where men and women from all over mingled in work camps and told "lies" and played music. Zora thrived there until, in danger of losing her life to the fury of a jealous woman, she hopped in her coupe and drove fast to Louisiana.

Early in her Floridian sojourn, she had first investigated hoodoo—also known as voodoo—in the Lake George port town of Sanford with a female practitioner who specialized in woman-man problems. Now, in and around New Orleans, she devoted herself to hoodoo, underwent several initiations involving lying naked face-down upon a snake skin, sacrificing chickens, and drinking potent libations concocted, of course, from nature. The Florida stories, many of them suffused with bears, snakes, and giant birds—animals actual and imagined—and the Louisiana hoodoo combined to make a fascinating, often hilarious book, *Mules and Men* (1935).

While Zora wrote her first book she also published popular and scholarly articles and began to develop plays and musical shows that elaborated on the Gulf coast stories and songs she had learned. The sprawling ensemble, not least her own drumming, singing, and dancing, made her a star of the Harlem Renaissance. She knew everyone: Langston Hughes was a dear friend. He rode with her on the long drive from New Orleans to New York, and while they once fell out over credit for a collaborative theatrical creation, their correspondence was frequent and long-lasting. Carl van Vechten, white hanger-on and chronicler of the renaissance, took her photograph more than once. Yet Zora could seldom support herself. The stock market crash and descending Great Depression strangled and killed off magazines that paid, straitened existing theater, discouraged investment in new drama and musicals, and dried up philanthropic sources. Black artists certainly suffered more than white ones, and single dark women such as Zora Neale Hurston could not survive in Manhattan. Once she tried Hollywood (just as William Faulkner and F. Scott Fitzgerald did),

*Zora Neale Hurston, ca. 1930. Courtesy Florida State Archives.*

but she did little work as a contract screenwriter and felt isolated on the West Coast. So as before, time and again, Zora fled to Florida, and wherever she could, she gardened, out of sheer joy as well as necessity.

In May 1932, back in Eatonville, she effused to her New York benefactor, "I am happy here, happier than I have been for years. The air is sweet, yes literally sweet. Summer is in full swing. The days are hot but the nights are cool. The mocking birds sing off and on all night long and the honey suckle and magnolia are in bloom." She had put in a garden, too, beside the house she rented. By late July she wrote again, announcing that a "hot dry spell has killed my garden." But just two weeks earlier she had bragged that her pea crop was overwhelming. She had picked all she could possibly use and had thought of getting "somebody to take them to town and sell them for me," except, she wrote, she would love to mail a good batch to the Upper East Side, with directions for the benefactor's cook.[25]

Nineteen years later, Zora, now sixty (although she never admitted it), settled in a one-room cinderblock house with huge, albeit messy and tangled grounds, in a tiny town called Eau Gallie, Florida, two blocks from the Indian River, close to the Atlantic. She was "the happiest I have been in the last ten years," she wrote to a friend. "I am up every morning at five oclock chopping down weeds and planting flowers and things." Finding an artesian spring in the yard, she made an ornamental garden around it, planting butterfly ginger. Elsewhere she put in pink verbena. Zora also painted the house. She enjoyed feeding more and more birds and defending them from cats. And she petted her two dogs, Spot and Spot's daughter, Shag. She hired a man to grub out cane so she could plant papaya. Investing all of $75 in "knee high" papayas, she hoped to sell them in what promised to be a good market.[26] All this on rented property, property poor Zora hoped desperately to buy, where she already felt so wonderfully "at home." Sad to say, despite all her labors on a white man's house and fields, she lost it. Coastal property values, almost forever burgeoning, blasted off, as it were, during the 1950s. Eau Gallie was too close (for Zora's benefit) to Cocoa Beach and military installations, and she could never earn or save at a rate even slightly exceeding inflation.

Ironically, the only home she ever owned was a houseboat moored on the Indian River. It was thirty-eight feet long, tight but comfortable, and its engine was overhauled. There was no dirt for gardening on a boat, however. Zora never enjoyed the financial security of marriage to a wealthy man, as did Bernice Kelly. Zora was married three times (that we know of), but never for long, and although her first husband became a well-established physician in Los Angeles who responded generously to Zora's requests for loans, she had little luck. She died at last in Fort Pierce, in yet another rented place. Loving friends and neighbors buried her but never got around to setting a memorial stone. This came later, along with new appreciation from literary academics and a new generation of readers. In the meantime, poor Zora's heroic landscaping and gardening, both provisioning and ornamental, remind one of the heroism and determination of countless tenant and sharecropper women, feeding families, improving garden soils, and beautifying others' places.

The last of my literary gardeners is Marjorie Kinnan Rawlings (1896–1953), who knew and, like everyone, loved Zora Neale Hurston, from their first meetings in 1942. It was a strange, wonderful, and awful year for both women. The United States was at last in the new World War, and Marjorie's new husband, Norton Baskin, a St. Augustine hotelier, would soon depart for South Asia as a volunteer ambulance driver. Zora was already driving —across North America, giving up on Paramount and screenwriting and heading for Florida, her old refuge. Her vivid memoir, *Dust Tracks on a Road*, would appear toward the end of the year, but for now she was nearly broke, and there was a summer teaching opportunity at the Florida Normal and Industrial College in St. Augustine. Marjorie's luminous autobiographical essays, *Cross Creek*, copyrighted in 1942, along with *Cross Creek Cookery*, were on their way into print. *Cross Creek* became a best seller, and the witty cookbook apparently sold quite well, too. But one of the chapters in *Cross Creek* would give offense to a neighborhood woman with whom Marjorie had ridden on horseback to take the federal census years before. Her lawsuit dragged on, expensively, for years, before Marjorie finally lost an appeal and paid a nominal fine. Still, in 1942 her life was busy and satisfying. She was often away from Cross Creek, her orange grove, and her garden. She stayed with Norton atop the hotel; she kept a summer cottage at Crescent Beach, a few miles south of St. Augustine; and she bought and restored another summer house in upstate New York, for when she needed a cool northern respite from Florida's almost endless summer heat. And too, throughout the 1940s she enjoyed the services and companionship of her favorite maid, Idella Parker, who minded not only her house but the yard and the plants.

One day during the summer of 1942, in the meantime, Marjorie came by Florida Normal to give one of her frequent talks at the little institution for blacks. There she met Zora, whose work was well known to her, and the two women seemed instantly to have taken to each other. Marjorie invited Zora to tea at five o'clock the next afternoon, in the apartment atop the Castle Warden Hotel that she shared with her husband. The hotel was an elegant, five-story resort that stood on the present-day site of the Ripley's Believe-It-or-Not attraction, near downtown. Marjorie's enthusiasm for Zora's company was infectious, and Norton was eager to accommodate, yet a bit worried. The Castle Warden, like virtually all southern public accommodations during the long age of Jim Crow, was segregated, and Zora was lushly brown in color—"café au lait," Marjorie described her.

Norton's characteristically discreet solution was to stand watch himself at the front desk and to station at the hotel's entrance a black bellhop who would greet and escort Zora up to the fifth floor. Norton and the bellhop waited, then grew apprehensive when Zora did not appear. At 5:20 Norton phoned up to inform Marjorie she had been stood up, only to hear in his receiver a joyous roar. On her own initiative Zora had entered in back, by the kitchen, and walked up alone. She and Marjorie were already joking and howling with laughter. Marjorie's "teatime" was doubtlessly cocktail time for her, too; she loved to drink, smoke cigarettes, and make risque practical jokes. Sometimes she became a little rowdy. Zora, curiously, was not a drinker—or so she claimed—but possessed such an exuberant spirit, sober, as to fill rooms with laughter. She was, though, like Marjorie another heavy cigarette smoker, a flamboyant dresser, and an extravagant raconteur. Both were writers, too, of course, who shared many other passions.

Either that evening at the Castle Warden or from later talk with Zora, Marjorie came to understand that her newfound friend was displeased with her publisher's grossly intrusive deletions from her autobiography. J. B. Lippincott, insisting that angry descriptions of Jim Crow were incompatible with patriotism in wartime, had forced her to accept excisions from *Dust Tracks* while leaving in good-natured mockery of black folks. The truncated book provoked leftist critics such as Richard Wright, who excoriated her seemingly accommodationist attitudes. Zora needed funds, too. So Marjorie recommended her to Maxwell Perkins and her own publisher, Charles Scribner. Ultimately Scribner issued Zora's last book, *Seraph on the Suwanee*, in 1948. In the meantime Max Perkins's account to Marjorie of Zora's first visit to his Manhattan office confirms—if confirmation be needed at this late date—Zora's legendary magnetism. Zora made "the impression," he wrote, "of somebody so full of life and emotion and intelligence that whatever she did should be good. She roused up the whole office by the vitality of her presence." [27]

Months after their first meetings, meanwhile, Zora read *Cross Creek* aboard her houseboat. She wrote to Marjorie: "Twenty-one guns! . . . 'Cross Creek' . . . is a most remarkable piece of work. . . . Whether it pleases you or not, you are my sister. You look at plants and animals and people in the way I do. You are conscious of the three layers of life, instead of the obvious thing before your nose." Zora declared her special admiration for Marjorie's treatment of Cross Creek's black folks. "You *looked* at them," she wrote, "and saw them as they are, instead of slobbering over them as all of the other authors do." Zora hated "that black-face minstrel patter," still so common in white writing, and thought Marjorie had understood the "linguistic heirogliphics" of Afro-southern speech. A bit later, Zora invited Marjorie down to stay on her boat and, on another occasion, offered to come to Cross Creek to look after her while Marjorie's maid was on vacation. Marjorie probably did not get to the houseboat, but Zora was a guest at Cross Creek at least once.[28]

Neither woman seems to have written about the long, overnight visit. Idella Parker, a bright, educated woman and former schoolteacher, did, however, much, much later. Parker (who was African American) published two books about her decade-long association with Marjorie: *Marjorie Rawlings' "Perfect Maid"* (1992) and *From Reddick to Cross Creek* (1999). In the first book, Parker wrote, "Imagine this now! Here was a black author who had come to visit Mrs. Rawlings and had been treated like an equal all day long, talking, laughing, and drinking together on the porch for all the world to see. But when it came to spending the night, Zora would be sent out to sleep with the servants." She insisted, too, that Marjorie had no other guests and that there were two empty bedrooms in her house.[29]

Rawlings was indeed an imperfect "pioneer" (her term) against the color line, as Hurston's latest biographers and others have observed. Zora praised Marjorie's appreciation for rural black speech, yet writing to Max Perkins once, Marjorie ridiculed the pronunciation of a substitute maid. There is other stereotyping in her letters, too. Yet during the late 1920s and 1930s — if we are to believe other letters, most to friends and relations — she risked the disapproval of neighboring landowners by paying not only maids but farmhands and pickers more than the low local standard. Marjorie herself acknowledged a sometimes difficult relationship with Idella Parker, although it seems clear from both women's writing, Parker's so long after Rawlings's death, that they felt dear to each other. As for Zora, she was a genius at negotiating the color lines of all sections of the country, not least her native one, and her extant letters contain not a word of rebuke or disapproval of Marjorie Rawlings.

So-called race relations is not exactly our subject here — except that harmony and equilibrium among humans must surely contribute to equable and reciprocal relations between humans and the rest of nature. I think—noting well her failings—that Marjorie represents perhaps the best of her contemporary white Americans, especially southerners. What she and Zora shared seems more important than Marjorie's ugly lapses of ideology and friendship. They were both so passionately engaged (as Zora acknowledged after reading *Cross Creek*) with other people and with plants and animals. They were both generous, optimistic voluptuaries who wished that all God's children might be as fat as happy as they. One longs to know much more of their companionship. What did Marjorie and Zora talk about all day at Cross Creek? (And was Zora drinking liquor?) Oh, for a taped recording of their intensely languid exchanges. (And what if someone had audiotaped Zora and Langston Hughes during their long road trip?) Still, one may well imagine Zora and Marjorie on the Cross Creek porch, looking at each other and, before and below their rockers, many ducks; Marjorie's beloved Jersey cow, Dora; a dog or two; perhaps a caged raccoon; a few orange trees; flowering vines; roses; and a vegetable garden. Idella or a hired man apparently did most of the pruning, weeding, picking, and feeding and milking of the animals. Marjorie worked, too, when she was home. Principally, though, she was designer and boss of her self-provisioning and outdoor ornamentation, and she was a confident, even adventurous cook. It is likely that she, rather than Idella, did most or all of the food preparation during Zora's visit.

"Our Daily Bread," the *Cross Creek* chapter about gardening, foraging, hunting, and cooking, is the longest in the book and a delight to re-read again and again. "Cookery is my one vanity," she wrote, "and I am a slave to any guest who praises my culinary art." Her "literary ability," she averred, "may safely be questioned as harshly as one wills, but indifference to my table puts me in a rage."[30] As a girl and a young woman she had tried with little success to emulate her mother and grandmother in their kitchens. Then, probably while in upstate New York, before her migration to Florida, she read a book (Fannie Farmer's) and melded, finally, printed instruction, common sense, and talent with memory. In northern Florida, Marjorie found not only new ingredients but variety and freshness undreamed of, and however immodestly, by 1942 she could anoint herself a magician. She would consider anything. Rattlesnake, for instance, she tried and dismissed as not terribly good, citing William Bartram for authoritative backup. Steaks of alligator tail, on the other hand, she found delightful, instructing readers of *Cross Creek Cookery* (on page 111) to "cut strips lengthwise . . . four inches long and two inches wide, or cut cross-sections between the vertebrae." Then one should "roll in salted and peppered flour and fry quickly in butter." Bears had grown scarce even around Cross Creek, but when Marjorie was introduced to bear meat in the still-wild Big Scrub—as pot roast or steak—she also found that delightful and offered instructions on preparation. Her most outrageous animal-scavenging occurred seren-dipitously, during her first duck hunt, on nearby Orange Lake. Her neigh-bors—much better shots than she, she confessed—"were bringing down their ducks." Marjorie "had not touched a feather." Her eyes and mind wan-dered, and nearby she saw "hundreds of red-winged blackbirds . . . stirring in the tussocks." In a flash she thought of "the four and twenty blackbirds baked in a pie and wondered if these grain and seed eating birds might not be the edible ones of the rhymed fable." So she "slipped No. 10 shells into my shot-gun, and two shots brought down a dozen birds." Marjorie made the pie and found it "utterly delicious." Thereafter for several years, when-ever she lacked meat and ordinary game had disappeared, she repeated the slaughter and baking. At last, however, she "began to be ashamed of shoot-ing the cheerful chirruping things that were so ornamental in the marshes. I decided I would do no more of it." A little later, too, she discovered that on her hunting license, red-winged blackbirds—albeit under another name— were a protected species off-limits to hunters.[31]

Marjorie foraged relentlessly for vegetables and fruits, too. Northern Florida pokeweed flourished in late winter and early spring, and she went gathering with a basket. She knew that native southerners washed and ate leaves as "salat" or boiled them with bacon, but she preferred to remove the leaves and cook the shoots as one would prepare asparagus. She served it on toast covered with a creamy sauce, with fried bacon on the side. Marjorie also harvested the ubiquitous scrubby palm called swamp cabbage. Her ob-jective was the palm's heart, but since extracting the heart killed the palm, she took few and served the delicacy not often. Wild grapes and other fruits were plentiful, though, if got one to them ahead of birds and raccoons.

Marjorie's fenced garden was typically southern. She loved collard greens and seemed to have grown them as well as turnip and mustard greens. Cowpeas were a staple, and okra was a specialty in her kitchen. Next to her celebrated lemony hollandaise, Marjorie's culinary vanity was most invested in her ingenious treatment of okra. In her garden poetics, okra was "a Cinderella among vegetables." Living "a lowly life, stewed stickily with tomatoes, or lost of identity in a Creole gumbo," it still possessed potential to become a princess. Marjorie happened to possess "the magic wand" and knew "no other cook who serves it as I do." Selecting only the small, tender pods, leaving on the stems, she boiled her okra in salted water for precisely seven minutes. Service arrived on small plates for each guest, with little bowls of hollandaise in the center, the okra arranged spokelike around the hollandaise. One lifted each pod by its stem, then dipped it into the sauce "more daintily than is possible with asparagus," she wrote.[32] Brava!

Her genius with okra was actually born of frustration. Marjorie dearly loved asparagus and, finding herself in a presumptive Garden of Eden, assumed at first she might have all her fondest wishes here and now. Cross Creek was indeed close to but was not quite paradise. The asparagus bed she planted flourished—and flourished. It was quickly a tall forest of ferns, but lacking a Yankee winter's rest, there was never an edible spear. Okra was her substitute. Similarly, being in La Florida, Marjorie figured she should have her own avocados, mangoes, and plantains. Of course Cross Creek was too far north for successful cultivation of these tropicals. Her clever attempt to breed her own hardy avocado trees ended with freeze-blackened stumps. Marjorie's compensation was nearby seasonal markets, where at a fraction of the prices in Washington and New York she might have her tropical fruits. Sometimes Eden costs a little cash, and one will recall that Marjorie Rawlings was in the orange business, trying to provide a taste of paradise to the less fortunate to the north. In return, they might send her some asparagus each spring. Eden, it seems, cannot be a private garden but, rather, a very large space with cooperating parts.

Cooperation among provisioners in the long duration necessitates gardeners' and vegetable- and fruit-growers' cooperation with nature, too. Conservation—which is management of nature with a respectful, wary hope for permanence—is the word. Poor, heroic Zora Neale Hurston was a conservationist gardener, even on ground she had no hope of owning. The self-interest of victuals-in-return-for-exercise (and a bit of luck) may be the soul of equilibrium, but there is also beauty, accomplished by wise encouragement of nature's own power. Zora did both these well. Bernice Kelly Harris, Marjorie Kinnan Rawlings, and countless other owners of land, no matter how small, were the more obvious and the most rewarded conservationists.

Marjorie Rawlings interests me the most because in the high age of conservation she boldly confessed her own lapses. Not only did she shotgun red-winged blackbirds for pies; once she shot (with a .22, like Audie Murphy's rabbit) an endangered waterfowl, a brown crane called a limpkin. This happened not at Cross Creek but up by the Ocklawaha River in the Big Scrub, probably about 1930, when Marjorie was living with the cracker family who inspired her self-sufficient fictional characters. They had rhapsodized about roasted limpkin. Marjorie was collecting, as it were, for the sake of literature, so one day she spotted a limpkin, brought it down, and roasted it according to local custom. It was delicious, she declared. But by the early 1940s Marjorie was done with collecting and had become ashamed of her transgressions. She had never killed a deer or a bear, she wrote, but had participated in hunts, trying to absorb the lives of her hosts and companions in the doing. Claiming to be a poor shot (what of the limpkin?), she nevertheless helped butcher, prepare, and consume the meat of dwindling birds, amphibians, and mammals. Now she lived away from Cross Creek much of the time, and the great models for Penny Baxter and other old-time hunters were gone or quite old. Marjorie swore off hunting, except for quail and dove—she "dread[ed] the day when conscience shall triumph over palate"—but obviously, this was a question of ethics, perhaps morality, too, that awaited her answer.[33] Belatedly, she made her peace and became a part of twentieth-century game restrictions and an informed, wise user of nature's bounty.

Yet not quite. Cal Long, a legendary hunter and another Big Scrub friend and mentor, approached eighty about 1940, and while he may have defined quaint in every respect, he was by no means dead, not yet. So long as Cal and others like him lived on, in the few remaining Floridian places still wild and thinly populated by humans, Marjorie thought, then the Age of the Commons lived on, too. It would indeed live on in her fiction, and for a little while, at least, Cal and his ilk remained real, *vivant*. Such people's use of wild game "is an ancient and honorable and necessary thing," she wrote in *Cross Creek*. Cal had once killed wildcats and panthers—the former for meat, especially livers, and the latter for oil to treat rheumatism. Florida panthers had disappeared from the scrub, and poor Cal gave up on curing his own aches and pains. To make matters worse (for both Cal and Marjorie), much of Cal's own land had become a protected game preserve. "'The law,' Marjorie quoted Cal, 'says I cain't shoot a buck [deer] in my own potato patch!'" She observed, nonetheless, that "venison continued a staple meat on his table." Cal persistently complained, though: "'The law says I cain't kill me a wild turkey scratchin' up my cowpeas. The law this, that law that! Why, I'm too old a man to begin obeyin' the law!'"[34] Indeed.

Cal would pass. So would the last remnant of preserved venison in her own larder, Marjorie said; then she would give it up for good. She the Pulitzer winner and best-selling writer and paid lecturer had no need of the scrub's commons. There was plenty of cheap beef for sale, anyway, and it certainly tasted better. Marjorie had become disgusted with "sportsmen"—the very class she represented—who had been principal makers of hunting preserves and restrictions. Like herself, they had no compelling need for a deer's life. "When a clean kill is made," one "hardened hunter" said to her, the sportsman "takes pleasure in the sport." But most shots do not kill cleanly—"the fallen deer is yet alive . . . and [the hunter] must cut its throat . . . the big eyes turned on him with a stricken wonder."[35] Cal-style hunters, desperate and without alternative protein, might do such work quickly and honorably, leaving no waste and eating with profound gratitude. Throat-slitting is ugly business to most (although certainly not all) of us. To Marjorie—and some male hunters, she said—such business is justified only by necessity. She herself went on killing domestic ducks and chickens, but well before her too-early death in 1953, it seems clear, Marjorie Rawlings's version of conservation had come to include a definitive moral aspect.

This moral aspect was hardly unique to Rawlings. The American men (mostly) who created and named conservation, a cohort slightly older than Marjorie's parents, wrote and spoke of conservation in terms economic and political. Nature must be used, and wisely, for our self-interest and national security. Fouled waters sicken and kill people and livestock. Clear-cut forests not immediately replanted will leave the next generation short of wood —and the nation dependent on overseas sources. Clearing the air will reduce the costs of health care and bring forth healthy, productive workers, not to mention future soldiers. Yet I have yet to encounter the writings of a single prominent early-twentieth-century conservationist who was not also a Romantic. Spectacular nature (notably in the first national parks) defined the United States. Nature (mountains most of all) transported humans and put them closer to God. Wilderness was not only a healthy but a necessary check on urban civilization. Theodore Roosevelt, already quite famous for roughing it on the Great Plains and in Cuba, was famously photographed with John Muir in California, on the peak of a high Sierra, joining Muir, at least by suggestion, in the Christian metaphors Muir indulged: The natural world is blessed, sacred. Roosevelt had been a close student of nature since childhood, in fact, and would continue to be. His friend Gifford Pinchot, one of the American definers and exemplars of conservation, was no less the outdoorsman and worshiper of natural beauty both monumental and tiny. So was the southerner Hugh Hammond Bennett, premier soil scientist of the first half of the twentieth century and first chief of the U.S. Soil

Conservation Service. Born on a North Carolina cotton farm, Bennett remained not only the practical agrarian but the outdoorsman and effusive lover of wildflowers during all his decades in Washington, D.C.[36]

🌸 The most ambitious of nature's planner-protectors acknowledge that sudden disaster may occur any time. Consider the enormous New Madrid earthquake of 1811. Radiating from its epicenter near the Mississippi River in Missouri's southeastern "bootheel," the quake changed the courses of rivers and creeks, rearranged many square miles of rural ground cover, and shook shingles and bricks off buildings as far away as Cincinnati. Had not most of the broad territory along the New Madrid Fault been rural and thinly populated by humans, the quake's consequences might have been bloody indeed. Charleston, South Carolina, suffered major damage and more than a hundred human fatalities during its earthquake of 1886. Great storms, too, can make lasting, sometimes permanent changes in landscapes. The South's western fringe is subject to tornadoes that carry away not only buildings, animals, and people but tons of topsoil that humans have dared to uncover as farmland. Hurricanes have ever been the bane of the humid South. Arising from the southern Atlantic near West Africa, hurricanes may sweep over Gulf and South Atlantic beaches, their tidal surges inundating all before them. Poor Charleston has been regularly flooded and/or flattened throughout recorded weather history. Often the winds of such storms slacken but nonetheless persist far inland, still sodden, releasing prodigious loads of rain. Rivers in the piedmont overflow and return more punishment to already stricken tidewaters. Inland-meandering storms have wrought their worst mischief in the mountains, though. Fast-running streams carry down enormous loads of silt and rock from above. Farms and towns have been ruined, sometimes buried, by debris. Bridges are washed away and roads are blocked or undermined, leaving rural people, especially, isolated and helpless. When such inland storms occur after industrial-scale clear-cutting of forests, the landscape is more vulnerable and the damage to nature, people, and their works much worse.

Then there is fire, every temperate climate's ancient boon and bane. Humans have ever employed fire both small and large to accomplish tasks personally essential and communally ambitious. Most rural fires begin with lightning, however, so a huge, all-consuming "wildfire" may imply no human agency or blame at all. Still, human disturbance of landscapes often leaves behind debris that is potential fuel for fire, inviting holocaust where otherwise a more modest, perhaps cleansing and rejuvenating fire might have blazed. Fire was the one natural hazard that conservationists believed they could tame and perhaps even eliminate—thus the early-twentieth-century criminalization of forest arson and state and federal fire prevention and protection programs. Well before 1900, too, conservationists also understood that healthy forests reduced damage from extraordinary storms with rain. Likewise conservationists maintained that wind erosion of exposed farming soils might be reduced by an agronomy that included wise plowing techniques, crop selection, and layout. Such was the confident, authoritative thinking of the twentieth century: The world is lovely, opulent, but occasionally dangerous; practical science and prudent management will prevent—at the least mitigate—imbalances, helping nature maintain its own harmony.[37]

Harmony, or better, equilibrium—a natural, self-correcting system (with or without human participation)—is a persistent characterization of the natural world older than the twentieth century. Oddly, it coexisted with the scary, chaotic Sturm und Drang of Darwinism and flourished, actually, through much of the twentieth century's successive scientific triumphs. "Home," though, has been the dominant evocative metaphor, encompassing the human domestic ideals of harmony, equilibrium, mutualism, and interdependency. Ernst Haeckel, the best-known German admirer of Darwin, based his 1866 coinage, "Oecologie," on the linkage of "economy" with the Greek *oikos*, home. Almost three decades later, the International Botanical Congress adopted the more contemporary (and English) spelling, ecology. In the United States at the turn of the twentieth century, one of the most important popularizers of early ecological science was a Bostonian chemist named Ellen Swallow Richards. A homemaker as well as a professional, Swallow Richards's public rhetoric (which included a book, *Sanitation in Daily Life*, published in 1910) sought to extend modern home economics to public built environments and beyond, conjoining private domestic duties (and joys) with the broader world. Hers was an entwined human-natural universe in which humanity assumed responsibility for harmony.[38]

Following the creation of the American Ecological Society in 1915, however, a succession of midwestern botanists and limnologists (freshwater biologists) defined ecological science and gradually, with many missteps, moved the most precious, specialized research toward the concept of ecological systems. Frederick Clements was the early giant who gave the world the terms "succession" and "climax." The first describes the orderly development of small and large landscapes, in plant stages, from filled-in ponds, say, with grassy cover, to dominant woody shrubs and finally to a mature (climax) forest. "Succession" survives today, both in lay and professional parlance. "Climax" may have seemed unnaturally permanent even during the 1920s. The great English biologist Arthur G. Tansley of Oxford University grew troubled that Clementsian science took no account of human agency. Clements seemed biased against "the human tribes," Tansley wrote, and civilization itself.[39] Tansley's own immortal coinage, "ecosystem," in 1935, accounted for humanity as part of what is called nature.

Other Americans had anticipated Tansley, however. As far back as 1887, the Illinois limnologist Stephen Alfred Forbes had described a "community of interest"—that is, a self-regulating system—in the natural world. Chancey Juday analyzed a Wisconsin "lake as [a] system" in 1895. The ultimate midwestern limnologist was Raymond Lindeman (1915–42), who presented in his University of Minnesota dissertation means to quantify simultaneous death and life in the shrinking Cedar Bog Lake, near Minneapolis. Here and in two acclaimed papers he wrote principally at Yale, Lindeman brilliantly set forth a "trophic-dynamic" conceptualization of the lake that actually demonstrated Tansley's notion of nature as working "system," with measurable energy flows representing both death and creation in the mutuality of the lake's chemicals, minerals, plants, and animals. Contemporary studies in Germany also elaborated on the ecosystem concept.

In the broadest views of ideas about nature, Tansley, Lindeman, and others seemed to validate an optimistic symmetry seen long before and after, among otherwise disparate sources. The anti-Darwinian Russian prince Peter Kropotkin, for instance, author of *Mutual Aid: A Factor in Evolution* (1902), may have been wrongheaded about Darwin, but he is often credited with the invention of what is still called "mutualism" in biology. Mutualism, indeed, has become a demonstrated phenomenon in ecological science as practiced by confirmed Darwinians. The classic example is fungi on plant roots that provide nutrients for root growth, especially in poor soil, while the roots provide supportive homes to fungi. Without fungi, roots would die or remain much smaller than their potential, and soil would remain impoverished. In turn, mutualism shadows the naturalist "holism" of the South African Jan Christian Smuts. And certainly the mutual interdependency of organisms within systems informed the evolving "land ethic" of the Iowa-born game manager Aldo Leopold. If humans, ever a part of natural systems, behave knowledgeably as stewards, then earth might remain a harmonious home.

The creation of an ecological science of dynamic systems working toward equilibrium was an international accomplishment with principal American contributions originating in the Midwest. From the 1940s, however, ecosystem ecology would mature and flourish, and—one may well argue—as a *southern* concept, earnestly refined and promoted by southerners and practiced most ingeniously in the South. Doubtlessly serendipity explains some part of such an odd turn of geography and genius. But the southernization of ecology was propelled by historical situation and human self-consciousness of mission, too.

As already observed, for at least a long half-century, from about 1890 through World War II, the South was the great, nagging, seemingly impossible problem of the United States. Dixie was woefully out of equilibrium—the "nation's number-one economic problem," as President Franklin Roosevelt memorably declared in 1938. He might have added "social," "public health," and "ecological" to "economic." By that late date the fragmented plantation system was dissolving, the region's post–Civil War farm tenure system and gross maldistribution of wealth were an international scandal, and legions of the poor and near-poor (white and black, but disproportionately black) had already deserted the region. Among the legions remaining, pellagra surged again, a parallel to (and perhaps a result of) emerging mechanized agriculture. Poverty and illness were already old and widespread in the South by the 1930s. But in contemporary national public awareness as well as in memory, southern ills became much more vivid because of photography and popularized sociology. USDA and (much more famously) a temporary New Deal agency's photographers practically swarmed over the region, filing their documentary records of distress in regional offices and at Washington. The government published many photos. Some veterans of the New Deal project—Dorothea Lange being the best remembered—compiled coffee-table picture books with accompanying text. Lange's and her economist husband's excellent work about displacement and migration was titled *American Exodus*. Commercial photographers and writers took up the genre, most notoriously Margaret Bourke-White and her husband, the best-selling novelist Erskine Caldwell. Whatever the quality of such a torrent of documentary still photography, most of it is notable not only for the human subjects but for their vernacular landscapes: shabby houses weatherproofed with newspaper, tired mules drawing antique equipment over fields equally tired.

Arguably the best-known, most widely seen portrait of the South during the 1930s was a motion picture, a federally sponsored propaganda film on behalf of the TVA made in 1937 by West Virginia–born Pare Lorentz. *The River* was screened in Paramount theaters across the nation. The river of the title was the Mississippi, which had been flooding for eons, but with mounting volume and damage since the late nineteenth century. The 1927 flood along the river below Memphis devastated the Yazoo-Mississippi Delta, occasioned a gigantic relief effort, and led big planters fearful of losing their sharecroppers virtually to imprison them atop remaining levees, which had become islands. Another great flood came in March 1937, just as Lorentz was finishing filming. *The River* is elementally and passionately conservationist. It is also ecological. Rivers will flood from time to time, we are clearly warned, but when thousands of square miles of watershed—in this case the upper Middle West and middle Appalachian chain—are clear-cut of their forests, then runoff of rains mounts in volume and distant drainage systems carry extraordinary new excesses into the Ohio, the Cumberland, the Tennessee, and then the Mississippi itself. Throughout the vast valley, erosion had grown and spread, too, because below the clear-cut places, increased populations of humans had cleared more land and planted more cotton and corn. Whole farms, houses, and barns tilted into or were consumed by gullies that had grown into eastern canyons. (Georgia ultimately made a state park of a gigantic gully known as the Little Grand Canyon.) The vast territorial connectedness of the system proved dramatically what Lorentz's sonorous narrator intoned over such scenes, the music rising to signify tragedy: "Poor land makes poor people." [40]

Many southerners, white and black, were publicly engaged in work to restore equilibrium to the region's people and landscapes. These included progressive New Deal elected officials; federal TVA, Soil Conservation Service, and other agency employees; government foresters; county agricultural and home demonstration agents; administrators and faculty at colleges and universities; many newspaper editors; and more. To me, though, the exemplary engaged southerner of the time was a rumpled, bespectacled sociology professor in Chapel Hill whose lifetime—1884–1954—corresponded to his beloved South's long, grinding travail. This was Howard Washington Odum, who happened also to be the father of the great ecosystem ecologists Eugene P. and Howard T. Odum.

Howard W. was born to a line of small farmers in northern Georgia, near

Athens. His father and paternal grandfather had little formal education, and illiteracy seems not to have been uncommon among Odums. Howard's mother, a daughter of a former slaveholder brought low by the war, was better educated, and she was ambitious for her children. Scholastic opportunity brought a family move to nearby Oxford, Georgia, site of the first incarnation of Emory College, where all five Odum children went to school. Howard earned a B.A. in 1904, taught a while in rural Mississippi, then entered the University of Mississippi, where he received an M.A. in classics in 1906. His major subject notwithstanding, Odum was decisively bent toward social science at Mississippi by Professor Thomas Pearce Bailey, who was already beginning to apply social (including economic) statistics to an elaborate justification for the new age of Jim Crow. Under Bailey's influence Howard traveled to Massachusetts and entered Clark University's doctoral program in psychology. He defended a dissertation on African American folksongs and folkways in 1909 and took a second Ph.D., in sociology, at Columbia the following year. The second dissertation, which Columbia published as a book, concerned black "racial traits." In decades to come, Odum would become embarrassed by the racism of both dissertations, and he forbade the reissue of the Columbia volume. Jim Crow, like pellagra and erosion, became anathema to Odum's deepening liberal sensibilities and social-scientific practice.[41]

After his stint in New York City, Howard returned to his native ground and introduced an ambitious range of practical, socially engaged courses — for example, on rural public health, the tenure system, and crime — for apprentice teachers in the University of Georgia's education school. He had married Ann Louise Kranz of Tennessee, a fellow psychology graduate student at Clark, and their first two children, Eugene and Mary, were born during the Athens years. In 1919 Howard W. accepted the deanship of the new (and relocated) Emory University college of arts and science in Atlanta. His ambition to enlarge the faculty and school and engage in what is more recently called outreach far exceeded the vision and patience of Emory's conservative chancellor, however, and in 1920 the Odums moved on to their destiny: Chapel Hill.

During the 1920s the University of North Carolina miraculously, considering the times, emerged as the first post–Civil War southern institution of higher learning to become great. "The Hill," as it was affectionately called, was blessed with courageous and imaginative leadership during the interwar decades, and among its distinguished faculty — who created excellent science departments and a history department that professionalized and largely dominated the field of southern history—Howard Odum was by far the most prominent. He founded the sociology department, a school of social work, the Institute for Research in Social Science, and the immediately prestigious and politically risk-taking journal *Social Forces*. By the late 1930s and 1940s, when government and foundation grants vastly expanded academic sponsored research, Odum became the very model of the university empire builder. Neither his empire nor his goals were quite original. Odum was doubtlessly aware of the "Wisconsin idea" of his youth, when that Yankee state's principal public university was dedicated to public service and, by the standards of the day, lavishly supported and loved by Wisconsin taxpayers and politicians. Now North Carolina and the Southeast had their Madison. Odum broadened and deracialized Thomas Pearce Bailey's social science and applied it to the great complex of southern ills. *Social Forces* campaigned for cures with scrupulously gathered data. Odum's colleagues (the most prominent being his own former doctoral students) and graduate students published their larger works with the warmly receptive University of North Carolina Press.

During these two interwar decades Odum reprised—without Bailey's bias—his old love of Afro-southern song and lore, and he wrote a novel. His most important work, though, was the summative *Southern Regions of the United States* (1936). The "of" in his title might have been capitalized or rendered in bold, further to emphasize the author's departure from lingering southern white separatism. Odum, as every social scientist must, despised romantic essentialism and mischievous chauvinism. His South was definable as a region, demographically, economically, educationally, legally (in terms of crime, say), and by other data-based means. It was changing, too, and it required more change—preferably planned, well financed, and humane change. All elements of southern problems were linked—racial oppression, for instance, with economic and environmental matters. All were structural (as well as ultimately moral) matters, to be addressed both scientifically and democratically. *Southern Regions* was a master blueprint, then, for a massive transformation, a kinder-hearted version of what is called modernization, that would likely render the South less southern.

No wonder that Odum's magnum opus elicited howls of protest from older, conservative white newspaper editors and especially from a group of youngish poets and critics associated with Vanderbilt University and Nashville called the Agrarians. In 1930 twelve of them (including two historians) had published a "manifesto" against modernism in all its disturbing modes: alienating industrialization, urbanization, and the most insidious of evils, godless relativism. *I'll Take My Stand* had its points both principled and elegiac, and it deserves to be in print even to this day. Moral and ethical relativism, after all, have not gone away as issues; rather, the opposite. Still, the agrarian manifesto was simultaneously and unambiguously white-biased and naive on rural life, labor, and authority and hopelessly unconnected to issues of social justice, health, landscape, and much else. Odum and his colleagues—now known as the Chapel Hill Regionalists—were connected; they were, in fact, not only modernists but mutualists and holists.[42]

Howard Odum in his own home seems quite comfortably to have connected southern versions of pasts and futures. Forever in rumpled suits and unassuming of demeanor, he nonetheless built for himself, his family, and his omnipresent students and guests an enormous house near the campus in Chapel Hill. Maids, a cook, and a butler tended to cleaning, order, food, and protocol. In addition to a master bedroom for the lord and lady of the manor, there were separate rooms for each of the three children, for a couple of graduate students in sociology, and yet another for visitors—usually invited speakers, consultants, and officials. Among the Odums' guests, well before World War II, was the occasional black traveler who otherwise would have found no decent accommodation in Chapel Hill. So Odum, schooled in scientific racism, had grown democratic as well as practical. He did need, after all, the expertise of black professionals in his work. Black anthropologists and folklorists—notably Zora Neale Hurston—disparaged and dismissed even Odum's later, admiring, books on Afro-southern song and narrative. He had inadequate feel for tone and practically no understanding of common syntax, Hurston complained.[43] Certainly Odum's turn from cultural anthropology to social ecology was fortunate for all. Still, on the subject of color, justice, and harmony, one will remember that Hurston (if we are to accept Idella Parker's word) was sent to sleep among Marjorie Kinnan Rawlings's hirelings, while the Odums welcomed black peers under their own roof. Howard had already been active in a moderate interracial group devoted to maintaining contact and conversation across the racial divide: the Commission on Interracial Cooperation, founded in 1919. Ultimately, during the 1940s, he became president of its successor organization, which survives, the Southern Regional Council.

Ironically, too, Howard W. Odum was ever the agrarian, more legitimately, one must say, than Allen Tate, Robert Penn Warren, and other Agrarians of the late 1920s and 1930s. Agrarianism may be a formal philosophy and/or political position about the rural and agricultural foundations of wealth and the spiritual and social advantages of rural life. Agrarianism may also be merely a closely related sentiment. The Agrarians and the Regionalists shared the latter. Regionalists—Odum, Rupert Vance, Arthur Raper, Gerald Johnson, Margaret Jarman Hagood, and others—seemed to accept the agrarian premise regarding the origins of wealth even as they unmasked the legends of bucolic bliss and welcomed machines and industries as opportunities for unhappy peasants' escape.[44] Odum always cherished his farmboy origins and heritage, and in Chapel Hill he assumed a rural persona parallel to the academic one. Outside town he maintained a farm where he bred Jersey dairy cattle—and quite successfully. The American Jersey Cattle Club once conferred upon him the Master Breeders Award, and Howard also served as president of the North Carolina Jersey Cattlemen's Association. Such a tiny agrarian universe as his offers timely, almost perfect poetics, I think: The Odum farm was not extensive in scope. Little ground cover was disturbed, because cows consume principally grasses, which hold the soil. And while unproductive bulls and cows were doubtlessly sent to the abattoir, breeding-for-dairy and dairying themselves seem worthy and moral uses of animals, assuming (from Genesis) that humans are entitled to dominate and exploit them.

In *Southern Regions*, Odum declared early on, "In fine and in sum, the agrarian problem is *the region*, for better or for worse."[45] By this he meant, of course, not only a premodern land tenure system and low commodity prices but high birthrates, poor education, racial discrimination, politics variously feudal and demagogic, and not least, poor land. Odum was not the first of the Regionalists, however, to engage the "agrarian problem."

In 1929 the University of North Carolina Press published Rupert Vance's superlative *Human Factors in Cotton Culture: A Study in the Social Geography of the American South*. Farm-raised himself, like Odum, Vance was a beloved fixture in Chapel Hill for many years. Opposite his volume's title page is a beauteous, color-coded foldout map titled "Soil Regions of the Cotton Belt" southeast of latitude 37° and longitude 103°. From the preface onward, Vance anticipated much of the best, I think, of agro-ecological historiography during the last two decades of the twentieth century. One of his consultants was the most prominent historian of the South at the time, Ulrich Bonnell Phillips of Yale, who began his own last book, *Life and Labor in the Old South*, also published in 1929, with the famous determinism, "Let us begin by discussing the weather, for that has been the chief agency in making the South distinctive." Vance himself rejected determinism in the abstract; yet in the course of explaining his methodology and conclusions, he conceded that "one must admit that much that is distinctive of southern culture, its plantation system, its sectionalism, its agricultural life, its rural practices, has developed as a kind of complex around the cotton plant," whose culture the South's climate and soils had invited.[46] Cultivation of cotton (most deterministic of all southern commodities, perhaps) had perpetuated slavery and caused sharecropping and the impoverishment of both people and the landscape. By Vance's time cotton culture had contributed enormously to an environmental and social crisis. No less than Pare Lorentz's *The River* almost a decade later, Vance's first agrarian book demonstrated the causative interrelationships between weather, soils, and human economic activity.

After *Human Factors*, Vance undertook a more comprehensive environmental study of the region. *Human Geography of the South: A Study in Regional Resources and Human Adequacy* (also published by the University of North Carolina Press) appeared in 1932. More than 500 pages long, this work rivals Odum's opus of four years later in scope. Encompassing all agricultural subregions, it demonstrated correlations between topography and "culture" (broadly defined). It also described industries, subclimates, and human diets in comparative perspective, and finally, it presented Vance's grim assessment of the condition and future of "folk" culture in the South.

Only three years later, in 1935, Vance broached an issue he had not emphasized before, oddly enough. This was the South's persisting overproduction of children during the great interwar crisis. His memorable essay "Is Agrarianism for Farmers?" appeared in *Southern Review* and addressed the Depression-era "back to the land" movement. The press had reported that numbers of rural southern migrants to the industrial North, thrown out of jobs and unable to pay rent, had flocked back south, often to their families, to take up farming again. Vance and other Regionalists already understood that there was seldom room for more farm laborers and that clearing more land for them resulted in more soil erosion and exhaustion. More immediately, though, Vance was annoyed by some of the Nashville Agrarians' celebration of the phenomenon. His essay observed the timeless dilemma of rural proprietors: generational succession and the subdivision of farms that were already too small. "Southern farmers," he wrote, should "take a look at the French peasant," for whom the "farm is a permanent thing to be tended with loving care and handed down undivided." The French ideal scenario was "to rear to adulthood two children, preferably one son who will inherit the family domain and one daughter who will marry a neighbor's son who will also inherit." Then "no child of his will have to till another's land nor seek his fortune in that wicked Paris." There being in America no more western frontier for surplus children to claim, he concluded, "the challenge to agrarianism . . . is . . . a population policy." [47]

Here was dangerous language, indeed, boldly and maybe recklessly anticipating the zero population growth aspect of environmental politics during the 1970s. From the 1870s until 1930, dissemination of birth control information and devices was prohibited by federal law and, in 1935, remained illegal in many states. Clearly Vance implied birth control. He actually specified "population policy," that is, guidance and intervention into the most private of human social activities by governmental authority, whether directly, coercively, or by some indirect, persuasive means. Vance did not specify here.

A decade later, however, Vance published (again in Chapel Hill) his huge population study, *All These People: The Nation's Human Resources in the South*. The book was dedicated to Howard Odum and presented as a "companion volume" to *Southern Regions*. *All These People* resembles *Southern Regions* in its uncharacteristically (for Vance) wooden prose and almost smothering array of maps, tables, charts, and graphs. Toward the end, though, Vance regained his usual felicitous expression in his recommendations about policy. The federal government, he observed, had already limited population growth through immigration restrictions adopted by Congress in 1921 and 1924. Now stabilization and improvement of families' standard of living depended on a combination of private and indirect government initiatives. Both the private and governmental programs would be "democratic" instead of coercive. Middle- and upper-class couples had already decided on birth control. The poor (particularly the rural poor) were beginning to understand the relationship between family size, standard of living, and family farm security. The private Planned Parenthood Federation of America—founded by Margaret Sanger, a sometime correspondent of Howard Odum—would assist such people with information and other means of zero population growth, which might be achieved, Vance hoped, between 1960 and 1980. (It was.) State and federal public health agencies should assist Planned Parenthood in such work, he suggested. [48]

🌿 Among the other Regionalists, I think that Arthur F. Raper was, next to Vance, the exemplary link to our own Age of Ecology. Raper's time in Chapel Hill was relatively brief. Seldom an academician, he was instead a great field researcher in small places. Raper's two classic southern books, *Preface to Peasantry* (1936) and *Tenants of the Almighty* (1943), describe only two counties in Georgia. Yet his masterful applied interdisciplinarity illuminated what had gone terribly wrong in Greene and Macon counties. Macon, especially its soils and black residents, was poor. Greene was poorer still because it was part of Georgia's first cotton frontier and its clay dirt and had been mined and washed longer; thus all of its residents had been impoverished longer.

In 1940 Raper returned to Greene County, stayed for two years, and wrote *Tenants of the Almighty*. He hoped to reach a wide audience with this work, which he addressed to Greene's own people and wrote in an informal style that partly disguised his thick description and shrewd analysis. After a hasty summary of what he had found in 1936, he undertook a frank celebration of the late New Deal's Unified Farm Program in the county, which represented the ideal of the Regionalists, some of the Agrarians, and other small-farmer advocates. The Unified Farm Program selected promising tenants and a few sharecroppers and provided them with cheap credit to buy land, mules, and equipment. Then it offered advisory assistance on marketing (the government helped create cooperatives), help in achieving self-sufficiency in food, and not least, assistance (a requirement, actually) in farm practices that restored soils and fertility. In 1943 Greene's citizens were learning, Raper had reason to hope, to reverse their historically destructive ways and live harmoniously with nature, even while earning modest livelihoods. Raper credited a local black poet, a "tenant mother" named Louisiana Dunn Thomas, for the title of his book. Thomas had written,

> We are tenants of the Almighty
> Entrusted with a portion of His earth
> To dress and keep
> And pass on to the next generation.[49]

Sad to say, Arthur Raper's wartime optimism for Greene County and comparable southern places was already unwarranted. The Unified Farm Program and similar tenant-to-owner programs were underfunded from the start and were soon to be gutted. Federal policy instead was already dedicated to capital-intensive agriculture, which was moving toward farming on a large scale, specialization, and a relentless trend away from self-sufficiency in food. In hardly more than a decade after World War II, almost all American farmers, including the shrinking number with modest acreage, would buy their vegetables, milk, cheese, and meat at supermarkets. The Soil Conservation Service and thousands of local conservation districts survive, and water erosion, if not conquered, is essentially controlled. Wind

*Greensboro, Greene County, Georgia, on a Saturday afternoon, 1941.*

*Photo by Jack Delano. Courtesy Library of Congress (LC-USF34-046421-D DLC).*

erosion is not, however. By the 1950s, market forces (pushed by chemical corporations and agronomists) had compelled virtually all farmers to buy and apply petroleum-based fertilizers, herbicides, and pesticides for their soils. By the 1970s, when world grain prices rose and rose, even supposedly conservation-minded midwestern farmers had abandoned crop rotations in favor of "continuous corn," fertilized by nearly continuous doses of anhydrous ammonia. So much for conservation.

The great wave of "big ag" across the South since World War II—southern farms are second in scale only to the West's—may render hopelessly quaint the Regionalists' dream of a landscape of small proprietorships managed by prudent, soil-conserving men and women. Quaint is not the equivalent of wrong, however, and industrial gigantism in farming was by no means inevitable. Big ag was engineered politically by representatives of machinery manufacturers, chemical producers, fiber and food processors and shippers, and many institutional economists and agronomists. Not least of the engineers was the U.S. Congress, which beginning in 1933 created a commodity subsidy program that disproportionately rewarded big producers. By the early 1980s, Earl Butz, U.S. Secretary of Agriculture, declaimed honestly, albeit undiplomatically, that all farmers ought to "Get big or get out!"

The Chapel Hillians and their allies had a better idea that, given sufficient political weight, might have been realized. Now we can only try to visualize alternative American (not merely southern) rural landscapes, as they might appear today: a more substantial human, middle-class population; less wind erosion; mixed, rotated crops; fewer requirements for artificial chemicals; and safer produce and meats—healthy land and healthy people. Howard Odum died in 1954, still hopeful despite many disappointments. And he had children who carried on with an optimism that, considering the odds against optimism, seems simply astounding.

Eugene Pleasants "Gene" Odum grew up during the 1910s and 1920s in his father's Chapel Hill mansion. A rather mediocre student, his first idea of a vocation, he once said, was to be plumber. Young Gene was a shy fellow living in a human beehive, so he retreated from company to crawl spaces under houses, where he followed pipes and mapped water-supply and refuse-disposal systems. "I was curious about networks," he explained much later, when he had grown into a gregarious, storytelling maturity. Whether the plumbing tale was merely an arch take on his juvenile indifference to school or not, it was symbolically prophetic. Almost three decades after his crawl-space studies, Gene Odum published his revolutionary textbook in ecosystem ecology, *The Fundamentals of Ecology* (1953), which was illustrated with diagrams of energy transfers bearing no little resemblance to large, complex plumbing systems. The historian Donald Worster reacted to Odum's famous ecosystem "flow charts" in amazement: "All the energy lines move smartly along, converging here and shooting off there, looping back to where they began and following the thermodynamic arrows in a mannerly march toward the exit points. A traffic controller or warehouse superintendent could not ask for a more well-programmed world." [50] Worster understands well that Odum did not share his alarm at the charts' calibrated, automaton-like schematics. Rather the opposite, indeed: Gene called his ecosystem home. Had he never retreated to crawl spaces as a boy in Chapel Hill, the young Odum could not have escaped serious talk about systems and homeostasis as ideal, from his father and other Regionalists. Later, by the time Gene repeated his plumbing tale, he proudly and forthrightly acknowledged the generational continuity.

Young Odum studied other systems, too. He followed streams in and around Chapel Hill from their sources to their outlets. Along the way he became an expert birder and began a typewritten ornithological newsletter, finally contributing well-written bird columns to the town's newspaper. He was patient, observant, and interested more in animal behavior than taxonomy. His sister, Mary Francis, six years his junior, declared him a good teacher. This he would always be, plus an academic empire-builder to rival if not exceed his father.

After earning his degree in zoology at Chapel Hill, Gene Odum moved to the Midwest for graduate study—first at Western Reserve in Cleveland, then the University of Illinois, where he devised a clever mechanism to record birds' heart rates, and where he met and married his mate for life. After a field research appointment in the frigid Northeast, he landed his first and last academic job at the University of Georgia. An Odum had returned to the old sod.

During the 1940s, Georgia was only beginning to aspire to North Carolina's standards of faculty research and graduate education. The productive Gene was something of a star there from the beginning of his career, but he was also a frustrated one. Not only were teaching loads heavy, but Gene's crusty senior colleagues in zoology resisted his hope to instruct undergraduates in ecosystem ecology. Ecology was hardly a new scientific discipline (or interdiscipline), but the old boys believed that undergraduates must begin studies at the bottom, as it were, and labor toward the interactive systems at the top. Their model textbook was *Principles of Animal Ecology* (1949), by Warder Allee and others. Gene Odum's intellectual and pedagogical model was the opposite, the top-down approach, to which he would adhere the rest of his long life. Whether young student or mature scientist, one begins with the system, then proceeds to its parts. Gene decided, then, to create a textbook of his own. His *Principles of Ecology* finally appeared in 1953, the year before his father's death. The elder Odum, in fact, had puffed Gene's project to publishers he had known for years, encouraged his son at every turn, and cheered the appearance of what would soon become a classic.[51]

There was other family assistance, too, that found its way into the text of the first edition of *Principles*. While Gene labored at his classic-to-be, he was in constant contact with his brother, Howard Thomas, eleven years his junior and then a doctoral candidate in ecology at Yale. Tom (as he was called in youth, and later HT) was a student of none other than Professor George Evelyn Hutchinson, who had mentored Raymond Lindeman the last years of the young Minnesotan's life. The younger Howard had been a much more serious student than the young Gene. Now he was completing what was arguably the best scientific preparation available in North America at the time. Tom was also, as Gene understood well enough, a much better mathematician than his brother. Here was a significant family asset, then, since Gene's version of ecological systems involved measurable thermal changes and exchanges. So while still a graduate student, Tom became Gene's number cruncher and received principal credit for writing the critical energy chapter in *Principles*.

The brothers Odum were very different, as family members and friends often observed. Gene was informal, gregarious, and intuitive. HT was the serious fellow, precise, seemingly more aloof, and perhaps not the patient teacher his brother always was. On the other hand, both brothers were tall, long-nosed, lean and fit, and competitive and confident not only in their profession but in sport. They were aggressive and skillful tennis players. They were also fast friends and frequent collaborators. Once, on a federally sponsored research trip, they worked together among the corals at Eniwetok Island in the Pacific, measuring the ecological effects of atomic testing. They did not work at the same academic institution, however. HT spent much of his career at the University of Florida, but he also moved about, to Chapel Hill, to Duke, and to the University of Texas.

At Florida he replicated, in effect, many of his older brother's administrative and research accomplishments at Athens. Gene had been prin-

cipal founder of Georgia's Institute for Ecology, where he trained generations of graduate students from around the nation and the globe as well as
conducted and supervised laboratory and field research. In 1952 Gene won
a contract with the Atomic Energy Commission to study the 300 square
miles of vacated farmland and woods surrounding the new Savannah River
nuclear plant. The project occupied him, many colleagues, and squadrons
of graduate students for years. Both brothers were fascinated (and one must
say, enchanted) by wetlands. Gene produced a book about coastal Georgia,
while his talented wife, a watercolorist, painted Sapelo Island and other
tidal scenes. HT, holder of an endowed chair and director of the University
of Florida's counterpart of Gene's institute, famously described the steady-
state ecosystem of Silver Spring. The 1960s and 1970s were the heydays of
ecosystem studies, and the brothers Odum were arguably the greatest stars
of the International Biological Program, which sponsored huge and costly
biome studies. They traveled the world, often together, with their wives,
reading conference papers and accepting awards. There is no Nobel Prize
for ecology, but there was probably a worldwide consensus that Gene and
HT were de facto laureates.

It may seem ironic, then, that such globe-trotters remained profoundly
provincial. Gene was the ur-Georgian. And HT, descending from New
Haven, did a stint in Puerto Rico, rambled among other excellent institutions before settling (for three decades) at Florida, but spent his long career
entirely in the South, too. Surely either scholar might have left, but both
were not only self-consciously southern but committed, like their father,
to southern missions. Wetlands must be preserved, for instance, and if
endangered, saved by wise management. Virtually all the physical South
was threatened in some way—by overdevelopment, mining and other industries, outdated sanitation, or inadequate and compromised water supplies. The Odums would apply their expertise and versatility to solving their
homeland's persisting ills. They were not merely ecosystem ecologists but
unabashed environmentalists.

Both brothers insisted upon addressing their work not only to peers but
to students at every level, to public officeholders, and to the public. Gene's
*Principles* evolved through several editions for two decades, and even rather
late in his life he sought to make ecosystem ecology accessible with such
works as *Ecology: A Bridge between Science and Society* (1997). Likewise, HT
offered (in 1971) his Odumesque contribution to public education, *Environment, Power, and Society*. The work was dedicated to his father, "who suggested," HT wrote, "a synthesis of science and society." He also "acknowl-

*Eugene P. Odum greets a bronze bust of himself, Institute for Ecology, University of Georgia, 17 September 1984. Photo UGA Research Communications, courtesy of Kathy Underhill.*

edge[d] the shared effort toward this aim with my brother Eugene P. Odum, University of Georgia."[52]

By the mid-1970s, with the brothers Odum at the height of their influence, what now seems an inevitable scientific reaction against their paradigm had begun, soon mounting to a veritable onslaught against the notion that homeostasis was nature's own goal and norm. In 1973 the influential *Journal of the Arnold Arboretum* published an article with the disarmingly simple title "Succession," by William Drury and Ian Nisbet, scientists who worked with the Massachusetts Audubon Society. Frederic Clements, creator of "succession" as theory and model, was long gone but, as any smart reader knew in 1973, immortal within the concept of ecosystem ecology, which was crowned with Gene Odum's clever substitution of "mature ecosystem" for succession's "climax." Shockingly, wrote Drury and Nisbet, succession actually led, simply, nowhere at all. There is no purpose to change in the world, that is, simply unending change itself. Nor was there progress, only randomness, and no system but competing individuals.[53]

By the mid-1980s, it would appear, *oikos* had lost any metaphoric relevance to science whatsoever—except, of course, the gloomy news that American households were dissolving at an alarming rate, divorces were as frequent as weddings, the young had become wary of intimate commitment, and many homes were scenes of spousal and child abuse. Home, in other words, could be more chaotic and disharmonious than the opposite. By unhappy coincidence, in 1985 the scientists S. T. A. Pickett and P. S. White collected an anthology they titled *The Ecology of Natural Disturbance and Patch Dynamics*. Collectively, the essayists found "disturbance," or "perturbation," the signal constant of the natural world. Even without human mischief, other agents—fire, storms, drought, digging varmints, and ants, for example—kept the earth in perpetual turmoil. Systems and climaxes being ephemeral or nonexistent, then, the only legitimate ecological pedagogy and research program must concentrate on dynamic, erratic patches of landscape. And this is, indeed, something approaching scientific consensus today. In 1992, meanwhile, Joel Hagen, a historian, published a critical book on the ecosystem concept and practice.[54]

Throughout the crash of their paradigm, Gene and HT Odum persisted as long-lived and long-working men. (They died a few weeks apart, late in 2002.) Neither wavered in his devotion to ecosystem ecology, nature-as-(ideal-)home. Both were assured, lucid, and confident to the end. One of Gene's longtime colleagues at Georgia's Institute for Ecology, Frank Golley, published a detailed and respectful history of the ecosystem concept with Yale University Press that appeared hardly a year after Hagen's work. Gene himself, by all accounts, never betrayed a moment of perturbation with the young insurgents. He simply grinned, waved a hand, and incorporated "disturbance" into the system. As late as 1997, Gene wrote that disturbance was no more than individual competition within and between species; it had ever existed and ever would—yet *within* systems that, always greater than their parts, naturally sought equilibrium.[55] What could society and policy makers do, after all, with disturbance and chaos? Ecosystem ecology was from the start, after all, a *concept*, as Gene's colleague Frank Golley reminded us during the 1990s, and one that served environmentalism exceedingly well.

*The commencement of warm weather gives activity to
decomposition, and the soft air is redolent of its products: and
in sundry different spots of every town, the effluvia arising
from filthily kept yards, of stables and hog styes, of privies, and
sometimes the breezes tainted by a dead cat . . . are offered to our
sense of smelling.* —Edmund Ruffin, 1837

*I believe . . . we can make St. Augustine the Newport of the South.*
—Henry Flagler, 1885

*A city cannot be a work of art.* —Jane Jacobs, 1961

*The capital of Mississippi, Jackson, is deserted on Friday
afternoon. No one walks its streets. . . . The centers of many of the
most interesting Southern cities, the neighborhoods that make
them most distinct and attractive, have been forsaken for fast-food
places, gas stations, and shopping centers at the outskirts, which
resemble any other place in the United States.*
—Charles Simic, 2004

# 6

## CITIES OF CLAY

Throughout the temperate and tropical zones of the globe, agriculture made possible the highest expressions of civilization—that is, towns and cities. As the Mesoamerican Neolithic revolution diffused northeastward, first through what we call the South, thousands of towns and not a few large settlements we might term cities appeared. Cahokia, east of present-day St. Louis (and arguably southern), was the largest, but other populous, year-round, and well-fortified towns thrived across the South all through the Mississippian era and into the long period of European invasions. European and then African pioneers met native southerners who were civilized in the essential sense that they were to a considerable extent urbanized.

The great native towns are no more. Cahokia, Etowa, and other surviving mound sites are archaeological digs and government parks and attractions. Many others doubtlessly disappeared into nature, their rotted wood feeding and hastening inevitable encroachment. Countless other native settlements and burial sites were obliterated during the nineteenth and twentieth centuries by farmers creating and leveling fields, and by road builders. Other towns became the foundations of successor Euro-southern settlements for the most practical of reasons. Native southerners, after all, had located towns with the same instrumental sensibilities demonstrated by Europeans, Asians, and Africans—by water, usually at outlets to the ocean, at fall lines, at riparian mountain passes, and almost always at convenient heads of navigation. Creeks and rivers were the highways of communication, trade, and warfare amid heavily forested, sometimes barely penetrable landscapes. Euro-southerners perpetuated the geographical trope. And because they were the last Americans to construct large cities—New Orleans was long the sole exception—and the last regional population to become generally urbanized, we might consider very old waterside towns as best representatives of southern civilization until quite recently.

West Point, Virginia, visited here before, presents a fine example of small-scale urbanized continuity *as well as* of longitudinal tumult and discontinuity in all respects save occupancy of terrestrial space. John Smith named the place in English. Exploring the lower Chesapeake from his base at Jamestown in 1608, Smith and his men sailed westward on the river they had named York. About forty-five miles above the river's mouth, at the bay, the English spied a narrow peninsula ahead, and Smith named it from their maritime perspective. Terrestrial West Point actually points east. Here the meandering Mattaponi and Pamunkey rivers converge to create the broad York. Native peoples called Mattaponi and Pamunkey—these are probably somewhat Anglicized versions of the names—had long settled the riverbanks, the Mattaponi upriver from the point, and the Pamunkey along their own river down toward the tip of the peninsula, where their ethnic capital stood. Pamunkey territory was in fact the center of the great Powhatan "empire" that had expelled a Spanish Franciscan mission in 1572 and would nearly repel the English during the bloody wars of 1622 and 1644. Pa-mun-kee, West Point, Deleware [sic] Town, again West Point—by whatever name —has always been a place of beauty and marvelous potential for human advantage. Therefore, by destiny perhaps, West Point has alternatively thrived and clung to existence by bare threads.

The vast Chesapeake region's gloriously easy navigability and the early development of an export tobacco culture effectively discouraged English town development. Jamestown itself was ultimately abandoned to slip under the James's tidal muds and marshes. West Point became briefly Deleware Town, an experimental settlement named in honor of Thomas West, Earl de la Warr, a well-regarded early colonial governor. West's grandson, John, reputedly the first Englishman born on the York, patented the town, drew up a long rectangle of plats and streets, and took up residence there. Deleware Town languished, though, West's plats apparently never attracting enough buyers. West Point ultimately reverted to John Smith's perverse name, and over several human generations it barely survived on its lush fishery and some, never all, of the trade of its rural hinterland. The town never claimed but a small portion of the tidewater's tobacco-exporting business. In addition to the private shipping docks of great riverfront planters, there were at least a half-dozen other, similar settlements along the York and lower Mattaponi and Pamunkey in competition. One, called Brickhouse, stood opposite West Point on the Pamunkey. Also nearby were Newcastle and Cumberland Town. All save Yorktown and West Point were abandoned by about 1800. Some, perhaps all, of the vanished settlements had lost their river landings to siltation, a phenomenon well known throughout the colonial Chesapeake. Rivers change course without human agency, but nearly two centuries of tobacco and grain culture, half of that accomplished with plows rather than mere hoes, suggests not only considerable deforestation but exposure of soils to wind and water erosion. The very symbiotic commercial coupling of countryside with towns destroyed both, the towns first, as silt from farms and plantations altered rivers' courses, isolating many little ports and finally making them disappear.[1]

Towns that survived benefited from the general prosperity preceding the Revolution, and some, not all, turned from wood to brick as their principal construction material. Tidewater soils are generally sandy, but there was clay sufficient to bake bricks—that is, once sufficient involuntary labor was at hand, which was the case well before the middle of the eighteenth century. Thus significant parts of Revolutionary Yorktown survive today, despite periodic cannonading by Washington's rebels and, almost a century later, George McClellan's grand army. Always a lesser port than Yorktown, West Point was not quite so permanently built, except for the occasional church. More brick, pavement, spots of elegance, and the diversity and animation that defined Jane Jacobs's great cities awaited the initiative of self-interested local leadership and some sparkling good luck.[2]

Like most towns and cities, West Point depended on its surrounding agricultural and forested countryside, which sent overland to the port its corn, wheat, tobacco, and sawn boards that urban merchants, warehouse-men, and shippers needed. During the 1850s a dynamic group of planters, lawyers, and financiers from the counties surrounding West Point brashly decided to add to the town's shipping business the enormous grain milling, tobacco processing, iron manufacturing, and cotton transferring that had grown up in the extraordinary metropolis of Richmond, forty miles westward, near the falls of the Pamunkey. A rail line to West Point and the York would hasten Richmond's considerable transport of goods to the sea, West Point being on the shorter route, compared with James River steamers bound from the capital down to Hampton Roads. So the York valley entrepreneurs created the Richmond and York River Railway Company, hired the redoubtable naval officer and scientist Matthew Fontaine Maury as consulting engineer, and by 1860 had constructed a last bridge over the Pamunkey to West Point, completing the line. Enlarged wharves and ship tonnage accommodated the boom, which included a quickly expanded population of workers and professionals, and more rooming houses and hotels, restaurants, and agencies of many sorts. Soon came another dose of luck, however, worse than awful.

In 1862, during General George McClellan's massive and costly attempt to capture Richmond and end the rebellion by marching up the peninsula between the James and the York, retreating Confederates burned the railroad bridge at West Point, and then McClellan's army occupied the town. Both sides ravaged the strategically unfortunate Richmond and York River Railway much of the summer. By the end of the war the railroad was in ruins, its company bankrupt, and West Point was virtually derelict. As late as 1870, only about seventy-five people lived there.

About this time one of my great-grandfathers, Captain James Kirby, recently a battery commander of field artillery in the Army of Northern Virginia, and his young wife, Susan Moore, migrated to West Point from York County. Their families had long been mainstays of Charles Parish, near Grafton, a short distance inland from Yorktown. Both families were modest farmers and small-scale slaveholders before the war. Susan's people were the Moores whose farmhouse was the scene of Lord Cornwallis's surrender to Washington in October 1781. (The rehabilitated house is now part of the Yorktown Battlefield Park, and the little graveyard outside includes the remains of Susan's brother and James's friend, Dr. Watkins Moore.) Such farmers often engaged in other businesses, too—oystering, for example, and small-time storekeeping. James and one of his siblings had run such a store before the war. Afterward, according to my branch of the tribe's tradition, a dispute over business led to James and Susan's migration upriver. There, by the Mattaponi shore opposite West Point, James opened his own store, and the couple built a big house (for the time): two wood-framed stories, two rooms wide and two deep, with railed front porches up and down and a cookhouse out back, at the edge of the Pamunkey's tidal marsh. Their son, Walton Leon, was born there in 1871; a daughter born earlier did not thrive. The girl's tragic early death notwithstanding, James and Susan's transplantation was luckily timed.

In 1873 a pair of ambitious Philadelphia shippers purchased the remains and right-of-way of the ruined railroad, began its rebuilding, and assembled a holding company they named the Richmond & West Point Terminal Railway & Warehouse Company. The organization included traffic agreements with the Richmond & Danville Railroad and the organizers' own Chesapeake ship line. In a relatively short time the Richmond & Danville connection drew on almost 8,000 miles of rails stretching deep into the cotton South, routing thousands of bales northward to Richmond, then to Chesapeake Bay via West Point. Main Street, the central of the town's three long concourses that were parallel to the Mattaponi and Pamunkey, soon became a bustling and sturdy brick downtown of stores, offices, newspapers and printing plants, restaurants, and hotels, extending from the wharf- and warehouse-crowded York waterfront northwestward about five blocks. Thereafter Main Street was (and remains today) the most stylish residential stretch of the town. A three-story brick Masonic Hall, with peaked tower alongside, went up in 1884. (James Kirby served as Grand Master, as his son did later.) There were also public schools for white and black children and, over the decades, a variety of private academies usually divided by gender as well as color. In 1887 a 200-room, four-story, corner-towered hotel, the Terminal, went up on the York waterfront. Adjacent to the grand hotel were Beach Park and a fine boardwalk. West Point, already a great transport center, became a saltwater resort, too, attracting Richmonders especially, for weekends and longer excursions of swimming, fishing, promenading, and dining well.

Walton Leon Kirby worked for the Richmond & West Point Terminal as a young man, zestfully rolling back and forth between the capital and his birthplace and proudly acquiring a railroad man's big pocket watch with chain. James Kirby died in 1896, the same year that Lewis Puller, later called "Chesty" as a Marine Corps officer and commander in four wars, was born in West Point. By this time the Richmond & West Point Terminal was no more. The Philadelphia shipping magnates, like so many local and regional

*Postcard of Terminal Hotel and Beach Park, West Point, Virginia, ca. 1900.*
*Courtesy Virginia Historical Society, Richmond.*

railroaders, lost control of their network during the panic of 1893. J. P. Morgan, New York financier and merger maker, melded the terminal complex into the new Southern Railway System. West Point as cotton shipper survived only four years under the Southern's regime. In 1897 the railway's directors moved its seaport terminal to Portsmouth, Virginia, which had deeper water, better connections to more transport vessels, and excellent direct rail connections not only with Richmond but with the South Atlantic's coastal plain. Suddenly, then, West Point was reduced to a seasonal tourist destination and, again, a minor Chesapeake port and fishery.

Then in 1903—the year Walton Leon married—much of downtown West Point was destroyed by fire. The Terminal Hotel was spared, as was the Kirby house, but 300 residents of the town's midsection were rendered homeless. For all its relative wealth, the little city had been ill prepared for the scourge of fire. After the blaze (its origin still unexplained) was under way, men and women formed bucket lines. A woman saved one house by covering it with soaked blankets and quilts. The city of Richmond quickly responded with the loan of a steam pumper, but West Point had only brackish marsh water to feed the boiler and hose, so much of the town's center was consumed. This was in May. In August, naturally, the town's voters approved the sale of bonds to erect a water tower, apparently the first in West Point's considerable experience. Townsmen also, and at last, organized a volunteer fire company. Walton Leon was chief in 1905. By this time he had left the railroad's employ and, with a partner, had begun a sign-painting business. He was already father of a baby girl, and by 1910 he and his wife were parents of three sons as well. Supporting such a family was probably not easy, for by 1910 West Point was clearly in decline again. One of its banks had failed after the great fire. The Terminal's occupancy rate began to wane, too, as the town and the York fell out of fashion. Population declined proportionately, perhaps as much as one-third, by about 1913, when a new industry and new outsider knight appeared, fixing, in effect, West Point's destiny for at least a century.

That year an Ohio paper mill acquired Pamunkey-front land just north of town and began construction of a wood pulp mill. Local pines would be harvested, chipped, cooked, and digested, the resulting fibrous slurry then pumped into tanker cars and sped over excellent rail connections to the paper mill at Loveland, near Cincinnati. West Point's skyline—and skies—were thus changed, seemingly forever. The Chesapeake Pulp & Paper Company was built and ready for production early in 1914, its impressive complex of buildings and a water tower sprawling beneath a giant smokestack.

Digesting wood chips into pulp slurry is magical chemistry and one smoky, smelly business. Huge plumes, usually white but occasionally black, arose and drifted from the high stack. The odor was principally that of burned sulfur, the element most intimately associated with converting conifers to pulp and paper. Decades later, after means were found to make fine white paper (as opposed to brown boxing material) from yellow southern conifers, the U.S. paper industry would shift overwhelmingly to the Southeast. Meanwhile West Point became the pioneer maker of pulp, and its citizens were the earliest beneficiaries of—and sufferers from—this first successful experiment.

The mill is situated north-northwest of West Point's old residential and business districts. In winter especially, cold winds blow the mill's sulfurous cloud high and low over the town. Fall nor'easters blow effluences away, over rural and forested New Kent County. Spring winds from the Southwest send them to rural and forested King and Queen counties, and summer southerlies waft them over the tiny Pamunkey and Mattaponi Indian reservations in upper King William County. Yet I have never met a West Pointer or near-hinterlander who complained of the smoke or smell, even on the coldest February day, when chilly rains carry down sulfurous smog to streets and kitchen doors. Smoke and foul odor signified stability and prosperity—my father's madeleine—and the mill was welcome. Walton Leon went to work in the mill, as did, for a time, all three of his sons.

West Pointers became even happier with industrial life, labor, and their new overhead environment in 1918 when another outsider knight arrived to make the mill locally owned. Elis Olsson was an ambitious and visionary Swedish-born chemical engineer with papermaking experience in both Scandinavia and Canada. With financing from Richmond bankers, Olsson bought out the Ohio company, renamed the pulp maker the Chesapeake Corporation, and moved his family to Romancoke, the upriver Pamunkeyside plantation formerly owned and occupied by Robert E. Lee Jr. By the mid-1920s, Olsson had installed a so-called Big Machine to make kraft paper (meaning strong, for boxing) from the company's own pulp and the region's own pines.

Twenty years later, winter's smoke and fumes notwithstanding, West Point met many of the criteria Jane Jacobs would ascribe to healthy, working cities of much grander scale. I remember this West Point well, as a small boy visiting my widowed grandmother, my aunt, her husband, and my father's older brother. The town was laid out as before, with three long lateral streets extending from the York to the perpendicular state highway

30. (The mill is just north of the highway.) Jacobs prescribed short blocks, a convenience to pedestrians offering more corners, many of which would be attractive to small businesses. West Point's lettered cross streets were (and are) many, and a half-century ago, its corners were often home to small businesses among residences. Motor traffic there was, but the town was principally designed for pedestrians, whether residents or country people come to shop, socialize, or do business. During the 1940s there was no house-to-house mail delivery, so everyone walked to the U.S. post office, which was a grand meeting place amid others nearby. These included a drugstore with a soda fountain. Diversity of land use—mixtures of the residential, official, retail, and entertainment—is central to the Jacobsian canon, and West Point compares not badly with Jacobs's favorite late 1950s neighborhood in Manhattan. When I was six and seven years old, my elders permitted me to take the mailbox key to the post office and fetch the mail by myself. West Point (like Jacobs's own neighborhood) was safe because there were "eyes" everywhere, watching out for the unusual and the dangerous as well as the unexpected social pleasure. Before I returned, I might stop at the drugstore, where, since I had been introduced by my aunt, I could order a soda without cash money.

This was the low age of Jim Crow and Virginia's post-Prohibition prohibition. There were black people everywhere except at "white-only" public venues such as the soda counter, and there were no legal taverns or bars for either color. Both shortcomings—and there were others, too—complemented neither ambience nor diversity. Yet African Americans had been property owners in West Point for generations. Some would be numbered among the working poor; others were business and professional people. The mill awarded better jobs to whites; harder semiskilled occupations went to blacks. Still, the town was too compact to be rigidly segregated, like sprawling Portsmouth, where I lived and where the almost evenly divided population had little contact or interaction. In West Point, the lack of taverns, bars, and clubs and the disappearance of the old Terminal resort complex meant (among other things) that the town more or less shut down into private life each sundown, not unlike the typical American suburb today. But there are more warm months than cold ones, and before the coming of air conditioning, folks visited neighbors, strolled around those little blocks, and hiked down to the York waterfront. There, during the 1940s, in place of the grand hotel, park, and boardwalk of a generation and more before, were simply a small greensward and a long public pier. In quiet times of day or evening, the town's corps of retrievers—Labradors and Chesapeake Bays,

*Residential D Street, West Point, Virginia, ca. 1912.*

*Courtesy Virginia Historical Society, Richmond.*

mostly—took spectacular exercise singly and in small packs. Ambling onto the pier's shoreline planks, they galloped southeastward, attaining highest speeds at the end, before flying into the York. One dog, I recollect, who resembled my Uncle Forrest's "Laddie," would swim back, shake himself, and repeat the dash and dive several times. Their sheer instinct and sheer joy reminded me that back during the 1880s a venerable preacher, the Reverend Thomas P. Bagley, had declared of West Point, "Nature has provided along the shores of these three rivers all the elements for happy homes." And more indeed, so it seemed to me.

West Point is old even as a Euro-American settlement, although it hardly looks so. Other southern town sites are older yet, from the Eurocentric colonial perspective. Recently, for instance, the state archaeologist of Florida wrote with unprovocative simplicity that "the first permanent colony in North America" was "Fort Caroline at the mouth of the St. Johns River," established by the French in 1564 to pester Spanish fleets passing by the coast. Caroline was lost to the French the next year—the year Pedro Menéndez de Avilés slaughtered almost the entire surviving garrison, near the aptly named Matanzas River. The Spanish took over Caroline, renamed it, and maintained a slight presence there. Long after the Spanish had departed for the last time, English speakers resettled the site and its lush vicinity, including a little spot called Cowford (or Cow-ford). In 1832, with Andrew Jackson a candidate for reelection as president, Jacksonville was incorporated on the site, with all of about 500 citizens.[3]

Caroline-Cowford-Jacksonville's name changes and apparent gaps in urban occupancy render any claim to "first" or "oldest" assailable by anyone who cares about such status. Instead, the archaeologist seems to have been utterly ignored by the state (his employer) and by the government and chamber of commerce of St. Augustine, just thirty-seven miles to the south, all of whom blithely persist in identifying and glorifying St. Augustine as the "ancient city" and the oldest in the United States. Tourists' money, minivan-loads of it, is at stake in such contests. Tour guides, taxi companies (one is named Ancient City Cab), tourist-oriented publishers, owners of what are called attractions, hoteliers, gift and curio sellers, barkeepers, restaurateurs, real estate brokers, public officeholders, public employees, and doubtlessly others all have life-and-death stakes in a uniquely august urban identity. Such interests succeeded in defeating a similar, more serious claim to oldest by Santa Fe, New Mexico, the second-oldest by a narrow chronological margin. Jacksonville would seem to be beneath such bother as competitor.

Jacksonville does not *look* old, whereas St. Augustine has a few surviving, restored buildings dating to the seventeenth and eighteenth centuries and some evocative Spanish- and British-style houses and public buildings put up during the nineteenth and twentieth centuries. Many of these are situated along quaintly narrow streets and alleys, the very same once trod and remarked upon by William Bartram, William Cullen Bryant, and other notable visitors from times past. Most important, however, St. Augustine boasts a magnificent Spanish stone fort, Castillo de San Marcos, constructed of locally quarried coquina toward the end of the seventeenth century. Now a federally operated national monument, San Marcos stands on the same low promontory facing Matanzas Bay and the ocean on which previous, wooden castillos had bristled since the 1560s. Not far away, facing the town square and old covered market, is the stately Cathedral-Basilica of St. Augustine. It is a little more than a century old but, like the Castillo, stands on the burned ruins of a predecessor. Nearby are three large, bizarre "Moorish" style buildings, all originally hotels (one still is) constructed of poured concrete late in the nineteenth century by Yankee magnate-developers. St. Augustine is blessed with (for a place in Florida) relatively few other touristic attractions, but these include a so-called geological exhibit just north of downtown reputed to be the very Fountain of Youth Ponce de Leon supposedly discovered during his brief 1513 incursion into La Florida. Nearby is the Ripley's Believe It or Not museum. The Alligator Farm—the same from which came Marjorie Kinnan Rawlings's Christmas gift of a huge bag, ca. 1940—thrives, still, to the east on Anastasia Island. From downtown one gets to the farm via the Bridge of Lions, a splendid (albeit crumbling) relic of the 1920s, guarded at its western end by a large pair of stone lions, its span decorated with towers and flagpoles.[4]

Today and ever in the past, remnants of the once mighty Pamunkey people might drive down to West Point from their reservation to see what Euro- and Afro-southerners have made of their ancient capital. Not so the aboriginals of northeastern Florida and St. Augustine. These were the Seloy Indians, a substantial group belonging to the Timucua language group, who numbered, by best estimate, perhaps 200,000 souls ca. 1565. The Seloys, one of at least thirty-five Timucuan chiefdoms, lived in St. Augustine and its hinterland. Other chiefdoms extended over most of peninsular Florida above present-day Orlando and northward to St. Simons Island and the Altamaha River in Georgia, and westward past present-day Live Oak,

Florida, to the Aucillia River. There is evidence that dozens of Timucuan chiefs, perhaps more, occasionally confederated, rather like the Virginia peoples called Powhatan. The phenomenon was boldly illustrated during the Timucua Rebellion of 1656, when chiefs of the northern Florida interior mounted an attempt to throw off Spanish oppression. For a century, various Timucuan peoples had resisted Europeans whenever and wherever they had appeared. The rebellion failed, without doubt, because Spanish troops brutally repressed it, but the revolt was probably doomed by a century's exposure to the Europeans' invisible warriors: pathogens such as smallpox and measles. The Timucua were a much-shrunken language group by the middle of the seventeenth century. Many chiefdoms either disappeared or were so diminished in numbers that survivors joined new or reconstituted chiefdoms. At the time of the rebellion, there were only about 2,000 to 2,500 Timucuans. In 1700 hardly a few hundred survived, and by 1728 a census reported but 70. In 1752 the entire population of Timucua—29—lived in a single refugee camp near St. Augustine's walls. A dozen years later, when the Spanish left La Florida for the last time, one sole native boarded ship for transport to Cuba.[5]

During the terrible two centuries that Timucuans endured European hegemony in northeastern Florida, both Europeans and natives were transformed, particularly the natives. The French, Spanish, and British brought with them not only pathogens but European plants and seeds, such as wheat (which did not thrive), watermelons, peaches, figs, hazelnuts, garbanzos, and oranges, and animals, including horses, asses and mules, cows, sheep, goats, swine, and large dogs. Nonnative fruits and vegetables were incorporated into Timucuan diets. Oranges became ubiquitous, their groves practically covering Anastasia Island by the eighteenth century, before a great freeze ended Spanish hopes of citrus plantations. Vast landscapes between the Matanzas and St. Johns became cattle ranches, too, typically with Indian herdsmen and Spanish rancheros.

Colonial St. Augustine was never more than a military post with a fort. There was little effort to capitalize on its potential as a fishery and fish processor or to engage in transatlantic trade. Spanish occupiers were administrators and soldiers, seldom farmers or fisherman, and they were always hungry. To ensure food supplies, then, the colonial administration entered a partnership with the Franciscan Order, which established a mission for every Timucuan chiefdom. The friars persuaded natives to give up their pyramidal houses for board (or log) squares and rectangles and to accept Jesus and Spanish protection. Now, too, the chiefs were to supply tributes of corn in return for gift trinkets. Timucuan populations slid lower and lower as Spanish hunger and military requirements grew, so colonial governors and Franciscans early resorted to de facto enslavement. Big mission farms provided large crops of corn as requirement, or else. Natives also operated ferries across the region's many waterways for the Spanish. And Timucuans excavated and cut blocks of coquina in the Anastasia quarries and barged them over to St. Augustine to construct the Castillo and other longer-lasting built features of the Ancient City. Today the island itself is almost completely built up, suburbanized except for its commercial zones. In some of the suburbs, behind recently built houses, unexpected charm is to be found in dark ponds—formerly coquina mines—many of which are now habitat for alligators.

For some time before they were forced to mine coquina, however, the Seloys took their revenge on the Spanish of St. Augustine by impoverishing their domestic architecture. According to the principal student of the town's housing, harassing natives prevented logging and sawmilling crews from replenishing lumber supplies always needed for repair and rebuilding. For the longest period, St. Augustine's architecture was miserably, shabbily bare—jerry-built shacks of rough wood roofed in palm thatch. Such structures rotted quickly, if they did not first fall apart, blow down in heavy winds, or burn. Later, when forced labor provided soft blocks of coquina, the bounty went into the Castillo, seldom housing, except that for the governor and treasurer. Bricks, the stuff of near-permanence and signifier of prosperity in Virginia, were almost unseen in Florida, where clay and straw were scarce. Cuba supplied but a few. The beginnings of architectural distinction in St. Augustine correspond to shrinking numbers of native warriors, secure wood supplies, and sufficient security and building skills to adapt northern Spanish house forms and employ coastal materials such as lime made from oyster shells (for plastering wood and waterproofing coquina).[6]

The "St. Augustine Look" was developed by early in the eighteenth century, when Castillo de San Marcos was completed, when the town was safe for longer periods, and when Spanish administrators and others had the wherewithal to occupy offices and homes befitting their status. A pleasing look it was and is, in becoming variety. These were buildings of stone or wood or both; one, two, or two-and-a-half stories; square or rectangular. Houses had walls and fences, never doors, on the street, often with a charming balcony above. Entry was made via a fence door around the side, into an enclosed yard, then through a loggia or covered porch. Some fences were wood, others wattle, others coquina. Walls were plastered inside and out. Domestic shelter, in particular, was sited with seasonal weather a principal consideration. The private indoor-outdoor sector, with loggia and garden, faced south (preferably) or east, so winter's sun might warm the air inside and out. Walls were thick to insulate against both extreme heat and cold.

Before and after Americans took control of Florida, during the 1820s, other (and complimentary) subtropical architectural forms were blended with the Spanish Floridian. The British, after all, had ruled Florida for two decades, between the two Spanish periods, and American planters just north of Florida had adopted their own distinguished traditions of housing for hot climates. So among the northern Spanish-style buildings in the town were also to be found Anglo-style "plantation" structures—often large, two-story, central-hallway affairs with front galleries.

All this said, and simplifying a lengthy and complex nineteenth century in St. Augustine, the Ancient City several times became nearly extinct. Natives—this time the Seminoles—took their revenge again, waging three wars between the 1810s and 1860s, the second (during the late 1830s and early 1840s), virtually shutting down Euro-Florida. Two decades after the Civil War, St. Augustine was lightly peopled by the poor and by famously proud, long-established families, its structures approaching or already descended into dereliction. Then, and suddenly, the city was reinvented, its look simultaneously enlarged and transformed, by a savior-knight from afar. This was Henry Morrison Flagler (1830–1913).

Son of an itinerant Presbyterian pastor from upstate New York, Henry migrated to northern Ohio as a teenager to work for relatives who owned general stores. With little formal education, Henry learned his numbers and markets quickly. Fatefully, through business young Flagler met the young John D. Rockefeller of Cleveland, who before the Civil War brokered grain deals. Flagler and his kin made money consigning grain, too, much of it ultimately bound for their own distillery, which earned fortunes before and especially during the Civil War. Flagler paid a substitute to save the union in his stead and headed north, into Michigan, to the lucrative salt business. Cutthroat competition persisted into the postwar's falling salt market, however, and led to Flagler's near-ruin. Starting over in Cleveland, he worked for Rockefeller, now a petroleum trader, distiller, and shipper. Flagler soon recovered his fortune many times over. As full partner in the new, burgeoning Standard Oil Company, Henry Flagler was the genius who

*Street scene, St. Augustine, Florida, 1893. Courtesy Florida State Archives.*

took profitable advantage of competition among railroads for large cargo shipments. He was the transport negotiator whose prowess powered the emergent empire of petroleum in North America.[7]

At fifty-five (in 1885), his fortune made, Henry Flagler was privileged to play among the eastern elite and to experiment—and invest, too—in expansion of the playgrounds. That was when he came to St. Augustine and, almost enchanted, decided to make the place his own. In general, Florida's railroads remained frontierish, their track mileage barely exceeding Delaware's and Rhode Island's. But Jacksonville and St. Augustine were served well enough, with decent connections amounting to a de facto line down the Atlantic coast all the way from New England. With appropriate accommodations, Flagler figured, the Ancient City might become the winter playground for the fabled Newport, Rhode Island, summer crowd. The centerpiece of Flaglerized St. Augustine would be his spectacular Hotel Ponce de Leon. The designers of the hotel included first the visionary Flagler himself. It must suit the high Gilded Age notion of *haute resort* while maintaining somehow the local character, Flagler reasoned. There were also two young French-trained architects from the prestigious New York firm of McKim, Meade and White. Finally, though, the ruling inspiration of the collaboration was not northern Spain—native region of Pedro Menéndez de Avilés and other Spanish colonizers—but the Mediterranean. The Ponce de Leon, built (amazingly) in only eighteen months, arose as a sprawling "Moorish" assembly of arcades, gardens, and towers resembling minarets. How to construct such a marvel in a land still without bricks, however? The young architects suggested poured concrete containing local sand and shell. Nothing so large had ever been made of poured concrete, but Flagler, his architects, and his general contractor gained confidence from a successful experiment of smaller scale constructed only a few years before, just across King Street from the hotel site. This was Villa Zorayda, a large private residence built for another wealthy northern man. (Today it is a commercial building.) So Flagler's contractor set in motion the grand project. First he brought to the Ponce de Leon site enormous loads of fill, so that the ultimate structure would stand above flood-prone St. Augustine streets. Such is ever the necessity in porous, low, coastal landscapes. And now—as then, one is reminded—for every building that has risen on such terrain, there is a comparable hole somewhere in inland Florida or beyond. The Ponce de Leon opened in 1888, the largest poured concrete structure on earth, not only a marvel for the eye but a lavishly modern jewel. Electrically powered throughout, the Ponce de Leon was also supplied with healthful sulfuric water from artesian wells, and its towers stored 16,000 gallons of water in case of fire. (No West Point would St. Augustine be.) A local associate of Flagler's built another, much smaller hotel across King Street, almost simultaneously, called the Casa Monica. He shortly sold it to Flagler, who renamed it the Cordova. Then Flagler built next to the Cordova what he called a casino, the Alcazar. Beginning with the 1889 tourist season, the Alcazar offered shops and entertainment for Ponce de Leon guests but also rooms for rent at much lower rates than the colossus across the street. Flagler also built a number of private cabins for tourists less interested in society and promenades.

Flagler was ever the negotiator with rail companies, and his huge investment in St. Augustine made him a railway owner and, ultimately, the builder of the East Coast Line (later the Florida East Coast Railway) that reached all the way to Key West. Initially, however, he bought into an existing line from Jacksonville that concluded northeasterners' journey to St. Augustine. Flagler had been dismayed that St. Augustine had no decent depot, merely an open platform on the western bank of the San Sebastian River, which parallels the Matanzas and at the time marked the inland boundary of the city. Deciding he must build the depot himself for the benefit of his hotels' clients, Flagler calculated that he must have an interest in the railroad, too. So, inadvertently, began his late-life career of claiming vast acreages of public lands in return for rail mileage built southward, ever southward.

The other inadvertency leading to Flagler's railroading career was a series of natural calamities that prevented St. Augustine from becoming Newport. In January 1886, even as Flagler and his architects finished planning and began to build the Ponce de Leon, amid much fanfare a New York City newspaper printed not only the low local temperature for the day—16° Fahrenheit—but that for St. Augustine: 22°, only six degrees higher than frigid Gotham's. There was a yellow fever outbreak in 1888, the year the first two hotels opened for business. Then came more freezes during the season of 1894–95. By the time Henry James's *The American Scene* appeared in 1907, with James's complimentary bow to the Ponce de Leon, St. Augustine had become passé, and Palm Beach—another Flagler concoction— had emerged as *the* scene to make in winter. On his way to Palm Beach, Flagler had bought another big hotel, the Ormond, just north of Daytona. He doubled the Ormond's capacity, then redoubled it and changed the look of its sprawling grounds to suit his notion of La Florida: the indigenous pines came down, and palms were planted in their places.

*Hotel Ponce de Leon, St. Augustine, Florida, 1920. Courtesy Florida State Archives.*

Ultimately, though, Henry Flagler came back to St. Augustine. When he died in 1913, his remains were secured within the Flagler mausoleum at the Memorial Presbyterian Church downtown. Back in 1889 Henry's daughter had died while en route to St. Augustine. Typically, he persuaded the pastor and congregation of the First Presbyterian Church to permit him to build them a new sanctuary, with the mausoleum wing, and to change the church's name. Memorial remains a monument to the town's Flagler episode, with its great dome, Italian-tiled floors, and elegant leaded-glass windows. Nearby, the old Ponce de Leon lives on as a private institution, Flagler College. The Alcazar now houses the city government and the Lightner Museum. After decades of neglect, the old Hotel Cordova was restored to splendor, reopening in 1999 with its original name of Casa Monica. Juan Carlos II, King of Spain, visited in 2001. Hardly less exciting and newsworthy, in August 2004 Ringo Starr reportedly came to town, unannounced, stayed at Casa Monica, and sat in with a band at a nearby club. Sad to report, "Ringo" turned out to be an imposter.[8]

The sudden resurgences, glory days, and subsidences of the two old settlements of West Point and St. Augustine corresponded to a powerful regional trend also powered by rail construction and traffic. The post–Civil War political and business tumult across the South included reorganizations of old, battered rail lines and the founding of many new ones. By the 1880s, trunk lines were completed and vast construction of local connections was well under way. The South was becoming fully part of a national system, not only because owners and directors of its railroads were often Yankees and foreigners, but because rails pulled all regions into the conforming logic of business. It was railroad companies who imposed the standardization of national time, in four time zones, in 1883. Two years later, all major roads agreed to standardize almost 13,000 miles of nonconforming track gauge, most of it in the South. On a single weekend day— Sunday, 30 May 1886—workers moved mostly southern rails three inches closer together, so that practically any train from practically anywhere in the nation might easily roll anywhere. The two monumental standardizations hastened the opening, as it were, of the poorest, remotest places to the world. By 1890, nine-tenths of the southern population lived in a county with at least one operating rail line. Along these lines old settlements revived and enlarged, and many new towns came into being, all because the railroad came their way.[9]

During these decades and well into the twentieth century, the federal

Bureau of the Census defined a city as a settlement of more than 2,500 residents—a modest measure of the urban, indeed, yet one that still described relatively few southern rail towns. These remained towns or villages, then, but their enormous number and persistent growth indicates that while the region as a whole remained far from urban, by whatever measure, it was becoming, after 1890, somewhat less a rural South and much more a South of villages.

Railroads made money for themselves and for old and new villages lucky enough to have depots. Luray, Virginia—a tiny settlement on the Shenandoah side of the Blue Ridge range—grew suddenly rich, as historian Edward Ayers puts it, because of "a hole in the ground."[10] Luray Caverns were discovered (or rediscovered) in 1878 and became a successful business three years later, when a railroad company came through. The company built a large Tudor-style hotel and an electric dynamo to generate lighting in the majestic caverns. (Luray became another "first in the world" on this account.) By 1882, trains brought 3,000-odd visitors to Luray each month, and according to the local newspaper, they came from twenty-five states, Europe, and South America. A couple years later, a Luray merchant figured that stores' sales were tenfold greater than in 1879. Oddly, the depot, dynamo, hole in the ground, and hotel led to diversified growth of Luray's economy, too. By 1890 there were also a flour mill and two factories making furniture and cigars.

Rail-powered tourism created other boom villages, too. Blowing Rock, in the North Carolina mountains, got its grand hotel in 1884, and its summer population often tripled, with vacationers eager for rest and recreation in cooler air. Not far away, Asheville, upland Carolina's principal urban place, also became established as a summer tourist destination as well as a luxurious recuperative center for the ailing. Unpredictably, even the forlorn piney-woods South developed resorts offering tennis, golf, dubiously healthful waters, and clinics. By the early 1890s Thomasville, Georgia (of all places), had four big hotels for the trade. The little city left no visitor unimpressed, either, since Thomasville was fully wired for telephone service and its water was heated by steam. Jacksonville, Florida, allegedly the ugly stepsister to St. Augustine in terms of touristic interest, actually flourished around the turn of the century as a winter and spring destination where bathing, sports, and especially music and dancing attracted throngs of happy northerners.

Then there were the miraculous new towns-cum-cities, the best-known blown into being by the combination of rails and extractive industries. Consider Middlesboro, Kentucky, for example: During the mid-1880s a young Canadian capitalist persuaded English investors to buy up 60,000 acres of mineral rights. In 1889 Middlesboro still had but 50 residents, but the next year, when an extension of the Louisville and Nashville Railroad reached town, the population exploded to 15,000 in a few months. Iron and steel mills and hotels sprang up, the city installed a waterworks, and nearby towns built their own hotels and even a golf course. In 1892, however, the British investors suffered a failure and their capital infusions ceased; then the American panic of 1893 killed the Canadian's dream. Middlesboro resorted to its previous, modest incarnation.

The Middlesboro dream had been inspired by northern Alabama's great, smoky, flame-belching metropolis-out-of-nowhere, Birmingham. Barely in existence in 1870, the city leaped upward and outward during the following decade, gripped by a seemingly unstoppable boom. Birmingham had rail connections rivaling Atlanta's, and the hills of its hinterland shone darkly with deposits of coal and iron ore. Alabama capitalists persisted through trying times, built their homes upwind of the furnaces' and mills' acrid effusions, and succeeded. Barely a Census Bureau city in 1880, with 3,000 people, Birmingham had 26,000 in 1890, 38,000 in 1900, and (in part via annexation) an amazing 133,000 in 1910.

The upper South's minor-league counterpart to Birmingham was Roanoke, in southwestern Virginia. As late as the early 1880s, Roanoke's future site was the hamlet of Big Lick, home to about 400 souls. Then the railroad came, and within a decade a renamed hamlet became Virginia's fourth-largest city, at 25,000 and growing. Roanoke had its traditional southern businesses, milling flour, canning vegetables, and packaging tobacco. But its growth lay principally in the railroad's initiatives in Roanoke's hinterland: iron and zinc works from nearby Pulaski, farm implement and furniture factories from Marion, and so on, with all production funneled through Roanoke.

Louisville, a relatively old Ohio River port, long the rival of upriver Cincinnati in transferring and shipping, took off to become one of the South's largest cities after it became a rail terminal, too. Likewise Louisville's twin in late-nineteenth-century railroading, Nashville, Tennessee's capital by the Cumberland. It was the great Louisville and Nashville Railroad, most prominently among several, that not only took over so-called mid-South agricultural transport but hauled ore to Birmingham's mills and carried iron and steel out. It was the rise of these and similar interior railroad cities that accounted for the decline of such old cotton ports as Charleston,

Savannah, and Mobile. Charleston had been the South's second-largest city (after New Orleans) in 1860. It had fallen to third by 1880 and to thirteenth by 1910. Savannah, number six in 1860, fell to twelfth by 1910. Mobile, fourth in 1860, ranked fifteenth in 1910.[11] New Orleans remained throughout the half-century first among southern cities because it was the principal outlet for much of the midwestern grain belt as well as for the largest lower South and trans-Mississippi cotton growers. New Orleans had also become a railroad city, too, of course.

By 1910, however, Atlanta had already emerged as a serious contender for preeminence in the urban South. A young railroad city when Sherman's men burned it down in 1864, Atlanta had recovered and grown to the fifth-ranking urban place in the South by 1880. It was second in 1910 and already a marvel of civic ambition and technology. Atlanta had an all-electric lighting system by late 1886, and its electric street rail system, introduced in 1889, was well worth bragging about. Passenger cars were furnished with oak and plate-glass windows; their steel rails, bulkier than those of the Georgia Railroad, rested on stone foundation piers. There was a new waterworks and sewer system and then the South's first skyscraper, which opened in 1892; another one rose five years later. Both were equipped with elevators, naturally. In all these urban boasts Atlanta was merely bigger, never alone, and not always first. An electric trolley system opened in Montgomery, Alabama, before Atlanta's, Richmond's, and Nashville's, although not by much. By 1902, in fact, southern cities were ahead of other American urban regions in electric streetcar companies, electric lights, telephones, and other modern infrastructures.

On the other hand, southern cities resembled American cities generally in that modern transportation, communication, and sanitation were for central business districts and nearby well-off residential neighborhoods. Poor areas, whether outlying or close to urban centers—especially if they were predominantly black—contained steets that were never paved, irregular or nonexistent garbage collection, air fouled by smoke from trains and factories, latrines unconnected to sewers, and suspect water from private wells. Until gasoline-powered trucks finally displaced dray animals, city streets everywhere were covered with the urine and feces of horses and mules. Dead animals—usually equine but many other species, too—lying in streets and sometimes festering for days before city scavengers dragged them away, were common. Disposal of such poor creatures seems to have been various. A freshly dead horse could be economically recycled into meat, leather, insulation, glue, and many other products of value. The practice of simply dragging a carcass into the nearest river, however, was hardly unknown. Also not unknown in such urban environments were disease and disability.[12]

✿ Climates largely free of freezing temperatures encourage pests and pathogens, and urban places where strangers come and go facilitate exchange and spread of illness. Southern cities are properly associated with disease, then. The mountain South, rural and urban, is an exception, its higher elevations yielding ice and snow, and in tidewater and piedmont landscapes north of USDA zone 8, brief (at least) periods of winter freezing are common. Generally, however, its warmer climate has fated the South to distinctively pernicious afflictions. Europeans' insidiously invisible annihilators of native southerners we have observed more than once already. Many immigrants from Europe arrived already ill with endemic diseases brought from home. Seventeenth-century Anglo-Virginians may well have suffered from nonlethal malaria, common in Yorkshire and Essex, before they were reinfected in America. They were also poisoned by drinking from wells contaminated by saltwater. Many apparently were afflicted by typhoid fever. Then immigrants from Africa brought such tropical diseases as yaws, yellow fever, elephantiasis (caused by the imported filarial roundworm), the malignant form of malaria, and hookworm and dengue fever.[13]

All these save yellow fever are typically (and rightly) associated with rural areas. Certainly standing water in towns in summertime nursed mosquitoes that might afflict humans with both kinds of malaria. Cholera plagued country and city folk alike. And once hookworm was diagnosed and its etiology understood, during the 1890s, this ill was recognized among the barefooted in towns as well as in farm country. Elemental hygiene was lacking everywhere. Yet altogether, southern urban places, being warm and having greater concentrations of humans and animals—with all their wastes and parasites—must have been sicklier than the sickly countryside. No wonder that nineteenth-century southern white people, probably townspeople most of all (although not certainly, evidence being incomplete), suffered higher rates of addiction to opiates than other Americans and, according to one medical historian, rivaled the Chinese.[14] How else, one might ask by way of expiation, was one to endure life in alluring but dangerous places?

✿ Curiously, one of the antebellum South's premier advocates for urban public health was none other than its premier "agriculturist," Edmund Ruffin (1794–1865). Already weary of farming by the time he founded his newspaper, *Farmers' Register*, in 1833, Ruffin eagerly left his rural estate and moved his large family to nearby Petersburg, Virginia.[15] There he thrived. Erroneously thought of as cranky and confrontational, especially in his later years, Edmund Ruffin was actually affectionate with his family and devoted to friends, and allowing for the long spells of privacy every reader and writer requires, he relished company. Petersburg, on the Appomattox River near its confluence with the James, was also an early rail center, and Ruffin loved travel, too. Richmond was hardly twenty-five miles to the north, and by way of connections in Portsmouth, by 1840 one could easily ride the "cars" (as trains were then called) down into North Carolina, then catch a decent steamer to Charleston. Ruffin persisted in writing about the country, but he also long persisted as urban commuter and steadfast city man.

Petersburg had good printers and newspapers, a busy city center, a waterfront, a rail depot, and much red brick architecture as well as the usual wood. Notable among the former were magnificent warehouses, most down near the river; a few survived Yankee mortars and cannon and all the other ravishes to come. But Petersburg—also Richmond and every other town and city Ruffin knew—was filthy, foul, unhealthful, and ironically, he thought, wasteful of a potential resource everyone else called simply waste. To illustrate: Browsing dogs, cats, and pigs deposited their urine and fecal matter freely, as did horses and mules. Men relieved themselves in vacant lots—a scene that offended Ruffin morally as well as civically. (Like most Americans, perhaps, Ruffin would have been a Victorian without Victoria.) Men and women emerged early each day from their domiciles to empty chamber pots and buckets wherever they might. Stables accumulated mountains of animal wastes until they were simply shoveled up and dumped, as likely as not into wetlands and rivers.

Ruffin was astounded by these habits of inefficiency. All such offensive discharges, secretions, and excretions, even offal and dead animals, should be rendered neutral to the nose and useful in two ways, to both urban and rural society. Marl, naturally—Ruffin's calcareous panacea for worn-out farmland—was the answer. Sprinkle it regularly in stables and on the streets. Dig pits and erect privy enclosures on every corner, then have the police and public health officials enforce strict ordinances against public urination, defecation, and pot- and bucket-dumping anywhere but the public privies. Cities must then regularly clean stables, scrape streets, and empty privies. Marl would have reduced (if hardly eliminated) odor but also preserved the value of wastes as fertilizer for the farms of every town's hinterland. Some accumulations (as in Petersburg, he suggested) might be

*View of Petersburg, Virginia, featuring a railroad, ca. 1845.*
*Courtesy The Library of Virginia, Richmond.*

devoted to the city's poor farm. Others could be exchanged with farmers: Any cart entering town with a load of hay for the stable, for instance, or produce for markets should return home full of treated "manure."

However censorious he was on the subject of exposed private parts of human bodies, Ruffin was impatient with the prevalent taboo against fertilizing food and fiber crops with human wastes. The Chinese did it, but more important to the Eurocentric Ruffin, Europeans, notably the French, had long been at the business of creating *poudre* (dried manure) and simultaneously rendering cities sanitary. He discovered and reprinted an 1826 presentation to the Agricultural Society of Pennsylvania that included a translation of a 1791 patent on a *poudre* method by one M. Donat. Ruffin, who was competent in French, believed he had read a better treatise on storing and recycling wastes. This was the 1815 edition of Francois Rozier's encyclopedic *Cours Complet d'Agriculture, Theorique, Practique . . .* (originally 1781–91). So Ruffin translated and published Rozier's descriptive critique of the enclosed waste pits, or *fosses d'Aisance*, of French rural villages. Into these were deposited the bodily wastes and kitchen and other refuse of entire human communities, along with the wastes of domestic and farm animals and, apparently, offal and parts of animal carcasses. Accumulations effectively cooked themselves in their own hot gasses until annual cleanings, when the nitrogen-rich product was returned to nature, in this case the soils of crop fields. There were dangers in attending and emptying the *fosses*: Accumulated methane gas caused many poisonings of workers who opened the sealed lids of pits, and there were occasional fatal explosions. However, Rozier maintained, well-constructed community pits might easily be safely managed. Methane should be carefully released before excessive buildups, and foul odors might be neutralized by regular applications of lime. Lime —calcium carbonate—was the savior again. Ruffin well understood that American farmers did not live in villages. But Rozier's *fosses d'Aisance* bore more than passing resemblance to Ruffin's proposed privies for the streets of Petersburg.

Ruffin did not directly address standing, often putrid water in cities, although this problem is more than implied in his urban essays. He was a relentless advocate of drainage. Elsewhere he campaigned for years against rural standing water, especially the thousands of small millponds dotting the tidewater Virginia countryside. Without understanding that a species of mosquito, *Anopheles*, incubated in such waters and injected into humans the malarial virus, Ruffin rightly associated still, fresh, standing water with disease. Alas, as with the majority of his many proposed reforms of farming

*Edmund Ruffin, from a portrait by an unknown artist, ca. 1850.*
*Courtesy The Library of Virginia, Richmond.*

and the urban environment, Ruffin failed. Millponds may have ultimately given way to private fishing ponds in the country—little improvement, unless they were aerated—but cities, especially southern ones, remained filthy for another generation and more after Ruffin's time.

✾ In the long meantime, the most dreaded of ills regularly stalked the urban South. Petersburg's board of health (to which Ruffin referred), like similar boards in most warm-climate cities, probably existed because of yellow fever. Other diseases (as the medical historian Margaret Humphreys observes) claimed more lives than yellow fever. But this tropical horror killed more rapidly with such horrible suffering, and it shut down cities utterly, stifling business and trade. In 1900 U.S. army doctors Walter Reed and James Carroll confirmed that yellow fever is an arbovirus transmitted to humans by the mosquito species *Aedes aegypti*. Unlike the malarial vector, *Aedes* does not prefer marshes, lakes, or ponds for its incubation but urban cisterns, flowerpots, puddles, and buckets. The mosquitoes fly forth at maturity in July and die off with the first frost of fall—defining the fearful "season."[16]

A mild version of infection resembles influenza. Patients suffer muscle aches, fever, and chills but recover in a week or so. The classic version of yellow fever begins with the flulike symptoms but proceeds rapidly to liver failure; jaundice; hemorrhaging from the gums, nose, and stomach lining; then a final stage marked by dark-colored vomit. (English-speakers named the disease after the jaundiced complexions of victims; the Spanish, after the projectile eruptions from the victim's mouth—*vomito negro*.) Afro-southern victims may well have been underreported by eighteenth- and nineteenth-century authorities, but they may also have benefited from a genetic resistance to the disease. White people seem disproportionately represented in horrendous tallies of the dead. Mobile, in the outbreaks of 1843 and 1853, lost 750 and 1,191 people from populations of only 11,500 and 25,000, respectively. The twin cities of Norfolk and Portsmouth, Virginia, lost more than a tenth of their combined populations in 1855. Memphis was devastated in 1873 and 1878 when 2,000 and then 5,000 died. (Mary Harris—later self-styled Mother Jones, courageous champion of miners and other oppressed workers—lost her husband and all her children in the 1878 Memphis outbreak.) New Orleans, the South's largest city and perhaps the dirtiest, too, was regularly and sorely afflicted. In 1840 yellow fever accounted for a third of all the Crescent City's deaths, and during the early

1850s, for half. Charleston, Savannah, Jacksonville, and even Holly Springs, Mississippi, were scenes of epidemics as well. Holly Springs represented a new, post–Civil War, railroad-era scene in which towns distant from ports were counted in doleful statistics.

Yellow fever is not contagious, of course; American and European physicians declared this more than a century before Reed's and Carroll's discovery of the vector. Yet whenever an outbreak occurred, terrified peopled fled—or tried to flee—infected cities. Officials—mayors, the police, and by 1840, boards of health—declared quarantines and barricaded their boundaries to contain each epidemic. Naturally, few people willingly entered a yellow fever town. But why were quarantines declared against an ill not transmitted person-to-person? According to Humphreys, southern doctors interested in yellow fever concocted a theory justifying quarantines. Avoiding "contagious," they invented "transmissibility" to suggest certain environmental conditions, such as temperatures in ships' holds and cargo boxes, that in turn released and spread the disease. Therefore both people and trade goods in ports must be locked in place, lest they extend an epidemic's geographical scope. Another explanation for quarantines is that urban officialdom found them easier to impose than the systematic cleaning of cities. The Civil War occupation of New Orleans presented an enticing example of what might have been in the antebellum South. General Benjamin Butler, the occupying commander, ordered huge cadres of workers to scour streets and dispose of garbage, and New Orleans's public health was never better. Likewise, the gradual disappearance of yellow fever from the Atlantic coast north of Georgia, toward the end of the nineteenth century (but before the Reed and Carroll findings), correlates well with installation of urban water and sewer systems. And on the Mississippi, Memphis's catastrophic 1878 epidemic led directly to the city's first modern sewer system, built 1879–80.

Finally, discovery and confirmation of yellow fever's etiology, a famous adventure in tropical medicine, both corresponded to and caused a new, modern urbanism in the South. A Cuban physician, Carlos Finlay, had proposed the mosquito as vector in 1881, but his preliminary research and hypothesis were rejected by North American medicos. When a U.S. researcher, Dr. Ronald Ross, confirmed in 1897 that a certain mosquito bred in still, fresh water injected the malaria virus, however, the surgeon general of the United States, George Sternberg (himself a pioneer microbiologist), directed Reed and Carroll toward their experiments. At long last, then, but too late for so many thousands who had perished in such agony, cities were obliged to clean themselves—at least the neighborhoods of the well-off. The last southern epidemic occurred in 1905.

✤ Cleanliness approaches godliness, it is said, and beauty as well. The very civic exertions that built water and sewer systems, that provided garbage collection, that forbade free-ranging swine, and that began (at least) to complain about air pollution produced some version of the City Beautiful movement early in the twentieth century. The movement's beginning is usually associated with the gigantic Columbian Exposition in Chicago in 1894. The exposition presented a brand-new, dazzling array of faux Renaissance structures arranged in a park "like frosted pastries on a tray" (as Jane Jacobs put it). This was *design*, the magisterial signature of a new breed of planners. A beautiful city, indeed, *must* be planned, by men wise and brave—from boulevard to architectural and landscaping detail—in order to achieve the monumental. Civic pride and ambition—virtually always the possession and initiative of local business and professional elites—had been grandly demonstrated already, in expositions associated with southern cities' centennials and with farm products and manufacturing. Nashville and Atlanta, newer railroad centers with excellent transportation and sanitary infrastructure, shone brightly. The model was Atlanta's International Cotton Exposition in 1881, which featured a giant, cross-shaped structure built for the occasion in Oglethorpe Park. Then came the same city's Piedmont Exposition in 1887 and the memorable Cotton States and International Exposition of 1895, at which Booker T. Washington delivered a momentous address that seemed to sanction segregation. Nashville's triumphant show came two years later, with the Tennessee Centennial Exposition, where attendance and the monumental scale of the new buildings, such as the wooden "Parthenon" that remains today, outdid Atlanta.[17]

By these glorious times, the South had finally begun its takeoff toward urbanization. Such a historical turning point is defined as when the urban portion of a population surpasses 10 percent of the total. The Northeast's takeoff had occurred during the 1820s; the Midwest's, in the 1850s. By 1940, 35 percent of southerners lived in cities—a point the Northeast had achieved about 1860. The domestic demographic chaos of World War II, however, propelled southerners out of farming and lumbering and other rural callings and into cities. By the time the census of 1960 was completed and published, the South had become, at long last, urban, converging with other American regions.[18]

But by this date, too, *sub*urbanization was already under way in the

*Construction of a sewage disposal plant, Slagheap Village, Alabama, 1937.*
*Photo by Arthur Rothstein. Courtesy Library of Congress (LC-USF34-005945-E DLC).*

South, again mirroring other regions. By the 1980s the South's and the nation's populations were suburban-majority. What seems remarkable, thinking now of the glacial emergence of regional urbanization, is how briefly southerners were city people. Now, like other Americans, they are, and more and more so, suburbanites, with profound consequences, politically and ecologically.

Flight from city limits to new housing on newly cleared landscapes after 1945 represented more than swelling prosperity and population pressures on central cities. The federal government subsidized home ownership (as well as higher education) for veterans in thousands of local environments that were in rapid flux. In a huge swath of the southern piedmont, for instance, between 1939 and 1974, 10 million acres passed from farmers to other owners. Local and state governments both permitted and subsidized vast and ongoing transformations, eagerly collaborating with a class that, one must think, dominated the second half of the twentieth century: developers. Then Congress and President Dwight Eisenhower initiated the interstate highway system in 1956. Ostensibly a Cold War national security measure—the military must have rapid mobility within the continent—the interstates became the great enablers of suburbanization. I-85, for example, evolved into a teeming, long-distance corridor of bedroom communities, big-box malls, automobile dealers, gas stations, and interstate ramps, from Petersburg, Virginia, through Burlington and Charlotte, North Carolina, and on to Spartanburg, Atlanta, and Montgomery. Atlanta, once famous for its five rail lines, is now intersected by four numbered interstate highways and looped and bypassed by two more. (I-20 gets one over to Birmingham pretty quickly, traffic load permitting.) Early in the twenty-first century, metro Atlanta, meaning the city and its surrounding suburbs, ranked consistently at the top or near the top of national rankings for worst auto and truck traffic congestion. Richmond, with two interstates and three loops, is a more compressed version of the same. Houston, the Sun Belt champion of sprawl, so far exceeded federal accommodation that its great encircling so-called bypass is itself encircled by a gigantic toll road that bypasses the bypass. Farther north in Texas, the roadmap for greater Dallas–Fort Worth presents the illusion of an asymmetrical pair of gargantuan, blood-shot eyes. Dallas's intersected circle is much the larger, with a curious small circle, the city's iris, as it were, at the center.

What, meanwhile, became of downtowns and the oldest suburbs, which had come to be perceived as "central city"? Thriving business districts, such as Dallas's, are typically abandoned after about six o'clock each workday evening. Many other downtowns do not fare this well and have descended into dereliction. This was not inevitable, but the consequence of a series of political acts: taxpayer subsidization of the conversion of former forests and farmland into suburbs, of cheap mortgages to buy the new housing, and of new highways to get suburbanites to work. Such massive outlays of public money did not extend to maintenance and repair of the old built landscape. Rather, they accomplished the opposite. During the early 1970s, President Richard Nixon's New Federalism introduced "general revenue sharing" of treasury funds to be returned to states and localities, as opposed to direct grants targeted at central urban programs. The Housing and Community Development Act of 1974, meanwhile, permitted local officials to choose limited federal funding for projects that promised early, reportable successes. As a result, mayors, councils, and housing officials in Florida effectively wrote off at least thirteen neighborhoods as "too far gone" for action; so large swaths of Jacksonville, Tampa, Miami (the largest examples) were abandoned to permanent dereliction. The Ronald Reagan administration persisted with its version of a similar funding system, while cities watched their federal aid decline somewhat more than 20 percent. City officials, desperate to enlarge tax bases, usually spent reduced federal funds on the rebuilding of downtown business districts. Yet typically, cleaned-up streets and office buildings usually begged for foot traffic and renters, so everywhere (not just in the South), downtowns slid into blight.[19] Here is much of the explanation for the eerie silence of desertion in Jackson, Mississippi, on a Friday afternoon, when the poet Charles Simic came from New Hampshire for a visit in 2004.[20] Simic the literary man might have expected to see the likes of the late writer Eudora Welty toddling about, shopping or having an iced tea at a drugstore lunch counter. This was indeed Jackson's downtown of old, but no more.

The roots of urban dereliction are nourished, still, in certified accounting practices, depreciation schedules, and tax law. Before the 1950s, tax law permitted depreciation of buildings (domestic and commercial) over a long period, even if market values were rising (as they were). Amid the great boom of babies and 'burbs, however, law and accounting practices effectively reduced the period allowed for depreciation for tax purposes—in the case of commercial buildings, from forty years to twenty, thereby encouraging the construction of new buildings and abandonment of older buildings as soon as depreciations were exhausted as tax benefits. The urban geographers John Jakle and David Wilson suggest a revealing comparison that surely reflects post–World War II American priorities: maintenance workers, cleaners, janitors, and "handymen" receive low pay and low social status; carpenters and masons are well paid and respected.

Difficulty in finding renters for space in central-city office buildings is accounted for in the same depreciation schedules, yet more so. Corporations had begun to flee downtowns as early as 1945, separating themselves from labor unions while simultaneously finding cheaper land, lower rents, and fresh buildings with depreciation years in front. The great logic of build-depreciate-move generated by postwar tax law led, by the end of the twentieth century, to public admission by mall builders that new shopping centers were typically constructed to last but five years, ten maximum. Abandonment of malls, as everyone has observed, often proceeds in stages, with government offices renting some spaces, perhaps also a charitable flea market or old clothes store, and maybe a Pentecostal church sanctifying a former shoe emporium. Not-so-old malls became derelict, like downtowns, their massive parking lots—bane of drainage and source of toxic pollution—living on and on, although now sometimes revived as venues for illegal nighttime business. Suburban blight is the inevitable, visible effluvia of suburbanization.

Meanwhile, as downtowns and aging suburbs grew shabbier, rural places fared little better. First, from the 1960s onward, the most furious decades of interstate highway construction, many rural roads became ineligible for federal support, and many deteriorated in proportion to county and state governments' abilities or willingness to assume responsibility. Farms, rural communities, and woodlands were bulldozed everywhere, but the blight of neglect or abuse was most obvious in southern Appalachia. Corporate landholding outside cities and suburbia has usually been lightly taxed, so when coal companies control from one-half to two-thirds of the land in a county—the case in Logan, West Virginia; Harlan, Kentucky; and Wise, Virginia (in 1981)—not only do agricultural fields and country settlements disappear under strip-mine debris, but public services tend to deteriorate further. Garbage collection, for instance, was spectacularly absent in eastern Kentucky—spectacular because during winter and early spring, along the busy path of I-75, naked forests on populated mountain slopes revealed streams of assorted refuse, including household garbage (from rotting food to diapers), cans and bottles, scraps of wood and metal, old auto and truck tires, and rusting, abandoned cars and trucks. Such rural neighborhoods seldom had sewer systems, either, or inspections of private septic works. Like as not, drainpipes led from houses to the nearest creek, where untreated sewage began its course downstream. At the beginning of the twenty-first century, the government of Kentucky, mainly from civic embarrassment late expressed, fostered with other parties a great cleanup and institution of garbage collection and public inspection of sewage and water systems.[21]

Great cleanups were under way earlier in American downtowns, including southern ones, well before the end of the twentieth century. City governments hired such famous architects as John Portman (designer of, among other things, now-clichéd skyscraper hotels with glass elevators) to confer monumentality and confidence on central cities from Atlanta to Norfolk to Baltimore. Charlotte, Atlanta, and Nashville built skylines with stunning profiles. New Orleans, Norfolk, Portsmouth, and Baltimore converted derelict waterfronts into grand commercial-retail spaces that offered visitors opportunities to walk, ride bicycles, and take boat tours. Congress, meanwhile, had aimed to spark rejuvenation of old downtowns with the National Historic Preservation Act of 1966, which established a National Registry of Historic Places and offered tax and other incentives to restore buildings and neighborhoods. The legislation was partly responsible for ongoing "gentrification" of old neighborhoods: Youngish and middle-aged people (usually white) with money saved parts of many old seaboard cities, including Baltimore, Portsmouth, Norfolk, Wilmington, Georgetown, Charleston, Savannah, and Mobile. The durability and benefit of such return-to-the-cities movements is uncertain, however. Will supermarkets and other stores return from the suburbs to serve the reverse pioneers? Will there be schools, decent ones? Gentrification has tended to simplify demographics in formerly diverse neighborhoods. The poor, the working poor, the elderly with fixed incomes, and people of color tend to be replaced by middle-aged whites of the professional and business class. Their costly improvements cause rising taxation and market values, driving out the last of the former resident population. Diversity is not only the standard of strength and durability for the botanical cover of a landscape; it is (as Jane Jacobs insisted) the soul of a functioning city. Too, migrants from upscale suburbs to restored inner-city blocks often bring with them suburbanites' supersensitivity about security, so they install elaborate alarm systems and avoid walking the streets. Thus, paradoxically, some gentrified urban places are dissimilar from suburbs only in the absence of great lawns. The gentry do not walk their blocks but drive to the supermarket, often miles away, and drive children (if there are any) to distant schools. They may as well live in the (supposedly) most secure of automobile-centric suburbs, namely, gated communities.

By 1995 there were an estimated 150,000 private housing developments in the United States, 40,000 of them in Florida alone. Others are scattered, often densely, in other southern places: near the office parks along Atlanta's interstate loops; a few blocks from downtown Memphis; out in the country near little West Point, Mississippi; and all around Washington, D.C. From the mid-1980s to the mid-1990s, sixteen new gated communities appeared in San Antonio alone. During the 1990s, too, planners and property owners in Houston and Jackson, Mississippi, verged toward privatizing older streets—100 in Houston, 23 in Jackson. Robert Reich, then the U.S. secretary of labor, righteously decried this "secession of the successful." Community homeowner associations tax themselves and demand meeting time and talent, effectively depriving the larger urban or suburban community of their skills and financial assets.[22]

Not all enclosed and guarded neighborhoods are populated by "older, whiter, and wealthier" folks, as writer Evan McKenzie characterized gated communities in *Privatopia: Homeowner Associations and the Rise of Residential Private Government* (1994). Collegeville, a poorer quarter of Birmingham, actually has a public housing complex behind high iron fences and a gate where guards require identification of residents and visitors alike. Collegeville got its enclosure because it was a drive-through, crime-ridden project. The "cage" (as a few residents term the fence) brought safety, peace, and quiet. Such was probably the goal of middle-class neighborhood associations in Jackson, Mississippi, during the mid-1990s, since Jackson's crime rate was on the rise. Nearly everywhere else, however, violent and property crime declined throughout the decade and into the next century. Security in higher-end gated communities is likely a living fiction embedded in the minds of home buyers. Or it may have been merely the exclusivity implied by gate and fence or wall.

Exclusivity seldom applies to domestic architectural modes, however. Many of the most expensive houses in gated communities look about the same, except in minor (and community-approved) details of roofline, paint color, and trim. Architectural conformity suggests another significant aspect of security. A house is usually our largest financial asset, and expecting that no home is permanent—we may be transferred, we may retire from landscape maintenance to a condo, or we may move to be near the children —we fear for our investment's transferability. So the odd and unusual and avant in architecture are typically shunned. A vast conspiracy of developers, their designers, and real estate agents would seem to dictate also that the conformity of each community may or may not reflect anything indigenous to the subregion where the development occurs. Windrush, in Madison County, Mississippi, north of Jackson, an expensive project sold to doctors and businesspeople, presents housing in two styles, "Norman or Louisiana French." (Louisiana French may suggest galleries and wrought-iron fencing. Norman French—as opposed to Korean Normandy[?]—means fortresslike massivity and many roof levels and lines, often suggesting, too, the likelihood of roof leaks.) A yet more upscale gated community located between the Atlantic Ocean and Indian River in Florida, called Windsor, is actually described by its developers as an "Anglo-Caribbean village." One yearns to visit such places, to understand what design names actually look like—but of course one could not get inside.

Some houses in such exclusive neighborhoods rest on small lots. Developers squeezed them, as it were, among office parks, corporate "campuses," and malls, selling short commutes and (perhaps) less arduous and costly landscaping. From the beginning of the American suburbs in the nineteenth century, however, the urban migrant's hope and ideal has been the large, private greensward. Suburbs remain mostly true, I think, to their original promise: a leafy "borderland" (as John Stilgoe has put it) between the dirty, noisy, crowded city and the remote, isolated rural-agricultural realm.[23] There a house is better made a home because it is detached, its privacy assured by the surrounding yard, the bigger the better. Yards, dominated by expansive lawn, frame and present the home to the world, serving (paradoxically) as insulator from intrusion and private park. Backyards, sometimes side yards, too, better realized the insular, though. No wonder that these were typically women's places—to supervise children at play and to grow flowers, herbs, and vegetables for the family. Southern women have ever relished such spaces, but in the formal literature of lawns and gardens, it was northeastern women of the late nineteenth and early twentieth centuries who created the formal syntax. Among these, Beatrix Jones Farrand (1872–1959) was not only the private enthusiast but the professional landscape architect, becoming, during the 1890s, one of the founders of the American Institute of Landscape Architecture. Farrand studied at the Arnold Arboretum in Massachusetts and with Gertrude Jekyll, the English horticulturist. Farrand's aunt, the writer Edith Wharton, published a book about Italian gardens in 1910, influencing Beatrix. But like other famous but nonprofessional Yankee gardeners, Farrand may be regarded as a domestic feminist, or simply as ecofeminist, in her persistent view of the garden as decorative and useful outdoor "room." In this important way she lent authority to what Afro- and Euro-southern women of most social classes had created for many generations: privacy, security, and persistence.

Suburbs, no less than the densest cities, are arranged landscapes where inattentiveness to maintenance leads inevitably to dereliction and disgrace. Gardens and lawns are as susceptible as houses. They are, like farm crops, part of second nature—human-arranged and -maintained soils and plant assemblages—as opposed to first nature, which is unarranged or managed wilderness (of which there is little left on the earth). As a youth in suburban Long Island, Michael Pollan defied his gardener grandfather and planted his first flower seeds helter-skelter. After his seed had germinated and arisen, he discovered that he could not distinguish his infant cultivars from other, unwanted plants (i.e., weeds), and he lost his little garden to more aggressive plants. Thereafter he took care to plant in rows that revealed his intention and permitted crucial weeding. Pollan's nongardener father, meanwhile, was an early rebel against that anchor of the suburban yard, the lawn. He let it grow and, when family and neighbors complained, mowed amusing messages in the grass. There have been few of his ilk, though, while not only the lawn but the *perfect* lawn of one species of grass became the tyrant of the entire nation, the South included. Here is to be found the nexus of farm and suburb: chemistry.

The creation of DDT, an ally to Allied troops in the tropical Pacific and Asia during World War II, aroused interest in agribusiness and, combined with successful development of better hybrids of cotton and grains and both pre- and postemergent herbicides, made for a new and global capital-intensive farming. Labor requirements were minimal, since a single operator sitting atop a giant new tractor pulling a variety of implements might plow, cultivate, plant, and prevent weeds and insect pests. If strange new unwanted plants or bugs appeared, there would be new herbicides and pesticides to exterminate them. At the end of a crop season, the same operator, now driving a combine or other harvesting machine, could expect to bring in a heavy crop free of trash, rot, and insect damage. Agriculture's old industrial ideal was realized—if only the owner-operator could pay his huge debts.

Suburban America, emerging at the same time, was soon beneficiary and victim of the farming revolution. Corporations, some new and some the same as those catering to agriculture, rushed to tease a huge new market into (almost) labor-free gardening and lawn keeping. The front yard—the big, open one mowed and hand-weeded by men—could be sprayed or dry-pellet-treated to slay those dandelions or dollar weeds before or after they arose to spoil the perfect lawn of fine fescue, Kentucky bluegrass, or Bermuda or St. Augustine grass. There were general and specific poisons, too, for any number of flies, ants, and grubs that threatened perfection. By the late 1960s, here and there (including in the South), rebellions against suburban household borders arose: There should be no fences, hedges, or other barriers (e.g., garden rooms of roses and wisteria) to impede literally miles of perfect greensward. Now men and children could create communal ball fields and big playgrounds. I recollect the movement. Women had little or no part of it, since they, Farrandlike, were creatures of decoration and privacy. Male suburbanites, their garages and sheds bulging with riding mowers and bags and bottles of dangerous chemicals, would plant, feed, weed, and slay chinch bugs from tractor seats and, in triumph, call out, "Play ball!" Garden rooms got in the way of machine operations. And small-town-like sociability is encouraged by diminution of landscape barriers between private property holdings.

Another thing I observed—just north of the South but well within bluegrass country—was that by the 1970s, the lawns of my most chemical-dependent neighbors began to suffer sudden deaths. Independent landscapers and horticulturalists confirmed that pesticides, in particular, had "chemically locked" the soil. Earthworms, harmless grubs, and ants that perform essential aeration and mold-making functions had been exterminated by regular and excessive poisoning. Some mention was made of birds as victims of pesticides, too—but not much, a decade after publication of Rachel Carson's *Silent Spring*. In yet another decade, but especially during the 1990s, the word "diversity" had become common in political and also landscaping parlance as a hallmark of social *and* botanical good health. In other words, a diverse human community (including several racial groups, the young, the old, and representatives of several income groups) is more likely to thrive. Likewise, thriving landscapes consist of diverse, competing, but ultimately mutually supporting plants and animals. All this wisdom, now old, has made little difference in the business and practice of making and maintaining "perfect" lawns. Runoff from millions of them constitutes a major source of wetland and watercourse pollution everywhere.

Then, too, there is the roar of the four- and especially two-cycle gasoline engines that power the mowers, trimmers, edgers, blowers, and chainsaws that maintain this misguided aesthetic. Quiet had been the twin virtue of privacy in the happy old quest for borderlands, but now, throughout growing seasons—oppressively long in Dixie—decibel levels in suburbs rival those in the most raucous cities. Isolation within air-conditioned interiors became the alternative to sitting outside or gardening amid the smelly, grinding din. The resurgence of porches in new suburban developments during the 1990s changed not a thing.

🌸 The revolutionary introduction of mostly petroleum-based chemicals that sustained both the so-called Green Revolution and the endless American lawn has simultaneously placed much of the globe in grave peril. During the late 1970s, the world's press reported the discovery of irresponsibly dumped and buried chemicals in Love Canal, near Niagara Falls, New York. Residents of the community, unaware of what lay beneath their homes, suffered extraordinary rates of multiple cancers. Survivors abandoned the place. About the same time, in tiny Times Beach, Missouri, officials sprayed an oil concoction on roads to hold down dust. The formula included dioxin, a toxic by-product of the incineration of chlorinated wastes that is easily absorbed into animal (including human) tissue. Times Beach was abandoned, too. Halfway around the northern hemisphere, in November 1986, firefighters at the Sandoz chemical plant in Basel-Schweizerhalle, Switzerland, extinguished a warehouse blaze by flushing between ten and thirty metric tons of agrichemicals—fertilizers, fungicides, pesticides, and herbicides—into the Rhine River. The great river quickly flushed itself sufficiently to restore downstream drinking water to service; but the eel population was nearly exterminated, and many other surviving fishes starved in the spill's aftermath because the chemical scourge had killed the microorganisms that constitute the bottom of the food chain. The upper Rhine, particularly, was for years in painful recovery. Two years before the big Sandoz spill, in yet another hemisphere, the worst known chemical disaster had occurred. In Bhopal, India, an American (Union Carbide) plant engaged in producing an intermediate compound in the refining of both pesticides and herbicides exploded and leaked the substance over workers and townspeople. Three thousand, eight hundred people died, and an estimated 200,000 fell ill in what a witness termed "one vast gas chamber."[24]

In 1985—the year after Bhopal—another Union Carbide plant leaked, this one in Institute, West Virginia, near Charleston, albeit with far less catastrophic results. The Institute incident roused the U.S. Congress to order the Environmental Protection Agency (EPA) to develop a Toxic Release Inventory of more than 300 chemicals, to include not only chemical properties but precise locations of their productions. For those not already aware that the South was (and remains) home to some of the dirtiest and most dangerous industries, the Toxic Release Inventory detailed and mapped many "chemical alleys" across the region, all of them, naturally, along rivers. Southern workers feed the American (and the German and the Japanese) addiction to monoculture and pest killing, and they and their families and neighbors suffer consequences. There are, for instance, Buffalo Bayou in the neighborhood of Houston and Pasadena, Texas; a stretch of the Mississippi around Memphis; sections of the James, in Virginia; and the Kanawah in West Virginia, westward through Charleston past Institute and the perfectly named town of Nitro.

Once I spent a scary night in Nitro. Exhausted from driving, I rashly decided that it would be amusing to stop and see a place we had many times sped past. About eleven that night, strolling outside our motel with the dog, I was startled by flashing lights and alarm whistles across the river at the Monsanto plant. Back inside the room, we were instructed by the motel clerk to place dampened towels on the threshold beneath our door until an all-clear were sounded. There may have been a leak, she said; alarms occurred frequently. Earlier that same day we had driven past Hopewell, heart of Virginia's chemical alley and site of disaster in 1975. In July that year workers at the Life Science Products Company complained of alarming symptoms: unfocused vision, low sperm counts, tremors, and anxiety. Tests found the company's lethal product, a pesticide called Kepone (sold exclusively by contract with the giant Allied Chemical Corporation), in their blood. Then investigators discovered that not only had workers inadvertently inhaled or ingested Kepone, but there had been a large spill into James River. Shellfish sixty-five miles downstream, almost to Hampton Roads, were tainted with the pesticide, and the governor closed the eastern James to fishing. Kepone's "afterlife" was estimated at a century, so it endures yet and for some time more in the river's mud.[25]

The southern chemical alley ne plus ultra, though, is both banks of the broad lower Mississippi River between Baton Rouge and New Orleans. From the late eighteenth through the nineteenth and into the twentieth century, the banks blazed merrily each winter during holiday season, which was also when sugar planters' workers burned cane and fired their boilers. Beginning about the time of World War I, however, old sugar plantations became something else, and new fires something quite different. Southeastern Louisiana is blessed with extraordinary natural resources: not only lush alluvial land for farming but, farther down, petroleum and natural gas and, much farther down, giant domes of salt where many millions of gallons of oil may be stored and easily retrieved. Early in the twentieth century,

Standard Oil came to these riches, bought up old plantations, drilled into petroleum, and built refineries and strategic political domination of the state. Standard also conducted revolutionary research on petrochemicals from the refining process. Their chemists' isolation of hydrocarbon chains laid the foundation for the synthetic fiber industry and then much, much else, including the production of vinyl chloride (vc) and polyvinyl chloride (pvc)—plastics for a myriad of consumer goods from automobiles to carpeting, computer chips, diapers, furniture, luggage, medicines, paints, and water pipe.[26]

Over the next six decades, Standard's refinery flares were joined by those of other petrochemical corporations, American and foreign alike. All came to Louisiana because of its oil and gas but also because (except for the Huey Long era of the late 1920s and mid-1930s) government was generous to business in terms of taxation and labor law, and because the landscape on which this "American Ruhr" was constructed was populated by rural black folks eager for postagricultural work, no matter if refinery labor was at least as dirty. So into the valley came Dow, Ethyl Corporation, and W. R. Grace, among other U.S. firms. Japanese companies came here to escape environmental and health regulations at home, as did the German petrochemical giant BASF and the Anglo-Dutch behemoth Shell. By the 1970s it became apparent that Yankee and foreign companies had exported much more than capital and air pollution. vc and pvc are now long-proven carcinogens, and at least as early as the 1960s, the American Ruhr was being transformed, in the vernacular, to Chemical Alley and Cancer Alley. Local people, workers and residents, had become sick in extraordinary numbers, and while government and the corporations lied, obfuscated, and dodged responsibility, the African American civil rights movement became engaged, joining labor unions (notably the Oil, Chemical, and Atomic Workers International Union) in marches, demonstrations, and antipollution publicity. Environmental civil rights was thus born, and the struggle continues.

By the 1980s the international environmental troublemakers, Greenpeace, conducted their own research using public records and published a simple, documented observation: Following the Mississippi southward from its source to the Gulf, entering cancerous tumor rates along the way, Minnesota, with its very low rate, stood in shocking contrast with Louisiana. Could this be mere chance? asked Greenpeace. Essentially, public health officials and the corporations replied yes, citing Louisianians' supposedly poorer eating habits and heavier cigarette smoking. So organized labor and civil rights marches continued, featuring by the late 1980s war-horses from the 1960s such as Jesse Jackson and a second generation well represented by Martin Luther King III. All the marchers well understood human desperation and, not least, irony: that an American state, poor Louisiana, had become literally the sump for the world's toxic wastes, and poor New Orleans, so long the South's first city, was arguably the sump of the downstream sump.

Then came the terrorist attacks of 11 September 2001. In the aftermath, as the public and responsible officials investigated the security of seaports, airports, and military installations, the army's surgeon general's office conducted a study of the chemical alleys of the nation. An attack on a single chemical plant, the study found, might result in the deaths and dire woundings of perhaps a million and a half people. Early in 2003 the National Infrastructure Protection Center warned that chemical plants were likely targets. The director of the EPA identified 123 facilities where an attack—or an accident—might jeopardize more than a million people, and no fewer than 7,605 plants where catastrophe could harm more than a thousand people each. The director decided that the EPA could use the Clean Air Act to force chemical producers to increase security and to use less dangerous chemicals. At the end of 2003, however, the president overruled the EPA and assigned the matter to the new Department of Homeland Security. There the secretary reduced the threat presented by corporate chemistry by reducing the army's and the EPA's numbers of vulnerable plants and potential victims and by installing security cameras at plants in seven states. Florida, a state widely considered threatened, was not included.[27]

🌿 The evil twin of VC and PVC as late-twentieth-century scourge to public health has been petroleum-based pesticides. Here, too, the South and southerners were critical producers, users, and victims. Beginning with the wartime development of DDT for killing the mosquitoes and parasites that were sickening our troops in the southern Pacific, a peacetime miracle was beheld. Combined with petroleum-based herbicides (pesticides' great partner) and engineered grain seed, a Green Revolution could be made: super-productive agriculture accomplished by chemistry and machines and requiring little labor. It seemed a cause no less good than defeating the Axis, and it was happening by the 1950s.

Industrial-scale production and application of pesticides is actually much older than the Green Revolution, especially in California and the lower South. In the nineteenth century, European and American chemists combined arsenic with various solvents—Paris Green was a favorite in the United States—to kill pests in crops. During the 1920s, Central Valley, California and Mississippi Delta cotton "ranchers" and planters hired daring pilots to spread dried arsenic and other toxic pellets on fields from the air, and the dangerous profession of crop dusting was born. One young pioneer out of Sacramento reportedly guided a World War I trainer plane with his knees while heaving a lead-based pesticide out of his cockpit with a coal shovel.[28] Shortly, in both agribusiness regions, aerial application would become rather less haphazard and dangerous to pilots. Later, too, specialized aircraft would spray liquid treatments from tanks, a mode that continues today. While pilots still encounter utility poles and wires in their tight maneuvers, it is those on the ground beneath powders and sprays—worms, insects, fishes, reptiles, amphibians, and mammals—who are in more danger.

If arsenic and lead were not sufficient as toxic drift, the new, post–World War II generations of pesticides were crippling and lethal. Egregiously aggressive spraying of the agent parathion (especially during the 1950s) devastated wildlife populations and produced numerous human complaints of serious illness. As evermore, the corporate makers of pesticides steadfastly maintained the safety of their products, attributing mishaps to errors in application and/or failure to read simple warning labels. The USDA's Agricultural Research Service (ARS) had (and has) statutory authority to grant or to refuse permits to market, but instead of conducting thorough independent testing, the ARS persistently cheered the corporations' contributions to American and world food production. The federal Public Health Service and professional groups such as the American Medical Association and the American Chemical Society were also firmly lodged within the brotherhood of chemical solutions with acceptable risks. For a long while the chemical companies not only conducted virtually the only research on their products but wrote labels that the bureaucrats of ARS routinely accepted. Organized and politically articulate agribusiness, meanwhile, encouraged ever-larger spraying programs at taxpayer expense. The ARS and the rest of the USDA were eager collaborators.

In 1957, for example, the USDA announced an ambitious (and expensive) campaign to eradicate fire ants in the entire South by spraying the latest pesticide from the air. The ants won the war and live on, especially in sandy fields and suburban yards (such as my own). Pesticide makers obliged homeowners with handy cylindrical containers of specialized poison. One spies an anthill, grabs the can, gives the top a quarter-turn, and sprinkles white crystals directly onto the hill. Other ants will appear, but the diligent may respond again and control them. The undiligent—the lazy, perhaps—may be susceptible to the blandishments and broadcast sprays of lawn-service companies.

The USDA also remained committed to big spraying programs. During the early and mid-1960s there were massive fish kills in the lower Mississippi system from runoffs of the pesticide endrin. Some dead and dying catfish were nonetheless sold for human consumption, according to the historian Pete Daniel, and drinking water sources were compromised. Notwithstanding, in 1967 the USDA again declared war on the fire ant—this time not with the failed heptachlor but with mirex, a newish pesticide. The war was to last twelve years and cost an estimated $200 million, despite research that reported that mirex could be deadly to fin- and shellfish. All this occurred, too, five years after the appearance of Rachel Carson's *Silent Spring* and three years after a presidential report on pesticides and hearings in the U.S. Senate hostile to the chemical industry. In 1970, however, the EPA was born, and the next year its head canceled registration of mirex. Allied Chemical, mirex's maker, appealed, and in 1972 mirex's federal registration was restored, but its use near water was prohibited. Three years later the USDA finally abandoned the war.

The sorriest story in Pete Daniel's study of pesticides in the South, I think, has the smallest scope, namely, one man and his family. In 1956 there was a welder in Sunflower County, Mississippi, named Charles Lawler. One summer day as he labored on a farmer's building surrounded by crop fields, his head concealed under his welder's helmet-mask, a pilot sprayed malathion, endrin, and other pesticides suspended in a solvent called Xylene. Lawler thought no spraying would occur on the field next to his work, but the pilot came in low and close and loosed a cloud of poison over the work site and the gin house next door. Lawler's headgear and blazing torch prevented his hearing a warning from his helper, and the headgear doubtlessly trapped droplets of pesticide and Xylene around his breathing passages. He was never the same again: ill, weak, unable to work, and almost constantly under care of doctors and his family. Lawler's lawsuit was immediately and broadly understood as an elemental threat not merely to his employer but to Delta agriculture, the pesticide industry, and the USDA. All of these, directly and indirectly, fought the suit. Lawler lost, won an appeal, but ultimately lost in several ways. His health was ruined forever, the culture of big agriculture in the Delta went unchanged, and the cozy brotherhood of the USDA and corporate chemistry was unbroken.

✿ Still, there is now a middle-aged environmental movement, and it dreams on with mad persistence. Beauty, health, and permanence must be had. These brazenly utopian goals, according to one of the most insightful American historians, Samuel P. Hays, drove post–World War II environmentalism and environmental politics.[29] This ever-evolving movement was much preoccupied both with conservation—wise use of natural resources—and with preservation of wilderness, or a notion of natural wildness where humans might visit but not live. Even preservation was instrumental to human need and happiness, though. High, remote, protected mountains accumulate snow that melts and waters deserts below, permitting agriculture and sprawling cities, for example, and wetland preserves, salt- and freshwater, nurse fisheries while scrubbing and flushing wastes.

Meanwhile, beauty, health, and permanence in *built* landscapes—a matter not much formally considered by American environmentalists—surely would be best represented in clean, secure building materials tastefully rendered into form. Professor Hays, by coincidence, is himself a native of a rich landscape with lovely indigenous architectural materials: Corydon, the first capital of Indiana, in the limestone hills of the state's deep south, a short commute nowadays (via I-64) from Louisville. Not far north of Corydon is Bedford, heart of the region's great limestone quarries, which for generations supplied the building blocks of capitols, courthouses, and mansions but also modest housing for the middle classes. Southern Indiana's limestone is to be found in many places but most densely, elegantly, near its own source and across the Ohio River in northern Kentucky. A stone house is safe from wind and fire, a thing of beauty and a statement of strength suggesting health, too. There are other sturdy building materials in the South. Northern Georgia has granite. Florida floats upon a giant mat of porous limestone but is famous for its soft coquina, also porous and requiring plaster or stucco for waterproof construction. This seems a shame—the covering of fossil shells that tell of old seas—but solid shelter necessitates certain compromises.

Surely it is the sturdy brick, though, that for most southerners has signified security, freedom from most maintenance, stability in weather, and something approaching permanence. Southerners made brick from native clays and, later, clay and shale, too, as soon as their hold on the land seemed permanent. There were a few brick houses by the late seventeenth century and many more in the prosperous decades of the eighteenth. Baltimore had great brick kilns and drying yards. Clay mines were everywhere and spread westward with southern migrants. Three decades before West Virginia's creation, a brick factory was founded at New Cumberland. By the 1890s there were more than fifty clay mines in the state. Some specialized in firebrick for the steel mills of Pittsburgh. Others supplied the wherewithal for ordinary folks to realize their domestic dreams.[30]

Consider ordinary black citizens of Gloucester County, Virginia, who as late as the 1890s, thirty years after emancipation and male suffrage, still dwelled mostly in houses of wood with chimneys made of sticks and daub. These folks' champion—and a champion of brick—was Thomas C. Walker, born a slave in 1864, a graduate of Hampton Institute (a decade or so after Booker T. Washington), a schoolteacher, an attorney, a Republican office-holder, and a public-spirited entrepreneur. Walker founded the Gloucester Land and Brick Company, which during the 1890s bought up farmland as agriculture declined, sold it to aspiring black landholders, and made low-interest mortgages. "Brick" in the company name captured Walker's goal to rid his people of dangerous chimneys in favor of beautiful, permanent ones. A half-century later, in the aftermath of a modern exodus that took almost 5 million Afro-southerners away to other regions, many of those who remained in Gloucester and similar, small-town and rural places, had acquired brick houses. Down in eastern North Carolina, automobile commuters (black and white alike) to work in paper mills and factories lived in brick ranch-style houses strung along highways. For all the miles of aluminum siding on southern houses, the dream of brick had come true for many.[31]

Brick construction as a standard for civilization is ancient, and not without complex poetics. In 1881, for instance, Albion Tourgee published a sequel to his best-selling novel about Reconstruction in the South, *A Fool's Errand*, titling the new book *Bricks without Straw*. Tourgee, born on a northwestern Ohio farm in 1838, became a Romantic idealist while a student at the University of Rochester on the eve of the Civil War. Although blind in one eye since the age of fourteen, he eagerly enlisted in a New York volunteer company and a short time later was badly injured during the Union retreat from the field at First Bull Run. He nonetheless returned to war as a lieutenant in an Ohio outfit the next year, fought at Perryville, and was wounded. Tourgee was also once captured and spent four months in Confederate prisons before he was exchanged; then he returned to war yet again and participated in the early stages of the struggle for Chattanooga, before

*Cabin with mud chimney, Gees Bend, Alabama, 1937. Photo by Arthur Rothstein.*
*Courtesy Library of Congress (LC-USF34-025349-D DLC).*

suffering a crippling reinjury of his back. So at last he left the army, studied law in Ohio, and in 1865 moved to Greensboro, North Carolina, to practice and attend to the business of completing the development of democracy for all in the South. He became a founder of the North Carolina Republican Party; served in the "radical" constitutional convention of 1868; wrote law transferring local authority from the legislature to the counties, towns, and cities; and manfully resisted constant threats to himself and his family from the Ku Klux Klan. Tourgee served on the state's superior court past the return of conservative Democrats to power, and after President Grant conferred an appointment to a pension commission in Raleigh, he persisted in a place ceaselessly hostile to him. He was a brave, determined, and impetuous man, not unlike southern white extremists who had lost the war but were determined to win the peace. Finally, after fourteen years, Tourgee and his wife, who was pleading for peace elsewhere, moved to New York. There, ultimately, lawyer-judge Tourgee became a literary man, what he had always wanted.[32]

The title of *A Fool's Errand* more than suggested the failure of civil rights and justice in the South following the war. So did *Bricks without Straw*. The North and the federal government failed black and unionist white southerners; Reconstruction was a brick that crumbled too easily before the relentless opposition of defeated but brash ex-secessionists. Neither Tourgee during the 1880s nor his principal twentieth-century biographer (Otto Olsen) nor the literary historian Edmund Wilson (both writing during the 1960s) felt a need to explain the allusion of the novel's title. Now (I suspect) one does. It was the Old Testament's second book, Exodus—most dramatically the fifth chapter. The Hebrews had long been in Egyptian captivity. Moses, an escapee, met the Lord, Jehovah, who conferred upon him a magical rod, an eloquent spokesman named Aaron, and the mission to free his people. So, returning to Egypt, Moses commanded Pharaoh to "let my people go" (5:1), but Pharaoh instead ordered his subalterns to harden slaves' principal task, the manufacture of bricks, by requiring "them to gather straw for themselves" (5:7). Ancient Egyptians (and modern ones, too) sun-dried clay brick shaped in forms. Nile alluvium was their clay, and the ancients learned that when the alluvium was too rich in clay—that is, lacking sand and impurities—bricks dried too slowly, shrank, and lost shape or crumbled. Chopped straw became the essential additive for regularity of size and dependable strength; straw might also be added as a simple binder that, combined with the heat of baking, made the product long-lasting.

Meanwhile, until Moses' impertinence, enslaved brick-makers had been provided straw; now they would have to gather straw and meet the same quotas of bricks in the same time (5:18). The dismayed Hebrews suffered; but as we learn in later chapters of Exodus, Jehovah made Pharaoh and his ilk suffer more, and at last the slaves were delivered out of Egypt. Difficulties in making good bricks were compensated, then, by cataclysmic horrors visited upon Egyptians that anticipate merciless vengeance upon sinners in the last book of the Christian Bible. Still, details about good bricks were obviously not forgotten. "Feet of clay," after all—a poor foundation for a building or a person—survives as a metaphor without mention of straw. And the passing of sun-drying bricks bound by straw in favor of furnace or kiln firing does not exactly antiquate the old usage either, because artificially fired clays become something other than mere crumbly earth. They are *bricks*.

This helps mold our own final large question: Are the built landscapes of the South merely clay, or brick? To be most inclusive, one might fairly say both. New Orleans, the shocking-charming example—and no matter how it is rebuilt after the deluge of 2005—may be sinking into its own sewage and PVC-heavy groundwater and is, despite some recent reforms in the police force, a scary place to walk at night. Yet central and old-suburban New Orleans flaunts its diversity of population and land use, its distinctive architecture and elegant plantings, and its music and food sublime. One can walk the town (wisely in company) invigorated. Elsewhere, re-gentrification may be working in a few places, too: in Norfolk's Ghent section; in the Shockoe waterfront in Richmond; in Main Street and environs in Lexington, Kentucky; in Memphis's near-downtown; and so on. And—allowing for the annoying and dangerous necessity of driving for elemental needs—many suburbs are pleasant places to live. My own, on Anastasia Island southeast of St. Augustine, is an assemblage of "Floridian" style houses, most with balconies and all with verandas, from which neighbors of various ages and backgrounds greet and meet. There are no sidewalks—typical of American autocentric sprawl and developers' parsimony—so we take to foot on the street, morning and evenings during the long summer, leading our mutts and holding what we call impromptu dog conventions. There are other communities like this.

Yet many suburbs consist of isolated, tightly closed houses, their occupants' interaction with neighbors minimal, perhaps waving from car windows twice each weekday. Everyone works hard and afar. The timetables of such bedroom communities are the inverse of most downtowns and of so-called edge cities—those new, ring-road business centers where many suburbanites work. The suburbs shut down by day; the cities, by evening and night. Woe, then, to visitors—such as hotel-bound conference-goers—to most central cities. As conference business subsides after 5:00 P.M. and conferees are eager to walk, drink, and eat, the downtowns of not only Jackson but Dallas, Little Rock, Birmingham, and Atlanta are closing doors and turning out lights. New Orleans, New York, Chicago, and San Francisco are the great exceptions among American cities, proving the rule.

Mostly, I conclude, cities and suburbs are clay in the varied and dreadful environmental impacts they have on themselves and on thinly populated countrysides. Consider, for instance, the use of urban sewer sludge as fertilizer: Disposal of the enormous effluvia processed by the nation's sewage systems is a major sanitary issue. Application of sludge, usually in dehydrated form, to crop fields seems an excellent disposition indeed, and Edmund Ruffin, relentless champion of recycling, might have been joyful at the realization of a frustrated dream. Ruffin knew not of the uptake of heavy metals from soil to plant to animal, however. Beginning during the late 1960s, ecologists at Miami University in Ohio—led by Gary W. Barrett, recently a star graduate student of Eugene Odum—found that sludge often included heavy metals (lead, copper, cadmium, and zinc) from the blending of industrial with household wastes, and that the contaminants traveled up the food chain from soil to plants to animals. The EPA, however, from 1978 through the 1980s and 1990s and into the twenty-first century, encouraged so-called biosolids companies and farmers alike to accept the safety of sludge, and by 2003, 60 percent of the more than 5.5 million tons of sewer sludge was disposed of in agriculture. Farmers surrounding Augusta, Georgia, spread sludge from the city's sewer and helplessly watched their dairy cattle die. Down in Dublin, Georgia, a man grew so ill building roads with materials that included tainted hay in the slurry that he was forced into months of disability leave. Lawsuits abounded.[33]

Then there are airborne toxic effusions from blatantly scofflaw industries operating in poor, usually black-majority fringe sections of southern cities far from Louisiana's petrochemical corridor. In the Northside of Jacksonville, Florida, the Millennium Specialty Chemicals plant is the oldest continually operating manufacturer in the city. Its principal products, ironically, are scents: fragrant soaps, shampoos, gum, and toothpaste. By-product wastes, however, are literally breathtaking. "Horrible" or "The smell will just knock you down" is repeated by down-wind residents over and over. Generations of complaints have yielded no relief. Northside folks

—black, white, and brown—are working class or poor; Millennium is well connected with city government, and government responds to its burgeoning affluent constituencies south of St. Johns River.[34]

Then, too, there is the yet-unmeasurable but frightening cost of powering the region's electrical grid. Coal has been absurdly cheap for years, and most southerners' homes, offices, and shops buzz and whirr with electricity from coal-fired plants. The air above Jacksonville is hazy most days, not from the foul effusions of Millennium, but from auto and truck exhausts and great smoky plumes from giant electrical power plants. Jacksonville is hardly unusual. The residue of burning so much coal has been falling for years, accumulating on land and water. Then in 2003 and 2004, reports on soil and especially water studies from around the nation began to appear. Rivers, creeks, lakes, and ponds contained so much mercury that many should be closed to fishing, or at very least, heavy consumers of fish should have their blood tested, and all who eat fish should severely restrict their intakes.

One of the most severe reports concerned the sleepy Blackwater River in rural southeastern Virginia. The Blackwater is broad and cola-colored where it joins the Nottoway to form the Chowan at the North Carolina state line. Upriver, by Franklin, Virginia—where there looms a large saw-, pulp, and paper mill, the only industrial plant along the river's entire length— the Blackwater is substantial although not so broad; a few miles north, at Zuni, it barely deserves a bridge for U.S. Route 460. From there the river meanders northwestward through swamps, pine flatwoods, and pine plantations toward its murky origins in Prince George County. In 1996, state officials' testing of Blackwater fish tissue yielded methyl mercury readings of nearly zero. In 2002 and 2003, however, Virginia's environmental quality testers were shocked to find dangerously high mercury contamination in Blackwater fishes, especially largemouth bass and red-ear sunfish, which are local anglers' favorites. In response, the Blackwater's paid riverkeeper posted signs all along its course, warning anglers and consumers to limit themselves to a maximum of two eight-ounce meals of such fish per month. Mercury at high levels is a dangerous neurotoxin—that is, a poison affecting the brain and central nervous system. Pregnant women will pass the toxin to fetuses, which may suffer irreparable mental retardation, lack of coordination, inability to speak, blindness, and seizures.[35]

During the 1990s there had been a dioxin scare and fish warning at Franklin and downriver. The source was the Union-Camp mill (now International Paper), which spent more than $100 million installing new paper-

bleaching equipment in order to eliminate dioxin. This investment succeeded and restored Union-Camp's reputation as good corporate citizen in
the area. The source of mercury poisoning, however—not only downriver
from the mill but miles north of Franklin—remained a mystery. The fact
that waters remote from any industrial site all over North America suffer
comparable mercury pollution may have inspired the riverkeeper's theory
that airborne mercury has been accumulating in the Blackwater for many
years, settling into its muddy bottom. In 1999 came two large hurricanes
back-to-back—Dennis and Floyd—dumping so much rain that downtown
Franklin was inundated and (here the theory) tons of mercury were flushed
from wetlands, creeks, and the Blackwater's own bottom into the river's
current and the food chain. The riverkeeper is not a trained scientist but an
experienced and patient observer of landscape, and his theory seems more
than plausible. Such is the cost, it must be said, of the revolution in southern living introduced by air conditioning.

Finally, there is the tiny panhandle Florida town of Apalachicola and
its lovely bay—and the bay's oysters, arguably among the best in the world.
The head of the bay is the mouth of the Apalachicola River, which meanders
(rather like the upper Blackwater in Virginia, but much longer) through
piney woods and great swamps, much of these within the Apalachicola
National Forest. At the Georgia line there is a large impoundment called
Lake Seminole interrupting the Apalachicola's natural confluence with the
Chattahoochee and Flint rivers. The Chattahoochee is the same so beloved
by the poet Sidney Lanier, who chanted its beauteous source in Appalachian Georgia and its magnificent course down through what is now metropolitan Atlanta to Macon to the Georgia-Alabama border and finally into
Florida. All along its long trip south, the river collects nutrients for deposit
in Apalachicola Bay—once they are released from Lake Seminole, of course.
The bay's abundant life, most famously its banks of succulent oysters, de-
pends on ever-flowing waters from faraway Appalachia.

Now the bay and its oysters are threatened by Army Corps of Engineers
dredging (to enable slight barge traffic) and with loss of water in the river.
Reduced flow, expected in drought years, has become a constant, owing to
drawdowns by metro Atlanta, Macon, Columbus, and other sprawling suburbanized places, especially greater Atlanta. There, particularly in upscale
suburbs, demand for water has time and again reduced the Chattahoochee
to a proverbial trickle.[36] To be sure, human population has veritably exploded, and people must drink, bathe, and launder, drought or no. Affluent

people, however, are usually the great despoilers of nature because, given their wherewithal, they demand, use, cast off, and waste more resources than middling folk and the poor. In this case they have semibeautiful, permanent-looking mansions of brick and stone with huge kitchens and many baths. Inside their many garages are big vans and sport utility vehicles in need of frequent washing. There are swimming pools, too, and perfect lawns that are not only toxic fields but probably the most voracious wasters of precious water. Rain, after all, is so unreliable when one's turf *must* remain brilliantly green from March into December.

The desert West has ever been the scene of battles over ownership of water. By the 1980s, however—amazingly to those of us easterners who recall—comparable scarcities, scares, and struggles over water and ownership came to every region of the East. Population pressures, but also depletion and pollution of watersheds by industries and developers, made water suddenly precious (and more expensive). Too, when rivers coincide with and/or cross state lines, as in the case of the Chattahoochee-Apalachicola, eastern states such as Georgia, Alabama, and Florida have negotiated endlessly and then resorted to litigation equally protracted. One wishes that judges had the wisdom (also the power) to make decisions far simpler than Solomon's: In return for the survival and abundance of perfect oysters, give up your perfect lawns.

*You can't change history if you are [weighed down by history].*
—Clint Mathis, May 2002

*Zeus! Give me coolness! Give me the . . . [sic] will to avoid!*
—Conrad's prayer in Tom Wolfe, *A Man in Full*, 1998

## EPILOGUE

# POSTMODERN LANDSCAPES

The suburban Georgian Clint Mathis, only twenty-five, addressed the U.S. experience of invisibility (or humiliation) in quadrennial World Cup competition on the eve of 2002 match play. A fleet and improvisational striker whose boyhood hero was the unglued Argentinian star Diego Maradona, Mathis was instrumentally blunt about U.S. soccer's unglorious past: Deal with it and move on, he advised. At little later, in South Korea, Mathis—suddenly appearing with a badly fashioned Mohawk haircut before at least 3 billion *futbol* fans on global television—scored the goal that put the United States into the cup quarter-finals. By 2004 he had left the Metrostars of American professional soccer for the Hanover 96 team in Germany's premier Bundeslige. Mathis's practical philosophy of history lingers, meanwhile, reminding us of the literary historian Fred Hobson's take on southern postmodern fiction writers. Beginning with Walker Percy, Hobson figures, southern literary imagination became autochthonous, which means indigenous yet free of cultural and territorial entrapment. Unlike modernists such as William Faulkner, who were possessed by and obsessed with history, postmodernists interrogate memory in relative independence and discover the funny as often as the morbid. If with Faulkner, Pickett's Charge is still happening, with Percy it is over yet still signifying everywhere, often in absurd manifestations.[1] (In *The Thanatos Syndrome*, Percy's last novel, published in 1987, moldy, crumbling former slave quarters are converted to hip $300,000 condos.) The autochthon is genuine native, sprung from this earth, but never the captive and ever more interested in *how to* than *why*. So postmodernism as fiction or historiography might dismiss the past as casually as the mature writer Richard Ford or the maturing athlete Clint Mathis. More often, postmodernism engages and questions history with a wit and improvisation resembling Mathis's flamboyant play. Which brings me again to the brilliant work of a pair of Minnesotans and to a poetically imagined historical southern landscape.

The brothers Coen, Ethan and Joel, have been making what I would call comic regional films for years—for example, about the sentimental working classes of the Southwest in *Raising Arizona*, about southern California slacker culture in *The Big Labowsky*, and most famously, about maddeningly bland yet redemptively persistent Nordic midwesterners ("You betcha!") in *Fargo*. Finally, early in 2001, the Coens brought forth a southern version, *O Brother, Where Art Thou?* which is more historical than their previous regionals—and, one might add, allegorical, since the script is "inspired by *The Odyssey*, by Homer." The scene is the Yazoo-Mississippi Delta during the 1930s, high age of the "American Congo,"[2] when tiny white minorities coerced enormous black majorities in cotton fields and on chain gangs; when Dixie demagogues roused the rednecks with oratorical vacuity and fiddle tunes; when the legendary Robert Johnson, having exchanged his soul for virtuoso guitar licks at a Delta crossroads, riffed and yowled in smoky juke joints; and when publicity-hungry rural outlaws roared over the countryside in V-8 Fords, sticking up banks, exchanging heavy fusillades with the cops, and providing witty summaries to the press. *O Brother* offers bits of all this and more—a Klan ceremony, for instance, that resembles the overture to "Springtime for Hitler" in Mel Brooks's *The Producers*. There is even a public works project typical of the 1930s: a new dam will flood a hidden "treasure" sought by the film's three hapless protagonists. And the Delta's low, flat profile itself figures large throughout, conferring a sultry, dangerous verisimilitude. Except the summer outdoors does seem a bit yellower and mellower than searing-white reality.

*O Brother*'s landscape is really a *mondo bizarro* in which almost everything is wrong. The film opens with a chain-gang scene of black men making large rocks into small ones beside a dusty road. Then three white guys, just escaping, pop up, and we follow their wacky odyssey thereafter. A blind, elderly black man (The Oracle, a likely representative of Homer himself) appears memorably but briefly. Robert Johnson—here rendered "Tommy Johnson"—accompanies the escapees' vocal group, The Soggy Bottom Boys, as the only persistent African American character in a very Afro place and time. None of Johnson's or his contemporaries' blues are heard, either. Instead we get T Bone Burnett's remarkable assemblage of "ole-timey" white music, which is the film's plot motor and pleasure. And this, too, is wrong in another way.

Ole-timey—the descriptor spoken by the movie's blind white radio station manager and recording engineer—hardly seems appropriate to Jimmie Rodgers's "He's in the Jailhouse Now" or Louisiana governor Jimmie Davis's "You Are My Sunshine," both new in the 1930s. Ole-timey really means traditional *mountain* music, the death-y lamentations of Appalachians such as the Carter Family and the Stanley Brothers. (Ralph Stanley himself won a Grammy for his rendition of "Oh, Death" on the film's soundtrack, which became a hit CD.) I am persuaded that differing elevations and geologic morphologies yield differing sensibilities and musical styles. Not that flatlanders and highlanders were unaware and/or unappreciative of each other's musical traditions in the age of automobility and radio. Rather, I suggest, the Coen brothers and musical director Burnett were engaged here in a playful homogenization of upland and lowland white Souths. A historical Appalachian band, the Foggy Mountain Boys, becomes the ad hoc Soggy Bottom Boys, rather like one of Walker Percy's characters' hilarious misappropriations of legend. The "South," then, always a singular idea despite its irreconcilable varieties, is effectively leveled. And O Brother becomes, to me, a wistful poem to us about southern landscapes in our own lifetimes.

Consider first southern Appalachia. Never a great agricultural commodities empire like the South's piedmonts and deltas, the mountains nonetheless were home to many farmers for a long time, many of them participating in remote markets. Deep Appalachian farmland (i.e., not on plateaus and broad river valleys) was typically "cove land," narrow, fertile streamside settlements. Hardly anyone lived on heavily forested ridges and peaks. This land held rains, filtered water, and provided fuel, building materials, and selectively cut timber for downriver markets. Then came railroads and timber and coal corporations. Forests were clear-cut, and mines, whether "slope" or "deep," brought forth not only coal but slag wastes including toxic minerals that tumbled down ridges onto farms and into streams. Farmers went to work in the mines or left for the Midwest, and by 1960, agricultural census takers designated most of the subregion as either "industrial" or some rural-undeveloped descriptor.[3]

Then appeared a quantum leap in mining technology: giant machines that could strip away vegetation, dirt, and rock to reach seams of coal approximately parallel to horizon or slope. Federal and state legislation during the 1970s required operators to "restore" landscapes once coal seams were depleted, but legislators did not intend replication of original morphology and ground cover. Instead they insisted that mined landscapes be returned to some economically useful form, and this usually meant near-flat, grassy (i.e., treeless), would-be beef pastures.[4] What is called "restoration ecology" bears little or no resemblance, in any of its forms, to preservation, anyway. And so the literal leveling of the South was under way.

Now, after four decades of eastern strip-mining and "restoration," coal operators have engineered ever-larger machines and a new (during the 1990s) method called "mountaintop removal." Actually, miners now refer to mountaintops as "overlays," since peaks and ridges cover seams of low-sulfur coal; so "overlay removal" is the interchangeable term. The removal procedure begins with blowing up mountaintops; then teams of towering machines, each twenty stories high, manipulate monster drag-lines to dump millions of tons of rubble into valleys, most with streams. People living below such overlays are typically bought out, their villages to become "valley fill." The Army Corps of Engineers, which issues permits for filling watersheds in coal country, concedes that about 1,000 miles of Appalachian streams have disappeared as a result of landscape leveling. The concession may be too modest, and destructive flooding in southern West Virginia during the spring of 2002 suggested to many a causative relationship with wholesale obliteration of forests. In 1999 and again during the floods of 2002, the chief judge of the federal district court of southern West Virginia condemned government permits for valley filling as an "obvious perversity" of the Clean Water Act. The judge's first ruling was overturned on appeal, and King Coal marched on, imperiously confident in a cozy consensus with the rest of the federal judiciary, not to mention the entire executive branch.[5]

Now consider the coastal South. Here a much older and pervasive perversity of several clean water acts is evident everywhere, from Chesapeake Bay and the Delmarva Peninsula to Key West to Padre Island.[6] Mile after mile, as any beachgoer or gliding pelican has observed, any patch of land, dry or soggy, not already built upon is for sale and development. Since World War II, but explosively since the 1960s, the eastern riviera has risen, quite literally (even as parts of the mountains have fallen). Most of this low landscape consisted of wetlands of one sort or another: floodplain pine barrens, pocosins, tidal marshes, and estuarial swamps. Ocean and Gulf beaches themselves are deserts, of course, delicate, shifting, and wind-blown. Yet ironically, even as wetlands' ecological functions and beaches' impermanence became generally understood—during the 1960s—Americans herded to the coasts to live, permanently or on regular or extended holidays. Private developers and eager local and state governments obliged private landowners, but it was the Army Corps of Engineers (again) that sanctioned the dredging and straightening of creeks, the digging of canals, and the draining of thousands of acres of wetlands, using spill from massive excavations to build (relatively) high and dry landscapes for safe homesites and convenient business districts. When environmentalists recoiled in horror at losses of wildlife habitat, natural fish hatcheries, and estuarial function—as early as the mid-1960s—the corps resisted or ignored checks by Congress, the Fish and Wildlife Service, and private conservationist groups.

Florida, the lowest southern state with the longest coastline, was (and remains) the epicenter of reengineered hydrology and runaway development. During the late 1960s and early 1970s, however, in a move astounding in its secrecy and state-corporate collusion, the Walt Disney company bought miles of orange groves and wetlands near Orlando, established a private government for its domain, and built Disney World, transforming a low, pastoral landscape into a soaring tourist attraction, the biggest in the East, that supports a year-round population in sprawling suburbs. Northeast of Orlando, along the I-95 corridor from Jacksonville toward Daytona Beach, good well-drained farmland is now under wholesale conversion to gated golf course community developments. This despite the shocking news, in 2001, that Florida's water supply is compromised by pollution and limited in relation to population growth, which passed 15 million in the 2000 census, heading for at least 20 million by 2010.[7]

It is South Florida, however, that has become the most elevated of all southern coastal places. Limestone foundations support impressive skylines of office towers and multistory condominiums, from Palm Beach to Miami and from Tampa–St. Petersburg to Naples. Canalization sanctioned by the Army Corps of Engineers yields more and more (and more expensive) "waterfront" property, which is essentially fill from canal digging. Truck and auto traffic—and air pollution—renders life hectic and dangerous to all but the sequestered wealthy. Recall that Gail Fishman, the Miami native, writer, and conservationist, can no longer bear to visit her hometown and has fled to Tallahassee. Carl Hiaasen, another Miami-Dade native, famously remains, and his arch send-ups of South Floridian life appear in the *Miami Herald*. Hiaasen likely finds release, too, in his series of over-the-top "ecological" novels featuring a disaffected ex-governor, now gone feral in the Everglades, and a mad young man obsessed with highway litterers and fat-cat patrons of private hunting clubs where, for large fees, one may shoot large, exotic animals. Both characters are avenging nemeses not only of the publicly messy but of developers and their shady political enablers.[8]

What is called development in South Florida includes also a well-drained agriculture empire. Below Miami, around Homestead and Florida City, down the eastern border of Everglades National Park, endless fields of vegetables and citrus stretch out between arrow-straight canals. Workers speak *en español* and live in *colonias*. Were the air not so humid, and were the canals not carrying water away from rather than to the croplands, a visitor might mistake this surreal scene for the Imperial Valley at the bottom of California. More disorienting—is this another aspect of the "postmodern"?—on my road atlas this landscape is part of the Everglades, indicated by not only a printed label but a cartographer's symbol for wetlands. So, too, is the rural countryside northwest of Miami, up to Lake Okeechobee. A drive along U.S. Route 27 from Miami's suburban fringe reveals not grass, standing water, or alligators, however, but forty miles of continuous sugar plantations. Then, from the western shore of the lake, down Florida Route 80, which shadows the dredged and locked Caloosahatchee River toward Fort Myers, spread more miles and miles of orange groves—also in territory designated Everglades. All this inland agricultural gigantism, like the sprawling coastal built landscape, results from the twentieth century's ingenious engineering, armed with remarkable machines of war against nature. The recent multibillion-dollar, multiyear plan to restore the Everglades' natural hydrology could be termed a profoundly postmodern dialogue: The latest techno-genius engages older techno-genius in order to condemn techno-genius, sort of. We must wait and see. As observed before, there is no such thing as perfect restoration of historical landscapes, and the pressures of migration and greed are never to be underestimated.[9]

Now move a short distance inland, to the Atlantic and Gulf coastal plains, to the piney woods of legend and fact, an enormous southern subregion always rivaling Appalachia in rustic poverty. With a few notable exceptions, little of this tidewater landscape was under cultivation before the Civil War. Instead, entrepreneurs established naval stores industries, especially turpentining, among towering stands of longleaf pines. Then came rolling destruction, as we have noticed, which began in North Carolina about 1850 and then moved down through Georgia, into northern Florida, and across into Texas's big woods. Next came tobacco, sometimes peanut farming, and, later, short-lived assembly plants. The young, able, and ambitious (or desperate)—always at the forefront of migration—fled. The next big thing, beginning in West Point, Virginia, early in the twentieth century, was pulp and paper mills. They persist. (See more of them below.) Then came the industrialization of chicken and pork production, a disaster for workers and for watercourses, land, and air. The tidewaters are cursed, their people—recalling Linda Flowers's eastern Carolina-ism—"throwed away."[10]

Meanwhile, in these same sandy, piney landscapes—and indeed, into the piedmonts here and there—piney-ness itself was transformed after about 1960, as an enormous and economically powerful paper complex took shape. Denizens of (say) West Point and Franklin, Virginia; Plymouth, North Carolina; Georgetown, South Carolina; Savannah and St. Marys, Georgia; Jacksonville and Palatka, Florida; or Bogalusa, Louisiana, needed no reminders of the complex's existence. They see and smell the smoke from the mills, and they live in the physical monotony of loblolly culture, where sometimes for miles all plants are one species and all the same size—unless they drive past the ugly remains of a recent harvest. Nearly everyone else, I suspect, especially drivers on I-95 (all the way from Fredericksburg, Virginia, to Jacksonville) or I-75 below Atlanta to Lake City, Florida, or I-10 from Jacksonville to Beaumont, assumes they travel through forests. Not so. Forests—even predominantly coniferous ones—are complex ecosystems including many plant and animal species. Plantations are single-plant constructions; they are effective deserts—except (again) my allusion gives deserts an undeserved bad name. Even after the banning of the notorious pesticide DDT and the harsh herbicide 2-4-D during the early 1970s, the paper complex's vast loblolly plantations remain absolutely chemically dependent. Other pesticides assault pine pests, and Roundup—the same ubiquitous weed-killer of the suburbs—eliminates deciduous competition with conifers. A pine plantation, then, is nature grotesquely simplified, a monochromatic grid bearing little similarity to original landscapes—unless the original were (somehow) a corn or cotton field. White oaks, for instance, are not permitted, and neither is the stately longleaf, which is nearly gone. Animal life is also impoverished. Woodpeckers that normally feed on insects that damage trees have been reduced if not nearly eliminated by pesticides, along with dozens of species of ground animals, worms, fish.[11]

Automobile tourists bound for (say) Disney World who dread the hours spent among the South's endless pines might take heart, though. Disney World is likely to outlast the paper complex and its landed dominion because today there is a global oversupply of paper, and the American industry is in flux once more. West Point's pioneer mill has passed out of local ownership, changing hands twice in the past decade. Other takeovers and mergers seem to have achieved certain efficiencies, but there is little promise, really, of survival in the international market. This, in turn, is owing to the emergence of paper complexes in tropical America, which enjoy the enormous advantage of climates yielding tree "rotations" even shorter than the astounding fifteen years U.S. geneticists have achieved in loblollies. American paper production is not likely to end altogether; Americans remain the most egregious consumers of paper in the world. But if the complex is reduced substantially, one must wonder what future tidewater landscapes might have.

There is another wood products industry in the South that (one must hope) does not survive for much longer. This is the production of wood chips, virtually all for export and manufacture into composition board abroad, and the industry is unlike the paper complex altogether, with no resemblance to the complex's chemically maintained, monochromatic sprawl. It is a new industry, too. In the Pacific Northwest, timber corporations have blown sawdust and chips into the holds of Japanese vessels at Coos Bay, Oregon, for years. Southeasterners chipped their pulp bolts (as lengths of loblolly are known) but cooked and digested nearly all to make paper. Then in 1985 the Tennessee-Tombigbee Waterway opened to navigation. At $2 billion the most expensive public work to date, the project was to enrich the impoverished counties along the Alabama-Mississippi state line, from remote Tennessee hill country down to Mobile Bay. After a decade, though, it became obvious that the waterway would never replace, much less rival, the Mississippi (not to mention the rail lines and interstate trucking) in delivering midwestern commodities to the Gulf. Of operating barge traffic by the late 1990s, more than half consisted of wood chips or wood-for-chipping loads that had been harvested in those border counties, where the poverty rate, sad to report, had actually risen since the waterway opened.[12]

American corporations with familiar names, such as Weyerhaeuser and Scott Paper (now merged with Kimberly-Clark), sell the chips to (usually) Japanese buyers in Mobile. But chip suppliers are small, simple-technology operators who buy the woody cover on small private properties within easy reach of the waterway. Pine, oak, sweetgum, poplar, and hickory—any species of any size will do. All these are bush-hogged or bulldozed and then dumped into large, barrel-like contraptions with spikes inside that tear off bark and reduce sticks and logs to chips. These in turn are poured into "Tenn-Tom" barges bound for Mobile. The government of Alabama "advises" landowners to replant stripped plots, but so far as we know, few oblige. Those who do replant pine, which grows to harvestable size years before deciduous trees. Thus pine cover in the South expands yet further, far beyond fall lines, past the piedmonts and prairies into the hill country. In such country, generations of local, family-sized sawmillers, often the backbones of rural communities, find themselves without mature hardwood to cut and sell and with grim prospects for the coming generation.

Finally we come to the old plantation heartlands: the red clay piedmonts, the blackland prairies, and the deltas. It was here, during the 1960s, that sharecropping ended and that plantations, after generations of functional subdivision, were recentralized in a new regime of mechanization closely resembling big agriculture in the West. Then, during the 1980s, cotton culture suddenly returned to many parts of the South, from southeastern Virginia out to Texas, following introduction of an effective new boll weevil pesticide. Cotton had been abandoned for so long in the northeasternmost sectors of its renewed domain that no one alive during the 1980s could remember what a harvesttime field looked like. Maybe the most bizarre aspect of cotton's revival appeared in Southampton County, Virginia, the site in 1831 of the antebellum South's best-remembered slave rebellion, named after its leader, Nat Turner. About 1995, a black farm laborer named Turner was photographed driving a cotton-harvesting machine belonging to a powerful white planter, not far from Courtland, the county seat once called Jerusalem and the objective of Nat Turner and his men. No worker insurrections have been reported; on the contrary, Southampton and neighboring counties produced such bumper crops that regional gin companies were backed up so far that planters dumped truckloads onto the runways at Franklin's airport, to wait their turn at the gins. More gins were soon built, and Franklin's little airport was at last cleared for aircraft.

A few folks in revived cotton country worried about the new pesticide, which is applied aerially. Mostly they were relieved to have a substitute for tobacco, which had come upon hard times, and peanuts, which had failed too often. The earth seemed peaceful again, especially around Thanksgiving. The cotton is in and there are traces of "snow" along roadsides and in the fields. It is really cotton, of course—the debris that escaped from the harvesters or blew from trucks—but festive in a way, if one can forget the pesticide residues.[13]

🌼 More typically, however, the former plantation South is no longer recognizable as such. In the sprawling Georgia lower piedmont, the old

Natchez district, much of central and northern Louisiana, and other stretches, commodity agriculture of any specialty is largely abandoned. Pine plantations and (more likely) suburbs sprawl over thousands of disappeared Taras. Within the paper complex's conifers it is often possible to find, between the straight rows of loblollies, the remains of other straight rows, where corn and cotton once grew for generations of men and women. And the suburbs' shade-making ornamentals flourish where trees were prohibited for eons of extensive agriculture. Out in the Yazoo-Mississippi Delta, where cotton but especially corn, soybeans, and rice cultures survive, remnants of a formerly large but scattered farmworker population are now re-centralized, like the plantations themselves, in housing proximate to machinery sheds. Yet even in the Delta most people are no longer employed in farming but in a variety of industrial and service jobs, and they live in along-the-highway hamlets (as the geographer Charles Aiken terms such settlements) close to churches in clean country air.[14]

Yet is there such a thing as clean country air in any part of the contemporary South? Actually, not much. For many decades the tall stacks of midwestern electrical power plants have sent sulfates, nitrates, mercury, and other particulate matter to the Northeast, not only poisoning trees and water in the Adirondacks but penetrating the lungs of Pennsylvania farmers and Brooklyn pedestrians. More recently the vast expansion of power capacity in the South itself (as well as in the lower Midwest) has conferred on a large subregion called the mid-South the dubious distinction of having the worst air in the nation. The atmosphere over central and western Kentucky, middle and eastern Tennessee, most of western North Carolina, and most of the upper halves of Alabama and Georgia commonly contains more than six micrograms per cubic meter of particulate matter from power plants —compared with, say, zero to one microgram on average in the western half of the United States. (We do not address air pollution from autos and trucks here.) So now trees and water in southern Appalachia suffer the same grim fate as those resources in the Adirondacks. There have been massive tree die-offs in the mountains before, from disease epidemics, and there is now an epidemic of human denial that TVA smokestacks might cause tree deaths in the Great Smokies and the Black Mountains in North Carolina. There, and along the Skyline Drive in Virginia, the Park Service conspires to present evidence. Most effective, I think, are glassed-in displays at pull-offs that used to present grand vistas. Dated photographs demonstrate clear, thin air revealing those grand vistas, back in the day, alongside recent pictures that usually replicate what tourists can see for themselves: gloomy shrouds, more of the stuff of "eco-pessimism."[15]

🐾 Some things never change, though, such as humans' apparently irresistible propensity to transport and transplant exotics. The phenomenon was mentioned here in the Prologue, in reference to times long gone. More recently, southerners have demonstrated continuity. Consider first two animals, the nutria and the monk parakeet, and then an otherworldly plant.

Nutria (*Myocastor coypus*) are semiaquatic rodents native to Argentina, Brazil, Bolivia, Paraguay, and Uruguay. Smaller than beavers but larger than muskrats, nutria adults average about twelve pounds in weight. They breed year-round, and females require only 130 days to produce litters averaging 4.5 (but ranging up to 13). They are herbivores estimated to consume a quarter of their body weight each day. Nutria are also known to devour water hyacinth, tempting some wetlands managers to introduce them in order to reduce another introduced species. But nutria will eat virtually anything herbaceous, including sugarcane seedlings and other farm crops, and because of their fecundity and voracity, their populations can cripple, even destroy, wetlands' cover.[16]

During the 1930s, nutria were purposefully introduced into Louisiana to develop a "fur farming industry." The state government cooperated by listing the creature as a protected species. Before the decade was out, some had escaped—or were released—and in the bayous their numbers grew prodigiously. They indeed ate some water hyacinth, and the rodents entered sugar and grain fields and, worse, denuded natural levees at the mouth of the Mississippi. By 1950 Louisiana wildlife officers calculated the nutria population at no fewer than 20 million. In 1958 nutria were dropped from the state's protected species list, but the fur industry prevailed in returning its raw material to the list in 1965. Feral nutria populations grew exponentially, while industry captives gave up many thousands of pelts for collars, cuffs, and coat linings. Then during the mid-1980s the international fur business went bust. (The American stock market crash of 1987 was apparently the coup de grace.) By this time wild nutria damage to natural levees appeared to be permanent, and wildlife officers observed further wetlands destruction. In addition to natural levees, nutria were denuding tidal islands and shoals, which then readily washed away in storms. Nutria were a causal element in the disastrous flood of 2005.

Meanwhile, in 2000 U.S. Senator John Breaux of Louisiana persuaded Congress to fund much of a plan to control nutria and conserve (or restore) wetlands function. There would be more money for studies, replanting, and the encouragement of trapping and removal. Since then I myself have observed a grisly aspect of the last: Every day about 3:00 P.M. at St. Augustine's Alligator Farm, a large crowd flocks to witness the big-show feeding. The biggest 'gators—each addressed by its given name—hasten to the base of a raised platform from which a voluble farm employee calls the monsters to feast. The treat comes in smelly buckets full of skinless nutria carcasses. Louisiana alligators, despite their own improved population, have been unable to control now-native pests, so hardly feral Florida alligators receive the dessert.

Monk parakeets (*Myiopsitta monachus*) would seem the more agreeable introduction. Native to most of the same parts of South America as nutria, especially Argentina, monk parakeets were sold as pets and private zoo attractions some time before about 1970 in Florida, New York City and nearby New Jersey and southern Connecticut, Chicago, and probably Texas. (They also live in parts of Europe and on the island of Tenerife in the Canaries.) Inevitably some escaped or were released. By 2004, friends had spotted a few on bare winter tree limbs in Washington Park, Fort Green, Brooklyn. Other reports confirmed year-round Monks in eastern New Jersey and Connecticut, and a graduate student in Chicago did his master's thesis on the local (and growing) Monk population. In Florida, meanwhile, where few tree limbs are bare in winter, the feral Monk population is estimated at 3,000.[17]

Monks are actually parrots and are rather larger and somewhat less colorful than domesticated parakeets. Bright yellowish-green or perhaps what is called "bottle" green, adults are usually eight to ten inches long, beak to tail-tip. They eat berries, seeds of almost anything, and fruits. The graduate student in Chicago believes that there, in winter, Monks nourish themselves entirely from "backyard" bird feeders. This may be true in the Northeast, too. Some celebrants of the Monk parakeet proclaim the return, in effect, of the long-extinct Carolina parakeet, which once (like passenger pigeons) darkened the skies as it swept in force from orchard to orchard. The Monk, however, is a sedentary creature, not a migrator. It does, however, multiply rapidly, so the Monk's territories will likely increase. Here appears the problem.

Monk parakeets are sweetly domestic birds, and there is something akin to mad genius in their domestic architecture. Nests are large, relatively heavy, intricate assemblages of mainly sticks. The nests are marvels in themselves, but the genius, arguably, is in the Monk's preference of location—not in trees or atop steeples but among the supporting wires of the electrical grid. So in Florida, where the nests are most numerous, electrical companies have blamed many nonstorm power outages on the Monks. This could be true, and conceivably, the parakeets' evident territorial expansion might threaten the very foundation of contemporary southern (human) living: air conditioning, of course. Imagine the reversal of development below the Mason-Dixon Line—massive human out-migration and staggering declines in acid rain and mercury contamination. More likely: imagine a new war on terrorism, this enemy godless (we presume) and colored green.

No less bizarre—yet entirely within reality—is a near-future South where ground cover consists almost entirely of creeping bentgrass. Bentgrass, of course, is the preferred cover for golf course greens because it may be mowed short, deemed an instrumental necessity for the pushing of golf balls short distances into the cup. Bentgrass is a horror to maintain, however; it is often sickly and vulnerable to invasion by other grass species (also known as weeds). Thus we witness the frightening scene at every golf course, first thing in the morning: Workers safely encased in what resemble space suits, spraying chemicals. Here, then, was another opportunity for the biochemical companies. Monsanto and Scott (the latter a dominant seller of lawn seeds, chemicals, and maintenance equipment) conducted research at an Oregon laboratory farm on a genetically modified (GM) bentgrass that might be maintained merely with occasional, light sprayings of Roundup. Unless one is Scottish or a member of the Anarchist Golfing Association—all hating primped grasses—GM bentgrass might seem a boon: preservation of a particular aesthetic with fewer chemicals. But then federal oversight of GM plant research revealed that pollen from the Monsanto-Scott farm had drifted as far as thirteen miles away. Pollen drift is no less problematic (arguably) than the toxic. Organic farmers are ruined by pollen from GM crops of soy, corn, wheat, and papaya; GM corn calibrated for pharmaceutical use is discovered among soybeans; American GM corn is found in Mexico, which prohibits GM plants, and so on. Now what? Roundup-resistant bentgrass could take over virtually every disturbed surface and spread everywhere, most disastrously in the South, American capital of golf.[18] When, one must ask, will we have had enough of tampering with nature, especially for our comfort, convenience, and monetary enrichment, as opposed to elemental necessities of life?

🐾 This is the central question, I think, in Tom Wolfe's sprawling Atlanta novel of 1998, *A Man in Full*. Wolfe, a native of Richmond, was educated at the South's preeminent neo-Confederate college, Washington and Lee, then at Yale. Now long a stylish Manhattan boulevardier, he is a writer of breadth and witty passion. Best known perhaps for his portrait of the Mercury astronauts, *The Right Stuff* (1979), Wolfe had pilloried the hip white counterculture and the New Left during the 1960s and early 1970s. He took up fiction—most notoriously *The Bonfire of the Vanities* (1987)—but also made himself an authority on architecture and decor, as demonstrated in his *The Painted Word* (1975) and *From Bauhaus to Our House* (1981).

These last expertises crowd endless pages in *A Man in Full*, which is fiction about possessions as much as anything. The title character is Charles (always "Charlie") Croker, who is sixty years old during the late 1990s year the novel takes place. Croker is a cracker, or a plain old redneck, from way down in Georgia's southwest, the endless piney woods of Baker County. He is a big man with sturdy legs, huge arms, a shockingly expansive chest, a tree trunk of a neck, and a back that suggests to everyone that of another species. Charlie relishes comparison with a folkloric character described by country folks down in Baker, a character also named Charlie Croker: "Charlie Croker was a man in full / He had a back like a Jersey bull." The physique (and high school heroics) won him a football scholarship to Georgia Tech, where he became the legendary "60 Minute Man" during the late 1950s and early 1960s. Charlie played linebacker on defense, running back on offense. After graduation and a tour in Vietnam, he returned to Atlanta and became a real estate salesman. Tireless, crude, aggressive, reckless, and gregarious, Charlie did well and became a developer himself, and fabulously wealthy. "People don't think of Charlie as clever and shrewd," his ex-wife reflects, "they think of him more as a force of nature."[19]

At sixty Charlie has grown a paunch and suffers recurrent pain in his right knee—football casualty, naturally. But there are compensations: He has dumped his longtime wife and separated himself from their three children in favor of a new wife, a bit less than half his age, and their baby girl, whom he also ignores. Charlie runs his business, Croker Global, from a marble, glass, and dark wood office in a tower high above downtown Atlanta. Croker Global includes his vast real estate holdings, a development company, and Croker Global Foods, a coast-to-coast (not global, really) collection of warehouses from which he distributes food, mostly frozen. Charlie also has what the Internal Revenue Service accepts as an "experimental farm" down in Baker. It is called Turpmtine [sic], suggesting the landscape's industrial beginnings as turpentine plantation. Actually Turpmtine is a 29,000-acre private quail-hunting retreat for Charlie, his friends, and clients. There is a big house, a guesthouse, a gun house, stables for fifty-nine horses, shelter for hunting wagons with shock absorbers and fine leather seating, accommodations for countless dogs, servants' cabins, and not least, a "Snake House" with walls covered in snakeskins and a large glass box for live specimens, all vipers. All structures, inside and out, are designed and embellished only with the best accoutrements New York and other entrepôts of luxury purvey or skilled craftsmen may fashion from local hardwoods.

In Atlanta's most prestigious suburb (to the north, naturally), Buckhead, Charlie, his gorgeous new wife, their baby, and a company of live-in servants occupy a towering mansion of stone surrounded by many shady acres and ever-primped gardens. All this lies within a wall. The winding driveway is marked by stone pillars, and atop these are stone avians in flight, so outsized only country folk and wealthy sportsmen can identify them as quail. Charlie gets to Turpmtine from Buckhead via a private airport nearby, where he keeps a small fleet of jets, a giant Gulfstream-5 his personal one. On the G-5 Charlie keeps a flying office. His desk is the same highly polished, burled wood that adorns Turpmtine, and on the wall opposite is the possession he prizes second only to his Baker plantation: N. C. Wyeth's painting of Jim Bowie's last moment at the Alamo. On another lush avenue in Buckhead, meanwhile, Charlie's ex-wife lives in a mansion nearly as huge as his new one. Once Charlie's own abode, it is now part of his divorce payoff, in addition to what ordinary people would call staggering monthly emoluments, which permit the ex to pursue yoga, restaurants, and high culture downtown.

Wolfe loads page after page, chapter after chapter, with intimate descriptions of the shapes and contents of offices, airplanes, houses, and more— the stuff that signifies power, prestige, comfort, and quality. If this were not enough, other denizens of haute Atlanta not only do other scenes but discuss the politics and poetics of high art and male sartorial presentation. Roger White is Wolfe's master aesthete. A partner at one of the city's oldest and most powerful law firms, Wringer, Fleasom & Tick, he exudes knowledge and finesse. (Beginning with the name of the law firm, one might think Wolfe too cute. There is also an architect named Peter Prance who flatters clients' megalomania. A slimy, scheming accountant is Peepgass. A menacing prison bully is Rotto. On the other hand, Wolfe may have found monikers no less outrageous in any telephone directory or court docket.) Roger, also known as Roger Too White, is a light-complexioned African American, a Morehouse man, fraternity brother to the incumbent mayor, a graduate also of Georgia Law, a devotee of Western aesthetics, the first non-Caucasian to be a partner at Wringer, Fleasom & Tick, and probably the best-dressed man in the South—or the North, too, with the exception of Tom Wolfe. Like Wolfe, he knows clothes and their labels, exquisite automobiles, furniture and interior decor, and the history of architecture; although White is modest and careful in public, the world knows that he knows what is good in the material world.

Except for his Wyeth and his Turpmtine, and perhaps his riding boots, Charlie, possessor of so much, is actually rather indifferent. Both his wives have burdened him with things he cares little about, except when they get in his way. He has indulged the women with their dreams of delight, but to demonstrate his power rather than enjoy material delights himself. Now, however, Charlie approaches his own Alamo. A few years before, he had borrowed billions in a brash move to extend Atlanta's suburban satellites to the far north, way up into Cherokee County, at the end of I-575, which is not a loop or ring road but a dead-ending four-laner into the hills. Charlie had built edge cities above downtown before. (Wolfe actually cites Joel Garreau's paeon, *Edge City*, in the novel's text.) Now he would top everyone with a multiuse development crowned with an office tower named for himself: Croker Concourse. Charlie's timing was bad, however, and as his enormous banknotes come due, Croker Concourse is 60 percent vacant. A special team of his bank—a "workout" crew—call him to heel, then send deputies to confiscate his G-5 and its precious artwork. What to do?

Charlie cannot give up his food distribution business—justification for the Internal Revenue Service that Turpmtine was an experimental farm. Desperate and in hope that any economy in his business empire would show good faith to the bank, Charlie orders a 15 percent layoff of Croker Foods employees. One of the thousands to get his notice the next day is a young Californian, Conrad Hensley, who, hundreds of pages later, will converge with Charlie himself in Atlanta and settle many matters great and small.

Conrad is twenty-three years old, mild of temperament, hard working, physically brave but rather hapless, married to a discontented young wife, and the father of two. Briefly a community college student, Conrad experienced a shining week of recognition in a literature class taught by a generous and imaginative professor. Then his domestic circumstances sent him off to work full time in the Suicidal Freezer Unit at Croker's warehouse near Oakland. There the slightly built youth acquired enormous arms, wrists, and hands hoisting eighty-pound packages of frozen food. The workers' name for the warehouse is defined by cold, the dead weights of the goods, the frequency of spills and new ice on floors, and accidents. Only moments before Conrad received notice he was laid off, he had saved the life of a fellow worker, at great risk to his own. A few pages later, following a cursed series of breaks, Conrad is in prison for felony assault—the absurd end to his attempt to retrieve his car and to protect his honor from bonehead bureaucrats.

The East Bay jail is a nightmarish scene of claustrophobia, ceaseless howling and blasphemous chanting, and surly gangs organized by complexion. Conrad hopes to be alone, at least in his head, and pleads with his wife to send him a particular book to read. The wrong one arrives—an old scholarly collection of Stoic philosophy. Conrad is bitterly disappointed until he comes upon the section devoted to the Greco-Roman Epictetus. Brought to Rome as a slave, Epictetus, once free, later served time in jail. Perhaps experiences 2,000 years old might still apply, so Conrad, starving for distraction, reads on, and his life is changed. Epictetus instructs the desperate not how to overcome but how to endure and accept. Conrad commits to memory what he judged the essential paragraph of the philosopher's message, in the words of Zeus himself: "If it were possible I would have made your body and your possessions (those trifles that you prize) free and untrammeled," the god began. "But as things are—never forget this—this body is not yours, it is but a clever mixture of clay. I gave you a portion of our divinity, a spark from our own fire, the power to act and not to act, the will to get and the will to avoid."[20] Epictetus was autochthonous.

Avoiding the prison gangs soon becomes impossible, however, and Conrad acts, coolly and mercilessly, employing his Herculean arm strength to defeat and humiliate Rotto, the Nordic Bund bully and rapist of other prisoners. Now the Bund will demand Conrad's life. Sleepless and sweaty on his cot deep into the night, Conrad prepares himself for more of the unavoidable when a devastating earthquake wrecks the prison. Buried for a while, Conrad and his cell mate finally wriggle free. The cell mate is too badly injured for running, so Conrad, fearing the Bund more than recapture—and confident that the earthquake is Zeus's work—escapes. A little later, Conrad has found the coworker whose life he had saved at the Suicidal Freezer Unit at Croker Foods. The buddy, who has shady connections, arranges further flight and a new identity for Conrad.

Now called Connie, Conrad is in the hands of a southeast Asian underground that funnels immigrants (mostly illegal) to chicken disassembly plants and felons to faraway places and sells excellent birth certificates and drivers' licenses. The network flies Connie/Conrad to (where else?) Atlanta, then puts him into temporary quarters in nearby Chamblee, or "Chambodia." Most of his housemates—Vietnamese rather than Cambodians—work at a nearby chicken plant, but Connie's handler advises him not to work there. (Good advice.) Instead he finds a job with an agency that supplies helpers to elderly people still living at home who require assistance with maintenance, cleaning, or shopping. Connie, a man both handy and kind, becomes the most successful and popular employee. Thus came Epictetus at last to Buckhead, of all places.

By this time Charlie Croker is morbidly depressed—bankers and their lawyers are hounding him—and literally pained. His gimpy old football knee requires surgery. Charlie uses the painful recovery from knee replacement to retreat into self-pity. He will not talk or take messages, and worse, he will not walk, preferring atrophied muscles and ligaments to more pain. His wife has called Connie's agency, and Conrad arrives—polite and attentive, his new copy of the Stoics (the old was lost in the earthquake) in hand for idle moments. Of course the bored Charlie wonders what occupies the young man and persuades Conrad to read aloud a sample. Charlie will soon understand that he needs Epictetus. For he is anguished over other things, too—there are more subplots in this doorstop—particularly an offer to gain miraculous relief from his enormous debt (and avoidance of the loss of all his stuff), but in return for a public sacrifice of his honor, in this case the betrayal of his word to a friend. Charlie asks the loan of Conrad's book and, for perhaps the first time in his life, is engrossed in reading. He drives (his plane now gone, recall) down to Turpmtine with his wife, baby, Conrad, and Epictetus to study and gain the resolve to initiate settlement of his own fate.

Later—in time and in Wolfe's engrossing epilogue—it is Wes Jordan, mayor of Atlanta, who explains Charlie's reincarnation to us and to his amazed fraternity brother, Roger Too White. Instead of betraying his word to a friend, Charlie had appeared at a televised press conference and announced the abandonment of all his property—"The keys are on the table!" He declared himself a servant of "the Manager" and, furthermore, affirmed that "it's better to be a tranquil beggar by the side of the road than a perturbed plutocrat in Buckhead." "I mean," Wes declares, "he walked away from a corporation worth *hundreds of millions*. Of course, his debts were even greater . . . but still, it was unbelievable. Now he's an evangelist." Roger is incredulous: "What in God's name is he preaching?" "Nothing in *God's* name," Wes answers. Charlie had gone back to Baker County (with young wife and daughter) and begun teaching the crackers about Zeus and Epictetus, "and now he's moved into the Florida Panhandle and southern Alabama. Apparently he's dynamite, at least among white folks who go in for that sort of thing. . . . He's about to sign a syndication deal with Fox Broadcasting. . . . It's going to called *The Stoic's Hour*." So Charlie was reborn as the force of nature, a man full in himself, free at last of things not necessary—unless, of course, Fox will corrupt him with excessive cash money. One hopes, and somehow believes, this will not be.

But what of Conrad Hensley, Charlie's own messenger from Epictetus? Wes showed Roger a press clipping from an Oakland paper. The article's headline read TURN ME LOOSE, ZEUS. After Charlie had thrown off material trifles, Conrad returned to California and turned himself in to the police. In court, his sentencing judge inquired if the prisoner had thoughts about himself, his crime, and his fate. Conrad did: "It's up to you to do your part, Judge, and it's up to me to do mine." When the judge expressed surprise at Conrad's calm, Conrad averred that, indeed, "I'm completely tranquil. I feel completely in accord with nature. My body, it's nothing but a clay bowl with a quart of blood, and it's only on loan in the first place. But Zeus has given each of us a spark of his divinity, the ability to say yes to what is true, and no to what is false, and no one can take that away from you, not even in prison." "Zeus, hunh," said the judge, and then set Conrad free with two years probation—"in the custody of Zeus."[21]

Amen.

# NOTES

## PREFACE

1. C. Vann Woodward, *American Counterpoint: Slavery and Racism in the North-South Dialogue* (Boston: Little, Brown, 1971), 69.

2. See (for this and following paragraphs on the subject) Charles Reagan Wilson, "Mockingbird," in *Encyclopedia of Southern Culture*, ed. Charles Reagan Wilson and William Ferris (Chapel Hill: University of North Carolina Press, 1989), 386–87; Donald and Lillian Stokes, *Stokes Field Guide to Birds (Eastern Region)* (Boston: Little, Brown, 1996), 342 (mockingbird), 427 (white-throated sparrow); <www.mbr-pwrc.usgs.gov/id/framlist/i7030id.html>; <www.lsjunction.com/bird.htm>; and <www.birdwatching.com/stories/mockingbird.html>.

3. See William Cronon's marvelous essay, "The Trouble with Wilderness, or Getting Back to the Wrong Nature," in *Uncommon Ground: Rethinking the Human Place in Nature*, ed. William Cronon (New York: Norton, 1996), 69–90.

4. See Cronon's introduction to *Uncommon Ground*, esp. xvii.

## PROLOGUE

1. On Rawlings at Cross Creek and vicinity, see *Selected Letters of Marjorie Kinnan Rawlings*, ed. Gordon E. Bigelow and Laura V. Monti (Gainesville: University Press of Florida, 1983)—e.g., to Alfred S. Dashiell, March 1930 (pp. 36–37), on the swamps as "cracker" frontier, but especially the memoirish nature essays in her *Cross Creek* (New York: Scribner, 1942).

2. Much early writing in the field of environmental history followed a bipolar "man vs. nature" narrative, but more recent works present humanity as natural within nature and grant the nonhuman natural agency. See, e.g., the essays in William Cronon, ed., *Uncommon Ground: Rethinking the Human Place in Nature* (New York: Norton, 1996), and A. Dwight Baldwin Jr., Judith De Luce, and Carl Pletch, eds., *Beyond Preservation: Restoring and Inventing Landscapes* (Minneapolis: University of Minnesota Press, 1994). Also see Jack Temple Kirby, *Poquosin: A Study of Rural Landscape and Society* (Chapel Hill: University of North Carolina Press, 1995), esp. 1–34.

3. I refer here to the effective overturning of the "stable ecosystem" ecological science of especially Eugene P. Odum, which prevailed from the late 1940s into the 1970s, by a new science of dynamic local "patches" and unpredictability. See S. T. A. Pickett and P. S. White, *The Ecology of Natural Disturbance and Patch Dynamics* (Orlando: Academic Press, 1985), and historian Donald Worster's summary essay, "Ecology of Order and Chaos," *Environmental History Review* 14 (Spring/Summer 1990): esp. 4–16.

4. This and the following paragraph on storms are based largely on Ted Steinberg, *Acts of God: The Unnatural History of Natural Disaster in America* (New York: Oxford Uni-

versity Press, 2000), 3, 61, 70 (on Galveston), and esp. Raymond Arsenault, "The Public Storm: Hurricanes and the State in Twentieth-Century America," in *Paradise Lost? The Environmental History of Florida*, ed. Jack E. Davis and Raymond Arsenault (Gainesville: University Press of Florida, 2005), 201–32.

5. A pleasurable introduction to the St. Johns is Bill Belleville, *River of Lakes: A Journey on Florida's St. Johns River* (Athens: University of Georgia Press, 2000).

6. William Bartram, *Travels through North and South Carolina, Georgia, East and West Florida* (Charlottesville: University Press of Virginia, 1980; facsimile of the 1792 London edition), 68. Bartram's St. Johns trip consumes the following 100 pages; the travels in Alachua Indian country, 168–213; his encounters with alligators, 117–24; rattlesnakes, 262–64. For historical, scientific, and literary context, see Thomas P. Slaughter, *The Natures of John and William Bartram* (New York: Knopf, 1996). This prologue features three St. Johns voyagers—Marjorie Kinnan Rawlings and Gail Fishman, in addition to Bartram—but readers will understand that the St. Johns is famously traveled and written about. See, e.g., Charles E. Bennett, *Twelve on the River St. Johns* (Jacksonville: University of North Florida, 1989), and Belleville, *River of Lakes*, in addition to citations of Rawlings and Fishman below.

7. Audubon's binge shooting and Cooper's fiction are conveniently excerpted in Carolyn Merchant, ed., *Major Problems in American Environmental History* (Lexington, Mass.: D. C. Heath, 1993), 172–77. On nature-slaughter as endemic to frontierspeople, see Alan Taylor, "'Wasty Ways': Stories of American Settlement," *Environmental History* 3 (July 1998): 291–310; on southern white men's barbarism into the twentieth century, see Ted Ownby, *Subduing Satan: Religion, Recreation, and Manhood in the Rural South, 1865–1920* (Chapel Hill: University of North Carolina Press, 1990), esp. 21–102, 167–93.

8. Mikko Saikku, "The Extinction of the Carolina Parakeet," *Environmental History Review* 14 (Fall 1990): 1–18. The association of apples with brandy in the nineteenth-century Midwest is celebrated in Michael Pollan's essay "Johnny Appleseed" in *The Botany of Desire: A Plant's-Eye View of the World* (New York: Random House, 2001), 1–58.

9. See James Gorman, "Deep in the Swamp, an 'Extinct' Woodpecker Lives," *New York Times*, 29 April 2005. As the *Times* and other media reported, however, by mid-summer 2005 some experts judged the evidence of the sighting insubstantial.

10. In addition to Bartram, see John McPhee, *Oranges* (New York: Noonday Press, 1991).

11. See *Cross Creek*'s essay on snakes, "The Ancient Enmity," 166–79. Other incidents appear in the *Selected Letters*.

12. For the correction of "trout" with large-mouth bass, see Francis Harper, ed., *The Travels of William Bartram: Naturalist's Edition* (1958; Athens: University of Georgia Press, 1998), 355.

13. Gail Fishman, *Journeys through Paradise: Pioneering Naturalists in the Southeast* (Gainesville: University Press of Florida, 2000), provides a useful brief overview of Florida's alligator population, 49–51, 55–56. *New York Times* Photo Archive offered copies of the Ruth "Bags a 'Gator, Florida 1932" photo in advertisements in the paper—e.g., 5 July

2001, A16. On sport hunting on the St. Johns, see James J. Miller, *An Environmental History of Northeast Florida* (Gainesville: University Press of Florida, 1998), esp. 170–71, 173.

14. On "No fool, no fun," see Rawlings to Maxwell E. Perkins, 3 March 1933, in *Selected Letters*, 63–65. "Hyacinth Drift" first appeared in *Scribner's Magazine* in September 1933, then in *Cross Creek*, 342–58.

15. See Linda Flowers, *Throwed Away: Failures of Progress in Eastern North Carolina* (Knoxville: University of Tennessee Press, 1990); Deborah Fink, *Cutting into the Meatpacking Line: Workers and Change in the Rural Midwest* (Chapel Hill: University of North Carolina Press, 1998); Richard P. Horwitz, *Hog Ties: Pigs, Manure, and Mortality in American Culture* (New York: St. Martin's Press, 1998); and Rodney Barker, *And the Waters Turned to Blood* (New York: Simon and Schuster, 1997).

16. Alonzo Thomas Dill, *Chesapeake, Pioneer Papermaker: A History of the Company and Its Community* (Charlottesville: University Press of Virginia, 1968); Dill, *York River Yesterdays: A Pictorial History* (Norfolk/Virginia Beach: Donning, 1984), which is largely an illustrated history of West Point, including its early fire department.

## CHAPTER 1

1. On Tupelo, Memphis, and *Flaming Star*, see Peter Guralnick, *Last Train to Memphis: The Rise of Elvis Presley* (Boston: Little, Brown, 1994), 11–158, and Guralnick, *Careless Love: The Unmaking of Elvis Presley* (Boston: Little, Brown, 1999), 78–80, on the Presleys' lack of prejudice. For all his detail, Guralnick does not discuss Elvis's reputed Cherokee ancestry. See instead Elaine Dundy, *Elvis and Gladys* (New York: Macmillan, 1985), xv, 12–29. On "half-breeds" and the paradox of status, see Theda Perdue, *"Mixed Blood" Indians: Racial Construction in the Early South* (Athens: University of Georgia Press, 2003).

2. A useful summary of archaeological and other research is Jay K. Johnson, "The Chickasaws," in *Indians of the Greater Southeast: Historical Archaeology and Ethnohistory*, ed. Bonnie G. McEwan (Gainesville: University Press of Florida, 2000), 85–121. An apparently very large cache of Chickasaw artifacts, privately held in Tupelo, has recently been collected and returned to the tribe in Oklahoma, according to Richard Green, official historian of the Chickasaws, speaking at the Southern Historical Association annual meeting in Memphis, 5 November 2004.

3. On the evolution of agriculture among Eastern Woodland peoples of the Chesapeake region, see Helen C. Rountree, *The Powhatan Indians of Virginia: Their Traditional Culture* (Norman: University of Oklahoma Press, 1989), esp. 46–47, and James Axtell, ed., *The Indian Peoples of Eastern America: A Documentary History of the Sexes* (New York: Oxford University Press, 1981), esp. 130–33.

4. Unless noted otherwise, the summary of de Soto's adventures is derived from Charles Hudson, *Knights of Spain, Warriors of the Sun: Hernando de Soto and the South's Ancient Chiefdoms* (Athens: University of Georgia Press, 1997).

5. Quoted in typescript (p. 2) of 1747 memoir of Thomas Story (the missionary), Thomas Story Papers, North Carolina State Archives, Raleigh.

6. Karl G. Lorenz, "The Natchez of Southwest Mississippi," in McEwan, *Indians of the Greater Southeast*, 142–77.

7. On the cultural metaphoric pairing of darkness and light in ancient forests, see the essential Robert Pogue Harrison, *Forests: The Shadow of Civilization* (Chicago: University of Chicago Press, 1992), esp. 3–10; on fire in native and Euro-America, see Stephen Pyne, *Fire in America: A Cultural History of Wildland and Rural Fire* (Princeton: Princeton University Press, 1982).

8. A useful introduction (with extensive bibliography) of Amerindian cultural systems is Theda Perdue and Michael D. Green, *The Columbia Guide to American Indians of the Southeast* (New York: Columbia University Press, 2001), esp. 20–33, 151–220 passim.

9. Unless noted otherwise, this discussion of agriculture is derived from the geographer William E. Doolittle's authoritative *Cultivated Landscapes of Native North America* (New York: Oxford University Press, 2000). North America here means the present United States and Canada, although Doolittle necessarily ventures often into northern Mexico. On crop fields, see esp. 85, 87, 121–74; on gardens, 82–117; on swiddens, 174–90; and on protection, encouragement, and cultivation, 56–81.

10. On Euro-southerners' agronomy, its chemistry, and similarity to native method, see Jack Temple Kirby, *Poquosin: A Study of Rural Landscape and Society* (Chapel Hill: University of North Carolina Press, 1995), esp. 95–161. An eccentric essay on the garden model of native agriculture that goes so far as to suggest that native aesthetic wiring must have been different from Europeans' is Kirby, "Designs Necessary and Sublime: Aesthetic Meditations on Agriculture," *Harvard Design Magazine* 10 (Winter/Spring 2000): 41–46. The essay was composed and published shortly before Doolittle's *Cultivated Landscapes* appeared.

11. Doolittle, *Cultivated Landscapes*, 190.

12. Ibid., 183. Doolittle does not name the Guale, but see Rebecca Saunders, "The Guale Indians of the Lower Atlantic Coast," in McEwan, *Indians of the Greater Southeast*, 26–56, esp. 35–38, in which Saunders tilts toward characterizing the Guale as shifting farms and houses, opposing another scholar (Grant D. Jones) who argues for permanent-field agriculture.

13. See Kirby, *Poquosin*, 61–125.

14. On protection/encouragement/cultivation of sunflowers and many other small herbaceous plants (goosefoot, sumpweed, ragweed, et al.), grapes and other fruits, and nut trees, see Doolittle, *Cultivated Landscapes*, 23–81.

15. Francis Harper, ed., *The Travels of William Bartram, Naturalist's Edition* (1958; Athens: University of Georgia Press, 1998), 254.

16. Ibid., 227.

17. Mark Derr, "Network of Waterways Traced to Ancient Florida Culture," *New York Times* (Science Times NE), 23 July 2002. The report of the investigating scholars, Robert Carr, Jorge Zamanillo, and Jim Pepe, appeared in *Florida Anthropologist*, March 2002.

18. The authority on the Calusa is Randolph J. Widmer, *The Evolution of the Calusa: A Nonagricultural Chiefdom on the Southwest Florida Coast* (Tuscaloosa: University of Alabama Press, 1988), but the historian David McCally provides a perceptive brief updating in ecological context in *The Everglades: An Environmental History* (Gainesville: University Press of Florida, 1999), 31–57.

19. See Lorenz, "Natchez of Southwest Mississippi," 142–77, esp. 142, 154–55.

20. Shepard Krech III, *The Ecological Indian: Myth and History* (New York: Norton, 1999), esp. 201–8, 312. The following discussion of native hunting is based on Krech unless noted otherwise.

21. See Doolittle, *Cultivated Landscapes*, 190–92, and Rountree, *Powhatan Indians of Virginia*, 47.

22. Paul S. Martin, "Pleistocene Overkill," *Natural History* 76 (December 1967): 32–38 ("Blitzkrieg" appearing on 36); Martin, "The Discovery of America," *Science* 179 (1973): 969–74; but esp. Krech's excellent summary of Martin and his critics in *Ecological Indian*, 29–44. The following discussion of bison and the white-tailed deer is based on Krech, *Ecological Indian* also, 123–50 (esp. 121–31, 136) and 151–73.

23. James Merrill, *The Indians' New World: Catawbas and Their Neighbors from European Contact through the Era of Removal* (Chapel Hill: University of North Carolina Press, 1989), 32 (also quoted in Krech, *Ecological Indian*, 158).

24. Harper, *Travels of William Bartram*, 213–21 (quotations in order: 215, 214, 220–21).

25. Makko Saikku, "The Evolution of a Place: An Environmental History of the Yazoo-Mississippi Delta" (Ph.D. diss., University of Helsinki, 2001), 103.

26. Figures from Krech, *Ecological Indian*, 159–60. (The trade historian Krech cites is Kathryn Holland Braund.)

27. Native numbers, cultures, names, and identities during the pre-contact and early contact period, ca. 1500–1700, remain the difficult frontier of American studies, but substantial progress is being made. See Daniel Usner's important *Indians, Settlers, and Slaves in a Frontier Exchange Ecology: The Lower Mississippi Valley before 1783* (Chapel Hill: University of North Carolina Press, 1992); Patricia Galloway's exemplary *Choctaw Genesis, 1500–1700* (Lincoln: University of Nebraska Press, 1996); and the significant exploratory anthology of Charles Hudson and Carmen Chaves Tesser, eds., *The Forgotten Centuries: Indians and Europeans in the American South, 1521–1704* (Athens: University of Georgia Press, 1994).

28. The principal authority of transcontinental pathogenic exchange is Alfred W. Crosby. See his *The Columbian Exchange: Biological and Cultural Consequences of 1492* (Westport, Conn.: Greenwood, 1972), and the summative chapter, "Ills," in Crosby's *Ecological Imperialism: The Biological Expansion of Europe, 900–1900* (Cambridge: Cambridge University Press, 1986), 195–216. The following discussion of native population estimates is derived from Krech, *Ecological Indian*, 83–99.

29. Krech, *Ecological Indian*, 99; McCally, *The Everglades*, 59.

CHAPTER 2

1. See Numan V. Bartley, *The Creation of Modern Georgia* (Athens: University of Georgia Press, 1983), 1–15, esp. 12–13, on the land lottery (the descriptor "democratical" is quoted on 12). On persisting legal struggles with remaining natives and the rise of a cotton kingdom, see 16–26. Bartley quoted a slightly different wording of the frontier plantation ditty (15) used as the first epigraph. The song's first stanza is virtually ubiquitous in the literature and usually includes "Indian nation" or "Cherokee nation."

2. For dating and definitions of "plantation," see first the *Oxford English Dictionary* (compact ed., 1971), 2:2197–98. Also see Edgar T. Thompson, "The Plantation" (Ph.D. diss., University of Chicago, 1935), chap. 1, but esp. Philip D. Curtin, *The Rise and Fall of the Plantation Complex: Essays in Atlantic History* (Cambridge: Cambridge University Press, 1990), which includes references to Muslim as well as Christian European agricultural colonies in the Mediterranean, Atlantic, Caribbean, and both American continents. Since Curtin's definition of the "complex" includes slavery as constant, emancipations brought about the "fall," but Curtin well understands that slaves neither were nor are the only sort of coerced labor. This chapter charts the life of the "complex" well beyond emancipation.

3. On the London-centered global business of land speculation, the getting and marketing of plantation-made commodities, and the slave trade, see (e.g.) Charles Royster, *The Fabulous History of the Dismal Swamp Company: A Story of George Washington's Times* (New York: Knopf, 1999), esp. chap. 5, "The Age of Paper." (Royster's book title has little to do with contents.) See also Jack P. Greene, *Pursuits of Happiness: The Social Development of Early Modern British Colonies and the Formation of American Culture* (Chapel Hill: University of North Carolina Press, 1988), esp. chap. 1, and Elizabeth Fox-Genovese and Eugene D. Genovese, *The Fruits of Merchant Capital: Slavery and Bourgeois Property in the Rise and Expansion of Capitalism* (New York: Oxford University Press, 1983), esp. chaps. 1–4. The following discussion of Atlantic islands and sugar plantations is derived principally from Alfred W. Crosby, *Ecological Imperialism: The Biological Expansion of Europe, 900–1900* (Cambridge: Cambridge University Press, 1986), 70–103.

4. Philip Curtin, *The African Slave Trade: A Census* (Baltimore: Johns Hopkins University Press, 1979), remains (in my opinion) the best estimate of Africans imported into the New World. On prisoners, see Robert Reps Perkinson, "The Birth of the Texas Prison Empire" (Ph.D. diss., Yale University, 2001), esp. chaps. 1, 2, 4. An excellent (and brief) introduction to the Fujianese diaspora is Kenneth Pomeranz and Steven Topic, *The World That Trade Created: Society, Culture, and the World Economy, 1400 to the Present* (Armonk, N.Y.: M. E. Sharpe, 1999), 9–11.

5. Strickland quoted in John Taylor (of Caroline), *Arator: Being a Series of Agricultural Essays, Practical and Political: In Sixty-Four Numbers*, ed. M. E. Bradford (1813 and later dates; Indianapolis: Liberty Classics, 1977), 66. See also Taylor's subsequent references to Strickland, and editor Bradford's notes, 65, 72, 75, 99, 105–6. Following paragraphs on Taylor are based on *Arator* (page numbers for quotations are provided in the text);

Robert E. Stalhope, *John Taylor of Caroline: Pastoral Republican* (Columbia: University of South Carolina Press, 1980); and esp. Taylor's agronomy, Avery Craven, *Soil Exhaustion as a Factor in the Agricultural History of Virginia and Maryland, 1606–1860* (Urbana: University of Illinois Press, 1926), 99–103.

6. On the East Anglian "revolution," see G. E. Mingay, ed., *The Agricultural Revolution: Changes in Agriculture, 1650–1880* (London: Adam and Charles Black, 1977), 1–68, 115–25. On the Anglo-centricity of Chesapeake planters, see T. H. Breen, *Tobacco Culture: The Mentality of the Great Tidewater Planters on the Eve of the Revolution* (Princeton: Princeton University Press, 1985). On the switch to grains, see Carville V. Earle, *The Evolution of a Tidewater Settlement Pattern: All Hallow's Parish, Maryland, 1650–1783* (Chicago: University of Chicago Geography Department, 1975), esp. 24–30; Allan Kulikoff, *Tobacco and Slaves: The Development of Southern Cultures in the Chesapeake, 1680–1800* (Chapel Hill: University of North Carolina Press, 1986), esp. 48; and esp. *The Diary of Colonel Landon Carter of Sabine Hall, 1752–1778*, ed. Jack P. Green, 2 vols. (Charlottesville: University Press of Virginia, 1965), 1:157–62, 172, 337 (on English agronomy), 2:611 (on turnips in rotation). An important demurrer to an English agricultural "revolution" is G. E. Fussell, "Science and Practice in Eighteenth-Century British Agriculture," *Agricultural History* 43 (1969): 7–18.

7. See David F. Allmendinger Jr., *Ruffin: Family and Reform in the Old South* (New York: Oxford University Press, 1990), esp. 8–56. Quotation from *Incidents of My Life: Edmund Ruffin's Autobiographical Essays*, ed. David F. Allmendinger Jr. (Charlottesville: University Press of Virginia for the Virginia Historical Society, 1990), 192.

8. On European chemistry, esp. Liebig's in England, see J. D. Sykes, "Agriculture and Science," in *The Victorian Countryside*, ed. G. E. Mingay (London: Routledge and Kegan Paul, 1981), 1:260–72. Ruffin's response and significance is summarized in *Edmund Ruffin: Nature's Management—Writings on Landscape and Reform, 1822–1859*, ed. Jack Temple Kirby (Athens: University of Georgia Press, 2000), xxiii–xxv.

9. Ruffin's South Carolina Institute address was printed eight years later in *Southern Planter* 20 (July 1860): 401–8, and (August 1860): 481–86. This version (slightly different from the original text) is reprinted in Kirby, *Edmund Ruffin*, 323–44 (quotation, 337).

10. On nineteenth-century agricultural "improvers" north and south, and the significance of guano, see Steven Stoll's invaluable *Larding the Lean Earth: Soil and Society in Nineteenth-Century America* (New York: Hill and Wang, 2002), esp. 188–90. Ironically (I think), Avery Craven acknowledged and applauded the introduction of guano and credited it above marl in the Chesapeake's successful "reform." See Craven, *Soil Exhaustion*, esp. 148.

11. William M. Mathew, *Edmund Ruffin and the Crisis of Slavery in the Old South: The Failure of Agricultural Reform* (Athens: University of Georgia Press, 1988). I have treated Craven, Ruffin, and historical memory of "soil exhaustion" in somewhat more detail in *Poquosin*, 114–19, and *Edmund Ruffin*, xii–xviii. On the antebellum southern food supply and exports, see the works of the historical geographer Sam Bowers Hilliard:

Hog Meat and Hoecake: Food Supply in the Old South, 1800–1860 (Baton Rouge: Louisiana State University Press, 1972) and Atlas of Antebellum Southern Agriculture (Baton Rouge: Louisiana State University Press, 1984), pts. 5–7.

12. Frederick Law Olmsted, A Journey in the Seaboard Slave States, with Remarks on their Economy (New York: Dix and Edwards, 1856). My larger treatment of Olmsted in Poquosin, esp. 95, 105–11, 114, 116, and 123–24, considers Olmsted's travel accounts, his published letters, and Laura Wood Roper's biography, FLO: A Biography of Frederick Law Olmsted (Baltimore: Johns Hopkins University Press, 1973). On Bodenlosigkeit, see Simon Schama, "The Unloved American: Two Centuries of Alienating Europe," New Yorker, 10 March 2003, 34–39 (quotation, 35).

13. On the rhetoric of eastern "improvers," see Stoll, Larding the Lean Earth. On southern migrants (and Lyell), see James David Miller, South by Southwest: Planter Emigration and Identity in the Slave South (Charlottesville: University Press of Virginia, 2003). On migration and health, see Conevery Bolton Valencius, The Health of the Country: How American Settlers Understood Themselves and Their Land (New York: Basic Books, 2002), esp. chap. 5. Quotation from Don H. Doyle, Faulkner's County: The Historical Roots of Yoknapatawpha (Chapel Hill: University of North Carolina Press, 2001), 103. Rosa Coldfield quoted in William Faulkner, Absalom, Absalom! (1936; New York: Vintage, 1951), 17.

14. Population data from Hilliard, Atlas of Antebellum Agriculture and Historical Statistics of the United States, Colonial Times to 1957 (Washington, D.C.: GPO, 1961). Ruffin genealogy generalized is derived from Allmendinger, Ruffin, chap. 1. The following discussion of landscape is indebted to J. B. Jackson, Discovering the Vernacular Landscape (New Haven: Yale University Press, 1984), esp. 1–8, and the work of Jackson's successor, John R. Stilgoe, e.g., Common Landscape of America, 1580–1845 (New Haven: Yale University Press, 1982).

15. On sugar plantations and labor, see J. Carlyle Sitterson, Sugar Country: The Cane Sugar Industry in the South, 1753–1950 (Lexington: University of Kentucky Press, 1953). On Virginia grain planters, see Kirby, Poquosin, 46–47, and Gregg L. Michel, "From Slavery to Freedom: Hickory Hill, 1850–1880," in The Edge of the South: Life in Nineteenth-Century Virginia, ed. Edward L. Ayers and John C. Willis (Charlottesville: University Press of Virginia, 1991), 109–33.

16. Jack Temple Kirby, Rural Worlds Lost: The American South, 1920–1960 (Baton Rouge: Louisiana State University Press, 1987), esp. 52–53, 66, 140–44, 147, which summarizes and extends a large literature; also Thomas D. Clark, Pills, Petticoats, and Plows: The Southern Country Store (Indianapolis: Bobbs-Merrill, 1944). C. Vann Woodward, Origins of the New South, 1877–1913 (Baton Rouge: Louisiana State University Press, 1951), 178–85, suggests the bucket line of exploitation ending with soils.

17. My information on velvet beans is derived from my maternal grandmother (1884–1969), who cherished them and whose father, a large farmer in Florence County, S.C., faithfully planted them in his corn, and from e-mail exchanges (January 2000) with Dr. Marjatta Eilitta, a Florida-based biologist conducting research to assist small

farmers in the South and Mesoamerica. She suspects that velvet beans produced more L-dopa the nearer they were to the equator; so South Carolina beans likely had percentages closer to 3 than 9.

18. See Kirby, *Poquosin*, esp. 110–14.

19. See Kirby, *Rural Worlds Lost*, 67, 139 (on through-and-through), 148–50 (on commissaries), and 188–90 (on diet, re discussion following), and Pete Daniel, *Breaking the Land: The Transformation of Cotton, Tobacco, and Rice Cultures since 1880* (Urbana: University of Illinois Press, 1985), 240–55 (on the context of reconfiguring cotton culture).

20. Discussion following of the demise of the postbellum plantation complex is derived from Daniel, *Breaking the Land*, bk. 4; Kirby, *Rural Worlds Lost*, 1–24; and esp. the historical geographer Charles S. Aiken's *The Cotton Plantation South since the Civil War* (Baltimore: Johns Hopkins University Press, 1998), esp. pt. 1.

21. H. L. Mitchell, *Mean Things Happening in This Land: The Life and Times of H. L. Mitchell, Co-Founder of the Southern Tenant Farmers' Union* (Montclair, N.J.: Allanheld, Osmun, 1979), 344–45.

## CHAPTER 3

1. On Beverley, Byrd, and hogs in southeastern Virginia and northeastern North Carolina, see Jack Temple Kirby, *Poquosin: A Study of Rural Landscape and Society* (Chapel Hill: University of North Carolina Press, 1995), 98–99, 17 (Byrd quotation), 102–3.

2. Grady McWhiney, *Cracker Culture: Celtic Ways in the Old South* (Tuscaloosa: University of Alabama Press, 1988), 51–79, esp. 53, 55, 66–67, 69. (McWhiney's readers are not obliged to accept his Celtic-centric ethnography to appreciate the importance of his other treatments of the white-majority culture.) See also Forrest McDonald and Grady McWhiney, "The South from Self-Sufficiency to Peonage: An Interpretation," *American Historical Review* 85 (December 1980): 1095–1118.

3. Frances Anne Kemble, *Journal of a Residence on a Georgian Plantation in 1838–1839*, ed. John A. Scott (1863; Athens: University of Georgia Press, 1984), 110–11, 182 (last quotation). For the larger landscape and context, with considerable detail on Butler and especially his managers, see Mart A. Stewart, *"What Nature Suffers to Growe": Life, Labor, and Landscape on the Georgia Coast, 1680–1920* (Athens: University of Georgia Press, 1996).

4. [Edmund Ruffin], "Publication of the Byrd Manuscripts," *Farmers' Register* 9 (31 October 1841): 577; A. B. Longstreet, *Georgia Scenes* (1835; New York: Sagamore Press, 1957); Joseph G. Baldwin, *The Flush Times of Alabama and Mississippi* (1853; New York: Sagamore Press, 1957), 2 (quotation). Definition of "cracker" from McWhiney, *Cracker Culture*, vii.

5. Daniel R. Hundley, *Social Relations in Our Southern States*, ed. William J. Cooper Jr. (1860; Baton Rouge: Louisiana State University Press, 1979).

6. On swine perspiration and propagation, see Merrill K. Bennett, "Aspects of the Pig," *Agricultural History* 44 (April 1970): 223–35. On feral hogs' aggressiveness and (in

text following) their omnivorous tastes, see Gordon Grice, *The Red Hourglass: Lives of the Predators* (New York: Delacorte Press, 1998), 175–202. Also, on barbeque, swine, and religious tradition and swine as factotums in eastern North Carolina, see Michael D. Thompson, "High on the Hog: Swine as Culture and Commodity in Eastern North Carolina" (Ph.D. diss., Miami University, 2000), esp. 8–13, 94–138.

7. Documents relating to Ruffin's antirange campaign are available in *Edmund Ruffin: Nature's Management: Writings on Landscape and Reform, 1822–1859*, ed. Jack Temple Kirby (Athens: University of Georgia Press, 2000), 47–99. On the demise of relatively egalitarian rural communities in the North, see John Mack Faragher, *Sugar Creek: Life on the Illinois Prairie* (New Haven: Yale University Press, 1986), esp. pt. 5.

8. See Kirby, *Poquosin*, 32–33, 205, and Cecil C. Frost and Lytton J. Musselman, "History and Vegetation of the Blackwater Ecologic Preserve [Isle of Wight Co., Va.]," *Castanea* 52 (1987): 16–46.

9. These paragraphs on the naval stores industry are based principally on Robert Outland's outstanding work on the subject: *Tapping the Pines: The Naval Stores Industry in the American South* (Baton Rouge: Louisiana State University Press, 2004). His chap. 4, "Suicidal Harvest," depicts the sudden crash of North Carolina's longleaf forests. On northeastern North Carolina turpentining and complaints about overboxing, see my *Poquosin*, 32–33, 204–5. "First Wave" industries (in contemporary parlance) are nineteenth/early-twentieth-century ones, such as lumber and cotton textiles; "Second Wave" describes post–World War II enterprises such as auto and airplane manufacturing, communications, etc. See Philip Scranton, ed., *The Second Wave: Southern Industrialization from the 1940s to the 1970s* (Athens: University of Georgia Press, 2001).

10. This section on the Civil War as environmental experience is based largely on "The American Civil War: An Environmental View," my online article for TeacherServe, the National Humanities Center's website. But see also Charles Royster, *The Destructive War: William Tecumseh Sherman, Stonewall Jackson, and the Americans* (New York: Knopf, 1991), esp. on the burning of Columbia, S.C. On animals, disease, and death, see G. Terry Sharrer, *A Kind of Fate: Agricultural Change in Virginia, 1861–1920* (Ames: Iowa State University Press, 2000), esp. 9–18.

11. On New South economic expansion, see C. Vann Woodward's classic *Origins of the New South, 1877–1913* (Baton Rouge: Louisiana State University Press, 1951), chaps. 5–6, and especially Edward L. Ayers, *The Promise of the New South: Life after Reconstruction* (New York: Oxford University Press, 1992), esp. 9–13 (on railroad expansion).

12. See Michael Williams, *Americans and Their Forests: A Historical Geography* (Cambridge: Cambridge University Press, 1989), 193–237 (on the Great Lakes), and for following paragraphs on the South, 238–88 (242, 264–67 on J. H. Kirby). On the Midwest and the lumber business, see also William Cronon, *Nature's Metropolis: Chicago and the Great West* (New York: Norton, 1991), 148–206. On the Hatfield-McCoy feud, see Altina L. Waller, *Feud: Hatfields, McCoys, and Social Change in Appalachia, 1860–1900* (Chapel Hill: University of North Carolina Press, 1988), esp. 158–234. On Camp Manufacturing, see Kirby, *Poquosin*, 210–16, 222–23.

13. On the spirit and definitions of early conservation, see (among many other sources) Char Miller's recent biography, *Gifford Pinchot and the Making of Modern Environmentalism* (Washington, D.C.: Island Press, 2001), esp. pt. 2. On the criminalization of firing forests and the concurrent final closing of the range in North Carolina, see Thompson, "High on the Hog," esp. 34–65.

14. Forest arson was my subject in Kirby, *The Countercultural South* (Athens: University of Georgia Press, 1995), 34–35, 52–56 (Shea quotation, 52; Camp quotation, 53). On the larger context of a southern woods-firing tradition, one is referred to Stephen J. Pyne's classic, *Fire in America: A Cultural History of Wildland and Rural Fire* (Princeton: Princeton University Press, 1982), 71–83, 143–60.

15. Bertrand and Baird (above) quoted in Kirby, *Countercultural South*, 54–55. On the scale and scope of moonshining in the South, see Jack Temple Kirby, *Rural Worlds Lost: The American South, 1920–1960* (Baton Rouge: Louisiana State University Press, 1987), 204–14.

16. Kathy Mason, "North Dakota's Accidental National Park" (paper, American Society for Environmental History, 28 March 2003, Providence, R.I.). See also Mason's dissertation, "National Parks before the Park Service" (Miami University, 1999).

17. On Muir and nature language, see Robert L. Dorman, *A Word for Nature: Four Pioneering Environmental Advocates, 1845–1913* (Chapel Hill: University of North Carolina Press, 1998), 103–72. On Smuts, see Peder Anker, *Imperial Ecology: Environmental Order in the British Empire, 1895–1945* (Cambridge: Harvard University Press, 2001), 41–75. Lyrics to "Bruca Manigua" in liner notes to Ry Cooder, prod., *Ibrahim Ferrer* (Nonesuch Records/Warner Music Group Company, 1999).

18. On early southern Appalachia, see Margaret Lynn Brown, *The Wild East: A Biography of the Great Smoky Mountains* (Gainesville: University Press of Florida, 2000), esp. 1–48 (Cherokee myth, 11), and Donald Edward Davis, *Where There Are Mountains: An Environmental History of the Southern Appalachians* (Athens: University of Georgia Press, 2000), chaps. 1–6.

19. Hear T Bone Burnett, prod., *O Brother, Where Art Thou?—Music from a Film by Joel Coen & Ethan Coen* (Mercury, 2001).

20. Timothy Silver, *Mount Mitchell and the Black Mountains: An Environmental History of the Highest Peaks in Eastern America* (Chapel Hill: University of North Carolina Press, 2003), esp. chaps. 3–4.

21. For the Smokies narrative here, I rely principally on Brown, *Wild East* (e.g., 1900 communities, 13; lumber estimates, 67). But see also Daniel S. Pierce, *The Great Smokies: From Natural Habitat to National Park* (Knoxville: University of Tennessee Press, 2000), and Davis, *Where There Are Mountains*, chap. 7. One might also reflect on Christopher Camuto's dense and ruminative *Another Country: Journeying toward the Cherokee Mountains* (Athens: University of Georgia Press, 2000). On 1930s TVA dams and community removals, see Michael J. McDonald and John Muldowny, *TVA and the Dispossessed: The Resettlement of Population in the Norris Dam Area* (Knoxville: University of Tennessee Press, 1982).

22. Quotation ("strip-mined") in Brown, *Wild East*, 264; for the wild boars' story, see 86, 249, 252–56, 264.

23. Larry Anderson, *Benton MacKaye: Conservationist, Planner, and Creator of the Appalachian Trail* (Baltimore: Johns Hopkins University Press, 2002); Paul S. Sutter, *Driven Wild: How the Fight against Automobiles Launched the Modern Wilderness Movement* (Seattle: University of Washington Press, 2002), esp. chap. 5 on MacKaye and the Appalachian Trail.

CHAPTER 4

1. Don Graham, *No Name on the Bullet: A Biography of Audie Murphy* (New York: Viking, 1989), 16. Murphy's father's desertion was devastating, but it did not occur until 1940. See ibid., 1–25, on Murphy's first eighteen years; 26–103, on his army service; quotation on Murphy's lack of religion, 81. Murphy treated his boyhood only briefly in *To Hell and Back* (1949; rpt., Blue Ridge Summit, Pa.: TAB Books, 1988), 4–9; Murphy quoted on killing the Italians, 10–11.

2. David D. Lee, *Sergeant York, an American Hero* (Lexington: University Press of Kentucky, 1985), 5 (York quotation), 1–26 (background and early life), 27–68 (war service and hero status).

3. On southern out-migration, see Jack Temple Kirby, *Rural Worlds Lost: The American South, 1920–1960* (Baton Rouge: Louisiana State University Press, 1987), 309–33. More specifically on "Okies" and "Texies," see James N. Gregory, *American Exodus: The Dust Bowl Migration and Okie Culture in California* (New York: Oxford University Press, 1989). On upland southerners, see Chad Berry, *Southern Migrants, Northern Exiles* (Urbana: University of Illinois Press, 2000).

4. Marjorie Kinnan Rawlings, *The Yearling* (New York: Scribner, 1938). On the ethics and rituals of elite sportsmen, see John F. Reiger, *American Sportsmen and the Origins of Conservation* (1975; 3rd rev. ed., Corvallis: Oregon State University Press, 2001). On hunting narratives in the South, see Stuart A. Marks, *Southern Hunting in Black and White: Nature, History, and Ritual in a Carolina Community* (Princeton: Princeton University Press, 1991).

5. Grady McWhiney, *Cracker Culture: Celtic Ways in the Old South* (Tuscaloosa: University of Alabama Press, 1988), 105–45. On Harry Crews, one should begin with *A Childhood: The Biography of a Place* (New York: Harper and Row, 1978). For cockfighting, see Kirby, *Rural Worlds Lost*, 300–301, 303–4, and Alex Haley, *Roots* (New York: Doubleday, 1976).

6. A. B. Longstreet, *Georgia Scenes* (1835; New York: Sagamore Press, 1957), 97–105 ("The Gander Pulling"), 100 (on the setting), 104 (on the climax).

7. See (on slaughter, extinctions, and market hunting, this paragraph and below) Nicolas W. Proctor, *Bathed in Blood: Hunting and Mastery in the Old South* (Charlottesville: University Press of Virginia, 2002); Marks, *Southern Hunting in Black and White*, esp. 36, 190; Reiger, *American Sportsmen*, 1–104; Mikko Saikku, "The Extinction of the

Carolina Parakeet," *Environmental History Review* 14 (Fall 1990): 1–18; and Jack Temple Kirby, *Poquosin: A Study of Rural Landscape and Society* (Chapel Hill: University of North Carolina Press, 1995), esp. 56–58 (quotation on duck gunners at Back Bay, 56). A fascinating addendum to the literature of apples (and alcohol) is Michael Pollan, *The Botany of Desire: A Plant's-Eye View of the World* (New York: Random House, 2001), 1–58. On apples at Hermitage, see Debi Back, "The Women of Hermitage" (M.A. thesis, Miami University, 2001).

8. John Mack Faragher, *Daniel Boone: The Life and Legend of an American Pioneer* (New York: Henry Holt, 1992), esp. 31, 28, 49, 54–55, 66–67, 315.

9. Reiger, *American Sportsmen*, is of course the premier champion of elite hunters and anglers as originators of conservation. See his introduction, 1–4, on the argument, and 5–44, on antebellum proto-conservationists, including William Elliott of South Carolina.

10. Elliott has been neglected by scholars, but Willie Lee Rose provided excellent context on the region and a few details on Elliott in *Rehearsal for Reconstruction: The Port Royal Experiment* (1964; New York: Vintage, 1967), 5, 9–10, 108, 110, 118, 119–20 (quotation, 120), 133, 242, 248, 358–59. A copy of the Sully portrait is frontispiece to William Elliott, *Carolina Sports by Land and Water* (1859; Columbia: The State Co., 1918); page numbers for subsequent references to the 1918 edition are provided parenthetically in the text.

11. A. B. Longstreet, "The Fox-Hunt," in *Georgia Scenes*, 152–71 (quotation, 152). A sketch of William Somerville is to be found in Sir Paul Harvey, comp. and ed., *The Oxford Companion to English Literature* (1952; Oxford: Oxford University Press, 1967), 676. Somerville titled his long poem "The Chace"; Longstreet Americanized the spelling to "Chase."

12. *Matanza* (singular) is, in the 1959 ed. of *Cassell's Spanish Dictionary*, "action of slaughtering; cattle to be slaughtered; massacre, butchery, slaughter," and colloquially, "obstinacy" and "eagerness of pursuit."

13. The historical literature on the Matanzas Massacre—the redundancy is accepted—is quite large. James J. Miller, *An Environmental History of Northeast Florida* (Gainesville: University Press of Florida, 1998), summarizes as well as describes cattle operations on the plain. See esp. 110–14, 122–26.

14. Quotations from Kirby, *Poquosin*, 56–57. Following paragraphs are derived from ibid., 56–58, and Reiger, *American Sportsmen*, esp. xi–xii, xiv, 98–102.

15. Important historians of honor and premodern southern culture are Bertram Wyatt-Brown, *Southern Honor: Ethics and Behavior in the Old South* (New York: Oxford University Press, 1982); Wyatt-Brown, *The Shaping of Southern Culture: Honor, Grace, and War, 1760s–1880s* (Chapel Hill: University of North Carolina Press, 2001); Edward L. Ayers, *Vengeance and Justice: Crime and Punishment in the Nineteenth-Century South* (New York: Oxford University Press, 1984); Elliott J. Gorn, "'Gouge and Bite, Pull Hair and Scratch': The Social Significance of Fighting in the Southern Backcountry," *Ameri-*

*can Historical Review* 90 (February 1985): 18–43; and McWhiney, *Cracker Culture.* My exposition here is based especially on Ted Ownby, *Subduing Satan: Religion, Recreation, and Manhood in the Rural South, 1865–1920* (Chapel Hill: University of North Carolina Press, 1990).

16. On fairs, demonstration, and home demonstration agents' work and influence, in addition to Ownby, *Subduing Satan*, 64, 188–93, see Lu Ann Jones, *Mama Learned Us to Work: Farm Women in the New South* (Chapel Hill: University of North Carolina Press, 2002), esp. 107–70. The vignette on Hertford Co., N.C., is from Kirby, *Poquosin*, 238–40, and the Ham and Eggs movement is from Kirby, *Rural Worlds Lost*, 116.

17. On farm women as producer-marketers during the 1920s and 1930s, see Deborah Fink, *Agrarian Women: Wives and Mothers in Rural Nebraska, 1880–1940* (Chapel Hill: University of North Carolina Press, 1992), chaps. 5 and 7, and esp. Jones, *Mama Learned Us to Work*, 171–84.

18. On the chicken business from the 1920s to ca. 1985, see Kirby, *Rural Worlds Lost*, 355–60, and, more recently, William Boyd, "Making Meat: Science, Technology, and American Poultry Production," *Technology and Culture* 42 (October 2001): 631–64.

19. Farmer quoted on p. 63 in Michael Specter, "The Extremist," *New Yorker*, 14 April 2003, 52, 54–58, 59–67, esp. 62–63 on contemporary Delmarva chicken farming; this chapter's second epigraph appears on p. 63. In addition, an excellent summary of the treatment of animals during the past three decades is Peter Singer, "Animal Liberation at 30," *New York Review of Books*, 15 May 2003, 23–26; comparisons of U.S. and European Union regulations on 26.

20. Donald G. McNeil Jr., "KFC Supplier Accused of Animal Cruelty: Rights Group to Release Film Showing Chickens Being Abused," *New York Times*, 20 July 2004.

21. On Tyson, see David Barboza, "Chicken Well Simmered in a Political Stew: Tyson Fosters Ties to Officials but Is Unable to Avoid Scrutiny," *New York Times*, 1 January 2001. On processing plants and labor, see Deborah Fink, *Cutting into the Meatpacking Line: Workers and Change in the Rural Midwest* (Chapel Hill: University of North Carolina Press, 1998), and Leon Fink, *The Maya of Morganton: Work and Community in the Nuevo New South* (Chapel Hill: University of North Carolina Press, 2003).

22. On the Chesapeake and oysters, see John J. Alford, "The Role of Management in Chesapeake Oyster Production," *Geographical Review* 63 (January 1973): 44–54, and esp. John R. Wennersten, *The Chesapeake: An Environmental Biography* (Baltimore: Maryland Historical Society, 2001), esp. chap. 4. (The observation on Indiana oyster consumption and shell paths is my own, supplemented by the recollections of the late Carrie B. Boggs [b. 1902] of Salem, Ind.)

23. See Rodney Barker, *And the Waters Turned to Blood* (New York: Simon and Schuster, 1997), an investigative journalist's account of Burkholder's ordeal; William J. Broad, "In a Sealed Lab, a Warrior against Pollution," *New York Times*, 25 March 1997, the *Science Times* profile of Burkholder; and on the growth of industrial swine culture, Michael D. Thompson, "High on the Hog: Swine as Culture and Commodity in Eastern North Carolina" (Ph.D. diss., Miami University, 2000), esp. pt. 3.

24. Jennifer S. Lee, "Neighbors of Vast Hog Farms Say Foul Air Endangers Their Health," *New York Times*, 11 May 2003 (Sunday news section).

25. *Forbes*, 13 October 1997, quoted in Thompson, "High on the Hog," 169.

26. On sows and space and the European Union, see Singer, "Animal Liberation at 30," 26.

27. Graham, *No Name on the Bullet*, 314.

CHAPTER 5

1. Michael Pollan, "The (Agri)Cultural Contradictions of Obesity," *New York Times Magazine*, 12 October 2003. On Mississippi's fatness rank, see the *Jackson Clarion-Ledger*, 18 September 2003.

2. On the late 2005 corn subsidy projection, see Alexei Barrionuevo, "Mountains of Corn and a Sea of Farm Subsidies," *New York Times*, 9 November 2005.

3. The great authority is Alfred W. Crosby, *The Columbian Exchange: Biological and Cultural Consequences of 1492* (Westport, Conn.: Greenwood Press, 1972); also his *Ecological Imperialism: The Biological Expansion of Europe, 900–1900* (Cambridge: Cambridge University Press, 1986). Below, on the diffusion of maize to Europe and other continents, see (e.g.) Felipe Fernandez-Armesto, *Near a Thousand Tables: A History of Food* (New York: Free Press, 2002), esp. 167, 169, 176–79, 185.

4. Elizabeth W. Etheridge, *Butterfly Caste: A Social History of Pellagra in the South* (Westport, Conn.: Greenwood, 1972), 43–48.

5. Daphne A. Roe, *A Plague of Corn: The Social History of Pellagra* (Ithaca: Cornell University Press, 1973), 41.

6. See Alan M. Kraut, *Goldberger's War: The Life and Times of a Public Health Crusader* (New York: Hill and Wang, 2003), and more compactly, on the pellagra studies, Roe, *Plague of Corn*, 99–127.

7. Kraut, *Goldberger's War*.

8. Quoted in Etheridge, *Butterfly Caste*, 76.

9. Etheridge, *Butterfly Caste*, 29, 48, 231 n. 15; Roe, *Plague of Corn*, 53–54.

10. See Roe, *Plague of Corn*, 128–29; Etheridge, *Butterfly Caste*, 202–3.

11. Among other works on the southern poor and the New Deal, see Jack Temple Kirby, *Rural Worlds Lost: The American South, 1920–1960* (Baton Rouge: Louisiana State University Press, 1987), esp. 51–79.

12. On food variety and supply, see Joe Gray Taylor, *Eating, Drinking, and Visiting in the South: An Informal History* (Baton Rouge: Louisiana State University Press, 1982), 3–14 (on frontiers); Sam Bowers Hilliard, *Hog Meat and Hoecake: Food Supply in the Old South, 1800–1860* (Carbondale: Southern Illinois University Press, 1972), 51 (on vegetables); plus Hilliard's invaluable *Atlas of Antebellum Southern Agriculture* (Baton Rouge: Louisiana State University Press, 1984).

13. Harriet Martineau quoted in Taylor, *Eating, Drinking, and Visiting*, 57; see also 53–64 in his chapter on plantation fare, called "High on the Hog"; 36–51 on vegetables available to nearly everyone; and 83–91 on slaves' food. In addition to remem-

bered rhapsodies to velvet beans by my grandmother (Theodosia Yarbrough Palmer, d. 1969), information esp. on velvets as hallucinogens is derived from e-mail exchanges with a tropical ethnobiologist, February 2001, who was conducting research in Central America and searching for velvets in the U.S. Southeast.

14. I am indebted here and in following paragraphs esp. to Richard Westmacott, *African-American Gardens and Yards in the Rural South* (Knoxville: University of Tennessee Press, 1992), but one might peruse also Henry Glassie, *Folk Housing in Middle Virginia: A Structural Analysis of Historic Artifacts* (Knoxville: University of Tennessee Press, 1975). "Gardens" does not appear in Glassie's index, but photographs of many of his predominantly Euro-Virginian buildings include spaces obviously once gardens. There is also a photo of a European walled farmstead, suggesting European as well as African precedence. On home demonstration agents and decorative gardens, see Lu Ann Jones, *Mama Learned Us to Work: Farm Women in the New South* (Chapel Hill: University of North Carolina Press, 2002), 19–20, 151.

15. Michael Pollan described the disaster that followed his willful dismissal of his grandfather-mentor's instruction to plant in rows, in 1960s suburban Long Island, in *Second Nature: A Gardener's Education* (New York: Dell, 1991), 9–41. On formal pleasure gardens, see Anne Scott-James and Osbert Lancaster, *The Pleasure Garden: An Illustrated History of British Gardening* (London: John Murray, 1977), esp. chaps. 6 and 8 (on Pope, pp. 52, 54–56), and Peter Martin, *The Pleasure Gardens of Virginia, from Jamestown to Jefferson* (Princeton: Princeton University Press, 1991), esp. chaps. 4–6 (Wythe's garden plan, p. 88).

16. Pollan, *Second Nature*. William Cronon and other scholar-contributors to Cronon, ed., *Uncommon Ground: Rethinking the Human Place in Nature* (New York: Norton, 1996), incorporated Pollan's construction into their own discourse.

17. Eugene Odum quoted in Betty Jean Craige, *Eugene Odum: Ecosystem Ecologist and Environmentalist* (Athens: University of Georgia Press, 2001), 143.

18. Edmund N. O'Rourke Jr. and Leon C. Standifer, *Gardening in the Humid South* (Baton Rouge: Louisiana State University Press, 2002), 38–39 (on hoses), 40–41 (underground irrigation), 255 (organic gardening), and 30–36, 197–99 (pests, chemicals).

19. John K. Crellin, comp and ed., *Plain Southern Eating: From the Reminiscences of A. L. Tommie Bass, Herbalist* (Durham: Duke University Press, 1988), xi (on Tullos's "discovery" of Bass), 22 (on sharing milk when someone's cow went dry, etc.). Westmacott's *African-American Gardens and Yards* does not feature gender, particularly, but men and boys are pictured at vegetable production and processing.

20. See Louis R. Harlan, *Booker T. Washington: The Wizard of Tuskegee, 1901–1915* (New York: Oxford University Press, 1983), esp. 207–8, and Linda McMurray, *George Washington Carver: Scientist and Symbol* (New York: Oxford University Press, 1981).

21. Theodore Rosengarten, *All God's Dangers: The Life of Nate Shaw* (1974; New York: Avon, 1975), 200 (quotation); see also 297–300. On Washington, see Harlan, *Booker T. Washington*, 14 (on his Farmers' Improvement Society), 207 (on farm demonstration), 213–14 (the Tuskegee Farm and Improvement Co.), 233 (on public health). See also

Earl W. Crosby, "Building the Country Home: The Black County Agent System, 1906–1940" (Ph.D. diss., Miami University, 1977).

22. Margaret Jarman Hagood, *Mothers of the South: Portraiture of the White Tenant Farm Woman* (1939; New York: Norton, 1977). See Anne Firor Scott's introduction and, on the single mother as successful tenant farmer and gardener, 56–59.

23. Bernice Kelly Harris, *Southern Savory* (Chapel Hill: University of North Carolina Press, 1964), 33. I am indebted also to Valerie Raleigh Yow's excellent biography, *Bernice Kelly Harris: A Good Life Was Writing* (Baton Rouge: Louisiana State University Press, 1999), esp. 23–24 (on Frederick Koch and the folk drama movement), 39–41 (her despair with childlessness and difficulties with her husband), 87–101 (her work with the Federal Writers' Project and its significance in her fiction), and 42–43, 207, 276–77 (gardening and canning). Also on Harris and the Writers' Project, note my own testimony in *Rural Worlds Lost*, 162–63, 370–71.

24. Zora Neale Hurston, *Dust Tracks on a Road: An Autobiography* (Philadelphia: Lippincott, 1942), 77 (first quotation), 287 (second quotation). See also her jolly declaration of her identity as "a Southerner," 142. A finely detailed and reflective biography of Hurston is Valerie Boyd, *Wrapped in Rainbows: The Life of Zora Neale Hurston* (New York: Scribner, 2003), used here for details on gardening (262, 264, 662–63, 667).

25. ZNH to Charlotte Osgood Mason, 6, 20 July 1932, in Carla Kaplan, ed., *Zora Neale Hurston: A Life in Letters* (New York: Doubleday, 2002), 262, 264.

26. ZNH to Jean Parker Waterbury, 9 July 1951; to Burroughs Mitchell, 15 July 1951; and to Waterbury, n.d. (marked "rec'd 8/8/51"), in ibid., 662–63, 667–68, 672–73.

27. The St. Augustine meetings and aftermath are recounted in Boyd, *Wrapped in Rainbows*, 348, 353. See also MKR to Maxwell Perkins, 11 August 1943; Perkins to Rawlings, 16 August 1943 and 16 April 1947; and Rawlings to Perkins, 30 April 1947, in *Max and Marjorie: The Correspondence between Maxwell E. Perkins and Marjorie Kinnan Rawlings*, ed. Rodger L. Tarr (Gainesville: University of Florida Press, 1999), 551–52 (quotation), 608–9. Hurston's letter to Langston Hughes is quoted by Robert Hemenway in his introduction to a new edition of Hurston's *Mules and Men* (1935; Bloomington: Indiana University Press, 1978), xix–xx.

28. ZNH to MKR, 16 May, 21 August 1943, in Kaplan, *Zora Neale Hurston*, 486–88, 494–95, and MKR to Maxwell Perkins, 26 August 1943, in Tarr, *Max and Marjorie*, 552–53.

29. Quoted in Kaplan, *Zora Neale Hurston*, 494–95 n. 2. Brief discussion of Rawlings and color is based on a variety of her letters about employing black workers during the 1930s and 1940s, and Boyd, *Wrapped in Rainbows*, 350–51.

30. Rawlings, *Cross Creek* (1942; New York: Touchstone, 1996), 215–16.

31. Ibid., 242–43. On plants wild and domestic, see 224–36 and Rawlings, *Cross Creek Cookery* (1942; New York: Fireside, 1996), 50–65.

32. Rawlings, *Cross Creek*, 225.

33. Ibid., 248.

34. Ibid., 248, 246–47.

35. Ibid. 248.

36. Hammond traveled much as soil surveyor, and his personal correspondence, especially to his wife, contained frequent references to wildflowers and other beauties to be discovered across the continent. See the Hugh Hammond Bennett Papers, Southern Historical Collection, University of North Carolina, Chapel Hill. On Romantic and other attachments to beauty in nature among instrumentalist conservationists, see Robert L. Dorman, *A Word for Nature: Four Pioneering Environmental Advocates, 1845-1913* (Chapel Hill: University of North Carolina Press, 1998), esp. 29-30, on George Perkins Marsh's mind and sensibilities.

37. On natural disasters (many of them southern), see Ted Steinberg, *Acts of God: The Unnatural History of Natural Disaster in America* (New York: Oxford University Press, 2000), 5-6 (on the Charleston earthquake); Stephen J. Pyne, *Fire in America: A Cultural History of Wildland and Rural Fire* (Princeton: Princeton University Press, 1982); and Donald Worster, *Dust Bowl: The Southern Plains in the 1930s* (New York: Oxford University Press, 1979).

38. See Donald Worster, *Nature's Economy: A History of Ecological Ideas* (Cambridge: Cambridge University Press, 1977), esp. 192. In this paragraph and below I rely also on Worster, but especially on Frank B. Golley, *A History of the Ecosystem Concept of Ecology: More Than the Sum of the Parts* (New Haven: Yale University Press, 1992), and Golley, *A Primer for Environmental Literacy* (New Haven: Yale University Press, 1998).

39. Tansley quoted in Worster, *Nature's Economy*, 239.

40. Among many others, I have written about southern poverty and migration in *Rural Worlds Lost*, and about documentary photography in *Media-Made Dixie: The South in the American Imagination* (Baton Rouge: Louisiana State University Press, 1978). All students of the documentary are indebted to William Stott, *Documentary Photography and Thirties America* (New York: Oxford University Press, 1963). On Georgia's Little Grand Canyon, see Paul Sutter, "Georgia's Little Grand Canyon," in *The Environment and Southern History*, ed. Charles Reagan Wilson (Jackson: University Press of Mississippi, forthcoming).

41. On Howard Washington Odum's life and intellectual development, see Rupert Vance and Katharine Jocher, "Howard W. Odum," *Social Forces* 33, no. 3 (1955): 1-15, and Wayne Douglas Brazil, *Howard W. Odum: The Building Years, 1884-1930* (New York: Garland, 1988). Eugene P. Odum's biographer, Betty Jean Craige, employing these and other sources, including interviews with Howard W.'s three children, argues convincingly that the holism of Howard W. profoundly influenced his sons' concept of ecosystem ecology; see Craige *Eugene Odum*, 1-20.

42. On the Agrarian vs. Regionalist contretemps of the 1930s, see (among many relevant works) Paul Conkin, *The Southern Agrarians* (Knoxville: University of Tennessee Press, 1988), and Daniel Joseph Singal, *The War Within: From Victorian to Modernist Thought in the South, 1919-1945* (Chapel Hill: University of North Carolina Press, 1982).

43. See Boyd, *Wrapped in Rainbows*, 172, 254-55.

44. On Odum's and the Regionalists' agrarianism, see Michael O'Brien, *The Idea of*

*the American South, 1920–1941* (Baltimore: Johns Hopkins University Press, 1979), 31–69.

45. Howard W. Odum, *Southern Regions of the United States* (Chapel Hill: University of North Carolina Press, 1936), 57.

46. Ibid., 7.

47. Rupert Vance, "Is Agrarianism for Farmers?" *Southern Review* 1 (1935): 41–57, reprinted with an introduction in John Shelton Reed and Daniel Joseph Singal, eds., *Regionalism and the South: Selected Papers of Rupert Vance* (Chapel Hill: University of North Carolina Press, 1982), 60–74 (quotations, 64).

48. Rupert Vance, *All These People: The Nation's Human Resources in the South* (Chapel Hill: University of North Carolina Press, 1945), esp. 466–88. On Odum and Sanger, see his letter to her, 22 April 1933, box 5, Howard W. Odum Papers, Southern Historical Collection, University of North Carolina, Chapel Hill.

49. Arthur Raper, *Tenants of the Almighty* (New York: Macmillan, 1943), v (Thomas's poem); Raper, *Preface to Peasantry: A Tale of Two Black Belt Counties* (1936; New York: Atheneum, 1968). Further evidence of Raper's ecological consciousness, I think, is the large collection of Farm Security Administration pamphlets and photographs on soil erosion and conservation, and Raper's own notes on the "Dust Bowl" in his papers. See the Farm Security Administration files and "Unarranged Notes—Dust Bowl," in the Arthur F. Raper Papers, Southern Historical Collection, University of North Carolina, Chapel Hill. The following paragraph on the inadequacy of New Deal tenant programs and the failure of self-sufficiency in food is summarized from Kirby, *Rural Worlds Lost*, 1–24, 334–60.

50. Craige, *Eugene Odum*, 12, repeats his story about "studying plumbing." Worster, *Nature's Economy*, 313.

51. See Craig, *Eugene Odum*. Also Eugene P. Odum, "The Emergence of Ecology as a New Integrative Discipline," *Science*, 25 March 1977, 1289–93, which recounts his frustration as would-be teacher of ecology at Georgia.

52. Howard T. Odum, *Environment, Power, and Society* (New York: Wiley-Interscience, 1971), viii. Eugene P. Odum's *Ecology: A Bridge between Science and Society* (Sunderland, Mass.: Sinauer Associates, 1997), appeared in earlier editions from the same publisher under a different title, *Ecology and Our Endangered Life-Support Systems*.

53. On the paradigm break, see Donald Worster, "Ecology of Order and Chaos," *Environmental History Review* 14 (Spring/Summer 1990): 4–16.

54. Joel B. Hagen, *An Entangled Bank: The Origins of Ecosystem Ecology* (New Brunswick, N.J.: Rutgers University Press, 1992).

55. Odum, *Ecology*, esp. 189–204. See also E. P. Odum, "When to Confront and When to Cooperate," *INTECOL Bulletin* 20 (1992): 21–23, which Golley also cites in his *Primer for Environmental Literacy*, 186–87. (On Gene Odum's demeanor and opinion regarding the new "disturbance" and "patch" paradigm, I observed moments as suggested during a slight acquaintanceship with him, beginning in 1986, and several of Odum's own acquaintances and colleagues reinforced and elaborated on my impression.)

CHAPTER 6

1. See Helen C. Rountree, *The Powhatan Indians of Virginia: Their Traditional Culture* (Norman: University of Oklahoma Press, 1989), and (on native occupance and the Euro-controlled York valley) Alonzo Thomas Dill, *York River Yesterdays: A Pictorial History* (Norfolk/Virginia Beach: Donning, 1984), 9–54. On twentieth-century West Point, see Dill's excellent industrial/urban history, *Chesapeake, Pioneer Papermaker: A History of the Company and Its Community* (Charlottesville: University Press of Virginia, 1968).

2. I refer to Jane Jacobs, *The Death and Life of Great American Cities* (New York: Random House, 1961), esp. pt. 2. The following detail on nineteenth- and early-twentieth-century West Point is based on Dill, *York River Yesterdays*, pts. 3 and 4 (55–126; Rev. Bagby quoted, 126), and certain Kirby family letters and documents from the era, originals in the Jack Temple Kirby Papers, Virginia Historical Society, Richmond.

3. James J. Miller, *An Environmental History of Northeast Florida* (Gainesville: University Press of Florida, 1998), 40 (quotation), 164.

4. In addition to ibid., see the works of St. Augustine's most revered authority on the old, Albert Manucy—e.g., *The Building of Castillo de San Marcos* (Washington, D.C.: National Park Service, 1942); *Seeing St. Augustine* (St. Augustine: St. Augustine Historical Society, 1937); and esp. *The Houses of St. Augustine, 1565–1821* (1962; Gainesville: University Press of Florida, 1992). On pictorial evidence of downtown St. Augustine's near-dereliction before Flagler, see Ron Puckett, Rod Morris, and Mary Lou Merritt, *Yesterday in St. Augustine* (Tallahassee: Yesterday in Florida Co., n.d. [ca. 2001]).

5. Jerald T. Milanich, "The Timucua Indians of Northern Florida and Southern Georgia," in *Indians of the Greater Southeast: Historical Archaeology and Ethnohistory*, ed. Bonnie G. McEwan (Gainesville: University Press of Florida, 2000), 1–25.

6. See Manucy, *Houses of St. Augustine*, 14–22. On the "St. Augustine Look," see 7–13.

7. Edward N. Akin, *Flagler: Rockefeller Partner and Florida Baron* (1988; Gainesville: University Press of Florida, 1991), 1–73 (early life and business), 111–33 (St. Augustine), and 134–42 (Flagler's Florida rail line).

8. See ibid., 125, on Memorial Presbyterian. Disposition of the Flagler hotels is standard in guidebooks. On the visit of "Ringo Starr," see *St. Augustine Record*, 7, 10 (on the hoax) August 2004.

9. See Edward L. Ayers, *The Promise of the New South: Life after Reconstruction* (New York: Oxford University Press, 1992), 9, 12–13, and on towns and cities (in text following), 60–61, 72–76. On comparative regional rates of urbanization, see Don H. Doyle, *New Men, New Cities, New South: Atlanta, Nashville, Charleston, Mobile, 1860–1910* (Chapel Hill: University of North Carolina Press, 1990), 1–21.

10. Ayers, *Promise of the New South*, 60.

11. See Doyle, *New Men, New Cities, New South*, 1–21, esp. 16, on regional rankings of cities and on comparative urbanization rates.

12. Ayers, *Promise of the New South*, 72–76.

13. Albert E. Cowdrey, *This Land, This South: An Environmental History* (1983; rev. ed., Lexington: University Press of Kentucky, 1996), 37–38.

14. Ibid., 104–5. The authority on opiates is David T. Courtwright, *Dark Paradise: Opiate Addiction in America before 1940* (Cambridge, Mass.: Harvard University Press, 1982), esp. 38–39.

15. David F. Allmendinger Jr., *Ruffin: Family and Reform in the Old South* (New York: Oxford University Press, 1990), esp. chaps. 1–3; *Incidents of My Life: Edmund Ruffin's Autobiographical Essays*, ed. David F. Allmendinger Jr. (Charlottesville: University Press of Virginia for the Virginia Historical Society, 1990). Ruffin's writings on urban sanitation appeared in *Farmers' Register* and later editions of *Essay on Calcareous Manures*. His two 1837 epistles (summarized and quoted below) are reprinted in *Edmund Ruffin: Nature's Management—Writings on Landscape and Reform, 1822–1859*, ed. Jack Temple Kirby (Athens: University of Georgia Press, 2000), 128–69.

16. Margaret Humphreys, *Yellow Fever and the South* (New Brunswick, N.J.: Rutgers University Press, 1992), 1–10 (description), 15, 27 (on boards of health and urban sanitation), 34–43 (on etiology).

17. Jacobs, *Death and Life of Great American Cities*, 24 (quotation), 93, 170, 374 (on City Beautiful); Doyle, *New Men, New Cities, New South*, 151–58 (on expositions).

18. See Doyle, *New Men, New Cities, New South*, 1–21, esp. 8–12, on relative urbanization, and Jack Temple Kirby, *Rural Worlds Lost: The American South, 1920–1960* (Baton Rouge: Louisiana State University Press, 1987), pt. 3, on rural-to-urban migration.

19. John A. Jakle and David Wilson, *Derelict Landscapes: The Wasting of America's Built Environment* (Savage, Md.: Rowman and Littlefield, 1992), 94–98, 137, 201; below, on accounting, depreciation, and maintenance, see 19–30; on deindustrialization, 57–92; corporate flight to suburbs, 101; rural dereliction related to suburbs, 196–221; and failures of urban preservation/gentrification, 223–56.

20. Charles Simic, "Down There on a Visit," *New York Review of Books*, 21 August 2004, 45–47 (epigraph quotation, 45).

21. Information on trash and sewage in mountain Kentucky, then the cleanup, is derived from personal observations, 1965–2004, and various newspaper reports, 2000–2003.

22. Robert A. Ivy Jr., "Locking Up the Suburbs: Gated Communities on the Rise," *Reckon: The Magazine of Southern Culture*, Fall 1995, 42–47 (Reich quotation, 45; Evan McKenzie quotation, 45; Windrush and Windsor quotations, 46).

23. John R. Stilgoe, *Borderland: Origins of the American Suburb, 1820–1939* (New Haven: Yale University Press, 1988). On Beatrix Farrand and garden "rooms," see Vera Norwood, *Made from This Earth: American Women and Nature* (Chapel Hill: University of North Carolina Press, 1993), 111–12, 114–17. On post–World War II suburban lawns, I rely on the charming first chapter of Michael Pollan, *Second Nature: A Gardener's Education* (New York: Dell, 1991), plus my own long and checkered past as designer and maintainer of suburban lawns.

24. On the Rhine spill, see Mark Cioc, *The Rhine: An Eco-Biography, 1815–2000* (Seattle: University of Washington Press, 2002), 109–10. On Love Canal, Times Beach, Bhopal, and (in the following text) Institute, W.Va., see Gerald Markowitz and Davis

Rosner, *Deceit and Denial: The Deadly Politics of Industrial Pollution* (Berkeley: University of California Press for the Millbank Memorial Fund, 2002), 248 (incl. quotation).

25. *New York Times*, 30 August 1975; Cowdrey, *This Land, This South*, 187.

26. This and following paragraphs about Louisiana are based on Markowitz and Rosner, *Deceit and Denial*, 235–62.

27. Rich Hind and David Halperin, "Lots of Chemicals, Little Reaction," *New York Times*, 22 September 2004.

28. John Turner, *White Gold Comes to California* (Bakersfield: California Planting Cotton Seed Distributors, 1981), 41–44. On southern crop dusting and the following text on agricultural chemicals, see Pete Daniel, *Toxic Drift: Pesticides and Health in the South, 1945–1970* (Baton Rouge: Louisiana State University Press, 2005).

29. Samuel P. Hays, *Beauty, Health, and Permanence: Environmental Politics in the United States, 1955–1985* (Cambridge: Cambridge University Press, 1987). Observations on Indiana limestone are based on my own long residence nearby and travels around southern Indiana and northern Kentucky.

30. See the following websites: <http://www.lostrivers.ca/points/Brickmaking .htm>; <http://www.epa.gov/ttn/chief/ap42/ch11/final/c11s03.pdf>; and <http://www .wvgs.wvnet.edu/www/geology/geoldvcl.htm>.

31. On ancient Egyptian brick making, see A. Lucas and J. R. Harris, *Ancient Egyptian Materials and Industries* (1962; Mineola, N.Y.: Dover Publications, 1999), 48–50. On Walker, see Jack Temple Kirby, *Darkness at the Dawning: Race and Reform in the Progressive South* (Philadelphia: Lippincott, 1972), 171–72. During years of travels in eastern Virginia and North Carolina, I have observed brick ranch-style worker housing.

32. See Otto H. Olsen, *Carpetbagger's Crusade: The Life of Albion Winegar Tourgee* (Baltimore: Johns Hopkins University Press, 1965), esp. 223–41 (on the Reconstruction novels); also on Tourgee as novelist, see Edmund Wilson, *Patriotic Gore: Studies in the Literature of the American Civil War* (1962; New York: Oxford University Press, 1966), 529–48.

33. Jennifer 8. Lee, "Sewer Sludge Spread on Fields Is Fodder for Lawsuits," *New York Times*, 26 June 2003. Lee did not check the EPA's contention that there was no or inadequate research on heavy metal uptake. See (as a small sample) J. Parizek, "Peculiar Toxicity of Cadmium during Pregnancy: An Experimental Toxaemia of Pregnancy Induced by Cadmium Salts," *Journal of Reproduction and Fertility* 6 (1965): 111–18; M. K. John, C. J. Van Laehoven, and H. H. Chubah, "Factors Affecting Plant Uptake and Phytotoxicity of Cadmium Added to Soils," *Environmental Science and Technology* 6 (1972): 1005–9; Elizabeth A. Kruse and Gary W. Barrett, "Effects of Municipal Sludge and Fertilizer on Heavy Metal Accumulation in Earthworms," *Environmental Pollution*, ser. A, 38 (1985): 235–44; and John D. Peles, Susan R. Brewer, and Gary W. Barrett, "Heavy Metal Accumulation by Old-Field Plant Species during Recovery of Sludge-Treated Ecosystems," *American Midland Naturalist* 140, no. 2 (1998): 245–51.

34. Tim Gilmore, "That Smell: How One Company's Powerful Stink Defeated a Northside Neighborhood," *Jacksonville Folioweekly*, 22 June 2004, 14–16, 18–20.

35. Scott Harper, "Blackwater River: A Poison Runs through It," *Norfolk Virginian-Pilot*, 19 July 2004.

36. See <http://ngeorgia.com/naturally/cnf.html> (on sprawl and acid rain's effects on the upper Chattahoochee and Chattahoochee National Forest); <http://www.audubonofflorida.org/action/2004actionagenda/apalachicola.htm> and <http://www.taxpayer.net/corpswatch/crossroads/Apalachicola.pdf> (on Corps of Engineers dredging); and David L. Markell, "ACF River System Is Novel Case for U.S. Supreme Court," *Tallahassee Democrat*, 21 November 2003, posted at <http://www.tallahassee.com/mld/democrat/news/opinion/7311740.htm> (on the Georgia/Alabama/Florida federal suit over water ownership).

## EPILOGUE

1. Jere Longman, "Feisty and Fearless, Mathis Swaggers onto World Stage," *New York Times* (Sunday Sports), 12 May 2002 (also the epigraph); Fred Hobson, *The Southern Writer in the Postmodern World* (Athens: University of Georgia Press, 1991).

2. The expression is borrowed from Nan Elizabeth Woodruff, *American Congo: The African American Freedom Struggle in the Delta* (Cambridge: Harvard University Press, 2003), which cites the NAACP's usage (during the 1920s), comparing northwestern Mississippi and neighboring eastern Arkansas with the notorious African colony of Belgian King Leopold II.

3. See Wilma A. Dunaway, *The First American Frontier: Transition to Capitalism in Southern Appalachia, 1700–1860* (Chapel Hill: University of North Carolina Press, 1996); Mary Beth Pudup, Dwight Billings, and Altina Waller, eds., *Appalachia in the Making: The Mountain South in the Nineteenth Century* (Chapel Hill: University of North Carolina Press, 1995); and on the near-end of mountain farming, Jack Temple Kirby, *Rural Worlds Lost: The American South, 1920–1960* (Baton Rouge: Louisiana State University Press, 1987), 80–113.

4. See A. Dwight Baldwin Jr., "Rehabilitation of Land Stripped for Coal in Ohio—Reclamation, Restoration, or Creation?" in *Beyond Preservation: Restoring and Inventing Landscapes*, ed. A. Dwight Baldwin Jr., Judith De Luce, and Carl Pletch (Minneapolis: University of Minnesota Press, 1994), 181–91.

5. See Michael Lipton (a West Virginia editor), "The Fight for the Soul of Coal Country," *New York Times*, 17 May 2002. Useful overviews of mountaintop removal and recent legal and administrative struggles are Francis X. Clines, "Judge Takes On Bush Administration on Strip Mining," *New York Times*, 19 May 2002, and Elizabeth Kolbert, "Comment: Bad Environments," *New Yorker*, 20 May 2002, 35–36.

6. Congress passed "clean water" acts in 1960, 1965, 1972, and 1977. Most singular references seem to be to the 1972 law. See Samuel P. Hays, *Beauty, Health, and Permanence: Environmental Politics in the United States, 1955–1985* (Cambridge: Cambridge University Press, 1987), 53, 58, 78–80, 153, 162, 252, 324, 420, 466, 496, 508, 517. On coastal development (below), see 148–51.

7. On the rise of Disney World, see Alan Bryman, *Disney and His Worlds* (New York:

Routledge, 1995). Observations on northeastern Florida, development, and water are my own (some based on local newspaper accounts) during four visits, 2001–2. See also John Sayles's film, *Sunshine State* (2002), which depicts scheming would-be developers of "Lincolnville" (actually the historically black American Beach) in northeastern Florida.

8. Gail Fishman, *Journeys through Paradise: Pioneering Naturalists in the Southeast* (Gainesville: University Press of Florida, 2000), 246; Carl Hiaasen, *Stormy Weather* (New York: Warner Books, 1995) and *Sick Puppy* (New York: Warner Books, 1999). On Florida (especially its south) as new American *mondo bizarro*—replacing California—see Michael Paternite, "America in Extremis: How Florida Became the New California," *New York Times Sunday Magazine*, 21 April 2002.

9. Most of this paragraph presents personal observation and local newspaper reading, especially in 2002; but see also David McCally, *The Everglades: An Environmental History* (Gainesville: University Press of Florida, 1999), esp. 154–81, and Andrew C. Revkin, "Stockpiling Water for a River of Grass: New Plan Redesigns Plumbing of Everglades," *New York Times* (Science Times), 26 March 2002.

10. Among many sources (see notes to Chapter 3 esp.), see Robert B. Outland III, *Tapping the Pines: The Naval Stores Industry in the American South* (Baton Rouge: Louisiana State University Press, 2004), and Linda Flowers, *Throwed Away: Failures of Progress in Eastern North Carolina* (Knoxville: University of Tennessee Press, 1991).

11. Jack Temple Kirby, *Poquosin: A Study of Rural Landscape and Society* (Chapel Hill: University of North Carolina Press, 1995), 197–235, also suggests social and political liabilities of the paper industry. The expressions "paper complex" and short "rotation" in tropical America are William Boyd's; see his "The Forest Is the Future? Industrial Foresty and the Southern Pulp and Paper Complex," in *The Second Wave: Southern Industrialization from the 1940s to the 1970s*, ed. Philip Scranton (Athens: University of Georgia Press, 2001), 168–218. On the costs of biodiversity in pine plantations, see Janisse Ray, *Ecology of a Cracker Childhood* (Minneapolis: Milkweed, 1999), which includes lists of extinct and endangered species in the lower South pine plantation belt.

12. Jeffrey Stine, *Mixing the Waters: Environment, Politics, and the Building of the Tennessee-Tombigbee Waterway* (Akron: University of Akron Press, 1993); but see esp. Eric Bates, "Exporting Southern Forests," *Doubletake* 3 (Winter 1996): 88–95. In text below, on the historical advance of conifers over deciduous forests, especially owing to farmers' use of fire, see Kirby, *Poquosin*, 95–125.

13. Personal observations since ca. 1982, plus press clippings and reports of one of my sisters, who is a school librarian in Southampton County.

14. Charles S. Aiken, *The Cotton Plantation South since the Civil War* (Baltimore: Johns Hopkins University Press, 1998), latter chapters.

15. Katharine Q. Seelye, "Senators Plan Joint Hearings on Clean Air," *New York Times*, 9 January 2002. On mountain tree deaths, see Timothy Silver, *Mount Mitchell and the Black Mountains: An Environmental History of the Highest Peaks in Eastern America* (Chapel Hill: University of North Carolina Press, 2003), 245, 249. On "eco-pessimism,"

see Otis L. Graham, "Again the Backward Region? Environmental History in and of the American South," *Southern Cultures* 6 (Summer 2000): 50–72.

16. See <http://www.nutria.com/site/php> (this site is created and updated by the Louisiana Department of Wildlife and Fisheries).

17. Information from <http://www.monkparakeet.com>, plus personal and friends' observations in Florida and New York City.

18. Charles McGrath, "Of Greens and Greens," and Andrew Pollack, "Can Biotech Crops Be Good Neighbors?," both in *New York Times* (Week in Review), 26 September 2004.

19. Tom Wolfe, *A Man in Full: A Novel* (New York: Farrar Straus Giroux, 1998), 510 ("force of nature"); ". . . had a back like a Jersey Bull" recurs.

20. Ibid., 398.

21. Ibid., 731–33.

# INDEX

Agrarians (Nashville), 243–44, 246

Agriculture, 75–112; genetically modified, 324; slash-and-burn, 56–59, 334 (n. 10); violence of, 4–5. *See also* Native southerners; Plantations

Aiken, Charles, xvii, 105–6

Alligators, 28; William Bartram and, 17–20; hunting of, 22–23; and pets, 23–24

Animals: extinctions of, 166–68; introduction of European, 16–17. *See also* Alligators; Hunting; Snakes

Apalachees, 42, 52–53

Apalachicola, Fla., 310–11

Appalachia: leveling of, 314–15; pollution in, 321–22

Appalachian Trail, 154–55

Apples, 14–15

Aquatic plants (introduced), 24–29

Arson of forests, 138–43

Audubon, John James, xii, 30; slaughterer of birds, 12–13

Audubon Society, 180

Ayers, Edward L., xv

Baldwin, Joseph G., 117

Barbeque, 46–47, 119, 121, 123

Barrett, Gary, xix, 308

Bartram, John, 11

Bartram, William, 1, 60, 69, 232; in Florida, 11–31 passim. *See also* Alligators; St. Johns River

Baskin, Norton, 229–30

Bass, A. L. Tommie, 218–19

Bennett, Hugh Hammond, 236–37

Berry, Wendell, xviii

Blackwater River (Va.), 309–10

Boone, Daniel, 163, 168–69

Brown, Margaret Lynn, xvii, 153

Bryant, William Cullen, 123–26

Building materials, 303–7

Burkholder, JoAnn, 195–96

Butz, Earl, 202

Byrd, William, II, 113, 117

Cahokia, 48–49, 57–58

Calusas, 61–63

Camp Manufacturing Co., 135

Camp, Wofford B. "Bill," 106, 109

Cardinals, xiii

Carson, Rachel, 296, 302

Carter, Colonel Landon, 83–84

Carver, George Washington, 219

Catesby, Mark, xii, 30

Chemical industry, 33–34; and air pollution, 308–10; disasters of, 297–98; in Louisiana, 298–300; and pesticides, 297–303; and suburban lawns, 295–96

Cherokees, 38–39, 67–68

Chesapeake Bay, 10; fishery of, 192–95

Chesapeake Corporation, 264

Chickasaws, 38–42, 46–47, 52, 67–68

Choctaws, 38, 68

Chowan, 68

Cities: and coastal development, 315–17; dereliction of, 289–92, 308; design and exposition of, 287; native, 257–58; sanitation and public health in, 279–87. *See also* Petersburg, Va.; St. Augustine, Fla.; Suburbs; West Point, Va.

Civil War: economic recovery from, 132; as ecological disaster, 128–32
Cobb, Ned, 219–20
Coen, Joel and Ethan, xviii, 145–46, 313–14
Cofitachequi, 43, 52
Coosas, 43, 52
Corn: and obesity, 201–3; and pellagra, 203–10
Cowdrey, Albert, xvi
Craven, Avery Odell, xvi, 88–91
Creeks, 38, 45, 60, 68, 70
Crews, Harry, 165
Cronon, William, xviii, xix
Crosby, Alfred, xviii

Daniel, Pete, xvi, 302
Davy, Sir Humphry, 84
Dillard, Annie, xviii
Disney World, 316, 318
Doolittle, William, xvii, 57
Dorman, Robert, xvii
Doyle, Don, xvi, 93

Ecology (scientific), xiv; ecosystem concept, 251–55; as equilibrium, 238–44; southernization of, 240–56. *See also* Odum, Eugene P.; Odum, Howard T.
Elliott, William, 169–71, 177; hunts manta rays, 171–75; hunts other animals, 175–76
Eppes, Dr. Richard, 99–101
Ethridge, Robbie, xvii

Fairs and circuses, 180–83
Farrand, Beatrix Jones, 294–95
Faulkner, William, xviii, 9, 23, 38, 93, 226, 229–32, 312
Fences. *See* Open stock range
Fishman, Gail, 29–32, 316
Flagler, Henry M., 2, 271–76

Food, supply and variety of, 210–14. *See also* Gardens
Forestry, 136–37, 143
Fox-Genovese, Elizabeth, xvi

Gaither, E. W., 183
Galloway, Patricia, xvii
Gardens, 214–20
Garreau, Joel, 327
Genovese, Eugene D., xvi
Goldberger, Dr. Joseph, 206–9
Golley, Frank, 255–56
Great Smokey Mountains: air pollution in, 321–22; national park, 150–54
Green, Michael, xvii
Grice, Gordon, 120
Guale, 60
Guano, 89

Hagood, Margaret Jarman, 220, 222, 224
Haley, Alex, 165
Ham and Eggs movement, 182–83
Hammond, James Henry, 91
Harper, Francis, 30
Harper, Roland, 31
Harris, Bernice Kelly, 223–25, 234
Harrison, Robert Pogue, xviii
Hatfield, Anderson "Devil Anse", 134–35
Hays, Samuel P., xvii–xviii, 303
Herty, Charles, 126
Hiaasen, Carl, 316–17
Hilliard, Sam Bowers, xvii, 213
Hobson, Fred, 312
Hookworm, 204
Hudson, Charles, xvii
Hundley, Daniel R., 118
Hunting, 156–65; as blood sport, 65–66; of foxes, 173–74; for markets, 68–69; by native southerners, 65–71; pot-shooting, 178–79; reform of, 178–80; as war on wilderness, 13–14

Hurricanes. *See* Natural disasters

Hurston, Zora Neale, xviii, 7, 201, 225–29, 234, 244

Jackson, John Brinkerhoff, xviii
Jacobs, Jane, xvii, 257, 259, 264–65
Jakle, John A., xvii
Jefferson, Thomas, 216–17
Jewell, Jesse Dixon, 186–87, 191, 197
Jones, Lu Ann, xvi

Kemble, Frances Anne "Fanny," 115–17
Kirby, John Henry, 135
Kretch, Shepard, III, xvii, 73–74
Kudzu, 112

Lanier, Sidney, 310
Lee, Harper, xii
Longstreet, Augustus Baldwin, 117, 166, 173–74
Lyell, Sir Charles, 92

MacKaye, Benton, 154–55
Martin, Paul, 65–66
Mathew, William M., 90
Mathis, Clint, 312–13
Mattaponi, 258, 268
McCally, David, xvii, 74
McKibben, Bill, 29
McPhee, John, xviii–xviv
McWhiney, Grady, xvi, 114–15, 124, 164–65
Menéndez de Avilés, Pedro, 72, 177, 267
Merchant, Carolyn, xviii
Mitchell, H. L. "Mitch," 109
Mockingbirds, xi–xiii
Moscoso, Luis de, 51–52
Mountains, as spiritual refuge, 143–46
Mount Mitchell, N.C., xvii, 146; and air pollution, 321–22; as park, 148–49
Muir, John, 30, 143–44, 236

Murphy, Audie Leon, xv, 156–58, 163, 199–200, 234
Murphy, Wendell, 197–99

Native southerners, 38–74; and agriculture, 55–61; "ecology" and, 64–71; human sacrifice among, 62–63; Mississippian culture of, 52–55; populations of, 72–73; "racial" mixing among, 39–40, 43, 52. *See also* Apalachees; Cherokees; Tula; *and other peoples*
Natural disasters, xiv, 6–8, 237–38, 310
Naval stores industry, 124–28
Newkirk, Ingrid, 189
Norton, Grady, 7–8
Norwood, Vera, xviii
Nutria, 322–23

O'Brien, Michael, xvi
Odum, Eugene P., xix, 201, 217, 220, 241, 250–56, 308
Odum, Howard T., xix, 241, 252–55
Odum, Howard W., 217, 220, 241–45, 247, 250
Odum, Mary Francis, 251
Olmsted, Frederick Law, 91, 98, 113, 115, 137
Open stock range, 2, 113–19; effect of Civil War on, 129–31, 149
Oranges, 1–2, 16
O'Rourke, Edmund N., 218
Ortona, 61
Outer Banks (N.C.), 32–33
Outland, Robert, 126
Ownby, Ted, xvi, 179–80

Pamunkey, 258, 268
Paper industry, 133; as redemption of coastal plains, 35–37; social ecology of, 33; threats to, 317–20

Parakeets, xi–xii; Carolina, 14–15, 323;
    monk, 323–24
Parker, Idella, 229, 231–32, 244
Passenger pigeons, 14
People for the Ethical Treatment of
    Animals (PETA), 188–89
Percy, Walker, 312–13
Perdue, Theda, xvii
Perkins, Maxwell, 2, 25, 230–31
Petersburg, Va., 281–82
*Pfiesteria piscicida* ("red tide"), 34, 194–96
Phillips, Ulrich Bonnell, 245
Pinchot, Gifford, 113, 136–37
Plantations: Civil War and, 99–100;
    demise of, 105–10, 320–21; improve-
    ment of, 79–90, 103–4; labor systems,
    78–79, 101–10; migrations of, 91–93,
    98–99; origins and definition of, 76–
    78. *See also* Edmund Ruffin; Edward
    Strickland; John Taylor
Pollan, Michael, xix, 201–2, 295
Ponce de Leon, Juan, 71–72
Poultry industry, 182–84; cruelty of,
    189–90; industrialization of, 185–92
Powhatan, 68
Presley, Elvis, 38–40
Prunty, Merle C., Jr., xvii
Pyne, Stephen, xviii

Quigualtam (Natchez), 50–52

Railroads, 274, 276–79. *See also* Flagler,
    Henry M.; St. Augustine, Fla.; West
    Point, Va.
Raper, Arthur F., 247–48
Rawlings, Marjorie Kinnan, xviii, xx, 113,
    131, 214; as hunter/gatherer/cook,
    232, 234–36; on hunting, 164; on St.
    Johns River, 25–29; settlement in
    Florida, 1–4; *The Yearling* as environ-
    mental history, 5–6, 8–10; and Zora
    Neale Hurston, 229–30

Reiger, John, xviii
Roosevelt, Theodore, 136, 169
Rountree, Helen, xvii
Ruffin, Edmund, 59, 177; as agricultural
    reformer, 84–92; as enemy of open
    range, 114, 121, 123; on public health,
    257, 280–85

St. Augustine, Fla., 267–76; meeting of
    Zora Neale Hurston and Marjorie
    Kinnan Rawlings in, 229–30
"St. Augustine Look" (architecture),
    270–71
St. Johns River, 10–12, 14–29 passim
Sanger, Margaret, 247
Seminoles, 15–16, 38, 69
Shama, Simon, xviii
Shay, William W., 196–97
Silver, Timothy, xvi, 148
Simic, Charles, 257, 290
Simms, William Gilmore, 91
Small, John Kunkel, 30–32
Smith, John, 58–59, 72, 258
Smithfield Foods, 191–92, 198–99
Smuts, Jan Christian, 144, 239–40
Snakes, 9, 17
Soto, Hernando de, xv, 71–72; La Florida
    expedition, 42–51
Sparrow, white-throated, xiii
Spira, Harry, 188
Standifer, Leon C., 218
Stewart, Mart, xvi
Stilgoe, John, xviii
Stoicism, 328–30
Stoll, Steven, xvi
Strickland, Edward, 79–81
Suburbs, 287–89, 291, 307–11; gated,
    293–94; lawns of, 294–97, 310–11
Swine, 46–47, 119–23; as carnivores, 120–
    21; and the Civil War, 129; ecological
    impacts of, 118–19, 123; as industrial
    meat, 195–99

Tascaluza ("Black Warrior"), 45–46, 52
Taylor, Alan, xviii
Taylor, John (of Caroline), 58, 80–85
Tennessee-Tombigbee Waterway, 319–20
Thompson, Michael, 196
Timber industry, 133–37, 140, 319–20
Timucua, 15–16, 60, 68, 258–59
Tourgee, Albion W., 304–6
Tula, 50, 52
Tullos, Allan, 218–19
Turner, Frederick Jackson, 89–91
Turner, Nat, 320
Turpentine. *See* Naval stores industry
Tyson Foods, 191

Usner, Daniel, xvii

Valencius, Conevery Bolton, xvii
Vance, Rupert, 245–47

Washington, Booker T., 219
Water pollution, 192
Webb, Walter Prescott, xvi
West Point, Va., 258–68; as paper mill
    town, 35–37, 263–67
Weyerhaeuser, Frederick, 134–35
White, Richard, xviii
Wilson, David, xvii
Wolfe, Tom, 312; *A Man in Full*, 324–30
Woodpeckers, ivory-billed, 15, 70;
    pileated, 15
Woodward, C. Vann, xi, xv–xvi
Worster, Donald, xviii
Wright, Richard, 230
Wyatt-Brown, Bertram, xvi

Yellow fever, 285–87
York, Alvin, xv, 157–58, 160–63, 178–79